Tenacious of Their Liberties

Tenacious of Their Liberties

The Congregationalists in Colonial Massachusetts

James F. Cooper, Jr.

OXFORD

UNIVERSITY PRESS

OXFORD
UNIVERSITY PRESS

Oxford   New York
Auckland   Bangkok   Buenos Aires   Cape Town   Chennai
Dar es Salaam   Delhi   Hong Kong   Istanbul   Karachi   Kolkata
Kuala Lumpur   Madrid   Melbourne   Mexico City   Mumbai   Nairobi
São Paulo   Shanghai   Singapore   Taipei   Tokyo   Toronto

and an associated company in Berlin

Copyright © 1999 by James F. Cooper, Jr.

First published in 1999 by Oxford University Press, Inc.
198 Madison Avenue, New York, New York 10016

First issued as an Oxford University Press paperback, 2002

www.oup.com.

Oxford is a registered trademark of Oxford University Press

Library of Congress Cataloging-in-Publication Data
Cooper, James F. (James Fenimore), 1955–
Tenacious of their liberties : the Congregationalists in colonial
Massachusetts / James F. Cooper, Jr.
p.   cm. — (Religion in America series)
Includes bibliographical references and index.
ISBN 0-19-511360-8; 0-19-515287-5 (pbk.)
1. Congregational churches—Massachusetts—History—17th century.
2. Congregational churches—Massachusetts—History—18th century.
3. Congregational churches—Massachusetts—Government.
4. Congregational churches—Massachusetts—Membership.
5. Massachusetts—Church history—17th century.   6. Massachusetts—
Church history—18th century.   I. Title.   II. Series: Religion in
America series (Oxford University Press)
BX7148.M4C66   1998
285.8'744'09032—dc21   97-42441

1 3 5 7 9 8 6 4 2

Printed in the United States of America
on acid-free paper

For Harry S. Stout

Acknowledgments

THOUGH RISING INDIVIDUALISM is one important theme in the study that follows, the completion of this project has been anything but an individual effort. Over the course of many years, I have received considerable support from friends, colleagues, institutions, and family members, whose assistance it is my privilege to acknowledge.

This study has received generous financial support from a number of research institutions and foundations, including the John Carter Brown Library, the American Council of Learned Societies, the American Philosophical Association, the Oklahoma Foundation for the Humanities, the Pew Foundation in Religion and American History at Yale University, and the Department of History at Oklahoma State University.

I am also indebted to many research libraries for use of their facilities and collections, including the American Antiquarian Society, Worcester; the Beinecke Rare Book Library at Yale University; the Boston Public Library; the Congregational Library, Boston; the Connecticut Historical Society, Hartford; the Connecticut State Library, Hartford; the Essex Institute, Salem (in particular, I wish to thank William T. La Moy and the late Anne Farnam); the Houghton Library, Harvard University; the John Carter Brown Library, Providence; the Massachusetts Historical Society, Boston; and the New England Historical and Genealogical Society, Boston.

For all of the support of these fine institutions, this study nevertheless would have been impossible if not for the assistance of countless smaller local libraries and local historical societies throughout Massachusetts and, most importantly, the help of dozens of local church historians, secretaries, and pastors who located and provided me access to their church records. I will always remember fondly the warmth and cooperation of the many individuals who expended great time, energy, and enthusiasm to assist a total stranger who happened to have an interest in the history of the local church.

I am also pleased to acknowledge the many friends and colleagues who have helped me in the course of my research and writing. During my graduate career at the

University of Connecticut, I benefited greatly from the instruction and counsel of R. Kent Newmyer and, especially, Richard D. Brown. More recently, I have received support and many useful suggestions from W. Roger Biles, Patricia U. Bonomi, Louise Breen, Jon Butler, James L. Huston, George F. Jewsbury, Merja Kytö, the late Paul Lucas, Elizabeth Reese, Linda Smith Rhodes, and George Selement. I am pleased to extend special thanks to my dear friend and colleague, Kenneth P. Minkema, who has provided me with counsel for fifteen years, and has greatly improved this study through his thoughtful reading of my manuscript.

My family has assisted me throughout in more ways than I can possibly enumerate. I owe great debts (figuratively and literally) to my parents, James F. Cooper, Sr., and Janice H. Cooper, and also wish to acknowledge the encouragement of the late Hazel Harred. My wife, Rebecca, has assisted and encouraged me every step of the way, from accompanying me on various adventures during the Salem days to reading and criticizing my manuscript in the years that followed. My sons, James III and Nathan, show every indication of being able to read this book by the time they turn five; I hope they are willing at least to give it a glance by the time they end their college years.

My greatest thanks are reserved for my friend and mentor Harry S. Stout, to whom this book is dedicated. I cannot begin to describe the time, patience, faith, and effort that he devoted to my scholarship through my graduate career and beyond; whatever successes I have enjoyed as a teacher and a scholar I owe largely to his abilities and his generosity in sharing them. To an uncanny degree, his advice and observations have always been on the mark, except in one area: he informed me a number of times during the 1980s that his obligations to me as an advisor were more important than his obligations to me as a friend. Looking back, it has been in the latter capacity that I have most keenly felt his influence.

Portions of the introduction to this study have appeared previously in James F. Cooper, Jr., "Higher Law, Free Consent, Limited Authority: Church Government and Political Culture in Seventeenth-Century Massachusetts," *New England Quarterly*, 69 (June 1996), 201–222. Portions of chapter 3 appeared in Cooper, "The Confession and Trial of Richard Wayte, Boston, 1640," *William and Mary Quarterly*, 3rd ser., 44 (April 1987), 310–332, and "Anne Hutchinson and the 'Lay Rebellion' Against the Clergy," *New England Quarterly*, 61 (September 1988), 381–397. Portions of chapter 10 appeared in Cooper, "Enthusiasts or Democrats? Separatism, Church Government, and the Great Awakening in Massachusetts," *New England Quarterly*, 65 (June 1992), 265–283.

Stillwater, Oklahoma   J. F. C.
June 1998

Contents

Abbreviations and Editorial Policies

Colonial Massachusetts church records remain in a variety of incarnations. Though a number of sets have been published, most remain in their original manuscript form, and I have used the abbreviation "ms" in the notes when referring to those original manuscripts. A lesser number of church records, though unpublished, have been transcribed, a pastime that appears to have been rather popular among local church historians during the late nineteenth and early twentieth centuries. In some instances the transcriptions were the only records made available to me. I have used the abbreviation "msc" in reference to manuscript copies or manuscript transcriptions of the original records. At times I relied upon transcriptions for simple reasons of legibility. Particularly useful were a number of typescripts that were completed by historians employed by the Works Progress Administration. I have used the abbreviation "ts" when referring to these records.

Most manuscript church records are both dated and paginated, though some entries lack page numbers, or dates, or both. In a few instances, as explained in the endnotes, I used surrounding entries or internal references to determine the year (or month and year) of an entry.

The differing forms of church records complicated my efforts to adopt a consistent editorial policy—when relying upon published or manuscript copies, for example, my editorial policies were circumscribed somewhat by those employed by the original transcriber. Fortunately, most transcribers appear to have taken few liberties with the original records and generally sought to produce verbatim transcriptions. Throughout, I have attempted to remain as close as possible to the records themselves while normalizing slightly for purposes of readability. Original punctuation, capitalization, and spelling have been maintained. Superscripts have been lowered. The use of u and v, i and j, has been standardized. Ampersands have been rendered "and," while the "y" or the English thorn has been transcribed as "th." Archaic abbreviations and contractions have been extended: "ch" has been rendered "church," for example, "Xt" has been rendered "Christ." Punctuation has been silently added or omitted for purposes of intelligibility. Conjectural readings and obvious omissions have been placed in brackets.

Tenacious of Their Liberties

Introduction

IN 1639, JOHN COTTON preached to his Boston congregation on the subject of their relationship to church authority. After addressing a number of issues concerning Congregational church government and lay-clerical relations, Cotton turned to the practical lessons that churchgoers might take from the discourse. Let every man be "studious" of the boundaries the Lord had set around leaders, Cotton urged, for the Bible taught that "if a Church or head of a Church could have done worse, he would have done it: This is one of the strains of nature." Churchgoers must never forget, he concluded, "that all power that is on earth be limited, church power or other." Whether in church, state, or even the family, Cotton continued, "let there be due bounds set." For though "it is counted a matter of danger to the State to limit Prerogatives . . . , it is a further danger, not to have them limited: They will be like a Tempest, if they be not limited."[1]

Recognized by historians as the father of New England Congregationalism, Cotton frequently employed sermons on church government to address larger political principles. In discussions of the nature of authority, he urged his followers to recognize higher laws by which leaders' prerogatives might be limited, such as the higher laws found in the Bible or, later, in the *Cambridge Platform*, which the Puritans would come to describe as their "constitution" of church government. Perhaps most important, Cotton justified the principle of free consent, affirming that New Englanders gathered their churches voluntarily and reached no formal church decisions without the consent of the laity.[2]

Ordinary lay people understood and embraced these political principles. In 1669, several dozen laymen in Newbury announced that they "stood unmoveable" regarding the teachings on church government advanced by Cotton and the other Congregational "fathers." They employed those principles to suspend their pastor from office, complaining that in violating the members' right of free consent he had refused to acknowledge the higher laws of the *Cambridge Platform* and "the mind of Christ." "We own Mr. Hooker's Polity, Mr. Mather's catechisme, and Mr. Cotton's

Keyes," the members wrote, justifying their decision to a ministerial council. "Our controversy," they continued, "is whether God hath placed the power in the elder, or the whole church, to judge between truth and error, right and wrong, brother and brother, and all things of church concernment." Massachusetts' civil and church authorities eventually acknowledged the legitimacy of the members' grievances, upholding the principles of limited authority and free consent. Well into the next century, churchgoers remained "tenacious of their Liberties," as Cotton Mather observed, refusing to accept any innovations in church government in the absence of lay approval, and resisting any effort to abridge their rights.[3]

The implications of Congregational practice and theory have fixated historians of colonial New England. Pointing to the prominent role of Massachusetts in the American Revolution, writers have traditionally described the colony as a seedbed of democracy. In attempting to trace the roots of New England's libertarian ideology, a generation of early historians asserted that the democratic principles and practices espoused by Cotton and the other Congregational fathers explained why Massachusetts emerged as the birthplace of the American Republic.[4] Later historians dismissed these Congregational writers as quaint "filiopietists," whose distorted accounts represented celebrations of their own religious tradition rather than serious explorations of relevant themes of early American history. Scholars such as Perry Miller admitted that, in theory, seventeenth-century Congregationalism contained "democratic stirrings." But in practice, Miller argued, a number of "provisions that could effectively stifle those impulses" permitted ministers to control church affairs. When it came to the actual implementation of church government in New England, Miller wrote, the seventeenth-century Hartford minister Samuel Stone "hit happily upon a perfect description" of Congregational practice: "'a speaking *Aristocracy* in the face of a silent *Democracy*.'"[5]

A generation of scholars writing in the 1960s and 1970s agreed with Miller that, notwithstanding ministerial claims to the contrary, Congregational principles of limited authority, free consent, and, especially, popular participation remained largely confined to theory. While church government may have been initially "democratic" (that is, lay controlled), most asserted, unpleasant New World experiences such as Anne Hutchinson's attack upon the clergy during the "Antinomian crisis" of 1636–1638 motivated ministers to draw in the reins of authority and assume a more aristocratic control of church affairs, which they maintained throughout the colonial era. Lay people consequently enjoyed little genuine influence in the administration of church government.[6]

Having apparently set aside the larger significance of Congregationalism in shaping political culture, scholars still faced the challenge of uncovering the roots of New England democracy. They responded by turning their attention to analyses of secular or civil politics. A barrage of studies in the 1960s and 1970s demonstrated that the vast majority of freeholders in Massachusetts and Connecticut enjoyed the right to vote for elected officials and upon local issues. These conclusions seemed to reinforce the long-held notion that the town meeting served as the birthplace of New England's democratic tradition.[7] But Kenneth Lockridge has pointed to the obvious limitations of these findings. Town meetings convened irregularly, often meeting only four times a year. When local freeholders exercised their right to vote, their main purpose was to choose selectmen, who then reached most decisions for the town. While this arrangement certainly represented a step in the direction of republican or representative government, it hardly constitutes an example of participatory democracy; in fact, Lockridge argued that local elites discouraged ordinary people from participating in town politics. More important, there is every reason to question the extent to which secular politics served as a training ground that shaped popular political attitudes; historians have produced little evidence to suggest, for instance, that townsmen discussed larger political principles at town meetings.[8]

Since the middle 1970s, studies on the origins of New England democracy have nearly ground to a halt. In monographs, textbooks, and in survey courses, the vast majority of American historians express the simple and conventional wisdom that "the Puritans were not democratic." It is hardly the purpose of this study to refute that conclusion, or to suggest that Puritans practiced a seventeenth-century version of modern American grassroots democracy in either church or state. It is well known that the Puritans equated unrestrained democracy with "anarchy," and that Puritan spokesmen such as Cotton strongly believed in deference and the hierarchical nature of society. "Democracy," Cotton observed, in his widely quoted letter to Lord Say and Seal, "I do not conceyve that ever God did ordeyne as a fitt government."[9] In their analyses of specific practices in local churches, historians have looked beyond the disclaimers that Miller offered to point out that Congregationalism disempowered women completely, denying them the right to vote in church affairs and forbidding them to even speak in church. Even among the men, only full church members were allowed to participate in the decision-making process. Given the cyclical pattern of membership rates, the proportion of churchgoers eligible to participate in government was greater in some periods than in others. Moreover, in a hierarchical, deferential culture, we might expect that more prominent local figures would wield more authority in church affairs than ordinary farmers, and in fact they did.[10]

In both practice and theory, then, Congregationalism contained strong undemocratic elements. But in focusing so heavily upon those elements, scholars have missed an important link between Congregationalism and New England's libertarian ideology. Congregational thought and practice in fact served as one indigenous seedbed of several concepts that would flourish during the Revolutionary generation, including the notions that government derives its legitimacy from the voluntary consent of the governed, governors should be chosen by the governed, rulers should be accountable to the ruled, and constitutional checks should limit both the governors and the people.[11] Moreover, while by no means democratic, Congregationalism certainly encouraged a significant (if varying) degree of popular participation.

Notwithstanding its undeniable debts to the Enlightenment and the English dissenting tradition, Revolutionary ideology in Massachusetts emerged from a political culture that contained deeply rooted libertarian traditions stretching back to its founding generation of Congregational settlers. And while local "secular" institutions also contributed to those traditions, Patricia U. Bonomi has correctly observed that "all that has been said and written about the New England town as the 'school of democracy' can be applied with equal or greater force to the church congregation."[12]

Congregationalism has appeared devoid of larger political significance to modern scholars primarily because of historians' particular focus in studying the history of early New England: until recent years, they have examined Puritanism mainly from the vantage point of the ministry. Previous analyses of Congregationalism have relied almost entirely upon ministerial tracts and treatises, which historians have read so selectively as virtually to ignore clerical affirmations of the lay role in church government. Scholars have been so obsessed with Cotton's letter to Lord Say and Seal, for example, that they have overlooked the fact that Cotton defended a strong popular *component* in church government in every description of Congregationalism that he ever wrote. Like Perry Miller, many writers have accepted ministerial discussions of clerical authority at face value, while insisting that ministerial descriptions of lay rights were "only theoretical." Finally, historians have overestimated the strength of clerical unity on issues of church government (particularly during the eighteenth century), and they have underestimated the significance of the lay right of consent. Consequently, scholars have mistakenly equated the desires of some ministers to force changes in church government upon the laity with actual developments in local churches.

In addition to their preoccupation with the clergy, many modern historians of Congregational church government have also shared an assumption that ministers and their flocks came to inhabit separate and even competing worlds of meaning, and so suggest that church government became an arena primarily characterized by lay-clerical contention and competition.[13] The implications of this conflict model have been called into question by a more recent group of studies that focuses instead on the extent to which leaders and followers shared a "collective mentality" or a "popular religion." Lay people, we have learned, were not merely passive receptacles of elite culture but were "active makers of their own world view." But although they have successfully demonstrated that churchgoers shared their ministers' theology of conversion, sense of "mission," and other religious values, recent historians of popular religion have offered little analysis of lay and clerical interchanges on the important subject of church order, and they have ignored lay initiatives in the actual government of Massachusetts churches.[14]

Far different conclusions concerning lay-clerical relations and the relationship between church practices and political culture emerge if we remember that Congregationalism, like Puritanism in general, placed an extraordinary emphasis upon the role of the laity. Just as Puritan ministers sought to kindle lay spirituality and to enhance lay understanding of the sermon through the use of an easily comprehensible "plain style" of preaching, so they sought to foster lay commitment to church government by teaching Congregationalism to the laity, by grounding the system in popular consent, and by granting churchgoers a central role in Congregational practices.

Consider how the restoration of the laity alters the significance of John Cotton's discussion of the limits of authority. Historians might easily dismiss these comments as mere theory had they only appeared in a treatise on church government directed at a clerical audience. But Cotton delivered them publicly, in Sunday sermons, before Boston's open congregation, and it is precisely the implications of this crucial point that historians have neglected to explore.[15] The public setting of Cotton's observations on the boundaries of authority calls into question assertions that clerical discussions of church government remained confined to theory just as it casts doubt upon suggestions that competing conceptions of church power and struggles over lay rights divided authoritarian ministers and rebellious churchgoers. To the contrary, Cotton's comments demonstrate that from the early years of settlement ministers themselves shared a healthy distrust of authority and *taught* the laity to demand lay participation and to resist the abuse of authority and the subversion of higher scriptural laws, whether by magistrates, other church members, or ministers themselves.

While overestimating ministerial authoritarianism in church government, historians have left the laity out of the equation nearly altogether, again reflecting, as David D. Hall has observed, the "contempt" for popular religion that has "infiltrated the telling of the history of New England Congregationalism."[16] This study seeks to demonstrate, for the first time, that ordinary church members in fact learned their lessons well, put ministerial teachings into practice, and shared the government of their churches with the clergy. It is not, however, *merely* a study of the laity, nor does it suggest that lay people, rather than ministers, dominated church affairs. While such a conclusion would represent an exciting reversal of existing interpretations, it would only perpetuate the myth that early Congregational church government can be neatly reduced to a division between the ministers and "the people."

Congregationalism's driving dynamic was in fact one of lay-clerical *interchange*. Although lay people and ministers frequently tested the boundaries of each other's authority, few struggles during the colonial era pitted a united laity against a united clergy. Throughout this period, ministers, to greater and lesser degrees, supported lay participation, if sometimes grudgingly, and advanced principles of higher law, limited authority, and accountability, if not always unanimously. During most controversies (whether local or colonywide), a significant proportion of lay people usually supported the ministers. Likewise, important voices in the clerical community always remained concerned with the popular response to threats upon lay rights, tempering their colleagues in times of rising ministerial authoritarianism. In general, church government did not divide New England culture along lay-clerical lines but served instead as a powerful component of a popular religion and a shared political ideology—an ideology whose fundamentals of constitutionalism, free consent, limited authority, an informed citizenry, and popular participation were shared by lay people and most ministers throughout much of the colonial era.

In attempting to illuminate the laity's contributions to Congregational church government, this study supplements ministerial sources, whenever possible, with an examination of manuscript church records where, in the minutes of local church meetings, lay participation is evident and where theories of government were put into practice. For all that has been written on New England Congregationalism over the last century and a half, no previous scholar has analyzed church government from the vantage point of these records and the church practices they describe. Scattered throughout Massachusetts in countless town libraries, local historical societies, banks, church vaults, private attics, and, in one horrifying case, on the floor of a pastor's coat closet, these manuscripts provide a far clearer picture of the inner workings of Congregational churches than the centralized and largely published sources historians have utilized in the past.

In tracking down useful church records, I have relied heavily upon Harold F. Worthley's "Inventory of the Records of the Particular (Congregational) Churches of Massachusetts gathered 1620–1805," an invaluable tool that provides descriptions of and locations for nearly all extant colonial Massachusetts church records.[17] Unlike Worthley, I cannot claim to have examined all remaining church records; as Worthley makes clear, dozens of these manuscripts are so fragmentary as to be nearly useless for the kind of analysis I have undertaken. But I have examined all extant church records for churches gathered prior to 1700 and nearly all of the eighteenth-century records that, according to Worthley, were likely to contain useful information. In all, I have examined over one hundred sets of local church records.

Church records are by no means a perfect source. In some cases, ministers or lay leaders took extraordinary pains to leave greatly detailed summaries of church meetings, even including verbatim dialogues of church proceedings. At their best, such records offer an unparalleled glimpse at the decision-making process within local churches and at times provide a portrait of lay-clerical relations strikingly different from the one that historians have previously presented. Unfortunately, church records that are sufficiently complete to offer an open window to the past are as scarce as they are illuminating. Most church records are of a far more cursory nature. Some, though very regular, include largely line-a-day entries that are so brief as to be of little utility for the historian. Others are clearly fragmentary in nature. Gaps in local church records often extend for years and even decades. Internal cross-checking sometimes turns up references to disciplinary repentances for which no previous church censure remains on record. Though the records of some individual churches appear to be sufficiently regular to sustain quantitative conclusions, such analysis is always tricky and often impossible.

It is also important to acknowledge that ministers generally kept the church records, raising the question of whether they left slanted accounts of church affairs. I have seen little evidence to support such a conclusion. It was not unusual for lay people to keep church records, and there is no discernable difference in the content or tone of records kept by ministers relative to those kept by ruling elders or other lay officers.[18] Likewise, verbatim accounts of church trials, such as those recorded by the Boston merchant Robert Keayne, contain little to contradict summaries that appear in the "official" records.[19] Although some ministers added church records to their private diaries, most church records were public documents. Lay people seldom (if ever) complained that their ministers recorded unfair accounts of church affairs.[20]

A more telling difficulty concerns the geographically uneven nature of the records: a relative paucity of records remains from western Massachusetts and Plymouth Colony, making lay-clerical relations in those areas far more difficult to assess. The problem of the representativeness of the records is further complicated by the principle of Congregational autonomy. As is well known, Massachusetts churches were not required to adopt identical procedures and, in fact, some variation in admissions, discipline, and other church practices was a constant in the seventeenth and eighteenth centuries.

Nevertheless, historians have perhaps made too much of the theme of variability within Congregational churches. Scholars have heavily emphasized the dissent to Congregationalism offered by figures like Solomon Stoddard, for example, but no historian has even attempted to demonstrate that significant numbers of churches in western Massachusetts (much less the colony as a whole) practiced the autocratic principles of church government that the Northampton minister advocated in his published writings. Little is known even about specific practices within Stoddard's own church. Caution must also be exercised in considering church government in Plymouth Colony. Richard Mather observed in 1639 that he was aware of no significant differences in church practice in Plymouth and Massachusetts Bay, a position that fragmentary evidence supports. We know that Duxbury pastor Ralph Partridge assisted in the construction of the *Cambridge Platform* of church discipline, and the more complete records for Plymouth Colony dating from later in the seventeenth century suggest that church government varied little from practices in the Bay. Nonetheless, while it is my belief that lay-clerical relations and church practices overlapped considerably in Plymouth and in Massachusetts Bay, a definitive assessment cannot be offered in the absence of early church records.[21]

The geographical distribution of the remaining records reflects the simple fact that the vast majority of churches and churchgoers were located in eastern and central Massachusetts. And these many volumes confirm that in the overwhelming majority of churches, variations in practice pertained largely to procedural details rather than the larger decision-making process. Little evidence exists in the records to suggest that lay people in one Congregational church frequently exercised a fundamentally greater or lesser degree of authority than lay people in neighboring Congregational churches. The records do confirm that throughout the colonial era virtually all congregations elected ministers and lay officers, held their leaders accountable to higher laws, and reached church decisions by popular consent.

Congregationalism operated in many shifting contexts over the course of the seventeenth and early eighteenth centuries, as churches introduced innovations such as the Halfway Covenant, England imposed religious toleration, ministers advanced claims of lay "declension" in spirituality, churches came to vary in their specific practices in worship and admissions requirements, and a spirit of individualism eroded the communitarian ideals in which Congregationalism was grounded. But in matters of church government, most ministers and churchgoers continued to inhabit a shared space. Despite the reservations of some clergymen, ministers continued throughout the colonial era to emphasize to the laity the basic conceptions of limited authority, the accountability of leaders, and free consent. And churchgoers continued to learn the Congregational system and to participate in the decision-making process. For nearly a century and a half, church government served as a political training ground for ordinary churchgoers, one that profoundly shaped Massachusetts political culture up to the American Revolution.

1

The Implementation
of the Congregational Way

LOOKING BACK AT THE PURITANS' painful decision to abandon their home-land for the uncertainty of a New World, Cambridge pastor Thomas Shepard and Dedham pastor John Allin singled out church government as the primary consideration for churchgoers and ministers alike. "Popish" practices in the Church of England had grown to such "an intolerable height," they recalled, that "the consciences of God's saints and servants . . . could no longer bear them." The mere "hope" of "enjoying Christ in his ordinances" persuaded thousands of dissenters to "forsake dearest relations, parents, brethren, sisters, Christian friends and aquaintances, overlook the dangers of the vast seas, the thought whereof was a terror to many," and "go into a wilderness where we could forecast nothing but care and temptation." Echoing the ministers' sentiments, the layman Roger Clap praised his "wonderous" God for prevailing upon the first planters to "remove themselves, and their Wives and Children, from their Native Country, and to leave their gallant Scituations there, to come into this Wilderness, to set up the pure Worship of God here!"[1]

According to these founders, in short, the Puritans left their country not to pursue their own system of economics, politics, or even theology. They ventured to Massachusetts to establish and practice a "purified" system of church discipline, a system stripped of all Catholic ceremonies and "humane inventions," and ordered instead entirely according to the "perfect" model contained in the Bible.

While later historians have identified a host of other motives for migration, church government would nonetheless be of transcendent importance in New England. As historians from Perry Miller to Avihu Zakai have observed, the founders regarded their New World venture as a sacred mission in the course of providential history, and the establishment of Congregational churches represented the central means toward the completion of their larger goal of world redemption.[2] As John Cotton, the "teacher" of the First Church of Boston later observed, the creation of a pure system of worship represented a duty and a privilege that would stand as nothing less than the crowning achievement and culmination of the Reformation:

> The Lord hath given us to enjoy Churches, and Congregational Assemblies
> by his Covenant, to worship him in all his holy Ordinances; that he hath given
> us to look for no Laws but his Word, no ruler nor forms of worship, but such
> as he hath set downe in his word; no platforms of Doctrine, but such as are
> held forth in the word of the Prophets and Apostles: It is such a privilege,
> that for 1260 years, the Christian world Knew not the meaning of it.[3]

Any deeper understanding of the Puritans' extraordinary efforts to establish the
"true" church—and their sometimes fanatical determination to preserve it—must
take into consideration the fact that church order, or God's "ordinances," stood at
the very core of the Puritans' mission, self-definition, and national identity.

Congregational spokesmen went so far as to suggest that the very success of the
Puritans in the New World would hinge upon their ability to establish and maintain
this scripturally based system of worship. "If God plant his Ordinances among you,
fear not, he will maintain them," Cotton assured his followers. But "as soon as God's
Ordinances cease," he cautioned, "your Security ceaseth likewise. . . . Look into all
the stories whether divine or humane," Cotton concluded,

> and you shall never finde that God ever rooted out a people that had the
> Ordinances planted amongst them, and themselves planted into the Ordi-
> nances: Never did God suffer such plants to be plucked up; on all their glory
> shall be a defence.

Thomas Hooker agreed that "the saints of God are marvelous importunate to keep
God in his Ordinances, . . . the want of which is under the penalty of death and
demnation."[4] The ordinances, Cotton continued, would represent the foundation
of government and social order in the New World. "It is better that the commonwealth be fashioned to the setting forth of Gods house, which is his church," than to
"accommodate the church frame to the civill state," he observed, expressing in
unmistakable terms his conviction that church government would serve as New
England's cornerstone.[5]

An understanding of the centrality of church government in Massachusetts is
especially important insofar as the system rested upon several revolutionary principles that would shape popular political perceptions for generations of churchgoers. These principles and their relationship to church order had gradually evolved
over the course of more than a century: first in Calvin's Geneva and later in sixteenth-
century England, where divines such as Thomas Cartwright, William Ames, Robert
Browne, and Henry Barrowe wrote freely on the need to reform and "purify" the
Anglican church.[6] Though English radicals and moderates differed over many particulars, most Puritan writers agreed upon several fundamentals that Browne described as early as 1582. The first of these was a belief in the sanctity of higher laws—
specifically, those of the Bible—over the laws of men. Echoing standard Reformed
sentiments, Browne and other Puritan writers based their analyses of church gov-

ernment and the larger nature of authority upon the assumption that the Bible contained a clear and specific pattern of church government, "not a partiall, but a perfect rule of Faith, and manners." The "calling" of reformers, Browne observed, was to initiate the "planting of the church" according to these New Testament principles. Every particular of worship and practice would be grounded in Scripture rules, and ministers and members alike were bound to obey them. In matters of church order, all earthly authority was strictly limited by the higher laws found in the Bible.[7]

English Puritans also agreed that reformed churches must be organized and operated voluntarily, on the basis of free consent. In general, as Edmund S. Morgan, among others, has observed, the Puritans strongly believed that popular consent must serve as the basis for government in both church and state.[8] English Puritans thus argued that individual churches should be organized "by a free mutuall consent of Believers joyning and covenanting to live as Members of a holy Society togeather." This church "covenant," a written agreement signed freely by all members, testified to their willingness to "geve up our selves to be of the church and people of God" and live and worship according to Scripture "by submitting our selves to [God's] lawes and governement."[9]

Since individuals contracted or "covenanted" only with God and one another in agreeing to submit to God's word, Puritans believed that no human authority outside this local covenant maintained a right to claim jurisdiction over internal church affairs. Unlike the Presbyterian form of church government, Congregationalism granted ministerial "Synods, Classes, Assemblies or Councils" no binding authority over local congregations. "We confine and bound all Ecclesiastical power within the limits onely of one particular Congregation," William Bradshaw wrote, affirming this principle of Congregational autonomy, "holding that the greatest Ecclesiastical power ought not stretch beyond the same." The same restrictions applied to the civil government: magistrates may "doo nothing concerning the Church," Browne professed. It "belongeth not to them" to "compell religion, to plant churches by power," or "to force a submission to Ecclesiastical goverment by lawes and penalties."[10]

Finally, English Puritans agreed that principles and practices of lay participation must stand as centerpieces in the government of true churches. "Every christian Congregation hath power and commandement to elect and ordeine their own ministerie," Henry Ainsworth and Francis Johnson averred. Local congregations also maintained the right to depose ministers guilty of "defalt" in "lyfe, Doctrine or administration," and might even "cut them off by excommunication." Christ also granted the congregation the rights to admit new members, and to remove offenders through the application of church discipline.[11]

For all its radical implications, early Congregational theory in England remained for the most part just that—theory. While Puritan thought was certainly revolutionary in its general stance toward the laity and in many larger principles of church order, few congregations enjoyed the opportunity to practice the new biblical form of government prior to New World settlement. As several scholars have noted, only a handful of Puritans, mainly Separatists in England and Holland, actually established Congregational churches. Because Congregationalism or "Independency" never achieved thorough preeminence in England, it could not influence English political culture to the extent that it stood to in Massachusetts, where Congregationalism would become the official state church and where, for the first time, Puritans enjoyed an opportunity to practice their new system of church order on a large scale.[12]

In Massachusetts, principles of free consent, limitations on authority, higher law, and popular participation would no longer remain theoretical notions debated in clerical treatises and practiced in a few isolated, outcast churches. On the contrary, these principles would influence the actual operation of government in virtually every church in the Bay. Consequently, the founders took a monumental step prior to the gathering of the First Church of Salem by reaffirming as their point of departure the single most important tenet of English Congregationalism, that of *sola scriptura*: "[T]he Reformation of the church was to be endeavored according to the written word of God." The faithful would base every decision bearing on church government upon the higher laws found in Scripture rather than the carnal whims of men. It is impossible to overemphasize the larger significance of this principle and its relationship to Puritan conceptions of authority in New England. Adherence to the principle of sola scriptura placed strict limitations upon all human authority, imposing a sacred duty upon ministers and members alike to make certain that all churchgoers adhered to these higher laws in matters of church government.[13]

The principle of sola scriptura required Massachusetts ministers to teach their followers that any practice of church order not drawn from the Scriptures positively violated the Scriptures and therefore abridged churchgoers' Christian liberty to worship in accordance with the biblical model. In order to preserve that liberty, John Cotton warned his Boston congregation, the people of God must never allow grasping men to usurp Christ's authority in the church. They must avoid and even resist "humane inventions": church practices created and justified by man rather than Christ and the Bible.

> They that bringe in an Invention of worship besids a Comand [i.e., not found in Scripture], thay will mayntayne it agaynst a Comand, and than he makes him Selfe a kinge [in] the church and thay will roote out Gods Command, and worship for thear own Invention. Those that will bringe in ther own Inventions will slight Gods Institutions . . . . You may better be a drunkard, Swarer, than to make Contience of a Ceremony.[14]

Once the churches wandered from the perfect system of government found in the Bible and strayed down the path toward "humane inventions," Cotton cautioned, disagreements would erupt over those inventions and God's vineyard would wither and die. In words that would later haunt Massachusetts churches during the controversy over the Halfway Covenant, Cotton warned that once Cerimonies and Inventions are brought in by the Sones of men, and men canot agre abowt thear owne Inventions: it will drive Christ owt of the Cuntry. If once yow begin to qwarell and Contend abowt Ceremonies and humane Inventions the next Newes is, it makes Christ leave the Cuntry, and depart into Gretia the Gentills Cuntry.[15]

In their efforts to understand whether ministers and ordinary people shared a larger world of meaning, or a "popular religion," historians have sought to understand the extent to which churchgoers internalized the sort of ministerial teachings that Cotton expressed in these sermons.[16] In the realm of church government, as we shall see, the laity not only shared Cotton's sentiments, but they accepted as a sacred charge his demands to practice a system of church order based upon the higher law of Scripture rather than the precepts of men, and to preserve their own Christian liberties within that system. For generations to come, nearly every churchgoer in Massachusetts—minister and layman, orthodox and dissenter—strove and sometimes battled to attain these higher goals.

Massachusetts Bay's first settlers formalized their commitment to biblical supremacy by making sola scriptura the basis of the voluntary covenants upon which they gathered their churches. The Salem founders solemnly vowed in their church covenant to

> give our selves to the Lord Jesus Christ and the word of his grace, fore the teaching, ruleing and sanctifyeing of us in matters of worship and conversation, resolveing to . . . oppose all contrarie wayes, cannons, and constitutions of men in his worship.

The Dorchester covenant, written by pastor Richard Mather, voiced the same themes in stronger terms:

> Wee do . . . promise . . . to endeavor the establishment amongst ourselves of all holy ordinances which [Christ] hath appointed for his church here on earth, and to observe all and every of them . . . opposing to the utmost of our power whatsoever is contrary thereunto, and bewailing from our hearts our own neglect thereof in former tyme, and our polluting ourselves with any sinful inventions of men.

While the few surviving covenants from the first decade of settlement vary slightly in particulars, all pointed to the necessity of establishing a system of church order based in every detail upon the higher laws of the Bible.[17]

In the act of covenanting, Massachusetts Puritans put into practice another theoretical tenet that was central to Congregationalism: free consent. The founders made clear that an adherence to Scripture rules alone did not give "essential being" to a church. Rather, as Cotton put it, "it is their mutual covenant with one another, that gives first being to a church." The point is crucial: for Congregationalists, church authority was grounded not only upon theological principles found in the Scriptures, but upon the congruent political principles of contractualism and mutual consent. As John Cotton observed,

> From the constitution [i.e., covenant] doth flow Jurisdiction. For in all relations a covenant is the foundation. I have no power over my wife, nor servant but by covenant. The magistrate hath no power over me, but by my consent. So in the Church, the Covenant is the foundation of that relation and power we have over one another.[18]

In signing the covenant, churchgoers thus bound themselves on political as well as religious grounds: any violation of Congregational precepts represented not only a sinful violation of Scripture law, but a violation of the principle of mutual consent as well.

While Massachusetts clergymen strongly supported free consent in principle, they also believed that voluntarism was a practical necessity in the wilderness of the New World, where few mechanisms of social control existed. As Thomas Hooker noted in a public sermon, ordinary people would be far more likely to bless their church and civil governments if they entered into them voluntarily and were granted the right to elect their leaders: "[B]y a free choice, the hearts of the people will be more inclined to the love of the persons chosen and more ready to yield obedience."[19]

In addition to their affirmations of free consent and sola scriptura, these early covenants institutionalized popular participation in church government. By affixing a signature to the covenant, each churchgoer pledged to assume an active role in church affairs. Congregationalism entrusted lay people with the duty of making certain that church officers governed according to the Bible, and granted them the right to add or refuse consent to church decisions on that basis. All formal church actions, from admissions to discipline to the adoption or modification of church procedures, required the consent of the membership.

The privilege of lay consent carried with it weighty responsibilities. For one, lay people could hardly offer informed consent in church affairs in the absence of a profound understanding of the Congregational way. As pastor George Moxon of Springfield pointed out, "[H]ow can a man be a judge if he be not acquainted with the law?" Free consent and lay participation would thus require members to learn the larger principles and specific procedures of Congregationalism, and its scriptural foundations as well. These requirements stood to shape fundamentally not only Congregational church government in Massachusetts but the larger political culture. During the founding of each church and later, as we shall see, during admissions procedures, election of officers, and discipline, ministers opened their Bibles and taught, explained, and, occasionally, debated Congregational principles and practices with the laity.[20]

The founders' emphasis upon free consent and an informed laity is well illustrated by the lengthy procedures leading up to the gathering of the First Church of Dedham in 1637. Pastor John Allin wove the themes of ministerial instruction, lay participation, popular consent, and higher law throughout his narrative of the foundation of his church, the only account we have from the 1630s that includes specific details of a church gathering. Most striking about this example is the effort Allin expended in discussing church order with his flock. The pastor recounted how, for months prior to the church's inception, he and a small number of prospective members gathered weekly to discuss Congregational practices, "that we might gaine further light in the waies of Christ['s] Kingdome and government of his Church."[21] He began the proceedings by preparing the founding members or "living stones" for active participation in government, making certain each individual understood every detail concerning the nature of the church, membership requirements, elections, administration, and the respective duties of members and officers. "Conscious of [their] duty to sett up every ordinance of christ in his church" and their "great need of the same," Allin and the founders rehearsed the Scripture grounds of even the most familiar practices. They considered the "right constitution of a church" and "the nature of the covenant," from the books of Genesis, Exodus, and Second Corinthians. Having defined and biblically justified the covenant, they discussed the specific "manner of gathering saints together." Turning to admissions, they reviewed the errors of the Church of England, which conferred membership at birth and confirmed it with baptism. According to the first chapter of Revelation, they believed, the local church ought to control admissions in New England. Likewise, though it had been practiced in New England for several years, they reaffirmed from First Corinthians that "churches should be churches of saints" and must therefore require of members a test of grace, or conversion. They finalized no decision until Allin and all prospective members were "clear" that the point under consideration indeed represented an "institution of Christ under the gospel."

Allin concluded by reminding the laity that free consent and the "general agreement" of the members would serve as the foundation for his office and church government in general. Though the settlers had recognized Allin as their unanimous choice for minister since their very arrival in Dedham, he nonetheless insisted that the membership "would seriously amonst themselves in his absence frely discusse whatever any of them might conceive materiall for or against [him] and so deliver what the lord suggested unto them which might either be ground of laying aside the motion or of admonition or advice concerning the faithfull disc[h]arge of such an office."[22] In the absence of objections, Allin proceeded to remind his followers of the significance of popular consent. The very "band of this society" that "knitt them together," he explained, was "a mutuall consent." He therefore offered the laity yet another chance "to propound any questions pertinent to the case or any objections or doubts remaining in any conscience" about the proceedings. Only then did the church extend invitations to the neighboring elders and proceed to a formal gathering. The church was born when the minister "publikely read" the covenant and the laity "consented thereto" by both a "lifting up of hands" and by signing the document.[23]

In writing his "brief history" of the Dedham church founding, Allin explained that he aimed his work at "future ages to make use of in any case that may occur wherein light may be fettched from any examples of things past." He and his colleagues perceived their roles in history as founders of a new order, and they foresaw the likelihood that future generations would subject their judgment to careful scrutiny. Recognizing that many of their precedents would influence church government for decades or even centuries to come, ministers attempted to establish a firm foundation. As the Dedham example illustrates, they accomplished this end by adopting a system that embraced and advanced several principles that would remain ingrained in the political culture of Massachusetts throughout the colonial era: adherence to fundamental or "higher" laws, strict limitations upon all human authority, free consent, local self-government, and, especially, extensive lay participation.[24]

In attempting to develop and justify the details of the New England Way, the ministers encountered a number of daunting obstacles. First, though from the outset Massachusetts ministers agreed on larger principles of church order such as free consent and sola scriptura, the early settlers apparently came equipped only with these general outlines of the Congregational Way. Salem's minister-historian William Hubbard, reflecting upon the "honest minded men" who gathered his church in 1629, asserted that the founders "were not precisely fixed upon any particular order or form of government, but like *rasa tabula*, fit to receive any impression," providing it "could be delineated out of the word of God." Hubbard overstated the colonists' lack of familiarity with Congregationalism, but he was correct in suggesting that neither church nor civil authorities had much practical experience with the new form of church government; a difficult challenge faced them as they attempted to untangle those "knotty places of the scriptures" in order to determine the specific forms, practices, and duties of church government that the Bible required.[25]

Ministers could not spend years debating or deliberating over proper forms and procedures of church order. They faced an immediate need to establish the foundations of church and state, which consequently forced them simultaneously to construct, instruct, and practice the Congregational Way. The early development of Congregationalism was consequently rather haphazard. It was not unusual for ministers to contradict one another during the first years of settlement or, on occasion, to reverse themselves, and many specific features of church order remained unresolved until the late 1630s and beyond. Questions as basic as membership and baptism requirements remained unsettled six or seven years after the Salem founding. In 1630, John Cotton insisted upon comprehensive baptism; he formally reversed his position in 1636. Richard Mather, another principal architect of New England Congregationalism, similarly demonstrated inexperience. He saw the gathering of his Dorchester church in 1636 delayed after authorities expressed concerns over his procedures and the spiritual state of prospective members, some of whom grounded

their hopes for conversion in works, others upon enthusiastical "dreams and rav-
ishes of spirit by fits."[26] Even greater confusion surrounded very specific provisions
of Congregationalism. Ministers understood that in principle a group of believers
gathered out of the world constituted a church. But how, specifically, was a church
to be gathered? They understood that the congregation maintained the right to elect
its officers. But how were elections to be conducted? What procedures did the Bible
require for ordination? Here, as Hubbard noted, "they had not yet waded into the
controversy of church discipline as to be very positive."[27]

The principle of Congregational independence represented another significant
obstacle to the early establishment of a shared orthodoxy in church government.
Before gathering the first church in the Bay, the Salem founders affirmed that while
they welcomed any assistance their Plymouth neighbors might provide, the Salem
church ought not acknowledge any ecclesiastical jurisdiction in the Plymouth church.
Likewise, the Dedham founders declared that should neighboring observers offer
any "just impediment" concerning their procedures in gathering their church, they
might "desist awhile from this our purpose," but they would do so "willingly of
ourselves" and "not by any autority of any one or all the bretheren Assembled." Here
the Dedham and Salem churches put into practice another central tenet of Congregationalism that would endure in Massachusetts for centuries: ideally, all decisions
affecting a particular church would be reached by that church. Churches frequently
offered "advice" to one another and expected this advice to be seriously considered.
But, at least in theory, no church, elder, or group of elders in Massachusetts enjoyed
binding authority over another church.[28]

A response to dissent from the church hierarchy in England, Congregational independence served an important function in Massachusetts, where the scattered
nature of settlement made self-sufficiency and autonomy especially desirable.[29] Ministers would soon discover, however, that Congregational autonomy created many
potential difficulties. The principle not only allowed for differences in specific practices but it also provided no formal machinery to discipline wayward churches. The
elders might attempt to persuade neighboring offenders to mend their ways, or deny
heterodox churches the "right hand of fellowship," cutting them off from all formal
interchurch relations. But as Presbyterians would later point out, little remedy beyond
voluntary compliance existed should a clergyman or even an entire church dissent
from the interpretations of the majority, a problem that would bedevil the Congregationalists later in the century.[30]

The founders, perhaps naively, did not expect the principle of Congregational
autonomy to create significant difficulties. The Scriptures, Puritan divines repeated,
contained a perfect, practical system of church government. While in some areas
the Bible might seem diffuse or even contradictory, in matters of church government the Scriptures would, upon careful study, prove perfectly clear. Because "every
verse admitted of but one interpretation," the founders expected "a general and

hearty concurrance" among the ministers who would construct New England's church government. Independent churches would thus voluntarily adopt and practice the same church order.[31]

The founders' hopes for total unanimity in the details of church government were quickly dashed: almost immediately individual ministers began to disagree with the majority's interpretations of the Bible, initiating a steady undercurrent of minor quibbles over procedural matters that occasionally grew into louder disputes. At the gathering of the Salem church, for example, civil and church officers discovered that "in some points of church discipline [Salem pastor] Higginson's principles" were "descrepant" from those of the Plymouth founders, while in Boston, John Cotton continued to vacillate on a number of topics ranging from membership requirements to ministerial maintenance. Later in the 1630s larger disagreements arose when individual ministers questioned the standard definition of a church covenant and the proper method of gathering a church.[32]

Settlement of these sorts of disagreements and standardization of procedures required ministers to circumvent some of the implications of Congregational autonomy by establishing lines of communication between churches and engaging in discussions among themselves about church order. As the Dedham example suggests, ministers often discussed issues of church government with their flocks. But there is little evidence in the early records to support the claims of some historians that ordinary church members played a dominant role in determining specific provisions of the ordinances.[33] Instead, the first settlers seem to have relied heavily upon clerical interpretation and expertise during the "invention" phase of Congregational development. At the gathering of the First Church of Cambridge in 1636, for instance, Thomas Shepard raised the question before neighboring elders and churchgoers of "what number [of initial members] were needful to make a church." John Winthrop's account of the proceedings includes nothing to suggest that lay people assisted in the formulation of an answer to this question. Rather, "some of the ancient ministers, conferring shortly together, gave answer": while the "scripture did not set down any certain rule for the number," they decided that "seven might be a fit number." Similarly, though Winthrop observed that "the neighboring churches" determined that Richard Mather's fledgling congregation was "not meet, at present, to be the foundation of a church," he also noted that the specific conclusions were reached "by the elders, and the magistrates"—that is to say, the elders acted on behalf of their churches in persuading the Dorchester church to delay its gathering.[34]

Ministers also standardized procedures of church government in more formal "meetings of the elders" that they convened for the express purpose of discussing church order. Winthrop noted in 1633 that "the ministers in the Bay and Saugus did meet once a fortnight at one of their houses, by course, when some question of moment was debated."[35] Concerns over violations of Congregational independence, however, surfaced quickly. Both ministers and laymen were sensitive to any possible infringement upon the rights of local churches and some believed these clerical "consociations" leaned in that direction. The elders denied the charge, pointing to their inability to implement any conclusion drawn from these meetings without the consent of their local churches; they intended these meetings only to be advisory. Nonetheless, the principle of Congregational independence had become so quickly ingrained that actions that even hinted of violation drew defensive responses from wary churchgoers and ministers alike. Meetings designed to discuss questions of church government became less commonplace in the 1630s than they would be in future generations, but informal communication among ministers remained frequent.[36]

In addition to these clerical conferences, ministers often resolved specific questions of church order by consulting by letter with neighboring churches. In 1632, for example, the Boston church sent queries to several churches in Massachusetts and Plymouth to determine whether an individual might hold the office of ruling elder and magistrate simultaneously. The neighboring elders (probably after consultation with their congregations, since the letters were addressed to "the elders and brethren") responded in the negative, prompting Boston ruling elder Increase Nowell to resign his church office. The Bostonians also inquired as to whether a church might employ "divers pastors together." The issue was not settled; the neighboring elders only commented that the practice was "doubtful." The First Church of Plymouth later wrote to the First Church of Boston to request advice from John Cotton concerning baptismal practices, while Peter Bulkley wrote privately to Thomas Shepard to ask, "What you judge concerning the teacher in a congregation, whether the administration of discipline and sacrament doe equally belong unto him with the pastor."[37]

The churches especially looked to the ministers of the First Church of Boston to formulate Congregational provisions and to help in establishing a procedural orthodoxy. As we might expect, John Cotton, the celebrated "Father of New England Congregationalism," was particularly influential in bringing the churches together under the New England Way. Prior to Cotton's arrival in 1633, William Hubbard believed, only George Phillips of Watertown was "acquainted with the way of church discipline since owned by Congregational churches." The Watertown pastor, "being then without any to stand by him," encountered "much opposition from some of the magistrates, till Mr. Cotton came, who, by his preaching and practice, did mold all the church administrations into the same form which Mr. Phillips labored to have introduced into the churches before."[38] In 1636, Salem minister Hugh Peter demonstrated his confidence in Cotton by petitioning the Boston church to "spare their teacher, Mr. Cotton, for a time," so that "he might go through the Bible" on his own and produce "a form of church government." There is no evidence that Cotton followed through on the idea, but he continued to play an important role in establishing and standardizing procedures throughout his career.[39]

John Winthrop described how Cotton established Congregational precedents during meetings of the First Church of Boston. In response to various questions of church order, Cotton opened his Bible before the congregation, stated his interpretations of Scripture, and often those interpretations became church law. In Winthrop's eyes, the Boston teacher enjoyed divine guidance in this process. In 1633, for instance, the governor recorded that "the Lord directed the teacher, Mr. Cotton, to make it clear by the scripture" that ministerial maintenance ought to be voluntary. Earlier Cotton had demonstrated from Scripture how "a minister hath no power to give the seals but in his own congregation" and that in admissions women need not "make open confession . . . which he said was against the apostle's rule." Included in Cotton's audience at any given time was an impressive number of future ministers. Richard Mather of Dorchester, John Eliot, Roxbury's famous "Apostle to the Indians," John Davenport, later pastor of New Haven, Edward Norris of Salem, Zechariah Symmes and Thomas Allen of Charlestown, John Knowles of Watertown, and numerous other future divines served as members of the Boston First Church during the critical invention years; all of them undoubtedly saw their own understanding of Congregationalism molded by John Cotton's preaching and his administration of church government.[40]

As a consequence of these ministerial efforts, the vast majority of clergymen gradually concurred in their biblical interpretations of church order and, as the founders predicted, the churches in Massachusetts Bay adopted the same general structures of government and most of the same basic procedures.[41] Though particulars would continue to evolve throughout the colonial era, by 1635 the churches had largely standardized practices in baptism, discipline, and the election of officers to the point where the General Court suggested that the elders produce a formal platform of discipline.[42] In an effort to avoid publicization of differences with the Church of England, the elders deferred the matter; undoubtedly they also anticipated the kinds of difficulties they would face in attempting to construct the *Cambridge Platform* of church government in 1646: some would interpret the move as an effort to bind them in violation of Congregational independence.

Because the founders left no formal platform of church order during the 1630s, many questions remain unanswered concerning the operation of the system once it began to assume a recognizable shape. Among the more intriguing questions are those concerning the role of the laity in the actual administration of church affairs. As we have seen, many scholars have pointed to the revolutionary implications within Puritan theories of voluntarism and free consent. Historians have cast doubt, however, upon the extent to which these principles extended beyond mere theory to shape specific church practices and to influence Massachusetts's larger political culture. To what degree was the decision-making process in local churches shaped by principles of lay participation, free consent, and limited authority implicit in Congregational theory? These signal questions can be addressed only by turning to the church records, examining the minutes of church meetings, and studying the details of church procedures during the first decades of settlement.

2

"A Mixed Form"

Clerical Authority and Lay Liberty

Rᴇꜰʟᴇᴄᴛɪɴɢ ᴜᴘᴏɴ ᴄᴏɴɢʀᴇɢᴀᴛɪᴏɴᴀʟɪꜱᴍ's first ten years of development in Massachusetts Bay, Richard Mather proudly described in *Church-Government and Church-Covenant Discussed* a system

> which the Philosophers that write of the best Common-wealths affirme to be the best. For in respect of Christ the head, it is a Monarchy, in respect of the Ancients [lay elders] and Pastors that Governe in Common, and with like Authority among themselves, it is an Aristocracy, or rule of the best men; in respect that the people are not secluded but have their interest in Church matters it is a Democracy, or Popular State.

Though this balanced or "mixed form" of government preserved order by vesting church officers with greater "managing" authority, Mather noted, it carefully limited the elders' prerogatives by granting members the right to elect and remove their officers, and by requiring popular consent in all church decisions. Because it limited the authority of both members and church officers, and entrusted lay people with the responsibility to make certain that all decisions adhered to the higher laws of Scripture, Mather concluded, the New England Way achieved its goal of ensuring the supremacy of the Bible.[1]

Mather wrote *Church-Government and Church-Covenant Discussed* not to rehash Congregational theory but to provide English observers with a description of actual practices in Massachusetts churches. Few contemporaries took seriously his celebration of the virtues of the New England Way. English polemicists shuddered at the privileges that Congregationalism granted to the laity in Massachusetts, denouncing in foaming diatribes the slide into democratic "anarchy" the system seemed guaranteed to produce.[2] Later historians have been equally skeptical of Mather's account, though on different grounds. They have dismissed it as a statement of ideals that bore little resemblance to reality. In practice, most have concluded, the clergy and the laity came to represent separate, competing groups in a system of church

government characterized far more by lay-clerical conflict than by the kind of balance described by Mather.

Analysis of remaining church records in fact sustains Mather's account and suggests that in the actual administration of church government the founders in Massachusetts practiced what they preached about lay rights and limitations on authority.
Ministers carefully instructed their congregations in both Congregational practices and principles; lay people, in turn, learned their lessons well and, as Richard
Mather observed, shared authority with their officers in reaching all church decisions. Far from the arena of contention historians have often described, church government largely united churchgoers and their ministers, especially during the first
decades of settlement.

An examination of the relative powers of church officers and members reveals how
the first settlers institutionalized basic Congregational principles of limited authority, free consent, and "mixed" government. In discussing the authority of members
and ministers in the administration of church government, spokesmen such as John
Cotton and Thomas Hooker observed that any "company or society of Visible Saints
confederate together in profession of the Gospel," constituted "a true church." Therefore, they acknowledged, "fundamentally" church authority resided with the laity.
But unless lay people elected officers, Puritan writers quickly reminded readers, their
churches would be incomplete. Just as a man destitute of "eyes [or] hands" was a
"true man" but not an "entire man," Hooker averred, so a church deprived of officers was "not complete, but lame and maimed in regard of the integrity of it."[3]

The specific offices that Hooker and other spokesmen described were taken in-
tact from Reformed practices as they evolved in Calvin's Geneva. They divided church
officers into two main categories: the "elders" (or "presbyters") and the "deacons."
They then subdivided the presbyters into "teaching" elders (i.e., the ministers—
pastors and teachers) and "ruling" or lay elders.

The distinctions between the office of pastor and teacher pertained largely to
preaching functions. According to the *Cambridge Platform*, the official "constitution" of New England church government written in the late 1640s, "The *Pastors*
special work is, to attend to *exhortation*; and therein to Administer a word of *Wisdom*:
the *Teacher* is to attend to *Doctrine* and therein to Administer a word of *Knowledg*."
Thomas Hooker distinguished between the two offices by suggesting that the pastor
directed his preaching to the listener's will or affections, while the teacher appealed
to the understanding. Even during the first years of settlement, Massachusetts
churches never universally practiced the dual ministry. Smaller churches in particular
possessed neither the need nor the wherewithal to hire both a pastor and a teacher;
by the eighteenth century most churches would employ only one minister.[4]

In matters of church government, as we would expect, ministers enjoyed considerable status. Beyond their duties in preaching and administration of the sacraments,
ministers set the agendas for church meetings and then served as guides or manag-

ers in the decision-making process, as churches debated matters of admission, discipline, dismission, and other administrative affairs. According to the *Cambridge Platform*, ministerial responsibilities further included the examination of candidates for membership, the reception of "accusations brought to the Church," the preparation of disciplinary cases, and the pronouncement of "sentence with the consent of the Church." In routine church decisions, as we shall see, ministers often formulated recommendations for their churches on the basis of familiar Congregational provisions and requested a perfunctory lay consent. When traversing unfamiliar ground, ministers explained, often at great length, why they believed the Bible and Congregational precedents justified a particular church action. If convinced that their ministers adhered to Scripture, lay people generally acknowledged their duty to add their approval to their elders' recommendations.[5]

Though clergymen obviously exercised considerable influence in church meetings, Massachusetts Congregationalists were careful to institutionalize the principle of limited authority. They strictly forbade ministers from governing their local churches unilaterally. As Mather's earlier comments suggest, the Puritans sought to balance the powers of the clergy by granting a number of "liberties" to the brethren that served as checks upon their ministers. The most obvious check upon the clergy was the laity's right to elect officers and to dismiss those who might commit "maladministration" by violating Congregational provisions. Though rarely executed during the seventeenth century, the laity's authority to dismiss officers was demonstrated when the Lynn congregation relieved Stephen Bachiller of his pastoral duties in 1636.[6]

A no less important check upon clerical control was the liberty that congregations enjoyed to elect lay people to assist ministers in managing church affairs. Throughout the colonial period, every church elevated a small group of "worthy laymen" from which they drew lay or "ruling" elders, deacons (whose duties initially pertained largely to financial concerns), and messengers to councils and advisory synods. Suggestions that laymen and church governors inhabited separate and competing spheres in government—a view that has commanded widespread acceptance among historians—ignore the extent to which the two groups overlapped: throughout the colonial era, many laymen *were* church governors.[7]

Many first-generation churches established governing committees comprising pastor, teacher, and ruling elders, or some combination of those offices. By ignoring this "presbytery" or "eldership" and instead offering descriptions of church government that assign control over the decision-making process to the ministers or the laity, historians have reduced a complex, multifaceted system of church order to a one-dimensional one.[8] Education, rank, property, and piety earned for these lay officers the same kind (if not the same degree) of deferential respect that ministers enjoyed. Though generally lay leaders wielded formal "managing" power only in the minister's absence, they assisted in government in significant ways throughout the colonial era, and any study of the dynamics of lay-clerical relations must take into careful consideration their influence and changing role in the system.[9]

In the first decade of settlement, worthy laymen often served in the office of rul-ing elder, a position of substantial church authority.[10] Like ministers, ruling elders were elected by the laity and ordained for life. The office was both prestigious and difficult, requiring men of unquestioned piety, sound judgment, education, and financial security, since churches rarely paid ruling elders.[11] According to the *Cam-bridge Platform*, ruling elders served as "guides and leaders to the church, in all matters whatsoever, pertaining to church administrations and actions." They assisted min-isters in the ordination of officers, admissions of new members, preparation of dis-ciplinary cases, and the moderation of "all matters in the church assembled, as, to propound matters to the church, to order the season of speech and silence, and to pronounce sentence according to the mind of Christ."[12]

John Cotton asserted that ministers and lay elders "Govern in Common, and with like Authority"; in fact, churchgoers commonly lumped both officers together under the category of "elder." Though they could not administer the sacraments, ruling elders and other worthy laymen could preach, and sometimes did in the minister's absence. Beyond a general ministerial authority, the specific duties of lay elders varied from church to church. In Boston and Charlestown, for example, the first lay elders kept the church records, a task ordinarily performed by ministers. The early Salem records contain one disciplinary trial that was managed entirely by the lay elder; in other cases he assisted the pastor.[13] The active role of ruling elders in managing church proceedings was less than that of teaching officers, and Massachusetts churches never employed ruling elders universally (in fact, by the second half of the seventeenth century most churches did not employ them). Nonetheless, Massachusetts Congregationalists never allowed ministers to govern their churches alone; deacons or other worthy laymen assisted pastors in churches that did not utilize lay elders.[14]

The founders further strengthened the checks upon ministerial control by elevat-ing a set of "higher laws" and more specific provisions that members and officers alike were bound to obey. Initially drawn from Scripture, these provisions would later be codified in the *Cambridge Platform* of church discipline, adopted in 1648. Though ministers devised the ordinances, they nevertheless expected to be held to them and to the Scriptures generally. It was not at all unusual for ministers to preach openly on the limitations that the "higher laws" of the Bible placed on their own authority. "The Largest grawnt and Comission of all the Apostells doth not give [ministers] Libertie to doe any thing of thear owne head," John Cotton explained to his Boston congrega-tion, adding that in matters of both doctrine and church practice the apostles "never gave them Comission to teach anythinge but what Christ Comanded."[15]

In addition to their emphasis upon higher laws, the founders reinforced the prin-ciple of limited authority by adding a strong component of popular participation to Congregational church government. Reminding their listeners that no elder, mem-ber, or church enjoyed absolute authority beyond public recall, ministers assigned churchgoers the role of God's watchmen in church affairs, entrusting them with the responsibility to make certain that churches based every decision upon the higher laws of the Bible or the *Cambridge Platform*. In Boston, John Cotton thus exhorted "the common sort of Christians" in his congregation to make certain that "neither doctrine nor worship of God nor Church Government be corrupt to your best discerning, but preserved by diligent examination of all things according to the patterne shewed in the Word." Ministers repeatedly cautioned their congregations not to follow their elders' recommendations blindly. Should churchgoers or officers stray from the Scriptures in matters of church government, members maintained a right to censure them, Richard Mather asserted, "even ministers themselves."[16]

The principal instrument through which lay people exercised watch over their officers was their right of free consent. All male church members (those among the "elect," who joined in covenant) enjoyed voting privileges, and in every Massachusetts church, all formal actions—election and ordination of officers, admission, dismission, and excommunication of offenders, participation in church councils, and even the transmission of official church correspondence—required lay consent. Unless convinced that the officers and church proceeded scripturally, the members were obliged to withhold their approval, instantly halting any church procedure.

These principles and practices of government, and the limitations on authority they included, profoundly shaped both day-to-day church practices and the larger nature of church government in Massachusetts. Congregationalism granted officers no authority to take formal church action without the members' permission, and the principle of Congregational autonomy prohibited neighboring churches from providing binding assistance to ministers unable to secure lay consent. Taken together, these restrictions rendered impossible any ministerial effort to assert unilateral control over an individual church, a critical fact that has been lost upon previous scholars who have asserted that at one point or another during the seventeenth and eighteenth centuries ministers "forced" changes in church government upon a reluctant laity. To the contrary, the clergy enjoyed few options but to work together with the membership in an effort to reach church decisions. Though in their tracts and treatises ministers sometimes contrasted their own powers with those of their congregations for the sake of analysis, Congregationalists acknowledged that in actual practice church power could not be so divided. According to Puritan spokesmen, the "organic church," consisting of the minister(s), lay officers, and membership, worked together in this balanced system to determine collectively what the Bible and Congregational provisions required in any given decision. When critics "demandeth whether we give the exercise of all Church power of government to the whole Congregation, or to the *Presbyters* alone," Richard Mather wrote, "our answer is neither thus nor so: neither all to the people excluding the Presbytery, nor all to the Presbytery excluding the People." "[Church] matters with us are carried," he concluded, "with the joint consent of the whole church."[17]

While Congregationalism clearly granted church members significant rights and liberties in this "mixed" form of government (indeed, church government would cease to function in the absence of lay cooperation), lay people did not immediately exercise all of their liberties to their full extent. Given the responsibilities incumbent upon them, churchgoers would have to learn the principles and specific provisions of the New England Way before they could determine whether church decisions adhered to "the pattern shewed in the Word." To prepare lay people for their role as watchmen and active participants in government, ministers took considerable pains to define and to justify the New England Way in open congregation. As the Dedham example illustrated, extensive instruction in Congregational principles and biblical justifications began during the founding process of local churches. But long after churches commenced operations, ministers continued to devote time and effort to explaining Congregational principles and practices, and they would do so throughout the colonial era.

In order to educate lay people in the details of church operations, ministers and their congregations agreed in the early years of settlement to perform and explain nearly all formal church actions in public. Significantly, churches often conducted procedures such as admissions, discipline, and repentances before the "mixed assembly" that included nonmembers (those as yet unconverted, who were not allowed to vote) as well as members, granting both groups an opportunity simultaneously to learn the system and to make certain church actions adhered to Scripture.

Numerous other procedures also served largely didactic purposes. Churches routinely received letters from neighboring congregations, for instance, requesting advice on points of church order. Congregational provisions required the elders to read these requests to their flocks. They then discussed recommendations with the laity, took a vote on the acceptability of the recommendations, and sent off their responses. When churches received advice, all such communications were read before the membership. In 1638, the Dedham church wrote to several neighboring churches for assistance in choosing a ruling elder. Upon receiving responses, the Dedham elders called a meeting and "delivered" their neighbors' suggestions "to the church," along with the "reasons thereof." After some public "debating and reasoning of the case and scanning one scruple" that a layman "cast in," the Dedham members voted to accept the neighboring churches' recommendations. From this experience churchgoers learned the method and rationale for choosing lay officers and, perhaps more importantly, how to resolve points of church order that the church was unable to settle on its own.[18]

Another example, drawn from minutes of proceedings in the First Church of Boston, also demonstrates how the elders utilized interchurch communication to instruct the laity in church practices. In 1641, pastor John Knowles of Watertown appeared in Boston—with formal letters of authorization from his church—to request information concerning the stance of the Bay churches on the subject of "prayinge with and such as are excomunicated."[19] Pastor Knowles informed the assembly that Captain John Underhill, recently excommunicated from the Boston church, "did affirme that it was the Judgment" of the Bostonians that "excomunicate persons might come and be present at prayers and Preachinge and at other Ordinances of the church." The Watertown church was especially concerned by Underhill's claim that other churches not only welcomed the captain in worship, but continued to exalt him as a man of honor and esteem as well. Upon his "returne home," Underhill had claimed, "goinge upon the Lords day to Salem and sittinge in a Lowe place under the Gallery, the [ruling] Elder of the church, Mr sharpe," sent to Underhill "to Come into a mor Eminent place" to sit. This account astonished Knowles and his congregation, who "scrupled" and "thought good to send to [the Bostonians] for the advise and resons" behind the solicitude the Salem church had shown the offender.

Knowles's questions demonstrate that, even ten years after settlement, the churches were still unclear on a number of procedural details, and in such cases they continued to look to John Cotton for answers. Cotton immediately saw through Underhill's misleading account: as "for the Elder at Salem," the Boston teacher responded, "it is like[ly] he did not know [Underhill] was then Cast owt." Cotton then offered a lengthy explanation of practices in Boston, explaining that "we thinke it not unlawfull to admit excomunicate persons to the preching of the word, for we allowe it to Hethen and Publicans." Citing First Corinthians 14–24, he patiently instructed Knowles and his Boston congregation in the proper treatment of excommunicates, whether in family prayers, when eating, or in "publike place[s] in the Comon wealth," noting that offenders should "Cary them selves soe Lowly and humbly as Cast owt of gods sight" and should not "aspier to any open or eminent places in church but to take some Lowe and meane place." Knowles accepted Cotton's interpretations but requested that the Boston elders "certifie thear Judgments by Letter," so he might share the information with the Watertown church that he represented.

The laity also learned many intricacies of the New England Way when they received requests to help resolve controversies within neighboring churches. In June of 1640, Cotton announced to his congregation that he had received letters from the laity in Plymouth concerning the claim of their interim teacher, Charles Chauncy, that "to use sprinklinge insteed of dipinge" in baptism represented "a violation of all Ordinance."[20] Chauncy's position generated considerable disagreement in Plymouth; Cotton might have been tempted to avoid publicizing these unorthodox views by responding privately by letter. But, again, Congregational provisions required all such requests and responses to be delivered publicly before the church. Consequently, in a remarkably lengthy discourse, Cotton explained to the Boston congregation the "Answers as god hath brought to our hands." In developing his exposition, Cotton offered a thorough review of Chanucy's position, a detailed account of his own views, a point-by-point rebuttal of all Chauncy's arguments, and a careful refutation of each of Chauncy's biblical justifications. As always, Cotton adhered closely to Scripture, offering dozens of biblical references in support of his interpretations. Upon concluding his discussion of baptismal practices, Cotton informed the Boston congregation that he would send all of his observations to the Plymouth church by letter.

In later decades, churches suffering from irreconcilable differences would send requests to neighboring churches for "messengers" in order to establish councils that would debate cases and offer nonbinding advice. Typically, upon notification of a dispute, the elders read the request for council to the members, who then chose representatives (usually the elders and perhaps a worthy layman or two). Upon returning from the council, the messengers stood before the church, related both the facts of the case and the positions of the various disputants and, in a process that could take hours, explained how the council arrived at its decision.[21] In the early years of settlement these kinds of discussions served to educate laymen in the nuances of the Congregational system and to further the development of orthodox church procedures; later in the century, during debates over changes in admissions standards, for instance, lay people would gain from these sessions an understanding of new ecclesiastical practices beyond their local church, a development that contributed to the diversification of Congregational procedures.[22]

Lay people also learned the details of Congregational practices through their observation of and participation in various proceedings within their local churches. Attendance at church disciplinary trials, for example, not only helped lay people to distinguish between acceptable and unacceptable behavior, but also provided ministers with an opportunity to instruct their congregations on the nature and biblical foundations of specific church procedures. In 1637, the Salem church considered a case that centered around the difference between a letter of recommendation and a letter of dismission. Churches granted letters of dismission to members who, for "weighty" reasons such as marriage or business, sought to remove permanently from one church to join another. While letters of dismission permitted admission to another church, letters of recommendation only allowed members to worship elsewhere for brief periods when they were away from their own churches.

The Salem elders hauled one Brother Cotty[23] before the church because he had signed the church covenant and claimed full membership even though he "was not dismissed but only recommended to the Salem church—which implied a purpose of stay for a time only." Salem's pastor Hugh Peter admitted that "for recommendations there are [biblical] texts, tho' not so manifest for dismissions." Nonetheless, he pointed out the important differences between the two procedures from the fourth chapter of Colossians. Cotty disagreed: "Dismission is but a term of distinction for recommendation; since letters dismissive are nothing but letters recommendatory." The pastor easily turned aside Cotty's defense:

> Our Lord hath diverse household. Now though the Lord sends a servant . . .
> upon a message or the like to the other, [and] those servants shall give him

entertainment . . . , he shall have no power of transacting anything in that house. Like as there from whence he came, so here.[24]

While the newcomer had every right to worship in Salem temporarily, Peter concluded, he could not become a member simply on the basis of a recommendation.

Finally, ministers frequently addressed questions of church government in their sermons, which served as a central source of information on the topic. Robert Keayne's notebook of John Cotton sermons, dating from the 1640s, includes numerous instructions from Cotton to the laity on specific church procedures such as admissions standards, disciplinary measures, and mutual watch. Ministers often employed the concluding or "applications" section of their discourses not only to explain or review Congregational principles and procedures but to offer commentary on larger political principles as well. Throughout his career in Boston, John Cotton warned his congregation that "men of power [are] apt to abuse their power to oppression," exhorted members "to be faithful in admonishing Magistrates when God leaveth them to scandalous fall," and taught "the people not to swallow downe all the Commandments of their Rulers, least sometimes they should rule you to evil."[25] Ministers continued to instruct lay people in church government throughout the colonial era, delivering their sermons on Congregationalism not only before voting members in full communion but before halfway members, nonmembers (or "auditors," as they were sometimes called), and women as well.[26] The fact is of crucial importance: while it is exceedingly difficult for historians to plumb the minds of the "unchurched" who rarely spoke up in the records, ministers prepared them for active participation in government in hopes that they would eventually join their churches in full communion. It seems safe to assume, in short, that the unchurched achieved familiarity with the basic Congregational concepts that helped to shape their political culture.[27]

An examination of the actual decision-making process within local churches demonstrates that churchgoers learned their lessons well from their ministers' instruction. Analysis of lay participation in decisions involving admissions, discipline, and other procedures recorded in surviving church records leaves little doubt but that members mastered both Congregational principles and practices, and they utilized their knowledge to decide whether to support or dissent from the recommendations of their officers. In actual practice, lay people participated in government in meaningful ways, and the right of consent acted as an effective brake upon the authority of the ministers.

While the members actively participated in government throughout the colonial era, their role in the decision-making process during the first years of settlement was less significant in some types of determinations than in others. Previous accounts of the establishment of New England church government have greatly exaggerated the extent of early democratization in claiming that in the 1630s the laity was uniquely "the font of church power" or that important church decisions were made entirely "by popular vote."[28] As early as 1636 John Cotton affirmed that New England churches were "administered not by the people, but by the governors."[29] Not in the first decade or in any decade thereafter would Cotton recognize democracy as a sovereign authority: "If the people be governors," he asked in his famous letter to Lord Say and Seal, "[w]ho shall be governed?" As for monarchy and aristocracy, Cotton continued, "they are both of them clearly approoved, and directed in scripture, yet so as referreth the soveraigntie to himselfe, and setteth up Theocracy in both, as the best forme of government in the commonwealth, as well as in the church."[30]

The elders were in fact especially careful in the early 1630s to maintain control of their churches. Perry Miller theorized that, as founders of a new order in a New World, ministers were never more jealous of their authority in the churches than in the first years of settlement.[31] On this point the records seem to bear him out. In Salem, the elders feared that "this wilderness might be looked upon as a place of liberty, and therefore might be troubled with erroneous spirits." Consequently, at the founding of the church in 1629, they made a point to "put in one article into the confession of faith" affirming "the duty and power of the magistrate in matters of religion."[32] Likewise, the ministers at both the Salem and Dedham church gatherings balked—at least momentarily—at the prospect of sharing authority with lay elders and deacons, concluding that the candidates were not sufficiently "gifted" for such important posts.[33]

Ministers recognized that they could not rely upon coercion to rule their churches, and they soon relaxed these positions. After receiving assurances from neighboring elders, both the Salem and Dedham ministers supervised the election of lay officers. Similarly, the elders clarified their position on the role of the magistrate in local churches, deciding in 1633 that no civil officer maintained a right to exercise formal church power.[34] Ministers added a large democratic component to New England church government by granting the membership the liberty of consent to all clerical decisions; the significance of this right cannot be overstated. Nonetheless, the elders made certain that lay consent was only one component in the larger decision-making process.

The lay role in the decision-making process was sometimes perfunctory during the first years of settlement, particularly when churches faced questions that involved theology or required the establishment of important precedents. In 1631, a dispute arose in Watertown that illustrates the respective roles that officers and members assumed in rendering these kinds of decisions. That year Watertown ruling elder Richard Browne voiced an opinion that "the churches of Rome were true churches." Though Browne's claim obviously deviated from Puritan orthodoxy, the worthy layman apparently enjoyed sufficient authority and prestige to win some supporters in the Watertown congregation. Pastor George Phillips opposed Browne and, in a scenario that would be repeated countless times in colonial New England, disagreement among the elders sparked a division among the laity.[35]

Unable to settle the dispute on its own, the Watertown church sent to their Boston neighbors for assistance. Because Boston pastor John Wilson had temporarily gone to England, the church sent its three worthiest laymen: ruling elder Increase Nowell, Governor John Winthrop, and his deputy, John Endicott. Winthrop reported that pastor Phillips and the representatives from Boston debated the matter "[b]efore many of both congregations, and, by the approbation of all the assembly, except three," they concluded that Browne was "in error." In describing the method by which they reached their decision, Winthrop's specific wording is crucial: pastor Phillips, ruling elder Browne, and the Bostonians debated the matter "before" the lay people, the governor noted, not with them.[36]

The Browne case demonstrates how in cases involving theology and interpretation rather than familiar church procedures, church officers "ruled more than the rest of the Congregation" insofar as "it is more to be a . . . guide or leader, than to be guided or led." But the example also shows how the elders carefully observed the combined restraints of Congregational independence and lay consent. Before the proceedings began, the elders acknowledged that any conclusions reached by their neighbors from Boston would serve only as "advice": the Bostonians would not participate in a way of binding authority, but "as members of a neighboring congregation only." And once the authorities reached their conclusions and explained them to the assembly, they were careful to obtain the consent of the members before formalizing the decision.[37]

While in Watertown the elders shaped the thinking of the "organic church" by providing scriptural interpretations to demonstrate Browne's errors, many important church decisions concerning admissions, church discipline, and the election of officers were discretionary in nature and did not admit of simple biblical interpretation. Indeed, a study of these sorts of church decisions reveals a far greater degree of lay participation, even during the early years of settlement. A paucity of sources somewhat complicates this kind of analysis: although Winthrop left some invaluable accounts of local church affairs in his *Journal*, actual church records dating from the early years of settlement are scanty. Useful accounts of church proceedings remain for only four of the eighteen churches gathered in Massachusetts Bay by 1640. Nonetheless, evidence bearing upon admissions and disciplinary practices strongly suggests that lay people participated meaningfully in government during the 1630s, enabling the system to approximate the mixed form of Congregational theory.

In church admissions, the Puritans maintained a carefully balanced set of procedures in which the laity and ministry shared decision-making authority. Initially, Massachusetts churches required candidates for admission to profess only "historical faith," that is, an assent to the major doctrines of Christianity. Within a few years of John Cotton's arrival in 1633, most churches added a test of "grace" or conversion.[38] Though assessment of the acceptability of conversion testimonials of prospective members fell principally to the ministers, Congregational provisions prevented them from making any decision on admissions on their own. Writing in the late 1630s, the Massachusetts lawyer Thomas Lechford noted that prior to public confession, each candidate delivered a testimony of his conversion in a private meeting that included not only the minister but the lay officers and perhaps a worthy layman or two, who served as witnesses. In 1644, the Chelmsford church "voted that [deacon] Read should be joined with the pastor in taking the first trial" of candidates for admission, and only "with both of their consents they are to be propounded" to the church. Permitting the pastor to conduct these private meetings alone, the church cautioned, "would be neither safe, comfortable, or honorable."[39]

We will never know precisely what occurred in these meetings. But in cases where the relation failed to satisfy the elders, the admissions process stopped: the candidate enjoyed no recourse but to seek to understand his shortcomings, wait upon the Lord, and try again. If the officers accepted the testimony, the minister or ruling elder announced the candidacy, or "propounded" the individual to the church, at the next public meeting.

Insofar as no candidate appeared before the church before satisfying the officers, the elders wielded considerable control over the admissions process. But the members exercised important prerogatives in admissions as well—just as the worthy laymen provided a check on their minister in private hearings, so the membership provided a check on the collective decision of their officers. Once the elders propounded candidates, members maintained a right to "except" if they held a grievance with a candidate or if they knew of some hidden "scandal" the elders did not. Ministers and members alike understood that "the wrath of God" might await any church that profaned his covenant by carelessly admitting hypocrites or "notorious and obstinant offenders." In the interest of maintaining church purity, Congregationalism therefore granted each member this powerful "veto," which instantly halted the admissions process until the candidate resolved the difficulty in private meetings with the aggrieved member and the elders.[40]

In the absence of exceptions, the elders next requested the candidate to "make knowne to the congregation the work of grace upon his soule" so that the congregation could witness what the elders heard in private. These "relations," or conversion testimonials, served a dual function. First, they provided the membership with first-hand evidence of the candidate's worthiness and the church's continued purity. Secondly, relations served an educational function. The elders recognized that admissions testimonials served as a "means" for the unconverted to grow in grace, and so they decided to make relations public in hopes of providing inspiration to the unconverted in the audience. Cambridge pastor Thomas Shepard applauded as a "special use unto the people of God" those candidates who "shew, Thus I was humbled, then thus I was called, then thus have I walked, though with many weaknesses since."[41] Later, Cotton Mather recounted how lay people soon came to regard both the educational benefits and the assurance of purity as cherished "liberties":

[I]n the year 1634, one of the Brethren having leave to hear the Examinations of the *Elders*, magnified so much the Advantage of being present at such an Exercise, that many others desired and obtained the like leave to be present at it; until, at length, to gratifie this useful *Curiosity*, the whole Church always expected the *Liberty* of being thus particularly acquainted with the *Religious Dispositions* of those with whom they were afterwards to sit at the Table of the Lord; and that Church which *began* this way was quickly imitated by most of the rest.[42]

The elders might ask questions of doctrine during these relations but usually only to help clarify the conversion testimonial "if the party be weak." After the relation, the officers requested congregational approval. In the absence of objections, prospective members then offered a "confession of faith," or a statement of the principal doctrines of Christianity. Ministers then called for a formal vote, often accepting the congregation's silence for consent. The minister or ruling elder completed the admissions process by reading the church covenant, to which the candidate granted assent.[43]

Some ministers may have regarded the public conversion testimonial as something of a formality—the candidates had, after all, already satisfied the elders in private. Cambridge pastor Thomas Shepard, who recorded the relations of fifty-one candidates in the late 1630s and early 1640s, considered admission as a foregone conclusion and expected the public testimonial to be "expeditiously formulated and run through." Shepard even cautioned candidates to refrain from taking up the congregation's valuable time with windy statements, reminding members not to burden the church with "Relations of this odd thing and tother" and to avoid the temptation to "gather together the heap, and heap up all the particular passages of their lives wherein they have got any good."[44]

While ministers and lay people in Massachusetts agreed on the necessity of a converted membership, both seem to have harbored reservations about the difficulties of these testimonials. Relations of grace required candidates literally to bare their souls in public, and lay people regarded these testimonials as taxing and sometimes agonizing ordeals. In 1639, the Dedham church encountered a candidate for admission who was "fearful and not able to speak in public but just fainting away." In Roxbury, the elders recognized that prospective members "stood out from the church for years" instead of facing the ordeal of a public grace testimonial. English critics, many of whom saw no need to require proof of "grace" as a condition of admission in the first place, complained that these strict admissions procedures contributed to a situation in which "more than one halfe are out of your church in all your congregations."[45]

Though Congregationalism granted members a right to question candidates and even to "except" against (and veto) their relations, churchgoers fully understood that the difficulty of relations undermined the larger goal of admissions by discouraging people from joining the church. Consequently, they sought to make the ordeal as painless as possible. Recognizing that the elders would not have propounded the candidate before the church unless the relation had been satisfactory, members rarely exercised their right to challenge candidates during their intensely personal testimonials. In fact, though lay people frequently vetoed candidates on the basis of unresolved scandal, the records for the entire colonial era contain few instances in which members excepted against a conversion relation that had previously satisfied the elders.[46]

The balance and limits of lay and clerical authority extended to church discipline. While church officers exercised considerable influence in determining which offenders came before the church and in determining appropriate penalties, disciplinary matters were by no means solely the province or the responsibility of the elders. To the contrary, every stage of the disciplinary process depended heavily upon lay participation. Disciplinary measures in the early churches revolved around a system of lay "collective watchfulness," in which members agreed to oversee the morals of their "brethren" and "sisters," and to heed the church's admonitions should they fall under temptation themselves. Failure to exercise "watch" over a fellow churchgoer represented breach of covenant—itself a grave, punishable violation—with the wayward sheep, whose soul stood in danger, and with the church, which stood to suffer corruption should sin seep in undetected and remain unpunished.[47]

The specific disciplinary procedures lay people followed in exercising "watch" mirrored those outlined in Matthew 17–18. Once aware (or even suspicious) of violations of God's law, churchgoers held a Christian duty to approach erring individuals in private and to labor with them in an effort to seek repentance. Should an offender refuse to offer satisfaction once approached, the Bible required the aggrieved to bring two witnesses to the next private consultation and, that failing, to bring the case to the attention of the elders. Even at this stage all parties hoped to settle the matter in private in order to avoid formal church proceedings. A case involving Watertown's John Masters, who in 1632 had "sinfully" withdrawn from communion, illustrates the Puritan ideal that, except for matters of great public scandal, disciplinary cases were to be settled "out of court," in sequestered meetings of the accused, the elders, and the aggrieved members:

> All [of the offenders] came in and submitted except John Masters, who, though he were advised by diverse ministers and others that he had offended in turning his back upon the sacrament and departing out of the assembly . . . yet he persisted. So the congregation (being loathe to proceed against him) gave him a further day; at which time, he continuing obstinate, they excommunicated him.[48]

Significantly, "diverse ministers" and "others" had met privately with Masters before acquainting the church with the case, illustrating the fact that both officers and lay people had fulfilled their duty of mutual watch. A fragment from Plymouth Colony, from which early records are exceedingly scarce, points to the same ideals and practices. In 1636, John Lothrop, pastor of the Scituate church, described a private meeting in which

> Mr. Tilden and some of [?] concluded peace with love be[tween] them at our Brother Gillson's. Divers of people have some dista[ste] with Mr. Vassell and he with them, were recon[ciled] and they and all of us in general renewed our covenant.[49]

Although churchgoers almost never recorded private discussions related to discipline, these fragments suggest that the lay people conducted much informal discipline on their own and settled many cases either by themselves, or with the assistance of the elders in private meetings. The absence of formal hearings in smaller churches like Dedham and Roxbury is striking. Even the populous First Church of Boston averaged only four or five formal disciplinary hearings each year through the 1640s; accounts from those proceedings include numerous references to lay mutual watch.[50]

In cases where private meetings failed, the officers faced the decision of whether or not to resort to formal church proceedings. Although the elders assumed a greater degree of control over the disciplinary process at this stage, they remained sensitive to the will of the laity, as the Boston officers illustrated in their handling of the celebrated case of the Boston merchant Robert Keayne. Before the General Court fined Keayne for overpricing his wares, the elders had privately decided not to pursue the affair in church. In the wake of the decision to drop the case, Keayne reported, a church member "made a great complaint to our elders" because "he thought they had been too favorable" to Keayne. In response, the elders reopened the case, held another private meeting with Keayne, and eventually proceeded against the merchant in a public church trial.[51]

Formal church hearings represented the final stages of the disciplinary process. In keeping with their superior "ruling" authority, the elders managed disciplinary proceedings almost entirely. After acquainting the church with the case, the officers offered recommendations for either a formal "admonition," which barred the individual from the sacraments; excommunication; or more time for the offender to consider repentance. (In practice, churches usually admonished offenders and waited several weeks for repentance. Continued "obstinacy" promised excommunication, "for purging out the leaven which may infect the whole lump.")[52] Throughout the colonial era, lay people participated in these disciplinary debates, and they formalized all decisions with their consent. But the laity would gradually assume a greater role in disciplinary hearings in the 1640s and 1650s, as they became increasingly familiar with church practices.

The best evidence of the respective roles of the members and the elders in the earliest church trials appears in the notebook of John Fiske, later pastor of the

Wenham church, who in 1637 described eight Salem disciplinary hearings. A remarkable source, Fiske's notes are the first extant records that contain actual dialogue of the accused and their judges. Of particular interest, especially in light of the greater degree of lay participation in records of later disciplinary hearings, is the relative lack of comments from ordinary members during these early proceedings. Salem's pastor and lay elder submitted nearly all of the questions and comments directed at the offenders.[53]

The case of Salem's Brother Walker illustrates not only how the elders directed disciplinary hearings but how they determined their outcome as well.[54] Arraigned in 1637, Walker had been "distempered in the head." During his distraction the church had suspended him from the Lord's Supper. When the authorities judged him "recovered thereof," they brought him before the church to face a number of charges stemming from his refusal to repent and his failure to "give thanks at his eating." Throughout the proceedings the defendant stubbornly justified himself against all charges. Finally toward the end of the trial, the ruling elder raised the issue of "giving thanks at meat."

> WALKER: That he is not bound to give appearance of it.
>
> ELDER: First in case of offense and second, in case of reverence, some gesture is to be used after eating.
>
> WALKER: That soul repentance suffices and the hat may be on, etc.
>
> ELDER: To that 1 Cor. 6, 20.

Since Walker "had nothing else to say in his defense," the elders "said he was convicted" and then "urged why he did not confess his sin." When he appeared before the church several days later, the pastor determined the outcome, concluding that Walker appeared to be "under a temptation" and that "twere fit his case were commended to God by fasting and prayer." The church presumably added its consent to these determinations.

In Salem, the elders both demonstrated the guilt of the accused and guided the church in affixing the penalties. The Boston elders performed the same functions in determining the outcome of the Robert Keayne affair, though in this case the members were apparently more vocal in expressing their opinions about the appropriate disciplinary punishment. The merchant had already been fined by the General Court for charging excessive prices. When he was arraigned before his Boston church for the same offense, "some [members] were earnest to have him excommunicated," while other churchgoers disagreed and "thought an admonition would be sufficient." This decision, as well as all others pertaining to church order, was to be based upon the Bible, for churches were not to perform any act "of their own head" but should "receive all as from the hand of Christ." The church turned to John Cotton to determine just what the Bible required. He "opened the causes that required excommunication out of that in 1 Cor. 5:11." The point in question now was "whether [Keayne's] actions did declare him to be such a covetous person." Cotton concluded that Keayne, having not sinned against his conscience, was not a swindler but, "being led by false principles," he had committed "an error in his judgment." In short, Cotton found him guilty of ignorance rather than malice. The Boston teacher decided that the Bible required only an admonition. The church, including enemies and magistrates who had fined Keayne, dutifully added their assent to Cotton's determination.[55]

We should not exaggerate the significance of the laity's relative inactivity during these early disciplinary proceedings. The members fully understood that their elders sought to avoid subjecting members and the community to the public humiliation of a church trial unless they strongly believed in the offender's guilt. These proceedings can hardly be considered "trials"; the members recognized that the purpose of these meetings was to acquaint the church with scandalous crimes or with lesser offenses that could not be resolved privately, generally because of the offender's "obstinate" temper. Usually the decisions churches faced revolved not around guilt or innocence, then,[56] but whether to admonish or excommunicate the offender, and here, as the Keayne case illustrates, lay people were willing to offer their opinions.[57]

In contrast to later decades, when ministers and lay people would at times misuse church discipline, bringing questionable rather than obvious cases before the congregation and even utilizing church censures as a means of pursuing personal vendettas, most early cases were of a clear-cut nature. In early disciplinary trials, as in other decisions of church government, the elders offered their recommendations and after some discussion generally persuaded the membership to formalize the decision with its unanimous and usually "silent" consent. The elders' efforts to achieve unanimous consent in disciplinary and other church decisions reflected the Puritans' belief that a right answer could be found in the Bible for any given question that came before the church. The members maintained a duty to accept that answer once the elders placed it before them.

But unanimous consent—by silence no less—has suggested to some historians that lay people may have been unwilling or unable to express their views, and has called into question whether the right of lay consent was in any sense a meaningful privilege.[58] In support of this contention, scholars have pointed out that churches maintained the right to censure members who refused to add their consent to church decisions, in order to dispose of "unjustified" opposition. According to Richard Mather, if the church believed that dissenters were "factiously or partially carried," the entire congregation labored to convince them of their errors. "If they still continue[d] obstinate," the church reserved the right to admonish them and, so standing under censure, their votes were "nullified."[59]

The practice of nullification is crucial, for the lay right to consent in all church decisions would obviously have been a meaningless privilege if dissenters stood to suffer censure whenever they disagreed. But suggestions that the clergy successfully stifled lay initiative with this instrument of coercion again illustrate the pitfalls of basing accounts of early Congregational history entirely upon ministerial tracts and Congregational theory rather than the actual proceedings within the churches. Though churches held a right to censure dissenters, in actual practice ministers almost never employed—or even threatened to employ—the nullification weapon.[60] Throughout the colonial era, thousands of disagreements erupted in the churches, sometimes dividing members and ministers, sometimes dividing factions among the membership. Yet clerical efforts to carry church votes by censuring dissenters are nearly nonexistent. Moreover, Congregational provisions never granted elders the right to censure members or nullify dissent unilaterally. Censures, like all church decisions, required the consent of the members. And churchgoers understood that discipline was to serve as a means to deter and reclaim offenders, not as a weapon to impose a particular brand of orthodoxy.[61]

In practice, not only did ministers shun the nullification weapon, they actually considered dissent foremost among the laity's rights and responsibilities, a critical understanding that has been lost upon previous historians who have suggested that once officers were elected they were merely accountable to God. Throughout the entire colonial period, few ministers challenged the laity's larger right to dissent. To the contrary, the clergy as a whole nourished and defended this crucial liberty, and from the outset church members demonstrated a willingness to hold fellow churchgoers and even ministers themselves accountable to the rules of church government they had been taught. Previous writers, mirroring the thoughts of some contemporary ministers, have described lay protest throughout the colonial era as evidence of "radicalism," "anticlericalism," and even a "declension" of lay spirituality. But in most cases lay people exercised their right to dissent in order to fulfill their duty as "watchmen," to hold their officers and churches accountable when they overstepped their bounds.[62]

A case in point occurred in 1637, when John Humphries traveled to Salem from neighboring Lynn to complain that his church received one Brother Tomkins into church communion "notwithstanding he excepted against him."[63] Already familiar with the Congregational system, Humphries responded to this obvious violation of lay rights in Lynn by withdrawing from communion. Salem pastor Hugh Peter arranged "to meet the elders at the church of Lynn to confer with them" about Humphries's complaint and then utilized the case to instruct and review Congregational principles for his Salem congregation. The elders rejected Humphries's notion that his grievances with his officers justified withdrawal from communion or that "irritation unfits for the sacrament." The layman had violated Congregational rules himself, the pastor announced, citing "I Cor. II, an examined man tis his duty to eat." But more important, Peter also informed his congregation that the church would write to the elders in Lynn to rebuke them for their violation of lay liberties. Once Humphries had excepted against Tomkins, the Lynn elders should have barred the latter from communion until they had investigated: the elders must never "take on members against [lay] opposition and privately." By infringing upon a "liberty which Christ hath given" to the membership, the Lynn elders had violated the principle that members and officers must not "do what themselves please, but they must do whatever Christ hath commanded" in the Bible. In ignoring exceptions, the Lynn ministers removed one of the most important checks on clerical authority and threatened to deny their congregation any say in determining with whom they communed. The church might thereby admit unworthy candidates and corrupt itself. Such "Oligarchy and Tyranny" on the part of the elders, ministers taught, was to be avoided at all costs.[64]

Another striking example of lay assertiveness, also dating from 1637, similarly demonstrates the intimate familiarity members attained with the new system of church government and their willingness to hold the elders to the rules. That year the Salem elders haled one Brother Weston[65] before the church on a charge of withdrawing from communion. The ruling elder began by demanding "the grounds of [Weston's] withdrawing." Weston wasted no time in turning the tables, challenging the elders in open congregation for neglecting to observe proper church procedures. The layman insisted that he withdrew from communion to protest the fact that "some are admitted" to the Salem church even though they "came disorderly away" from their previous church. Salem's chagrined pastor informed his congregation that the individual in question was his wife, whom the church admitted even though she "had no letters of dismission" from the Rotterdam church. Weston reminded the elders and congregation that even the pastor's wife "must come in" the Salem church "by way of God," or according to Scripture rules. A magistrate stood up in his pastor's defense: "Tis satisfaction enough that she be a member of another church." Weston dismissed the magistrate: even the Rotterdam church "manifested itself offended" at her "disorderly" manner of departing. Why was not "satisfaction first given"? Weston demanded. The layman's point was clear and inescapable. Humbled, Salem's pastor confessed that the layman was correct and "the fault was of negligence of the elders." He promised the congregation that "letters [would] be written to Rotterdam" to clear up the matter.[66]

In isolated cases, church officers refused to honor the lay right to dissent and sought to pursue their own agendas. But elders who attempted to rely on coercion rather than biblical justification and persuasion in attempting to secure lay consent could usually depend not only upon lively lay protest but reproof from other ministers as well. In general, if the officers overstepped their bounds in the administration of government, neighboring elders sided with the laity, not their clerical colleagues—and this held true throughout most of the colonial era. In 1635, for instance, a dispute arose in Lynn involving the minister, Stephen Bachiller, who had improperly gathered his church. A number of lay watchmen, upset with "the proceedings of the pastor," withdrew from communion. When Bachiller attempted to initiate disciplinary proceedings against them, a division erupted. Bachiller sought help from the neighboring elders, who flatly refused their colleague's request to hear only his side of the case. Instead, the elders urged that a meeting be arranged including representatives of both sides. Bachiller agreed, but then demanded that his opponents submit a written account of their grievances. Upon the dissenters' refusal, the enraged pastor canceled the meeting and formally announced to all nearby churches his intention to excommunicate the entire group of dissenters. The neighboring elders again thwarted Bachiller's plan. They proceeded to Lynn uninvited and managed to achieve a temporary reconciliation. A year later the Lynn church dismissed Bachiller, demonstrating that no church officer enjoyed power beyond public recall.[67]

Another case in point occurred at Dedham in 1638, when a controversy arose over the members' right to choose their officers. When Pastor Allin propounded Ralph Wheelock for ruling elder, the congregation refused to accept their minister's choice and elected John Hunting instead. A lengthy debate ensued over the next few days. Some suggested both be ordained, others neither. Finally Allin and the Dedhamites appealed to the neighboring elders, who without hesitation confirmed the congregation's decision. Allin accepted the elders' "advice" to ordain Hunting, who assisted the pastor in governing the church for the next thirty-two years.[68]

These episodes hardly represent isolated cases. Early Massachusetts church records make clear that from the first years of settlement lay people spoke out when they believed their officers violated the principles of Congregationalism, and at times they halted church proceedings on the basis of simple disagreement. As early as 1632, lay dissent delayed disciplinary proceedings against Watertown's John Masters. Members also complained that officers in Hingham, Cambridge, Charlestown, and Newbury violated Congregational provisions; in each of these cases the elders of the Bay defended the dissenters. In 1645, a group from the Weymouth church protested to the neighboring elders because their right to dissent had been ignored: the Weymouth officers, along with a majority of the members, excommunicated an offender even though a significant number protested the decision. The neighboring elders reaffirmed the rights of the minority and persuaded the Weymouth church to reverse the excommunication.[69]

As these cases illustrate, lay people held their officers accountable when faced with clear violations of the rules, and ministers defended the lay right to dissent. At the same time, laymen and ministers understood the potential dangers associated with the abuse of these privileges. Because churches endeavored to reach all decisions unanimously, dissent was a powerful right that stood to paralyze churches from taking actions. Churches generally avoided difficulties arising from dissent by adopting and maintaining a spirit of cooperation through which officers and members agreed to abide by "the mind of the church" or a sense of the meeting. In practice, ministers raised questions before the membership and invited debate. If sufficient dissent appeared, ministers concluded that the mind of the church was unclear and they refused to call for a vote. On the other hand, if only a handful of members objected, the dissenters' unspoken duty was to express their views and then accept the consensus of opinion. No written provision specified how much dissent was sufficient to halt church actions; the early Congregationalists allowed this spirit of cooperation, rather than rules and regulations, to guide them. Ministers generally refused to ratify church actions on the basis of a majority consent until the late 1660s and 1670s, and they preferred unanimity throughout the colonial period.

An episode from the First Church of Boston affirms not only the members' willingness to exercise their right of dissent, but demonstrates how the officers attempted to achieve a sense of the meeting and, eventually, a unanimous consent. In 1640, the Bostonians received a letter from settlers in a neighboring community requesting the preaching services of the layman John Oliver until they established a church.[70] Pastor John Wilson invited the members to debate the matter. In the discussion that followed, Oliver's father, Thomas, a ruling elder, requested a specific "Rule of gods word" to justify the church's consent. John Cotton, who clearly favored compliance with the request, cited Acts 16 in explaining how it was "an acceptable worke of god to send a Brother to Prophecy." Despite the recommendation of Boston's eminent teacher, shopkeeper Richard Fairbanks remained unmoved: "I desier to be spared if I Canot give my Consent," Fairbanks announced, in light of the "Helpfulnes and proffit" the church enjoyed from Oliver. Brother Thomas Buttolph, a glover, also dissented, arguing that sending Oliver to their neighbors would simply "keepe them from Ordinances hear [in Boston] or at Lyn." The elders quickly determined that the church was not sufficiently united. In deference to these lay objections they tabled the matter: pastor Wilson noted that although "it hath bine many times mooved to the church" to send Oliver, the church had not proceeded in consideration of the "scruples and doubtes in many."[71]

In a later meeting, Wilson announced that the doubting members had been "satisfied" in "meetings of the Bretheren in Privat" and so he again brought the matter to a vote, but not before once again inviting members to express dissent: "[I]f thear be any scruple yet remayninge on the brest of any Brother herin he hath libertie to expresse him selfe and to reaseve satisfaction." The motion passed unanimously. It remains possible, of course, that the members, though not truly persuaded, simply agreed in deference to the mind of the church. Or, despite reservations, they may have caved in under pressure from the elders. In fact, John Oliver addressed these issues specifically, and his comments point to the genuine unanimity and sense of mutuality that seems to have characterized most church decisions, particularly during the early years of settlement:

> I am glad that thear is universall Consent in the harts of the church, for if thear should have bine variete in thear thoughts or Compulsin of thear mindes, it would have bine a great discoridgment. But seinge a Call of god I hope I shall Imploy my weake Tallent to gods service and Consideringe my

owne yowth and feeblenes to soe greate a worke I shall desier my Lovinge
Bretheren to Looke at me as thear Brother and to send me owt with thear
Constant prayers.

In general, little systematic conflict divided lay people from their elected church
officers during the early years of settlement; ministers often bent over backward in
employing persuasion to achieve harmony and unanimity in their churches. Another
anecdote from the gathering of the Dedham church sheds light not only upon the
mutuality upon which pastor John Allin insisted, but upon the larger nature of lay-
clerical relations during the early years of settlement. In the course of the deliberations in Dedham, a question arose concerning whether Allin's "gifts" best qualified
him for the office of pastor or teacher. Allin left the decision entirely to the laity.
The members demurred, "press[ing] to have [Allin's] thoughts . . . and some further light on the nature and proper guifts of either office." Allin requested advice
from neighboring elders, who recommended the office of pastor, and the congregation "rested very well satisfied" with that conclusion. Previous historians have suggested that "anticlericalism" characterized the members' attitudes toward their ministers, who by the late 1630s grew fearful of lay authority in church government. This
case suggests a reversal of that model; the minister requested the laity to exercise its
liberty to render a decision, but the laity refused and asked the minister to resolve
the matter.[72]

We have seen, in sum, that Congregationalism placed a strong emphasis upon
higher law, limitations on authority, and lay participation. From the first years of
settlement, those principles found their way into practice. Though church officers enjoyed greater authority in managing church affairs, particularly during the
first years of settlement, they did not render church decisions unilaterally. They
encouraged the laity to take seriously its responsibility to learn the higher laws of
the Bible and Congregationalism, and to make certain that officers administered
their churches in accordance with those provisions. The "silent democracy" of the
1630s was never truly silent; from the outset, lay people exercised significant rights
in procedures such as admissions and dismissions, and when faced with violations
of the rules, or even just differences of opinion, members exercised their right to
dissent.

These conclusions have important implications for questions involving the development of early American political culture. It is important to remember that for
the laity in colonial Massachusetts, questions of church government represented the
most important kinds of decisions they would make, far outweighing the "secular"
concerns of the town government, such as the location of a bridge or a schoolhouse.
It is thus revealing to consider that, in contrast to most political cultures in Europe
and in other American colonies, ordinary people in Massachusetts played a central
role in rendering the most significant decisions facing their society. Moreover, they

made their decisions on the basis of principles such as limitation on authority, higher law, accountability, and popular consent.

These basic Congregational principles and the balance of powers that the founders established between churchgoers and their officers would remain essentially unchanged throughout the colonial era. This is not to deny, however, that Congregationalists would be forced to adjust details of the system in light of New World events. Undoubtedly the most serious challenge to the Congregational Way during the settlement period was the "Antinomian" crisis of 1636–1638. Convinced that rebellious lay people had abused their privileges, historians have suggested, ministers sought to modify practices in order to strengthen their authority in local churches. To the Antinomian crisis and its consequences we turn our attention next.

3

Lay "Rebellion" and Clerical Reaction

Antinomianism and Its Aftermath

THOUGH WRITING WELL AFTER "the monster" had been banished to Rhode Island and harmony had been restored to the colony, John Winthrop made certain that interested observers recognized the severity of the crisis Anne Hutchinson and her "multitudes" had precipitated:

> By a little tast[e] of a few passages . . . you may see what an height they were growne unto . . . and what a spirit of pride, insolency, contempt of author-ity, division, sedition they were acted by: It was a wonder of mercy that they had not set our Common-wealth and Churches on a fire, and consumed us all therin.[1]

Indeed, of all the examples illustrating the workings of clerical authority and con-gregational autonomy, the most notorious has been the "Antinomian" controversy. Essentially all historical analyses suggest that the episode extended well beyond theo-logical disagreement; scholars have traditionally described the Antinomian affair as a major turning point in the development of the Congregational Way and in lay-clerical relations generally. Those who supported Hutchinson, we have been told, challenged their ministers' roles as interpreters of the Word, rejected man's institu-tions, and, according to Darrett B. Rutman, "opened the door to a thrusting aside of all distinctions of birth, wealth, education." In response to this uprising, histori-ans have suggested, ministers concluded that Congregational church order granted too much authority to the laity, and they proceeded to reapportion responsibilities within their churches to tip the balance in favor of the clergy. This lay rebellion thus served as the critical factor in motivating the elders to curb their unruly congrega-tions and to initiate, in David D. Hall's words, "a quiet revolution" in the develop-ment of Massachusetts Congregationalism.[2]

A reconsideration of available evidence, however, indicates that both the lay re-bellion against the clergy and the ministers' assault on lay liberties within individual churches were more apparent than real. As they pondered the situation within their churches, ministers witnessed far less resistance to their authority than is commonly assumed. Even in Boston, which suffered a "contagion" of Antinomianism, the congregation continued to respect rather than flout the government of the elders throughout the controversy. Winthrop noted that at one point virtually all the church authorities in Boston sympathized with Hutchinson, and it is precisely the implications of this near-unanimous support that historians have failed to recognize. Moreover, despite the vast scholarship devoted to the topic, the actual impact the controversy made on evolving ecclesiastical practices also remains clouded; a careful examination of actual church practices in the aftermath of the Antinomian affair casts serious doubt upon historians' claims of rising ministerial control over their congregations.

Anne Hutchinson came to Massachusetts shortly after the arrival of John Cotton, whom she had regarded as her spiritual leader in England.[3] In the summer of 1635 she began holding weekly "prophecisings" in her home, where she discussed and elaborated upon the sermons of her beloved teacher. Such meetings, a common organizing practice in England, where the Nonconformist Congregational churches were opposed, were potentially more threatening in the New World, where the Nonconformist church was established. In these meetings Hutchinson posed Cotton's "sheer grace" sermons against the "preparationist" theology of other ministers, particularly that of Boston's other preacher, John Wilson.[4] In response to the preparationists, who preached that man could gain assurance of God's grace through voluntary adherence to covenant "conditions," Hutchinson insisted that such "sanctification was no evidence of justification." God granted salvation to whomever he pleased, she reasoned, and human actions could in no way influence his decision nor help establish proof of election. To argue that "good works" provided evidence of grace was for Hutchinson and Cotton theologically inconsistent, for no one could know whether works were a sign of election or hypocrisy. Hutchinsonians in Boston enjoyed the tacit approval (at the very least) of Cotton, the most prestigious minister in the New World. Whenever questioned, Hutchinson's followers simply cited Cotton's teachings, and Cotton did nothing to oppose the practice. Since, according to Roger Williams, most colonists "could hardly believe that God would suffer Mr. Cotton to err,"[5] his apparent support was central to the movement's taking root. Hutchinsonians, believing themselves neither rebellious nor heretical, felt that they were simply propounding the doctrines of their well-respected teacher.

By the fall of 1636, sympathy for Hutchinson's cause was growing within Boston. Several powerful church and civil leaders, like Henry Vane, the upstart English nobleman who in a moment of anti-Winthrop sentiment the colony had elected governor, joined Hutchinsonian ranks. More alarming to the civil authorities and the neighboring ministers was the fact that the Hutchinsonians enjoyed the perceived, if not actual, support of Cotton, and the avowed allegiance of Hutchinson's brother-in-law, the Reverend John Wheelwright, lately arrived from England. Eventually,

Hutchinson won over almost everyone in the Boston church, which nearly censured its own pastor, Wilson, for opposing her views.

Winthrop feared that the event would culminate in a popular revolt, but in describing the affair, he actually presented evidence that illustrates the extent to which the Boston congregation dutifully followed the lead of their elders during the challenge. In 1636, for example, after delivering a speech to the General Court that many deemed offensive, John Wilson was called by the Boston elders "to answer publicly, and the governor [Vane] pressed it violently against him and the whole congregation [joined in]."[6] Wilson was helpless to check an onslaught that the church elders not only approved but initiated. As Winthrop concluded: "It was strange to see how the common people were led *by example* to condemn him in that which (it is very probable) diverse of them did not understand."[7]

Even Wilson's closest clerical associate, Cotton, "joined the church in their judgement of the pastor." In spite of the members' eagerness to "proceede to censure," however, Cotton "staid them from that," defending the rights of the handful who opposed the measure.[8] This example provides an excellent account of how lay opposition could halt the majority's actions, but, more important, it demonstrates how the Boston congregation acquiesced to their elders. Throughout, the Boston congregation did not so much lead a rebellion against Wilson as follow the lead of Cotton and the ruling elders. After the proceedings Winthrop quickly wrote a letter to Cotton, offering "some reasons to justify Mr. Wilson." Cotton replied shortly, "persisting in his judgement" of the pastor's offenses. Winthrop composed yet another letter in which he "answered all Mr. Cotton's arguments." But instead of delivering the letter to Cotton, he handed it to the two ruling elders "whom the matter most concerned."[9] With Governor Vane, teacher Cotton, and the two ruling elders leading the charge, the laity had hardly acted rebelliously in attacking Wilson.

Outside of Boston, the elders unanimously denounced Hutchinson, and her doctrines received a frosty reception from the laity as well. Emory Battis's work on the social characteristics of male Hutchinsonians suggests, in fact, that while in theory Antinomianism may have threatened the ministers' position (it certainly suggested that lay people should be given more encouragement to make religious statements and judge the conversion of others than most ministers *or* laymen were willing to allow), this potential was scarcely realized anywhere outside of the immediate Boston area.[10] Of the thirty-eight loyal outspoken supporters found in Battis's "core group" of Hutchinsonians, twenty-six lived in Boston and six in nearby Roxbury. Newbury had three of these supporters,[11] three towns had one, and ten towns had none. Enlarging the frame to include Battis's "support group" changes the pattern little. Of the ninety-six in both groups, eighty-five lived in Boston, Roxbury, or Charlestown. The other eleven were scattered among the remaining thirteen towns. Although a couple of "peripheral" supporters (that is, those whose brief association with Hutchinson manifested no strong commitment to her doctrines) surfaced in most towns, Winthrop's "multitudes" that, he said, spread the heresies "into almost all parts of the country round about" were neither vast in number nor successful in infecting the countryside.[12]

Even in Boston, the battle lines were drawn over theological issues, not over questions of church power or lay usurpation of clerical authority in church government. These subjects were rarely addressed even in the various synods and trials surrounding the controversy. Winthrop, who confessed to being "lost" in the debates, claimed that few members of the congregation understood the theological issues raised during church meetings. But many *thought* they did. And the stakes were high. Under the terms of the corporate covenant, every Puritan was taught to believe that God might at any time raze the holy community should it forsake biblical prescriptions. Conversely, the Hutchinsonians taught that the elders' emphasis upon works righteousness denied the primacy of grace and, anticipating events of the Great Awakening, created tremendous anxiety by claiming that the path offered by the established "legal" preachers led to damnation. Both sides, then, taught that the end of their opponents' scheme was certain destruction, either of the commonwealth or the soul.

It is unlikely that the controversy precipitated in the neighboring ministers a crisis in confidence in their own relationships with their congregations that historians have described, for the neighboring elders recognized that, regardless of its intensity, the theological controversy was largely confined to the Boston church, which followed the lead of its officers.[13] The neighboring elders, it must be remembered, possessed no formal authority or jurisdiction to influence events in Boston; they could rely only upon persuasion to stem the Antinomian tide. But even in attempting to dissuade Hutchinsonians in Boston and potential adherents in their own congregations, the ministers faced two difficult obstacles. First, they recognized that effective action required John Cotton's active support. When the elders finally decided to mount organized resistance, they first went after the Boston teacher, not Hutchinson, but Cotton refused to acknowledge the seriousness of the problem. Standard Congregational disciplinary provisions raised the second obstacle, for they prohibited public criticism of any individual prior to private deliberations. This prevented the elders from discussing publicly their disagreement with Cotton's preaching before they had exhausted all means of resolving their differences with him privately. As Thomas Shepard noted, the ministers "publicly preached both against opinions publicly and privately maintained" only *after* "having used all private and brotherly means with Mr. Cotton first."[14] The elders' public repudiation of the Hutchinsonians consequently did not begin until sometime in November 1636, when copies of their "Sixteen points" detailing Antinomian errors began circulating, along with Cotton's reply.[15] Antinomianism, in short, had reached full flower before the elders even had a chance to warn their congregations of its dangers.

Despite the ministers' late start in confuting the Antinomians and Cotton's refusal to cooperate, the elders still managed to keep most churches free of Hutchinson's influence simply by means of their powers of persuasion. They dealt the movement its first blow in the spring of 1637 during that year's tumultuous general election, when, according to Winthrop, "Some did lay hands on others." Freemen from out-lying towns, turning out in large numbers in the cause of orthodoxy, soundly de-feated Vane, whom Salem pastor Hugh Peter had rebuked as largely responsible for the whole affair, and reelected Winthrop.[16] Several laymen from Newbury, for in-stance, followed their minister on a forty-mile trek to cast their votes against Vane.[17] According to Shepard, the elders swung the election by "opposing Mr. Vane and casting him and others from being magistrates."[18] The election results gave eloquent testimony to the clergy's power in shaping the political consciences of their charges.

Although restored to power, Winthrop was still unable to stop the Antinomians without further assistance from the elders. The governor first resumed his earlier efforts to persuade the Hutchinsonians to repent and avoid censure. He delayed sentencing Wheelwright, whom the General Court had convicted of sedition in March 1637 for his incendiary denunciation of the colony's ministers in a fast day sermon the previous January. Winthrop also refused to prosecute the Antinomians for their riotous election-day behavior. The conciliatory tactics failed. Throughout the conflict, nothing the civil arm tried—from persuasion to coercion—succeeded in convincing the Hutchinsonians to abandon their cause. Winthrop thus appealed to the elders for assistance, who agreed to assemble in Cambridge to discuss the issues.[19]

Even as late as September 1637, at the first meeting of the Cambridge Synod, Cotton continued to hamper the efforts of the elders to resolve the crisis by insist-ing that the differences between the two sides resulted from mere ambiguities. Dur-ing the course of the proceedings, however, an astonished Cotton discovered that Boston's ruling elders refused to condemn what he had to admit were flagrantly erroneous opinions.[20] At last Cotton had realized why the neighboring elders were so upset, and he moved quickly to right matters. At this point, recovery began. Hutchinson was finally defeated not because she stopped talking, but because Cot-ton started. Once the ministers had defined and confuted the Antinomian errors, the civil arm summoned Hutchinson to defend herself. For the most part the pros-ecution devolved upon the elders and, as is commonly known, Hutchinson was convicted and sentenced to banishment.

In seeking to document the final disintegration of Antinomianism, one finds a curious lacuna in both the contemporary and modern literature. It is widely assumed that the movement simply fell apart after Hutchinson's civil trial in 1637 or perhaps after her banishment. Modern historians have said little to challenge the seventeenth-century view that Antinomianism was a strange "affliction" which arose mysteri-ously and vanished of itself. The records suggest otherwise. They indicate that in contrast to the failures of the civil arm, the elders met with considerable success in stopping the spread of erroneous views.

Roger Clap, a layman who arrived in Massachusetts in 1630, indicated that the Cambridge Synod of 1637 contributed heavily toward ending the crisis:

God by his Servants assembled in a Synod at Cambridge in 1637, did discover his Truth most plainly, to the Establishment of his People, and the changing of some, and the recovery of not a few, which had been drawn away with their Dissimulations. Thus God delivered his People out of the Snare of the Devil .... *The Snare is Broken*, and we and ours are delivered.[21]

Although the Cambridge Synod may have resulted in the "changing of some," it did not destroy the movement. Nor did the civil trial that followed. Winthrop admitted that even after the civil arm had sentenced Hutchinson and the other leaders, her opinions continued to multiply and spread. "For all this," he lamented, the Hutchinsonians "strongly held up their heads many a day after." Recognizing their continued lack of success, the magistrates rushed to the elders for help and spent two full days "consulting with them about the way to help [stem] the growing evils."[22]

The movement's back was finally broken sometime in the four months between the civil trial of November 1637, after which the "evils" were still spreading, and the church trial of March 1638, during which the Boston congregation, formerly comprising almost entirely Antinomians, completely reversed itself by unanimously consenting to the excommunication of Anne Hutchinson. Again, Winthrop provides the clue for this change of heart. The same day on which he had noted the further spread of "evils," Winthrop reported that at long last Cotton was publicly speaking out against Hutchinson in open congregation:

Mr. Cotton, finding out how he had been abused, and made (as himself said) their stalking horse (for they pretended to hold nothing but what Mr. Cotton held, and himself did think the same), did spend most of his time both publicly and privately, to discover those errors, and reduce such as were gone astray.[23]

The fruits of Cotton's belated efforts became evident two months later during Hutchinson's first church hearing, when the elders convinced the vast majority of the congregation that she deserved a formal admonition. A few minor protests arose from time to time during the trial. Several members, including the ruling elders, wished to grant Hutchinson more time to consider a retraction. After one such protest, Zechariah Symmes, teacher from the Charlestown church, chastised the congregation: "I am much grieved that so many in the congregation should stand up and declare themselves unwilling that Mrs. Hutchinson should be proceeded against for such errors."[24] John Davenport of New Haven took offense at Symmes's impatience. The pastor leaped to the defense of the congregation's liberty, recognizing that Hutchinson would be truly defeated only if the elders succeeded in fully convincing the congregation that her opinions were indeed erroneous:

I think it is meet that if any of the Brethren have any scruples upon their Spirits about this or any other point that shall be discussed, that they should have free leave to propound it that it may be taken off and their doubts removed.[25]

No one challenged Davenport, who in defending the congregation's right to dissent had merely affirmed what everyone in the building knew was a primary tenet of Massachusetts church government. After reproving Symmes, Davenport turned to the members and sternly reminded them of another building block of church order: the elders were simply carrying out the will of Christ, and (as ministers said long before and would say long after) the congregation was not to prevent them from doing so unless they could demonstrate an error in their work:

> If the brethren . . . did consider that *admonition* is an ordinance of God and sanctified of him for this very end . . . to convince the party offending as well as arguments and reasons given, then they would not oppose it.[26]

The elders succeeded in removing the last doubts of the unconvinced. Had the members remained unpersuaded, nothing prevented them from voicing their objections; in fact, Davenport twice invited the congregation to do so. The votes of Hutchinson's sons were nullified through admonition. But this measure was taken to achieve the symbolic victory of unanimity. Once it was clear that the ministers were united in their opposition to the erroneous opinions, the vast majority of Hutchinson's supporters deserted her. Two weeks after it had begun considering Hutchinson's case, the Boston church excommunicated her, Winthrop noted, by "a full consent."[27]

Vane had asserted earlier that the colonists owed no allegiance to the authorities if they transgressed the laws of God or the King.[28] As the laity witnessed the elders' unanimous condemnation of Hutchinson, few dared conclude that all ministers from Massachusetts, Connecticut, and New Haven stood in violation of God's ordinances. As a result of Hutchinson's *public* abasement, Winthrop wrote, the laity finally "believed what before they could not, and were ashamed before God."[29] Hutchinson's words could no longer be accepted because she had been cut off from all lines of authority. First her brother-in-law had been silenced. Then Cotton announced to the Boston congregation that Hutchinson's doctrines

> [d]o the uttermost to raze the very foundation of Religion to the Ground and to destroy our faith. Yea, all our preaching and your hearing and all our sufferings for the faith to be in vain . . . . all is in vain, and we of all people are most miserable.[30]

Thus isolated, Hutchinson's words conveyed new meaning to her audience: "enthusiasm" instead of "inspiration."

In the weeks and months that followed Hutchinson's church trial, neither the civil arm nor the ministers responded to the crisis by instituting oppressive measures. The authorities held few beyond Hutchinson and Cotton accountable for the imbroglio. While they feared that the movement might become widespread, they were heartened that the overwhelming majority of laymen had followed their ministers in opposing the Hutchinsonians. Even most Boston Antinomians— strongly influenced by the church authorities themselves—were eventually brought into line.

Both Winthrop and Shepard cited the speed with which harmony was restored to the colony.[31] The General Court banished only two persons besides Hutchinson and Wheelwright, a fact that contradicts assertions by some historians that the civil arm ended the crisis by banishing dozens of the worst offenders. The Court also meted out a few fines and disarmed fifty-eight men who had signed a remonstrance in support of Wheelwright. As historians have pointed out, however, the penalties created "a deceptive appearance of severity." The disarmament order, which one writer called "ridiculously severe," was calculated to embarrass the offenders, not to annihilate them.[32] The Court claimed that, like Hutchinson, Wheelwright's supporters might be seized, in Hutchinsonian fashion, by an immediate revelation, a revelation that might command them to massacre the authorities. The offenders recognized the preposterousness of the claim, and thirty-five immediately acknowledged their error. The others were "troubled very much" by the humiliating order, especially since "they were to bring [their arms] in themselves." But finally, "when they saw no remedy, they obeyed." The leniency of the Court's punishments suggests that, contrary to the claims of later historians, the colony never approached "civil war."[33]

Like the civil authorities, the elders were careful not to overreact. Indeed, they trumpeted their own success in quelling the disturbance. Shepard insisted that the movement had been "crushed by the ministry of elders."[34] Cotton agreed, adding that although the civil authorities may have provided some "assistance," the "purging and healing of these evils . . . was the fruit of [the] church government." Arguing that his congregation was not to blame, he insisted that most "had only been misled," while others suffered from a "misguided conscience." Cotton further acknowledged his own centrality in the affair, as he "confess[ed] and bewail[ed] his own security, sloth, and credulity, whereupon so many dangerous errors had gotten up."[35]

Needless to say, Cotton had an interest in minimizing the entire affair, and his conciliatory comments must be regarded with caution. But the fact remains that neither Cotton nor any of his clerical brethren singled out a rebellious laity or congregational liberty as the root of the Antinomian controversy and, significantly, there is little evidence to suggest that the elders responded to the crisis by attempting important revisions of Congregational church order. During one of several sessions held at the Cambridge Synod of 1637, ministers convened specifically to address the question of whether the Antinomian controversy pointed to a need for modifications in the New England Way. They quickly concluded that despite the ongoing Antinomian threat they had no intention of abridging lay liberties in church government; there is no evidence to suggest that they even debated new coercive measures.[36]

The few conclusions reached by the synod were more a reaffirmation and a formalization of existing practices than a novel institutional "hardening." The elders determined that Hutchinson's weekly assemblies, "whereby sixty or more did meet . . . and one woman (in a prophetical way, by resolving questions of doctrine, and expounding Scripture) took upon her the whole exercise," were apt to foster disorder. But rather than prohibiting such assemblies altogether, they affirmed that still "women might meet (some few together) to pray and edify one another." "There are still [such meetings] in many places of some few neighbors," they later informed Hutchinson, "[b]ut not so public and frequent as yours, and are of use for increase of love, and mutual edification, but yours are of another nature."[37] Next, while the elders utterly condemned the Antinomians' interrupting ministers during church meetings "whereby the doctrines delivered were reproved, and the elders reproached, and that with great bitterness," they nevertheless reaffirmed the members' right to question clergymen after sermons, though "this ought to be very wisely and sparingly done, and that with leave of the elders." The ministers also stated that "a person refusing to come to the assembly to abide the censure of the church, might be proceeded against, though absent." Although this ruling may have been an innovation, it did not constitute much of an attack upon congregational liberties. Finally, they concluded that members ought not forsake the ordinance of the Lord's Supper for any opinion "which was not fundamental." This rule, which had been enforced at least since the John Masters case of 1632,[38] was apparently directed at the Antinomians' practice of withdrawing from communion on the grounds of "conscience." All of the rulings were directed at the Hutchinsonians' specific offenses rather than reversing lay privileges generally.[39]

Considering that the controversy was near its peak at this point, the elders exhibited considerable restraint at the Synod of 1637. Only the elders' desire to restrict the questioning of ministers may have led to new restrictions in some churches. In 1639, interested parties from across the Atlantic inquired of Richard Mather "whether doe you allow and call upon your people publicquely before all the Congregation to propound Questions, move doubts, and argue with their ministers?" Mather recognized that the question was offered by a critic of the New England Way who was determined to demonstrate that Congregationalism could only result in democratic "anarchy." He thus responded, perhaps conservatively, in *Church-Government and Church Covenant Discussed*:

> We never knew any Ministers that did call upon the people thus to do . . . .
> Some people think the people have a liberty to ask a question publicly . . .
> though even this is doubted by others, and all judge the ordinary practice of
> it unnecessary . . . . Such asking of questions is seldom used in any church
> among us and in most churches never.[40]

Earlier, however, in 1634, Cotton affirmed that "any young or old, save only for women," had liberty to propound questions. His written position had not changed as late as 1642. In addition, Robert Keayne's sermon notebook indicates that, in practice, lay people in Boston did ask questions after the sermon from time to time in the early 1640s.[41]

Far more remarkable than his qualms over the laity's right to question their ministers, however, was Mather's staunch defense of congregational liberties in *Church-Government and Church-Covenant Discussed.* The elders believed that England might call the colonists to account for their practices at any time,[42] so Mather would certainly have been tempted to overemphasize ministerial control at a time when England's worst suspicions of colonial unrest were being fueled by news of the Antinomian conflict. Even as Mather lashed out against Antinomianism in his own church, however, his writings defended every right of the membership in church government.

Ministers did not attempt to alter the balance of power within individual churches, in the final analysis, because they believed that balance was essentially unrelated to the Antinomian crisis. Far more significant developments occurred in the area of interchurch relations. The autonomy of Congregational churches had hindered ministers' attempts to deal with the Bostonians. In attempting to address problems associated with congregational independence, ministers faced the same obstacles they encountered whenever attempting to modify the New England Way. Neither ministers nor magistrates could institute changes that conflicted with the very biblical prescriptions that ministers had identified and taught to the laity. The most obvious means of dealing with another outbreak—the creation of binding ministerial synods with the authority to censure wayward individuals or even entire churches—was inimical to Congregational principles. Ministers also recognized that harshness or sudden claims of authority were more likely to alienate churchgoers than win their support and obedience.

Despite these obstacles, the elders did manage to develop a strengthening of interchurch ties, which remained as the most important legacy of the Antinomian controversy. This development had actually begun earlier, when the Boston elders joined with Thomas Hooker in laboring with the Salem church to dismiss Roger Williams. Another major step was taken in March of 1636, when the ministers and General Court agreed that no church could be formally gathered without the supervision and approval of the neighboring elders. After the Antinomian conflict, the elders again addressed the issue of congregational independence.[43] The ministers first revised their views of the acceptability of nonbinding ministerial conferences. Though, as we have seen, the elders met together with some regularity in the early 1630s, some ministers condemned such private conferences in 1633 and again in 1637. In 1639, however, Richard Mather formally announced that "we hold such meetings to be lawful and in some cases necessary." The assembled elders later affirmed Mather's position in 1643.[44]

Increased communication within the ministerial community represented the main benefit of such conferences. Antinomianism had been spreading for months, it must be remembered, before neighboring elders even knew about it. By strengthening interchurch ties, the elders hoped to achieve a better understanding of affairs within individual churches and thus prevent conflicts from building to crisis proportions. Moreover, consociation provided ministers with an opportunity to discuss and harmonize the doctrine that lay people would hear from them. As Robert Scholz and others have pointed out, significant theological differences existed within the ministerial community long before the Antinomian controversy.[45] In addition to the questions that eventually arose concerning sanctification and justification, for instance, ministers were divided over the relationship between the covenant of grace and church covenants. Unresolved differences also centered around the definition of experimental faith, which represented the main requirement for church membership. In this context, the Antinomian crisis appears to have been "an accident waiting to happen." Lay people inevitably recognized the significance of the differences between their ministers' views on theology and church practice, and even amplified them. In the late 1630s ministers witnessed for the first time the extreme divisiveness that could arise from these differences. Time and again during the colonial era, both within local churches and throughout the colony as a whole, ministers would have to come to grips with the fact that harmony could be insured only by strict unity and uniformity among the elders.

In the aftermath of the Antinomian controversy, ministers consequently strived to minimize whatever theological differences still existed. Cotton insisted that "there is among us all sufficient agreement" in matters of "faith and practice." Shepard and Allin agreed that "although Satan hath ben oft busie to make breaches among us, yet the ministers of Christ hath been hitherto generally (if not all) of one heart and mind in the main and principall things of religion." When Cotton was publicly questioned during a sermon in 1639, he refused to answer until he had an opportunity to consult with "all the Devynes" and construct an acceptable answer. He then answered the objection "by way of Addition" the following week. New England's ministers, the English Presbyterian William Rathband concluded, "agreed amongst themselves that none of them shall preach any doctrine that is not commonly received amongst them, till he have first communicated it with the rest of the ministers."[46]

In keeping with these efforts to control and standardize doctrine, ministers proved far more protective of their pulpits than of the government of their churches, which they continued to share with the laity. Even in the aftermath of the Antinomian affair, Mather reaffirmed the right of the laity to "prophecy publikely to the edification of a whole Church." Cotton also added his assent to lay preaching in 1640, urging in the "applications" section of a sermon that "if any Brother or straynger Prophesie . . . have no Scruples that way. You may hear him."[47] Despite their affirmations, however, clergymen did appear anxious to control these practices after the Antinomian excesses. As noted earlier, the Boston church voted to send a layman to prophesy to the farmers at Rummeny Marsh, but the individual selected was the son of longtime ruling elder Thomas Oliver, a close ally of Cotton. Boston authorities censured one Sarah Keayne later in the 1640s for "Irregular prophesying," and, in general, the church records manifest a decline in the number of references to the actual practice of lay prophecy as the century progressed.[48]

Although the elders concentrated their efforts on preventing another outbreak of heresy, they also adopted measures to fall back upon should another church repeat the errors of the Bostonians. Foremost was a strong emphasis on the "third way of communion" unseen in previous statements on New England church government. If in the future a "Church or Elders should refuse the testimony of other [neighboring] Churches," as in the Antinomian conflict, those neighboring churches could isolate the wayward church by denying "the right hand of fellowship." Offenders would be unable to commune (and, presumably, worship) with their neighbors' churches and thus would be less likely to "infect" them. But this emphasis upon the third way of communion hardly represented a bold or effective solution for potential difficulties arising out of Congregational independence. A denial of fellowship really amounted to little more than a public condemnation of an offending church, and despite the emergence of intense interchurch squabbling in the late seventeenth and early eighteenth centuries, ministers would prove extremely reluctant to employ this modest form of discipline.[49]

As generations of historians have pointed out, the Antinomian controversy certainly serves to remind us of the larger limits upon dissent in Massachusetts, particularly during the early seventeenth century. While the Congregationalists allowed and even encouraged dissent within the shared space of the church meeting, here they obviously contributed to a darker side of an ongoing American tradition by seeking to stamp out those who called into question the fundamental assumptions of their society. Historians' related thesis that the Antinomian affair motivated clergymen to strip rebellious members of their church liberties adds another dramatic dimension to the most sensational episode in early Massachusetts—but, as we shall see, the evidence in the church records flatly contradicts it. An examination of both clerical statements about Congregationalism and actual practices within the churches reveals that government witnessed little significant change in the 1640s. Massachusetts clergymen frequently offered modest adjustments to the Congregational Way in response to New World developments and (as is evident in the largely informal modifications in interchurch practices) their reaction to the Antinomian controversy represented no exception to this pattern.

If anything, the radicalism of the 1630s probably motivated ministers to strengthen the bonds of cohesion with their congregations. The Antinomian controversy certainly served as an uncomfortable reminder of lay power within individual churches. For one brief period Boston's Pastor Wilson had been stripped of his credibility and powers of persuasion, and without them he was helpless. In the absence of congre-

gational support, his office amounted to nothing but a meaningless title. Such might
be the result in any church where the consensus between minister and members broke
down. In Boston, Cotton prevented his overly zealous followers from wrongfully
censuring Wilson in 1637. But what was to prevent such a transgression in smaller
churches like Concord, where a lone minister depended entirely upon lay support?
As the elders would learn most dramatically a century later during the Great Awakening, nothing could prevent a wayward congregation from censuring or even dismissing its pastor. Most ministers understood from the first years of settlement that
there was no point in establishing an adversarial relationship with their flocks—they
would both lose in the end.

Some evidence of the ministers' attitudes toward church government and the laity
in the aftermath of the Antinomian controversy appears in the many tracts and treatises on Congregationalism that they directed at English audiences. Like Mather in
Church-Covenant and Church-Government Discussed, ministers stressed lay rights and
liberties as much or more than ever before.[50] But, again, it is impossible to fully
comprehend the operation and evolution of Congregationalism through an examination based largely upon ministerial treatises. As Williston Walker pointed out,
the possibility of an English decision to impose toleration loomed ever present in
the 1640s, leading ministers to carefully emphasize the orderly nature of the New
England Way.[51] When goaded by their critics, ministers sometimes equivocated on
particular lay rights. Asked in the early 1630s whether a congregation could excommunicate its entire presbytery, for example, Cotton answered in the affirmative. Years
later, he corrected himself, pointing out, quite logically, that in such a case no church
officer would be available to formally carry out the church's decision. Despite Cotton's
bitter denials and the fact that no congregation ever attempted to excommunicate its
entire presbytery, English critics (and later historians) seized upon these sorts of
"contradictions" in the Cotton corpus on church government to assert that New
World experiences motivated ministers to assume a more authoritarian stance toward lay rights.[52]

Ministers provided clearer and less inhibited comments on lay and clerical authority in the unpublished sermons they delivered before their local congregations.
And here, in addition to reaffirmations of traditional themes of lay consent, limits
on authority, and higher law, they stressed commonalities shared by ministers and
members alike. Though preaching in the very seat of Antinomianism, Cotton nonetheless offered a startling series of leveling, antiauthoritarian sermons in the early
1640s that stressed the spiritual heights to which lay people should aspire and
downplayed distinctions between pulpit and pew. Addressing his Boston congregation on the theme of limitations on ministerial authority, Cotton affirmed in 1639
that the principal duty of ministers was "to Teach men to become desiples of Christ"
and reminded his listeners that the apostles never granted ministers "Comission to
teach any thinge but what Christ Comanded." Any effort to "institute any Indiffer-

ent thinge" represented "a horible presumption and an abuse" of the minister's "Comission and Awthoretie."[53] In the administration of church affairs, he continued in a later sermon, "if we be Soe rufe, and sterne that we Canot be Content to be Servants to the church", and instead "wave owr owne endes and aymes, we are not fitt ministers of the Gospell."[54] Not only did Cotton describe ministers as "Servants to the Church" but, anticipating a major theme of the Great Awakening, he also insisted that neither a minister's office nor his education distinguished him from ordinary laymen. "Schools and Learning is [sic] not absolutely necessary to the ministry," he informed his Boston congregation, "for we see Christ can make fishers of men [i.e., ministers] without universities . . . . It is not the Learning Arts and Schools and Philosophy, nor all witty and Learning and parts that can restrain the devil in any part of his power."[55]

Both Cotton and Hooker stressed the spiritual equality of ordinary and more eminent Christians. "A weaker man . . . may offer seasonable advice to one that is far wiser," Hooker averred, while Cotton noted that "God doth sometimes reveal the greatest mysteries of Religion, not always to men of Eminent parts." Despite the recent excesses of Hutchinson, Cotton later offered a remarkable exhortation to the women in his congregation, urging them to recognize no limits in the spiritual knowledge and experience they might attain: "Godly women being attentive to the ministry of the word, may some times understand and be more apprehensive of the mysteries of Salvation than the best ministers of the Gospell."[56] These unpublished Sunday sermons, in sum, do not show the emergence of an eroded confidence in the laity or a suspicion of women in the aftermath of the Antinomian controversy.[57] Rather, both Cotton and Hooker discussed the spiritual equality among ministers and lay people and emphasized the capabilities of ordinary churchgoers to achieve a profound understanding of Christianity.

Given these clerical sentiments, it is unsurprising that an examination of actual church practices reveals little change in the decision-making process. In fact, records of church trials and proceedings suggest that lay people began to play a more *active* role in the decision-making process than they had during the previous decade. While sources dating from the 1640s remain slender, those that do survive are perhaps the most revealing of all the church records dating from the seventeenth century. The most important of these documents is the sermon notebook of the merchant Robert Keayne, who recorded numerous proceedings within the First Church of Boston. The nearly verbatim transcript of various church trials and hearings is probably the only one of its kind still extant, and it has not been incorporated into any previous account of lay-clerical relations and church government.[58]

Especially illuminating are the trial and confession of Richard Wayte, dating from 1640, and the later trial of Anne Hibbons, which both provide a sharply detailed portrait of lay understanding of and participation in the management of church affairs. The Wayte case demonstrates in particular how ministers taught the laity to rule, and shows that the specific role lay people played in the disciplinary process and in reaching church decisions had by no means diminished after the Antinomian controversy.

Wayte, a tailor, was born in 1600 and became a member of the First Church of Boston in 1634. Though disarmed in 1637 for his participation in the Antinomian conflict, he became marshal or sheriff to the colony in 1654. That Wayte could have risen to a position of public responsibility bears eloquent testimony to Puritan charity, given the tailor's long list of civil and church offenses in the 1630s. The Boston church excommunicated Wayte in 1639 for "having purloyned out of buckskyn leather brought unto him, so much thereof as would make 3 mens gloves." Wayte stubbornly refused to admit guilt and ignored the counsel and advice of his brethren, prompting the church to censure him. Fifteen months later he experienced a change of heart and sought readmission to the church.[59]

In recounting his long and tortuous journey from a state of sin to one of repentance, Wayte described in detail how several laymen came to him in private both before and after his excommunication and took "a greate deale of paynes" with him for his offense, offering another illustration of the mutual watchfulness church members promised one another when entering into a church covenant.[60] As we have seen, this watchfulness involved, in part, lay efforts to reclaim erring members; Wayte's church trial was only one of the later steps in a larger disciplinary process that required lay participation and understanding for its success. The Wayte account demonstrates that the exhortations of private brethren were as important to the process as formal church actions. Wayte thus explained to the congregation how the local innkeeper Samuel Cole[61] first dealt with him "in a private way," followed by the glover Thomas Buttolph, who urged him to "Give God the glory and confess" his theft. Several days later, Wayte explained to the congregation, Cole returned with one Richard Fairbanks, and the two "stayed up and pressed the things upon me till I could deny it no longer. I told them they burthened my spirit. They told me they desired soe to do. Then I confessed."

Though Wayte became so distraught that at one point he considered suicide, he explained how with God's help he "had some desier to see my Sine and to Loath my former abhominable Sines [and] this did still much mor astonish me that God should chaynge my mind from these things, and to admier God's patience to Soe vild a Sinner." He was then "desirus to be affected at the dishonor put upon [God's] Name" and to "lye downe at his foote stoole." Having witnessed Wayte's confession, the church faced the difficult decision of whether or not to readmit him. The respective actions of congregation and clergy in the case demonstrate the increased lay initiative in the decision-making process. As had always been the case, ministers enjoyed no means of implementing their recommendations except by persuading the congregation to add its consent. In a world where congregation and clergy shared the same goals, persuasion continued to be a powerful tool. But the Wayte hearing indicates that in church trials the elders no longer simply debated matters among themselves in front of the congregation, as they often did in the earlier years of settlement.

Wayte's confession had clearly impressed the elders. Cotton indicated to the congregation that the offender had manifested suitable "contrition," and ruling elder Thomas Oliver applauded his "humble carrigge ever Since his Casting out." Wayte's confession, they recognized, closely resembled in its basic outlines a portion of a sermon on the morphology of repentance Cotton had preached several months earlier. In November of 1639 Cotton had explained to the congregation that a "Contience that is afflicted for Sine but not affected with Sine, nor the Love of Christ will run any whither for ease" and might even lead the sinner to suicide. True repentance, Cotton continued, was characterized by an abhorrence for all sin "because it offends God" and sprang from "the sight of Gods favor" upon one so undeserving. Wayte must have been paying close attention, for his confession—from the thought of suicide to his "astonishment" at God's mercy—fit Cotton's formula almost perfectly. Wilson consequently employed the standard format for indicating that the elders expected the laity to approve readmission, announcing that if the membership "had not ought to say, then we will pronounce him a Leper no longer . . . and receive him in as a returning Prodigal."

The congregation saw matters in a different light, and in a striking affirmation of lay initiative refused to add consent. Francis Lyall, a barber surgeon, and John Milam, a cooper, insisted that Wayte's "keepinge Company with Lewde and wicked persons" required more attention, while William Tyng, representative to the General Court, desired to know why "thear was not a more showe of teares" on the offender's part.

In response to these reservations, the elders deferred Wayte's case for two weeks. At that time they again faced a considerable number of members who were determined to assert their own will in the case. When Pastor Wilson called for a vote to "take off [Wayte's] Censuer," Goodman Button, a miller, and James Johnson, a glover, dissented. The elders were displeased. Wilson reminded the congregation that the officers would not have brought Wayte before the church unless convinced of his repentance, but numerous members still remained unmoved. Though a majority agreed with the elders and even demanded "By what Rule we may Submitt to thease Brethren that Say they are not Satisfied?" the shoemaker and tavern keeper Thomas Marshall noted that the church was "divided." That being so, the elders were powerless to act, since ordinarily censures were to be exercised by the unanimous consent of the membership, a fact historians have overlooked in suggesting that ministers resorted to compulsion in church affairs in the wake of the Antinomian controversy. This case affirms yet again that Congregationalism granted ministers few alternatives but to rely upon persuasion and cooperation in managing their churches.

The dissenting members cleared up their remaining grievances with the offender in private, and two weeks later the church readmitted him with little fanfare. But that did not end the saga of Richard Wayte. Several months later the church excommunicated him again when they discovered that while repenting his various sins Wayte conveniently omitted his "manifold inordinate drinkings" with one Lesty Gunton. An exasperated lay elder noted in the church records that in response to the new charges Wayte "utterly denyed that ever he had beene therein gulty, no never, no never." As the evidence against him mounted, Wayte finally "acknowledged his guiltiness in a great measure (though not all at once) both of frequent wine drinkings, and that simetime with forsaking the lecture for it." Throughout, he carried himself "very high bravingly and stubbornly." When the elders and members exposed his hypocrisy in professing "a showe of Repentance" while keeping "Some groce Sine upon his Soule unconfessed," Wayte denied the charge, standing "like a deafe Adder stoping his eare agaynst the voyce of the church." The membership promptly excommunicated him again, this time for "grosse Dissembling before God and the Church," whereupon, "to the great grief and astonishment of all the brethren," Wayte aggravated his offense by professing that "his Conscience did not in the lest accuse him" for ignoring the warnings and advice of the church.

The elders had clearly blundered in ignoring the warnings of those who knew Wayte better and in insisting upon his readmission. While there is no outward evidence of embarrassment on the elders' part, they adopted a far different approach in the next church proceeding found in the Keayne notebook. Previous to the trial of Anne Hibbons, who was brought before the church on charges of slander and lying, the elders carefully prepared the congregation for the hearing, outlining the "four sorts of hypocritical humiliation," so that the Wayte error would not be repeated. And for the benefit of both the church and the sinner, the ministers preached on the example of "Mary Magdalene, that having sinned and given great offense she doth abase and humble herself; and the more penitent she was, the more honorable esteem she had in the heart of Jesus Christ."[62]

In Hibbons's church trial, the elders simply acted as moderators, leading the discussion and offering advice when asked.[63] The outcome of the Hibbons case, in essence, was determined entirely by the congregation. In a startling contrast to the Salem church trials of 1637 and the Hutchinson trials of 1638, in which nearly every comment was offered by a church officer, ordinary lay people dominated in the excommunication of Hibbons. Nineteen lay people participated in the trial in addition to the ministers. Thirteen of them were ordinary men who lacked the title of distinction "Mr.," and even though women were not ordinarily allowed to speak in church unless specifically requested by the elders, ruling elder Thomas Leverett's wife demonstrated her knowledge of Congregational provisions by openly rebuking the entire assembly for its "offensive" behavior in publicly discussing offenses that had already been settled in private.[64]

In contrast to the Wayte case, the elders offered little to prejudice the congregation. When, for example, Hibbons asked if she might express her defense to the church in writing, Pastor Wilson left the matter entirely to the church and refused to comment until asked: "The church is to consider whether they consent to her motion; if so, then we will draw to a conclusion." Winthrop then said, "[I]n this case your self should direct the church . . . and as you advise, I think the church will consent." As usual, Cotton provided the advice. "The practice of writing is uncouth in the church," Cotton responded, "[a]nd we have no precedent for it in Scripture." The church agreed.[65]

The suggestions volunteered by the various lay participants affirm once again that by 1640 church members had clearly achieved a remarkable depth of understanding of both procedural matters and of the various components involved in rendering a disciplinary decision. For this reason, the ministers were able to serve as mere guides. The lay discourses are often literate, informed, and reasoned, their vocabulary impressive. The shopkeeper Richard Fairbanks, for example, condemned the "averseness" of Hibbons's spirit, the "iniquity of her covetousness," and the "great obdurateness of her heart." References to the Bible abounded in nearly every lay statement. Two members even offered verbatim quotations from the Bible, interpreting and tying them into the case at hand in a manner indistinguishable from that employed by the ministers. Fairbanks recited Isaiah 57:17–18 and explained how "this place may somewhat suit our Sister's condition." Sergeant Oliver suggested that Hibbons's case was "somewhat like that of Miriam's, who rose up against Moses and Aaron [and] whose leprosy appeared in the face of the congregation," and argued for a sentence of excommunication. Finally, Hibbons's husband, William, spoke out in a moving plea for leniency:

> I would humbly propose one place to your consideration . . . and that is what the Lord sayeth concerning Ephraim and Israel: 'How shall I give thee up Ephraim? how shall I deliver thee Israel? how shall I make thee as Admah? How shall I set thee as Zeboim? My heart is turned within me; my repentings are rolled together; I will not execute the fierceness of my displeasure; I will not return to destroy Ephraim. For I am God and not man. The holy one in the midst of thee, and I will not enter into the city.'—wherein we see that though God was highly provoked at Israel, yet His bowels pittied them and He promised to spare them and not to deliver them up. So if the church would show their bowels of pity in sparing or respiting her censure for a time, the Lord may so bow the heart of my wife that she may give the church full satisfaction.[66]

The debate concerning whether to admonish Hibbons a second time or to proceed to excommunication not only demonstrates lay initiative but also underscores the necessity of unanimous consent and deference to "the mind of the church." The Hibbons decision, like all others, would be reached by the organic church, consisting of the elders and members. It was the job of the elders to lead the debate and pose questions about the disciplinary penalty in order to determine the collective opinion of the assembly. When enough people volunteered their views to give the elders a sense of the meeting, they took a vote. Though individuals might disagree in their interpretations, they were to go along with the mind of the church unless convinced that the church proceeded unscripturally.

In keeping with these goals, lay people of all ranks joined with the ministers in offering their opinions in the debates over the appropriate penalty. Virtually all participants hastened to add that they would support the collective decision of the brethren in whatever they decided. Winthrop, governor of the colony, expressed his agreement with Goodman Button, a common miller, who recommended excommunication. Pastor Wilson indicated that he was "of the same mind," but "would not be against any lenity the church should think meet to show." Edward Hutchinson asked Cotton to interpret a section of Scripture bearing upon a second admonition but added, "I do but only propose it, not intending to oppose, but to join with the church in what[ever] they shall determine and conclude therein." Cotton explained that if the church desired a second admonition, he would lend his support, yet if they opted for excommunication he would "freely join with them in that censure"— ministers as well as laymen honored their obligation to submit to the mind of the church. Several laymen supported "longer patience" with Hibbons, but they all indicated they would "willingly go along with the church" should it decide otherwise. Sensing the desire of the vast majority, Wilson called for an excommunication, to which the church added its silent consent.[67]

Throughout the proceedings, Hibbons's husband, who had desperately pleaded for leniency for his troubled wife, insisted he would not oppose any church decision. William Hibbons was so committed to the ideal of the covenantal relationship that prior to one hearing he called attention to

> an expression that I used in Calling one of my Bretheren sir insteed of Brother. How it fell from me I know not, but it was an expression unsutable to the Covenant I am in, and the mor unsutable for my selfe, because the Title of Brother is such a phras that I have fownd my hart many times inlarged when in the use of it.

Hibbons requested "that the brother to which I spake it would pardon it" and sought forgiveness from "all the rest of my Bretheren."[68] With the same spirit of meekness and mutuality, this respected gentleman reassured the church that his purpose in his wife's trial was "not to hinder the church in their proceedings; but whatever they shall conclude of I shall sit down contented with."[69] Hibbons, along with every other church member, agreed that failure to discipline a notorious offender risked "the wrath of God." They all understood that disciplinary cases involved the fate of the eternal souls of friends, neighbors, husbands, and wives, and that any violation of biblical church order amounted to nothing less than sacrilege. These concerns united ministers and laymen, high-placed officials and common farmers, and in the case of Hibbons they even transcended the matrimonial bonds between husband and wife.

Historians are fortunate to have a second major source that details the inner workings of church government in the 1640s: the Notebook of John Fiske of Wenham.[70] The Fiske Notebook is particularly valuable insofar as it illuminates procedures in a small frontier church that, like dozens of others, differed in several outward respects from older and larger churches like Boston, where church records were far more likely to survive. The Wenham church was organized in a small, homogeneous Essex county town that was, as one layman put it, "so little and so striken" that during the first years of settlement the church was forced to consider a number of requests to pull up stakes and move on to greener pastures. After only eleven years, the Wenhamites gave up the battle and the entire church relocated at Chelmsford. While the First Church of Boston, the colony's largest church, was managed by two ministers (including the most prestigious one in the Bay), two ruling elders, and three deacons, Wenham's Pastor Fiske received assistance in governing the handful of Wenham churchgoers from a lone deacon.[71]

While, at first glance, it might appear that, as the church's only "ruling" officer, Fiske enjoyed a position of greater authority in Wenham, we must remember that as a relative unknown assuming his first pastorate, he did not enjoy the deference that might accompany the colonywide reputation of Cotton or Hooker. Nor could he depend upon a half-dozen church officers to add the weight of their agreement to his prescriptions, as was often the case in larger churches. Despite these important differences, lay-clerical relations and church government in Boston and Wenham varied in no significant way: an examination of church procedures recorded in the notebook indicates that the respective roles and attitudes of the church officers and laity were virtually identical. This finding lends further credence to suggestions that, Congregational independence notwithstanding, the similarities that churches shared in lay-clerical relations and the fundamentals of government were far more striking than variations among churches, which remained largely insignificant during the seventeenth century.[72]

Lacking some of the tools of persuasion enjoyed by other ministers, Fiske had to work that much harder at winning congregational support and voluntary cooperation and, as in the Dedham case earlier,[73] he did so by operating under the assumption that if he demonstrated to his congregation that his every action proceeded according to higher law or "the Rule," then his congregation would support him. Fiske consequently met with his congregation on a regular basis to discuss and explain various points of church order, sometimes endlessly justifying seemingly insignificant points with a degree of detail that exceeded even John Allin's lectures prior to the Dedham church gathering. When a question arose concerning whether nonmembers should be allowed to attend the prayers between the sermon and communion, for example, Fiske offered three scriptural justifications in answering in the affirmative. Fiske then offered no less than five possible "Objections," which he proceeded to dismantle point by point. The church acceded to their pastor's wishes with little debate.[74]

Just as Fiske was careful to demonstrate to his congregation that church procedure adhered to the higher laws of the Bible, so the minister governed his church in
accordance with fundamental Congregational principles of lay consent and limitations on authority, including his own. Fiske not only refused to make decisions
unilaterally, he sometimes left decisions entirely to the laity. Like the elders in Boston, Fiske moderated church debates until he arrived at a sense of the meeting,
whereupon he called for a church vote. During one disciplinary case, Fiske attempted
to ascertain the mind of the church by simply sitting back and listening to the laity
debate their various alternatives. Fiske framed his own opinion in the case but determined that he would accept the mind of the church in whatever it decided. When
the congregation finally reached a conclusion, Fiske offered his support, but then
added pointedly, "[H]ad their views differed from mine I would have kept my silence."
Similarly, like the Boston elders, Fiske sought the unanimous consent of the brethren
for all church decisions and honored the rights of dissenters. In 1644, a question arose
concerning whether several Salem members had been properly dismissed to Wenham.
"Twas answered and agreed by most" that the newcomers should be free to join the
church, but, Fiske noted, "by reason everyone agreed not to this answer, the thing
was for present suspended."[75]

Church discipline in Wenham, as in other churches, revolved around lay participation. Rarely in the annals of the Massachusetts church records is lay devotion to
the church covenant and "mutual watchfulness" more evident than in the disciplinary case of George Norton. This single disciplinary case takes up almost one-eighth of
the entire Fiske Notebook. Norton had been brought before the Wenham church in
1646 for several counts of lying. He aggravated his offense by fanatical obstinacy, refusing
to admit guilt even in the face of overwhelming evidence against him. After suffering
aspersions from Norton for treating him "unfairly," the members lost patience and
excommunicated him.

Norton's case was a community affair. The entire church labored with the offender, in public and in private, for hundreds of hours over fourteen weeks before
finally censuring him, and, as the Wayte case demonstrated, even that did not end
the church's obligations to seek repentance from the offender. Pastor Fiske noted
how one church meeting devoted to the case was directed almost entirely by the laity;
eleven church members teamed up, spending two hours laboring with Norton "with
tears" in their eyes in an effort to inspire repentance. Norton simply could not bring
himself to admit to wrongdoing and continually exacerbated his case by offering false
confessions. One of these efforts, in fact, was so far-fetched that it left the church
"marvelling at such his answer."[76]

At one level, church discipline failed in the case of George Norton. Instead of
fostering understanding, repentance, and forgiveness, the church's censures left
Norton a broken man in a "desperate" mental condition.[77] But for the participants,
the failure could be laid at the footstep of Norton himself, not the pastor or the system as a whole. As in the Boston disciplinary cases, the entire church was united in

its understanding of the case and in its efforts to fulfill covenant obligations to Norton and to reclaim the offender.

Church procedures in Wenham, as in Boston, affirm that members and their elders inhabited a shared space in matters of church government that ministers defined in such a way as to encourage lay thought and initiative. The ministers taught the Congregational system to the members, who achieved a sufficient understanding to reach their own conclusions and assert their will while sharing responsibilities of church government. These features did not change as a consequence of the Antinomian controversy. To the contrary, lay people exercised more initiative in church affairs as they attained a fuller understanding of the workings of the system. Just as important, the church hearings we have examined reveal unmistakable evidence of profound lay commitment to the ideals of mutuality and cooperation expressed in the church covenant and in the Congregational system generally. We have seen lay willingness to labor for hours with offenders, even "with tears," tender apologies for forgetting to call a member "brother," and the determination of members and clergymen alike to forgo individuality and abide by the decision of the organic church. The unique degree of unanimity, lay participation, and mutual confidence among church officers and members are all manifestations of a larger group identity that characterized church government during the late 1630s and the 1640s. These shared ideals, just as much as the laity's understanding of specific practices and larger principles of limited authority and free consent, explain why the system worked so closely according to plan during the early decades of settlement. Later decades would witness the erosion of mutuality and communitarianism, a development that would be reflected in increasing contention in church meetings and divisions for which Congregational rules provided no ready cures. But in the decade that followed the Antinomian controversy, the effects of rising individualism among lay people and any efforts among ministers to initiate institutional "hardening" remained far off in the future.

4

The Presbyterian Challenge

Meeting privately in 1641, a group of Massachusetts ministers addressed a proposition that ought to have occasioned no debate whatsoever: "that the assembly of elders have power over particular churches." At length, the clergymen reaffirmed the long-standing principle of Congregational autonomy—that every church enjoyed "government within itself"—but not before pastor John Eliot of Roxbury offered a spirited justification for the binding authority of the collective elders.[1] Eliot was not alone in his belief that a decade of New World experiences pointed to the need for stronger consociational authority in church government. In general, "the brethren of New England incline more to synods and Presbyteries," insisted Robert Baillie, a noted English opponent of the Congregational Way, "driven thereto by the manifold late heresies, schisms, and factions broke out amongst them." Thomas Lechford agreed with this assessment, observing that "divers of the Ministerie have set meetings to order Church matters; whereby it is conceived they bend toward Presbyterian rule."[2]

Lechford, who addressed an English audience, was no more a friend of New England Congregationalism than Baillie, and their wishful descriptions of rising Presbyterianism in Massachusetts underscore the transatlantic influences that accompanied internal challenges to the New England Way in the 1640s. In 1643, the Westminster Assembly convened in London to define beliefs and a system of church order, advancing a Presbyterian form of discipline. That same year, Parliament established the Commissioners for Plantation, a board empowered "to provide for, order, and dispose all things" in the colonies. It seemed plausible that through the Commissioners Parliament might attempt to impose the results of the Westminster Assembly upon New England. New Englanders offered no objections to the Assembly's confession of faith; in fact, they heartily endorsed it. But the prospect of Parliamentary pressure to adopt Presbyterianism, following on the heels of the Antinomian controversy, emboldened a handful of Massachusetts ministers to challenge Congregational practices and forced orthodox elders to reassess several features of the New England Way. Ultimately, the Massachusetts clergy would strongly reaffirm Congregationalism and would codify the system in the *Cambridge Platform* of church government—but not before lay people made clear that they would tolerate no other alternative.³

Presbyterianism differed from Congregational church government in a number of fundamental respects. Most threatening to lay Puritans was the Presbyterians' belief that decision-making authority in discipline, admissions, and other church matters rested solely with the elders. The Congregational system, Presbyterians insisted, violated the Scriptures by granting the laity too direct a role in governing local churches. Their angry complaints remind us how radical the limited democratic components of Congregationalism seemed to many seventeenth-century minds:

> If all members . . . must judge and govern upon conscience, together with the Presbytery [i.e., church officers] 1) it must needs interrupt the work 2) It is work enough, a double Labor for the Elders to instruct the church how to judge. There is more time spent informing the church than in determining the case . . . Must Elders hold the hands of the common members (as the Masters teach the Scholars to write) and act only by them?⁴

The Presbyterians further pointed to the dangers created by the Congregational rule that forbade elders from intervening in the affairs of neighboring churches. Eventually, they warned, disputes would become so divisive that the English authorities would be forced to step in and impose toleration. Consequently, most Presbyterians demanded that the elders meet in regular, binding synods. Finally, most Presbyterians denied the necessity of regenerate church membership and would therefore admit all "non-scandalous" churchgoers to the Lord's Supper.⁵

The Presbyterian critique of Congregational autonomy in fact pointed with prophetic accuracy to weaknesses in the New England Way that would create difficulties in the next generation and would eventually contribute to the system's unraveling in the eighteenth century. In the early decades of settlement ministers achieved harmony within their churches by successfully promoting shared goals of mutuality and communitarianism. They also reinforced order by remaining united themselves on issues of church government and by relying upon the habitual deference paid to them as interpreters of the Word. Gradually ministers would enjoy less deference, especially when the clergy itself grew divided over critically important issues of church order. Without the recognized standards that ministers might produce in binding synods, churches were far more likely to experience divisions for which, the Presbyterians pointed out, Congregationalism offered no ready cures.

As their frequent discussions of the power of synods attest,⁶ the ministers of the Bay were hardly oblivious to these potential hazards. Presbyterian prescriptions for more coercive forms of control held a certain attraction for at least a few members of the Massachusetts clergy, including Peter Hobart of Hingham and, most notably, Thomas Parker and James Noyes of Newbury. Parker and Noyes formally accepted the results of the Westminster Assembly and openly demanded that the rest of the churches of Massachusetts Bay adopt a Presbyterian form of church government. The Newbury elders had in fact harbored Presbyterian inclinations since their election in Newbury in 1635. Emboldened by events in England, they began to lash out at the "confusion and disorder" that, they insisted, inevitably accompanied Massachusetts' "Democraticall [church] Government."[7]

By 1643, government in the First Church of Newbury had begun to lean in Presbyterian directions, as Parker and Noyes compromised the members' right to add their consent to church decisions. Predictably, the ministers' violations ignited a rebellion within the church among lay people who were well versed in their rights. No records remain from this period of Newbury's history that might cast light on the members' specific response to the elders' encroachments, but lay liberties and church government were clearly central issues of contention in a war that raged in the Newbury church for thirty years.[8]

The elders of the Bay Colony grew increasingly restive about these agitations in Newbury. On the one hand, few ministers in the Bay welcomed Presbyterianism; lay resistance in Newbury demonstrated to the elders the intense commitment to the New England Way shared by ordinary churchgoers. Other ministers, some of whom sympathized with Presbyterian calls to strengthen the elders' collective authority, pointed out that a total repudiation of the Newbury practices risked the alienation of Puritans in England, who kept a careful eye on events in Massachusetts, even publishing the results of the New Englanders' deliberations.[9]

In response to this touchy situation, the elders assembled at the Newbury Convention in 1643 to discuss the division in that town and Presbyterianism generally. Here the elders first unveiled a strategy they would pursue for the rest of the decade: for the benefit of the laity, they defended standard Congregational practices and principles at the convention, but they couched their positions in vague language that emphasized general points of agreement with the Presbyterians and could even be interpreted as supporting some of their positions.[10] According to an unnamed attendee, the elders concluded that the formal exercise of church power at the local level belonged to the church officers, "unless their sin be apparent in their work." To observers unfamiliar with Congregational practices, this statement seemed to differ little from the Presbyterians' stance toward clerical authority. But in fact, it hardly represented a shift in the position of the Massachusetts elders. Congregational officers all along exercised the "formal" power of admitting and censuring members; they differed from Presbyterians in that they exercised this power in the name and with the consent of the members, a fact they carefully omitted. The elders next attempted to cloud their conversion requirement for church membership, acknowledging that the well behaved constituted "fit matter" for the church, though not always able to make "large and particular relations of the work on doctrine of faith." All along Congregationalists had affirmed that faint measures of faith, not merely "large and particular" assurances, ought to entitle candidates to membership. The elders found it impossible to waffle their way around the issue of consent, concluding "the votes of the people are needful" in church decisions, "at least by way of consent."[11]

The determinations of the Newbury Synod hardly represented a stinging rebuke to Parker and Noyes; as Winthrop noted, the elders only "concluded against some parts of the Presbyterial way." The failure of the clergy to offer a stronger defense of Congregationalism has been subjected to conflicting interpretations among historians. Some have suggested that the elders' "soft" stance toward Parker and Noyes reflected widespread support among the ministers for the more authoritarian church government that Presbyterians advocated. Others have insisted that the ministers were simply exercising diplomacy at the Newbury Convention, in hopes of avoiding a strong public statement as long as events remained uncertain overseas.[12] While, as we shall see, the weight of the evidence supports the latter interpretation, historians on both sides of the debate have lost sight of the larger fact that no significant changes in the actual practices of church government could be instituted by the ministers themselves; any innovation would require the consent of lay people.

Ordinary churchgoers caught wind of the debates within the ministerial community and they fully understood the implications of the Presbyterian challenge. It is safe to assume that lay people followed the events in Newbury; Congregational provisions required churches to discuss the issues dividing that church in order to elect representatives to the Newbury Convention. Representatives then undoubtedly discussed the results of the meeting when they returned home. Letters condemning Presbyterian practices in Newbury, such as a series exchanged between the Salem and Wenham churches in 1644, were all read publicly before the laity, in accordance with standard Congregational provisions. Presbyterian practices were openly debated in Boston church meetings as well.[13]

Obviously, the more lay people learned about this system of governance, the less they liked it. Presbyterianism, they believed, not only violated the sacred system of discipline prescribed in the Bible, but it also stood to remove many liberties that churchgoers increasingly came to regard as inviolable rights. It should come as little surprise that in the few locations where Presbyterianism surfaced in Massachusetts Bay, church divisions soon followed. Contention not only racked the town of Newbury for decades, it also erupted in the church of Hingham, the only other Massachusetts church known to be run in a Presbyterian fashion. According to Winthrop, Hingham pastor Peter Hobart managed "all affairs without the church's advice." As in Newbury, the members fully recognized the violations of Scripture rules and their own liberties: the protests of "diverse of the congregation" left the church "divided into parts" until the elders interceded and declared Hobart "at great fault."[14]

Several other clues appear in the church records that suggest that lay people had no intention of sitting quietly while their ministers drifted off in the direction of Presbyterianism and excessive clerical control. In Boston, a remarkable exchange between minister and members flared when one Thomas Heddel[15] stood before the church in 1645 to challenge John Cotton on the topic of church discipline. In particular Heddell objected to disciplinary procedures that required aggrieved members to bring initial complaints before the elders, who then exercised unilateral authority to decide whether matters should be brought before the church.[16] "It is very dowbtfull to me," Heddel announced,

> whether by that place in math 18 goe to the church whan a Brother hath giuen offence and doth not giue satisfaction that we should first goe and tell the elders and thay must have the hearinge of the matter and offences befor thay are brought to the congregation. Then we shall make one injunction more than christ him selfe hath made, for he makes but 3. First goe to thy Brother thy selfe. If he satisfie not thee then, 2 take one or 2 mor with thee and if he will not hear them then, 3 tell the church. Therfor if we must tell the elders befor the church that is a 4th step or degre which christ hath not apoynted. If the elders must be told before the church that puts a defitiency upon christs order.

Apparently this question had come up in a previous, unrecorded meeting; Cotton responded that "yow have herd 2 of those Answers allready." The Boston teacher then defended existing practices, explaining that he "did not say tell the elders and not the church but tell the church by the elders," a procedure justified by the fact that "christ wrights to the churches by the Ayngells and reproves the churches by thear officers." Cotton based his conclusions, he insisted, on biblical authority, not his own. Having explained his position, he invited the layman to justify the practice of bringing an offence to the church "withowt acqwayntinge the Officers." "Showe me such a precident in the scriptuer and I will yeld to yow," the Boston teacher offered, "[b]ut I know no place nor president that warrants such a practise."

Reading between the lines, Cotton recognized that the issue Heddel raised extended beyond Scripture precedents to larger questions of lay and clerical authority. The point, Cotton said, in an effort to reassure the church, was not to "bringe it to the elders that they should kepe it from the church but that thay may prepare it for the church." The laity, or at least several members of it, appears to have been neither impressed nor intimidated by Cotton's response. Richard Hutchinson,[17] a town officer, cut through the formalities and seized the opportunity to bring the real issues—Presbyterianism and clerical control—into open congregation. According to his understanding of Congregationalism, the members and the elders stood on equal footing. But these procedures, he complained,

> put mor Awthoritie upon the officers than the church and this is that which both the Bishopes and Presbiterians attribute to them selves that thay are the church and all bussines of the church must be transacted by the Presbitery withowt the church.

What if the elders refused to bring a case before the church, Hutchinson demanded, even if the aggrieved remained unsatisfied?

In equating Cotton's declarations with those of the "Bishops and Presbiterians," the layman had hurled a stinging insult at the Father of New England Congregationalism. Cotton deflected this larger accusation before once again addressing the particular question. "You know owr judgment" concerning Presbyterians, Cotton scolded. "We bore witness agaynst thear practise." Again, he denied any sympathy for the Presbyterian belief that "the eldership should transact the publike bussines of the church withowt the Consent or knowledge of the church or thear assistance in it." The elders maintained a duty to prevent a case from coming to the church "if it not be ripe," Cotton insisted, but significantly, he reminded the congregation that if the officers prevented a "ripe" case from coming to the church, they were accountable to the members who held a right to censure them. Skeptical, the merchant Thomas Fowle[18] refused to relent. How, specifically, might a member bring a case before the church if the elders refused to do so? Cotton repeated the principle of accountability to the members: if the elders unjustly prevented a case from coming to the church, the aggrieved were to bring two witnesses to help assess the officers' behavior, and if the witnesses agreed, they were to call the elders to account for maladministration. At that point, the original case could be brought before the church.

The dialogue ended here. It is impossible to ascertain how many other Bostonians shared the reservations of the three protesting members. No further lay complaints of this nature appear in the Keayne Notebook. But the disciplinary procedures that Cotton defended were by no means new "coercive" measures; since the early 1630s, church officers brought cases before their churches only after determining that they were "ripe."[19] The members' hypothetical questions (the lay complaints cannot be explained by cases pending before the church) in protest of long-standing practices reveal far more than the members' ability to examine critically practices of church government and their willingness to challenge their ministers. They also suggest that the topics of church power and clerical authority troubled churchgoers who had grown sensitive, perhaps even hypersensitive, to Presbyterian suggestions that the laity enjoyed too much authority in matters of church government. No less than the lay rebellions in Newbury and Hingham, exchanges such as the one in Boston demonstrated to the elders that the "silent democracy" in the pews would not sit by idly should the "speaking aristocracy" decide to flirt with Presbyterianism and its challenges to lay liberties.[20]

Some ministers no doubt remained persuaded by certain elements of the Presbyterian critique, despite the kinds of lay resistance evident in Newbury, Hingham, and Boston. Like the Presbyterians, some clergymen continued to point to a need for strengthened interchurch ties, a topic ministers would continue to debate for the rest of the decade and beyond. Nonetheless, when push came to shove, the Bay clergy rejected Presbyterianism and continued to share with the laity a commitment to Congregational principles and the liberties of the brethren. Even on the subject of consociationalism, most agreed with Concord pastor Peter Bulkley that while ministerial consociations were "of singular use," their function was "to communicate light" and not "to authorize power." "Particular churches may want much light," he observed, "yet I thinke the power of execution must come from within." Addressing a number of ministers in a private meeting, Richard Mather and John Allin also remained firm in their conviction that the assembled elders maintained no authority in local church affairs other than to "direct and advise."[21]

The ministers in Salem and Wenham also faced Presbyterian challenges to the Congregational Way, and they also rejected them. In 1644, John Fiske noted that several members appeared in the Wenham church bearing written dismissals composed by Newbury's Parker and Noyes. Upon examination of the documents, Fiske discovered that the ministers had granted the dismissions without procuring the assent of their congregation. Obviously angered by this assault on lay liberties, the Wenham pastor sought the counsel of Edward Norris and Samuel Sharpe, Salem's teacher and ruling elder. He explained the plight of the Newbury members who, through no fault of their own, "could not have letters of recommendation or dismissal but in the name of the elders." Should they be allowed to join the Wenham church?[22]

The Salem elders were no more sympathetic to Parker and Noyes than Fiske. In a public letter to the Wenham congregation, the Salem officers reviewed their own practices and then urged resistance to the sinful assault upon the right of lay consent that the Presbyterians in Newbury advocated:

> When we call for letters dismissory they must come from the church as well
> as the elders. Otherwise, they will not be received here at any hand, it being
> no way fit to countenance their innovations in the church of Christ.[23]

The elders regarded the consent of the members, in short, as both vital to the maintenance of church purity and a required ordinance of God. They had no intention of violating the Scriptures and endangering purity by accepting Presbyterian practices, even in seemingly minor points of church order like dismissions.

Unwilling to drop the matter, Norris and Sharpe later sent the Wenham church a more detailed explanation of their views that included a further defense of lay liberties. The members and the elders, they noted, shared the authority to dismiss: "The church and not the elders without the church have this power." Furthermore, a dismissal testified to a member's good standing, and "none but the whole church can declare a member to stand in good state with the whole church." The Salem elders then "justified" the latter proposition by reminding the laity of its "watchmen" role: "Some are under offense and the offense is known only to some but not the elders." Norris and Sharpe admitted that "some members are of corrupt judgement," but, perhaps with an eye to Parker and Noyes, they reminded lay people of a fundamental lesson they had been taught since the founding: "Maybe the elders are corupt, too." Churchgoers, they repeated, were not to follow blindly the lead of their ministers. Finally, the Salem elders excoriated the officers from Newbury for their "carelessness and neglect" in violating "the liberties of the church of Christ."[24]

A month later, the Newbury elders addressed another letter of dismission to Fiske rather than to the entire Wenham church. And again, they refused to sign the letter "with the consent of the church." At the next church meeting Fiske produced the document and affirmed to the Wenham congregation his angry opposition to Presbyterianism and its emphasis upon clerical control of church government. "This dismission," he complained to his members, "is not to the church mentioned (and may as well [be] said to be unto the town as unto the church) but unto the pastor of the church only, as if the whole care and government belonged to him. Whereas by Mat. 16 and 17 it seems to belong to the church." Eventually, the Wenhamites voted to admit the former Newbury members but only after they publicly excepted against the form of the dismissions.[25]

Clearly, the elders in Salem and Wenham refused to budge even slightly from Congregational practices, a finding that contradicts the assertions of numerous historians who have argued that ministers not only advocated but actually implemented a significantly more authoritarian brand of Congregationalism in the 1640s. In fact, the grousing over the limits of ministerial authority that surfaced in private clerical meetings in Massachusetts was only sporadic; little evidence remains in the church records dating from the 1640s to suggest that any minister outside of Hingham and Newbury even attempted to introduce novel procedures in his church that stood to compromise lay rights and responsibilities in church government.

In the midst of this controversy over Presbyterianism, the General Court attempted to convene a formal synod of the elders for the purpose of constructing a written platform of church discipline. The Court's timing could not have been worse. Presbyterians insisted that synodical determinations enjoyed binding status, and news that the Court had ordered a synod to codify church government in the Bay only heightened fears among lay critics that the authorities were again showing their true Presbyterian colors. Several deputies questioned whether the civil arm maintained a right to command churches to send their elders and messengers to such a meeting. More important, some voiced fears that if the General Court stood to enforce the decisions of the synod, the ministers' pronouncements would bind individual churches, in open violation of the principle of Congregational autonomy.[26]

In fact, the motives of the authorities in church and state were far more complex. In the first place, it was the ministers who in 1646 petitioned the General Court to convene the synod, and the elders certainly had neither the intention nor the authority to foist Presbyterian innovations upon an unwilling laity. To the contrary, they hoped to offer a clear and concise alternative to Presbyterianism to English Puritans who had requested a definitive statement of Congregational church discipline. At the same time, the synod would present an opportunity to help standardize practices within

New England churches and to resolve a number of nagging questions that had arisen concerning admissions and baptism.[27]

The churches had addressed the latter questions several times since the first years of settlement and would continue to do so throughout the colonial era. In 1645, Massachusetts authorities faced pressure to reexamine admissions practices when confronted with a protest movement organized by William Vassal and Dr. Robert Child. Their complaint centered around the fact that Massachusetts limited the suffrage to church members and opened membership only to those who could prove their regeneration in the extraordinarily trying admissions test. Massachusetts leaders began to take the protests seriously when they learned of Child's intentions to take his case to Parliament, which never agreed with New England admission policies to begin with.[28]

While these sorts of pressures alone did not force the elders to reconsider admissions standards, the threat of parliamentary interference did add impetus to procedural changes many ministers had favored all along. As Stephen Foster has argued, the clergy had by the 1640s grown concerned with a steady sectarian drift in the churches that threatened to blossom into a dangerous overemphasis upon purity.[29] Though at this point no Congregational minister seriously considered the Presbyterian demand to abandon regenerate membership, most churches did begin in the 1640s to dismantle the elaborate obstacle course they forced candidates to conquer in order to become full members. Churches first began to allow women to read their conversion testimonials instead of requiring an oral confession of them. In time, some ministers would begin to write down the confessions in private and then read them to the congregation themselves. Later, beginning around midcentury, some churches began to offer the same options to men.[30]

Predictably, previous historians have explained these developments by arguing that ministers unilaterally decided to assume fuller control of admissions practices as part of a larger campaign to realign the balance of church power. There is, however, little evidence to support this conclusion.[31] Granted, in the absence of oral testimony, the members were no longer offered the opportunity to judge a candidate's sincerity for themselves, a right they continued to exercise in disciplinary repentances. Presumably, they were also no longer entitled to question candidates during admissions hearings.

Nonetheless, in allowing ministers to read private confessions, lay people surrendered little power that the elders did not already enjoy; churchgoers apparently favored these modest changes in admissions procedures. Public confessions, it must be remembered, had all along been something of a formality—once the elders approved of a conversion relation, a congregational rejection was almost unheard of. The difficulty of admissions tests never seemed fully justified to many lay people, and ministers and members alike recognized that the tests kept some from even attempting to gain membership.[32] Throughout the seventeenth century, lay people commonly requested the liberty to express themselves to the church in writing in matters of admissions and discipline, in hopes of avoiding an oral performance.[33] We can learn much of what was of real concern to lay people by examining the sorts of issues they fought over. We can also learn much by taking note of the sorts of issues they did *not* fight over. In sharp contrast to the resistance the laity offered in response to admissions changes in the 1660s, there is no evidence of serious debate, much less church division, over these earlier procedural modifications, which churches apparently implemented by mutual consent.

A far more volatile question facing the elders on the eve of the Cambridge Synod concerned the thorny subject of baptism. The General Court noted as early as 1646 that "many persons in the country are knowne not a little to differ" on the issue of "baptism and the persons to be received thereto." Though in "most churches" the ministers baptized "onely such children whose nearest parents . . . are setled [church] members in full communion," the Court noted that already "there be some who baptize the children if the grandfather or grandmother be such members, though the immediate parents be not." While other churches had not yet instituted changes in baptism, they did "much incline thereto."[34]

The ministers and General Court cited the varying practices in baptism and admissions as strong evidence for the need to create a formal platform of church discipline to standardize the most important church procedures in New England. Appeals for greater standardization were not entirely new. The Court had requested such a platform as early as 1634. The elders complied, but because countless specific procedural questions remained to be answered, they produced only a vague statement of principles rather than a detailed description of church practices.[35] Over the next ten years, however, ministers discussed the New England Way with increasing completeness and confidence. Richard Mather's *Church-Government and Church-Covenant Discussed*, published in 1639, contained a lengthy and accurate summary of church practices. Five years later the elders circulated Thomas Hooker's "magisterial" *Summe of the Survey of Church Discipline*, and privately approved it as an accurate overview and justification of the Congregational Way.[36]

The elders were not unprepared or unmotivated, then, when English Puritans asked them to supply a definitive statement of church discipline. The trick was to convince a wary laity—suspicious of civil interference in church affairs and sensitive to possible Presbyterian inclinations among the elders—to elect representatives to a synod. The Court attempted to ease lay fears by styling their request to the churches an "invitation" to send delegates, rather than an order. The Court also promised that it would not compel churches to abide by the finished platform; the civil authorities would add nothing more than their "approbation" to the final product. These concessions left some lay people far from satisfied. Three churches balked at the election of representatives to the synod, including Boston, the largest, and Salem, the oldest. Many, if not most, other churches elected delegates only because opponents chose to abide by the mind of the church rather than to exercise their right to dissent.[37]

In Boston, however, a large minority of some thirty to forty members formally voted in opposition to the synod, a number easily large enough to prevent the church from electing delegates, given the ideal of unanimous consent. The lay objections, according to Winthrop, mirrored those of several deputies, who feared that the elders and the Court stood to compromise the principle of Congregational independence:

> The order was expressed, that what the major part of the assembly should agree upon should be presented to the Court, that they might give such allowance to it as should be meet, hence was inferred that the synod was appointed by the elders to the intent to make ecclesiastical laws to bind the churches, and to have the sanction of the civil authority put upon them.[38]

The protest once again demonstrates that while lay people could be persuaded to submit to minor procedural changes such as those in admissions, they jealously guarded their liberties in matters they considered fundamental. In this case, the dissenters perceived a duty to defend both their own rights and church order in general from sinful "innovations." Should the churches ever accept the authority of synods as binding, the assembled elders, not the local congregations, would enjoy the last say in matters of government affecting local churches. This arrangement threatened (at least theoretically) to remove the laity from the decision-making process all together.

Though the Boston majority did not share these fears, they acknowledged that the dissenters had raised legitimate questions. They reminded the protesters that the synod stood only to approve a nonbinding description of New England practices. The elders had even promised to submit the platform to the individual churches for approval before forwarding the document to the General Court. But the minority remained unconvinced. They blocked several efforts to elect delegates, prompting the church briefly to consider sending the entire congregation to the Cambridge Synod.

In hopes of breaking the impasse, the Boston elders invited John Norton of Ipswich to plead their case in a Sunday sermon, demonstrating once again that persuasion, not coercion, stood as the ministers' primary means of advancing their positions. Norton started from scratch, reviewing "the nature and power of a synod" from the Bible. He assured the members that the synod would only be "consultative" and "declarative," not "coactive," attempting to soothe fears that Congregational independence stood to be sinfully compromised. Though Norton's sermon convinced most of the synod's opponents, the elders still failed to achieve a unanimous consent.[39]

The Boston church first confronted here a difficulty every church would eventually encounter. What was a church to do in the event of an honest disagreement that involved a small group of dissenters who refused to relent in the face of an overwhelming majority? What if the elders simply could not achieve a "sense of the meeting"? Theoretically, the church might censure dissenters for obstinacy and thus nullify their votes. But as mentioned, the collective elders and the laity agreed that this form of compulsion threatened to quash dissent altogether; throughout the colonial era, nullification was almost never attempted in an effort to settle disagreements. The church finally broke the impasse, passing a motion to send delegates "according to the minde of the greater part of the Church Declared by lifting up their hands." By employing a majority vote for the first time in its history, the Bostonians accepted the legitimacy of opposition but prevented the will of a small minority from paralyzing the church. This action by no means erased the ideal of unanimous consent in Boston or any other church: well into the next century, churches would often refuse to pass votes in the face of significant minorities. But already, in 1646, churchgoers began to recognize that legitimate differences could exist within Congregationalism and unanimity could not always be achieved. The Congregationalists hoped to prevent tyranny of the majority within church meetings by honoring lay dissent. By the same token, churchgoers saw the gradual implementation of the majority vote not as a symptom of "decline," but as a solution to a potential tyranny of the minority.[40]

In the first meeting at Cambridge, the elders immediately reaffirmed that the synod would be "advisory," not judicial, and then assigned Cotton, Richard Mather, and Duxbury pastor Ralph Partridge the task of preparing drafts of the platform. After some debate, the elders decided to table several important issues, especially those concerning baptism and church membership. Nearly all of the delegates agreed on the necessity of extending baptism to the grandchildren of the regenerate. But three prestigious ministers, John Davenport, Increase Mather, and Charles Chauncy, opposed the measure and, as the Antinomian controversy demonstrated, a position on such a troubling issue was best advanced by a united ministry.[41]

Having put off these controversial matters, the elders focused on composing a description of existing practices in their churches. Relying heavily upon previous descriptions of the New England Way, especially Mather's *Church-Government and Church-Covenant Discussed* and Cotton's *Way of the Churches of Christ in New England*, the delegates completed their work in 1648 and unanimously adopted the *Cambridge Platform* a year later. The General Court received the *Platform* in October 1649 and then went to extraordinary lengths to make certain that the laity approved of the finished document. Still sensitive to lay fears and criticisms, they offered nothing more than the cautious conclusion that the document was "meet to be comended to the judicious and pious consideration of the severall churches." The Court then requested to be informed, in writing, "how far its suiteable to [the churches'] judgments and approbations." Though some churches began to consider the *Platform* immediately, others dawdled and the Court found it necessary to repeat its order a few months later "that the said booke be duly considered [by] all the sayd churches within this pattent, and that they, without fayle, will returne their thoughts and judgments touchinge the particulars thereof."[42]

Over the next year, churchgoers throughout Massachusetts Bay read, reread, and debated the *Platform*'s every detail. The Wenham church records contain the only extended account of debate at the local level.[43] Most striking about pastor John Fiske's summaries of the Wenham deliberations is the careful scrutiny and depth of analysis to which the congregation subjected the *Platform*. The Wenham church studied the document in three separate meetings, dissecting every passage, sensitive to every semantical nuance. Fiske and his congregation were quick to note that isolated sentences and phrases were acceptable only if understood in context with other passages on the same subject:

> [W]e do declare ourselves that this our assent extends not itself to every particular circumstance in every chapter and section in the said platform according to that sense the letters sometimes might seem to carry as taken apart by itself and not explained by and compared with other places and expressions in the said platform touching the said matter.

Among several examples, the Wenham church cited chapter 10, section 8, on "the power which Christ has committed to the Elders," which includes an assertion that church members may not "oppose nor contradict the judgment of *sentence* of the Elders, without sufficient and weighty cause." The statement seemed overly authoritarian in tone, unless considered alongside other passages that describe limitations on the elders and the liberties of the brethren, including the right to "remove [an elder] from his Office."[44]

The vagueness of the *Platform* also concerned the Wenhamites, prompting the congregation to complain of some passages that they "wished had been otherwise set down or more fully explained." At length, they voted unanimously to ratify the document, with the understanding that they expected "the liberty of interpreting the same in our own sense." The bottom line in achieving consent in Wenham, then, was the fact that the *Platform* was simply a description of existing practices, not a binding set of laws. Like the Court and the other churches, the Wenhamites approved the document "for the substance thereof" and insisted "that there be no attempt as to impose in a way of authority and such[,] drafts or determinations from this or any other synod as binding canons or perfect platforms."[45]

Reservations from the Wenham members, along with those from the other churches, were recorded and sent on to the General Court, which in turn forwarded them to the elders. The lay questions, along with the elders' answers, have survived in the form of a forty-page document whose very existence is as significant as anything it contains. Here the authorities provided the laity not only with a forum to raise exceptions to possible innovations contained in the *Cambridge Platform* but, insofar as the *Platform* largely consisted of a description of standard practices, with the invitation to voice any scruples over church government whatsoever.[46]

The laity made very little of this opportunity to express doubts about Congregational practices. The detailed nature of the lay objections affirms that the churches analyzed the *Platform* carefully and indicates that some opposition to the document remained even after the churches had completed their debates. But it is important not to overstate the significance of this protest. The most striking feature of the "certayne doubts" concerns what the document does *not* contain: twenty-five of the twenty-nine churches in the Bay offered no objections to the *Platform* whatsoever. Nearly all of the objections from the other churches came from just three men.

No recurrent or overarching theme runs through these questions, such as a general fear that the *Platform* has usurped lay rights. One member from Malden—and only one—complained that the *Platform* rendered "the power of the people . . . as good as nothing." But at the same time, Edward Brecke, probably one of Presbyterian leanings, protested the fact that the elders "judge according to the will of the church." "If the people do not consent," he asked, "[w]hose will shall be done, the will of God or of the people?" One of the few topics upon which several members expressed doubts concerned, once again, the authority of synods. Some members of the Salem church, the Wenham church, and one John Johnson all "doubted whether synods be an ordinance of God." Apparently churchgoers entertained far more doubts about the process of convening the Cambridge Synod than its results.[47]

Still sensitive to lay concerns, the General Court refused to "[g]ive theire approbation" to the *Platform* until "such objections as were presented were cleared and removed." The Court also sought to mollify members from Wenham and elsewhere by unequivocally refusing "to impose any formes as necessary to be observed by the churches as a bindinge rule." After forwarding the lay objections to the elders and digesting the ministers' written response, the Court offered the modest conclusion that "the said Booke of Discipline . . . for the substance thereof is that we have practised and doe beleeve." Fourteen of the deputies voted against ratification, but their objections pertained to the Court's role in the entire process, not the content of the *Platform* itself. With but a handful of exceptions, lay people, despite their ongoing uneasiness with Presbyterianism and their fierce determination to defend their rights, voted, however cautiously, to ratify the *Platform*. Even the First Church of Boston, which witnessed such vociferous opposition to the Cambridge Synod, apparently approved the finished document with little fanfare. In the final analysis, lay support for the *Platform* is not surprising because churchgoers saw it as their duty to learn and enforce Congregational provisions, not to invent them. Lay people would have objected in large numbers only if convinced that the document contained important "innovations." The relative absence of such protest argues strongly that lay people believed that the *Cambridge Platform* contained, "for the substance of it," an accurate description of New England church practices.[48]

Generations of historians have subjected the tone and content of the *Platform* to scrutiny and debate in an effort to uncover its larger meaning and significance. Echoing the sentiments of nineteenth-century Congregational scholars, Henry Wilder Foote observed on the document's tercentenary that the *Platform* "laid down certain vital principles" that profoundly shaped "the development of American thought, political as well as religious." "It was inevitable," Foote averred, that Congregational autonomy and "principles of self government" contained in the *Platform* would strongly contribute to "a like spirit of political independence." From "the very small mustard seed of *A Platform of Church Discipline*," he concluded, "there grew the great tree of religious and civil liberty upon which, in the fullness of time, the American eagle could perch."[49]

Perry Miller acknowledged that the *Platform* represented "the pioneer formulation of the principle that a corporate body is created by the consent of constituent members" but repeated his warnings that, like the founders in the 1630s, "the authors of the Platform had no interest in political democracy or in religious liberty." Miller further observed, correctly, that the meaning of the *Platform* changed over time in keeping with shifting historical circumstances. Though in later centuries the *Platform* was "made over in men's minds in conformity with their changing political aspirations" and so was "interpreted as though containing those ideals of liberty," Miller asserted, the "Puritans in the Cambridge of 1648 had no such aims in mind." Miller believed that the *Platform* should be understood in its specific historical context, as a response to the Puritan Revolution in England, and as a means of preserving New England's unique brand of coercive communitarianism.[50]

More recent scholars have accepted this advice. In contrast to the Congregational historians' sweeping generalizations about the larger influence of the *Platform* in shaping American history, they have examined the document in the context of shifting lay-clerical relations in New England. Most have advanced the familiar argument that the elders had come to believe by the 1640s that the laity enjoyed too much influence in church affairs. The *Cambridge Platform*, they have suggested, ushered in a more authoritarian form of church government than the founders practiced in the first years of settlement; as Stephen Foster, among others, has summarized, the document "in small but significant ways takes back something of what the laity had gained in the last eighteen years."[51]

These more recent discussions of the *Platform* have been no more successful in capturing its significance than those which hailed the document as the harbinger of the American Revolution: though scholars have ransacked the *Platform* in hopes of discovering "authoritarian" innovations, the contemporary significance of the document cannot be located in procedural modifications that it supposedly introduced. In fact, the only area in which some elders at the synod hoped to strengthen their authority was consociationalism. Boston pastor John Wilson submitted a strongly worded recommendation to the assembled elders pertaining to the authority of synods and councils; if adopted, Wilson's proposals stood to compromise Congregational autonomy. Synodical "determinations," Wilson wrote, "if consonant to the word of God, are to be receyved with reverence and submission: not only for their agreement with the woord, but also for the power whereby they are made, as being an ordinance of God."[52]

Though some of Wilson's wording appears in the *Platform* itself, the elders watered it down considerably before placing it in the final draft. In introducing the topic, they immediately acknowledged that synods are "not absolutely necessary to the being" of churches, and then took further pains to note that such meetings would always include lay as well as clerical delegates: "Synods are to consist of both Elders, and other church-members . . . not excluding the presence of any brethren in the churches." Most importantly, on the fundamental question of binding authority, the *Platform* states unequivocally that synods are "[n]ot to exercise Church-censures in a way of discipline, nor any other act of church authority or jurisdiction" that might compromise the local churches' right of independent self-government. The elders hoped with this compromise to strengthen the prestige of synods and councils while making clear that they ultimately remained only advisory.[53]

The elders' judicious treatment of the subject of consociationalism is instructive, for in the final analysis, the *Platform*'s vagueness is far more conspicuous than any novel tone of authoritarianism. In many other controversial areas concerning the specifics of lay and clerical power, the *Platform* lapses into indecisiveness, as the Wenham church observed. Within the local church, for instance, the members are not to "oppose nor contradict the judgment or sentence of the Elders," unless they have "sufficient and weighty cause." Similarly, elders are "subject to the power of the church" if guilty of "mal-administration." Nowhere does the *Platform* even begin to explain what kind of causes might be "sufficient" to warrant lay opposition, or what kind of actions might constitute "mal-administration" and therefore open an officer to church censure.[54]

This vagueness was partly by design and partly a function of compromises forced upon the elders by the conflicting expectations of their audiences. A more authoritarian tone would certainly please English readers; the indecisiveness of certain passages reflects the elders' attempt to veil certain differences with the Presbyterians, as they had during the Newbury Convention of 1643. But the elders also had the needs and desires of their local congregations to consider, a crucial point that has been ignored in virtually all previous discussions of this important topic. Unlike earlier treatises on the New England Way, which ministers printed in London largely for an English audience, the *Cambridge Platform* was scheduled to be sent to every church in Massachusetts Bay (it probably turned up in every church in New England) for lay approval.[55] Whether they hoped to strengthen clerical control or merely to mask differences with the Presbyterians, the elders fully understood that the laity—still suspicious of Presbyterianism and synodical control—would refuse to ratify a more authoritarian document, and the finished product bears the impress of that recognition.[56]

Finally, it merits repeating that regardless of whatever the elders may have placed in the *Cambridge Platform*, actual changes in the practices of government would emerge in local churches only if churchgoers agreed to them. There is nothing in the records of church meetings to suggest that either the larger balance of power between the members and the ministers or specific practices within the churches shifted in the 1650s. And, significantly, relative to events later in the century, the years after the adoption of the *Platform* witnessed few struggles in the churches directly related to lay rights and clerical authority.[57]

The question remains, then, as to where the significance of the *Platform* rests, particularly for contemporaries. While it is true, as Miller noted, that future generations would reinterpret the *Platform* in keeping with their evolving political culture, the document nonetheless quickly assumed meanings that would endure essentially unchanged for much of the colonial era. Almost immediately, churchgoers would come to revere the *Platform*; lay people and ministers referred to it as the religious "constitution" of Massachusetts, a set of higher laws that contained written guarantees of the rights and liberties of members and church officers. Despite the incertitude of certain passages, the *Platform* stated decisively that "there may be the essence and being of a church without any officers" and affirmed in three separate places the concept of accountability: the members maintained not only a "power to *chuse* their officers and ministers" but they enjoyed "power also to *depose* them." The members' rights to participate and consent in admissions, discipline, and all other church decisions were likewise confirmed in unmistakable terms.[58]

The *Platform*, like church covenants, also enjoyed a constitutional status among lay people in that it drew authority from the consent of the churchgoers who ratified it. In discussing covenants and church government generally, the elders and lay delegates acknowledged in the *Platform* that they "see not otherwise how members can have *Church-power* one over another [except] mutually." The efforts of authorities in both church and state to secure lay ratification for the *Platform* and to resolve any doubts among the members further demonstrates that, no less than the founders in the 1630s, the elders still sought to base church government upon principles of voluntarism, mutuality, free consent, lay participation, and "higher law."[59]

As important as the *Platform* was in codifying Congregational principles of limited authority, free consent, and lay participation, its significance for churchgoers extended far beyond its constitutional status. All along, the laity had been taught that their church practices represented biblical ordinances, not creations of men. The ratification and adoption of the *Cambridge Platform* served only to strengthen churchgoers' commitment to the inviolable, biblical nature of the New England Way. "Our polity," Norton reminded his listeners, is "a Gospel polity," one "compleat according to the Scriptures, answering fully the word of God." Cotton went so far as to assert that "if the Lord Jesus were here himselfe in person," he would openly endorse the Congregational Way. The *Platform* itself affirmed that

> The partes of Church-Government are all of them exactly described in the
> word of God being parts or means of Instituted worship according to the
> second Commandement . . . . Soe that it is not left in the power of men, of-
> ficers, Churches, or any state in the world, to add, diminish, or alter any thing
> in the least measure therein.

So long as there "bee no errour of man" concerning "the partes of Church-Govern-ment," the *Platform* continued, "the determining of them is to be accounted as if it were divine." Ministers were so successful in convincing their congregations of the *Platform*'s scriptural basis that lay people would come to vest a sacred significance in the document as a virtual composition of God himself. Weaving together politi-cal and theological justifications, ministers and lay people acknowledged a sacred duty to adhere to the practices outlined in the *Platform* not only because members and ministers had mutually agreed to it but because God commanded it.[60]

Finally, insofar as church government motivated the Puritans to travel to the New World, and insofar as the *Platform* represented God's sacred plan of church order, the document would soon become for the Puritans a larger statement of religious purpose and national identity. When churchgoers discovered that England rejected the *Cambridge Platform* and the Congregational system it described, the document became that much more important as a set of principles and practices that distin-guished them as a unique people of God. "Tis that for which we are Out-casts at this day," Norton preached in his famous 1661 election sermon *Sion the Out-cast Healed of her Wounds*; the *Platform* "sheweth what *New-England* is."[61]

Any significant departure from the *Platform* advanced by ministers consequently ran the risk of ferocious lay resistance. Insofar as the *Platform*, like church govern-ment itself, was grounded and justified in free consent, lay people carefully scruti-nized efforts to modify the document and were quick to interpret such attempts as violations of the political principle of the limitation of authority according to higher law. More important, any challenge to the *Platform* represented a sinful attack on God's sacred plan of church order and an assault on their larger national identity as a people who defined themselves by the Congregational principles embodied in that document. Having vested the *Cambridge Platform* with secular, sacred, and national significance, in sum, lay people took this mere description of church practices and transformed it into the very binding document they so desperately feared when the idea was first broached to them.

Notwithstanding its sense of inviolability, the *Platform* by no means arrested the further evolution of Congregationalism. Through the rest of the colonial era, churches in Massachusetts would continue to tinker with procedural details of church government. Nonetheless, the codification of the New England Way certainly served as an obstacle to further "reformation," and it granted to the laity a greater hand in determining the direction of change. In the past, churchgoers enjoyed relatively little critical leverage with which to assess many clerical recommendations. Though in disciplinary cases and admissions church members did not hesitate to offer their opinions and to oppose their elders, sharp contention and outright lay resistance generally occurred only when ministers flagrantly flouted the practices that they had taught their congregations. With the adoption of the *Cambridge Platform*, the de-tails of Congregationalism became even more accessible for ordinary churchgoers. Though in some areas the document was vague, the *Platform* was certainly less open to interpretation, and therefore less open to ministerial monopolization, than the Bible, and it thus served as something more concrete to which the elders could be held.

Given the profound understanding of Congregationalism that lay people attained in studying and ratifying the *Platform*, churchgoers were far better equipped to scrutinize and challenge their elders' decisions, as ministers would discover in years to come. Any changes in church order would require ministers to close ranks among themselves and then persuade a well-informed laity that would draw careful distinctions between subtle procedural modifications (which churchgoers often approved) and larger violations of the New England Way (which they generally resisted). If the *Cambridge Platform* "took something away" from the laity, in short, it surely took more from the ministers by reducing their future role as interpreters and "inventors" of church government and handing the laity a clearer set of provisions to which the authorities could be held accountable.

It is doubtful that ministers foresaw serious difficulties emerging from the codification of the New England Way and the limits on clerical prerogatives included in the *Cambridge Platform*. The document, again, merely described a system that seemed to be working according to plan and presumably would require few wholesale changes. In convening the Cambridge Synod, the General Court explained that one purpose of the *Platform* would be to reaffirm existing practices, to consolidate the churches' current success, and to serve as a means of passing it on to future generations so that "glory may still dwell in our land, truth and peace may still abide in these churches and plantations." The *Cambridge Platform* would provide for the founders some assurance that their "posterity may not so easily decline from the good way."[62]

But the clergy, along with some members of the laity, never expected the *Cambridge Platform* to represent the last word in church government. The critical charge laid to the second generation was not only to abide by the *Platform*, or to avoid "decline" from it, or merely to pass it along. The founders made abundantly clear that they expected further refinements in church government, to "add to such beginnings of reformation and purity as we in our times have endeavored after."[63] For over fifteen years the elders had encouraged modest revisions of the New England Way, and most ministers recognized that the system would continue to evolve in response to changing New World realities. In codifying church order, the elders knew that they had only acted upon the light as they currently saw it. While in the future they could not expect to find new revelations in the Bible pertaining to church order, later generations might nonetheless see old biblical truths in a new light and consequently seek to modify the rules. Thus, while Dedham's John Allin aimed his elaborate description of the founding of Dedham "at future generations," he quickly added that he wrote "not to bind them" to his practices, but only to offer a point of departure. Similarly, Wenham's John Fiske noted that the signal purpose of Congregational independence was to allow each church to make decisions according to "its own light." His church had ratified the *Platform* with the understanding that the future might bring change.[64]

By the 1650s, then, the elders had established conflicting expectations among lay people concerning the future of Congregationalism: ministers demanded that their congregations further the Reformation by refining church government while simultaneously instructing them to avoid sinful "decline" by resisting innovations in the New England Way. Churchgoers accepted the *Platform* and the New England Way as sacred and everlasting, while they refused to be bound by canon or tradition. Varying perceptions of the meaning of the *Platform* and the inviolability of Congregational provisions represented a ticking time bomb, and would eventually come to divide ministers from a substantial proportion of the laity. The explosion occurred within a dozen years, when ministers pointed to a new "urgency" that required modifications of baptismal requirements that clearly conflicted with the teachings of the *Cambridge Platform* and thirty years of Congregational practice. The hostilities that followed would shatter the harmony within the churches and alter forever the course of lay-clerical relations in Massachusetts Bay.

5

Congregationalism in Crisis

The Halfway Covenant

SPEAKING IN BOSTON IN 1667, New Haven pastor John Davenport addressed a simmering controversy in Massachusetts churches that, he warned, threatened to develop into a crisis of colonywide proportions. Failure to maintain unanimity in purpose and practice, he averred, stood to jeopardize the entire Congregational system the Puritans had so painstakingly created:

> [I]f you fall into divisions amongst yourselves by different principles, some striving for one way, some for another, I feare and forwarne, that the Isshue will be a rent amongst you, unto God's great dishonor, to the Corrupting of the Church from the symplicitie that is in Jesus Christ.[1]

Davenport's "forwarnings" proved prophetic. The three decades of relative harmony among churchgoers in Massachusetts Bay ended abruptly in the 1660s, as ripples of disagreement over Congregational practices rose to a tidal wave of conflict within individual churches.

The "different principles" so threatening to Davenport concerned neither lay rights nor excessive clerical pretensions to authority in church affairs. In general, churches continued to govern themselves according to the provisions of the *Cambridge Platform* during the latter half of the seventeenth century. Instead, the crisis was triggered by baptism. Disagreement over the membership status of baptized but unregenerate "halfway" members and their children, a concern that first surfaced in the 1640s, would in the following decades extend and intensify throughout all of Massachusetts until a controversy arose whose intensity and longevity remained unrivaled until the Great Awakening.

Previous historians have amply discussed the debates surrounding the "Halfway Covenant," an innovation that permitted limited membership privileges to the children of baptized but unregenerate adults. But they have reached few agreements over the larger meaning and lasting influence of the shift in membership requirements. Writers such as Perry Miller and Darrett B. Rutman have seen in the easing of admissions standards proof positive of a decline in the spirituality of ordinary

88

churchgoers. Robert Pope and Stephen Foster have disputed such connections between the Halfway Covenant and "declension," and have described it instead as a necessary adjustment in admissions standards to shifting demographic patterns in New England. Many attribute surprisingly little significance to the controversy: David Hall described the Antinomian affair as the "main event" in the history of early Massachusetts and, in the most important study among recent overviews of Puritanism, Harry S. Stout devoted a scant three pages to the Halfway Covenant.[2]

Little attention in this literature has been devoted to the influence of the baptismal controversy upon lay-clerical relations and the evolution of Congregationalism. In this context, the Halfway Covenant generated a crisis in Massachusetts that surpassed all others in the seventeenth century in its breadth and lasting consequences. For the first time in the Bay's brief history, the Massachusetts clergy was significantly and publicly divided over vital issues of church order. This loss of unanimity permanently eroded clerical authority in church affairs, forcing a more active role in government upon ordinary churchgoers. The controversy also undermined the intellectual foundations of Congregationalism. Facing two openly conflicting interpretations of biblical warrant, many lay people could no longer understand Congregationalism as merely a set of procedures and principles that flowed inevitably from Scripture. The struggle over the Halfway Covenant, in sum, set into motion currents that would continue to reshape Congregationalism and lay-clerical relations for the rest of the colonial era.

As we have seen, the theory and practice of baptism had occasioned some debate among the founders from the first years of settlement. Virtually all of the elders agreed on the requirement to administer the seals to children of regenerate church members.[3] But ministers soon began to wrestle with an unforeseen corollary to the question of baptism: what was the status of a child whose parents had been baptized in infancy but had never experienced conversion upon attaining adulthood? Did these children of baptized but unregenerate parents retain a right to baptism? As early as 1634, John Cotton affirmed that "the Grand-Father a member of the Church, may claim the privilege of Baptisme to his Grand-Child, though his next Seede the Parents of the Child be not received themselves into Church Covenant." But that same year other ministers refuted such "halfway" membership, as it later came to be known, and within a few years Cotton reversed his position, arguing that only regenerate parents could baptize their children.[4]

Yet the elders remained uncertain. Though, in practice, churches baptized only those infants whose parents were converted, most first-generation ministers eventually came to agree with Richard Mather, a principal architect of the Halfway Covenant, who concluded that the children of baptized but unregenerate parents should receive the seals. Before declining church admissions had even emerged as a recognizable problem, nearly all of the founding ministers assembled at the Cambridge Synods of 1646–1648 agreed that baptism should be extended to these "children of the church," a fact that many seventeenth-century contemporaries and later historians glossed over in suggesting that in modifying baptismal practices second-generation ministers ran roughshod over the "fathers'" principles in order to address difficulties with the "rising generation."[5]

The elders' primary objective in seeking the extension of baptism was the preservation of the church covenant as a principal "means" of attaining grace and as the foundation of social order. By excluding the children of baptized, unregenerate members from their covenants, churches created a category of churchgoers who never entered into formal commitments with their "brethren" or "sisters," and thus did not enjoy the benefits of "mutual watchfulness" so essential to a Christian upbringing and social cohesion. They might never offer or enjoy the soul-saving "gracious admonitions" the community offered to scofflaws like Richard Wayte or George Norton to seek God and to obey his laws.[6] The Lord "hath given Officers and Churches a solemn charge to take care of and train" these children, Cambridge pastor Jonathan Mitchell warned, and failure in this duty to the children not only endangered souls but represented a sinful breach of the churches' covenant with God.[7]

Though the elders skirted the issue at the Cambridge Synod, the problem became more acute with each passing year. Familiar with the lines of debate among the clergy, increasing numbers of lay people began to push their ministers to offer the seals to the "children."[8] As early as 1655, Edward Brecke of Dorchester "called upon the church" to demand "why after so much waiting they did not put in practice their argument about Baptizinge church members children which not in ffull Communion." Five years later, several members pressed the issue again. Dorchester's ruling elder Henry Withington

> stood up before the Assembly was dismised and said that some breatheren had been with them that weeke and told them that they aprehended mr Mathers Arguments for baptizing of such children formerly spoken off was not [yet] answered and therefore desired that it might be now spoken to at this time.

Likewise, in Salem, the local cooper Samuel Williams, the innkeeper John Gidney and his son Bartholmew, and one John Massy "did stand forth" before the congregation to "modestly claim the right of their children upto baptisme and desired they might be baptized" in accordance with the new provisions. As was the case in most churches, some Dorchester and Salem members "weer unsatisfied" with the proposed revision. Given the ideal of unanimous consent, Salem pastor Higginson noted, ministers found themselves in a "streight."[9]

Eventually, disputes in Connecticut forced the hands of the Massachusetts elders. In an effort to stem a bitter division over baptism in the Hartford church, the Connecticut General Court in 1656 appealed to its neighbor colony for assistance, forwarding several questions concerning membership requirements to the Massachusetts clergy.[10] The ministers of the Bay responded within months, assembling seventeen clergymen in Boston to debate the issues. Their conclusion, *A Disputation concerning Church-Members and their Children in Answer to XXI Questions*, published in London in 1659 and commended to the churches by the General Court, contained a full endorsement of what later came to be known as the Halfway Covenant. Its provisions allowed unregenerate children of regenerate parents to baptize their offspring, providing that they led an upright life and agreed to own the church covenant before the assembled congregation. As adults, all halfway members assumed the benefits and responsibilities of mutual watchfulness incumbent upon those engaged in church covenant, but did not enjoy the privileges of voting or participation in the Lord's Supper until they experienced conversion and became full members. Hailed as a perfect compromise, the measure thus brought the children into the covenant and under the disciplinary "watch" of the church without corrupting church purity.[11]

In previous analyses of the Halfway Covenant, historians have raised a number of questions about the ministers' larger motives in relaxing admissions requirements. Some writers have suggested that, regardless of ministerial claims to the contrary, increasingly authoritarian clergymen "really" sought to bring a new and increasingly sinful generation under the coercive arm of the church in order to hold them accountable for their transgressions.[12] In fact, though ministers admitted that the extension of discipline would represent one principal consequence of the extension of baptism, they did not attempt to bring more lay people into the church primarily for the joy of casting them out. Several sets of disciplinary records that appear to be unusually complete indicate that while churches continued to maintain disciplinary "watchfulness" in the latter part of the seventeenth century, the rates of discipline remained constant. The First Churches of Boston, Dorchester, and Salem all extended disciplinary watch over the "children" before adopting the Halfway Covenant, yet none of these churches experienced a significant increase in the number of disciplinary cases.[13]

In press and pulpit, Massachusetts ministers articulated their support for the innovation and endeavored to prove its scriptural basis to ordinary churchgoers, many of whom were skeptical. In Salem, John Higginson assembled the congregation and professed the need to baptize the "children of the covenant," and admitted "if he had not grounds to believe that it was the Churches judgment that they were reall members, he had not ventured upon taking office in this Church." The pastor then reviewed for his congregation the principles

1. that the children of members born in the church or received in are true and reall members by divine institution
2. that their membership doth not ceas but by some other divine institution viz. excommunication.

The Dorchester elders similarly offered several "Arguments for the baptizing of such Children whos parents are not yet admitted to full communion at the lords table but yet are Judged members" and justified their assertions with a battery of scriptural references.[14]

Ministers further cajoled their flocks by warning of the dire consequences of inaction. Should New England preclude the rising generation from the church covenant, Jonathan Mitchell warned, "we should shorten and straiten the grace of God's covenant more than God himself doth, and be injurious to the Souls of men, putting them from under those Dispensations of Grace." Not only would the disintegration of mutual watchfulness and the church covenant threaten the welfare of the individual soul, but it might unravel the very fabric of society and bring the wrath of God down upon the nation. "Should the church education of your children by the want of your hearty concurrence [be] rendered either enfeizable or ineffectual," Mitchell pleaded, "we beseech you to consider how uncomfortable the account would be another day." Ministers did not routinely employ this kind of rhetoric in discussing church order and the Congregational Way; their consternation was rooted in a conviction that the Halfway Covenant was the most pressing issue of church government since the founding itself.[15]

Given the urgency ministers attributed to the measure, the Halfway Covenant represented a signal test for the lay right of dissent. In church after church, ministers refused to compromise this right, acknowledging that they were powerless to implement this vital innovation in the presence of significant lay opposition. Salem pastor Higginson professed that it was "clear to him to be his duty" to extend baptism but only "if he might doe it with the consent of the church in a peaceable way." In most churches, that consent was not forthcoming. Out of deference to the elders, the Salem congregation agreed to the "principle" of the change, but it refused to allow the implementation of the innovation for another thirteen years. Dorchester's Richard Mather began to press his church for adoption of the new practice in 1650, and five years later the members also agreed to it in principle. Yet as of 1660, Mather had still failed to convince dissenters to allow him to baptize the "children." The same pattern emerged in Boston and elsewhere.[16] The Ipswich church voted to extend baptism in 1656, and John Fiske's Chelmsford church soon followed suit, baptizing some seventy-five children of unregenerate members a year later. But apparently, by 1657, only these two churches offered halfway membership, testifying to the existence, if not the specific strength, of the opposition that ministers faced throughout the colony.[17]

In response to this lay reticence, the elders attempted to add the weight of a large, formal synod to their efforts to persuade the laity to accept the extension of baptism. The Massachusetts General Court convened the synod in 1662, which included lay messengers as well as clergymen. The elders sought to determine who "the subjects of baptism" should be, and they again brought up the troubling question "whither, according to the Word of God, there ought to be a consociation of churches." An overwhelming majority of the eighty lay and clerical messengers voted to endorse the Halfway Covenant, and reaffirmed as well the lawfulness of synods,

so long as they remained advisory.[18] The document to emerge from their deliberations was surprisingly dense. Though devoted only to the questions of baptism and
synods, the elders' published *Result of the Synod of 1662*, along with its *Preface*, is
longer than the entire *Cambridge Platform*.[19] The forty pages of closely reasoned
argument, replete with its dozens of scriptural justifications, again testify to the urgency with which the ministry regarded the Halfway Covenant.[20]

Clergymen read the results of the Synod of 1662 within every church and continued to lobby vigorously for the approval of its provisions.[21] They fully understood
that ministers themselves would come under attack for attempting to implement a
change in long-standing practices—they had, in effect, put themselves on the chop-
ping block. Were it for the elders' "own sakes, or Names, or Interest, we should not
be sollicitous to beg charity of you," Mitchell wrote to his lay readers in his preface
to the synod's results. "Do we herein seek our selves? Our own advantage, ease, or
glory? Surely the contrary!" Mitchell urged compliance as right and necessary "though
we be rejected."[22]

And rejected they were: many churchgoers, alarmed at the threat to church purity and the specter of sinful "humane inventions," saw a responsibility to exercise
their watchman duty and to dissent from the change. In the minds of many lay people,
no amount of ministerial persuasion could change the simple fact that the results of
this synod represented a clear departure from the sacred system of government the
churches had practiced over the previous three decades. It was, they feared, precisely
the sort of "cerimonie" that Cotton, along with the rest of the founding ministers,
had warned would "drive Christ owt of the Cuntry."[23]

Though rooted partly in a simple resistance to change, the laity's objections to
the Halfway Covenant ran far deeper than that. In learning the details of Congregationalism, churchgoers mastered not only a set of practices but the theological
underpinnings of the system as well. In justifying baptismal practices, Cotton and
the other founders had explained to their flocks that the covenant of grace included
both external and internal components by which church members communed with
other church members and with God. As such, the covenant of grace and the church
covenant were inextricably intertwined. As Cotton explained, "That which doth make
a people a joined people with God, that doth [also] make a church. [And] what is
that? The covenant of grace doth make a people, a joined people with God, and therefore a church of God." To allow those not engaged in the covenant of grace to enter
the church covenant served to drastically separate the two.[24]

Ordinary churchgoers understood and embraced these arguments. Chelmsford's
brother Thomas Adams mirrored Cotton's teachings precisely when responding to
his minister's scriptural justification of the Halfway Covenant, offering a seven-
point defense of his own opposition that pastor Fiske read to the church. In particular, the layman asked his congregation to consider "Whether the covenant of
grace doth not admit of a distinction in respect of the internal and external part of
it," and

> Whether this covenant of grace, in respect of the external part of it, was not given by God himself fore this very end: to engage a congregation in communion each with other, as well as, by the external part of it to engage them in communion with God himself?

Adams warned that it was hardly the "duty" of the Chelmsford church to "reform" the church by allowing the unregenerate to join in church covenant.[25]

Any chance of convincing churchgoers like Adams to accept a change of this magnitude would have required something close to unanimity among the clergy. But a small, important minority of clergymen was all too ready to confirm lay fears of sacrilegious innovation. The laity had never before encountered a significantly divided clergy, and it is impossible to overestimate the importance of this ministerial opposition. In addition to Davenport, a founder and respected Congregational spokesman, opponents included such noteworthies as John Warham of Windsor, John Mayo of the prestigious Second Church of Boston, John Russell of Hadley, a "second generation" minister, Charles Chauncy, president of Harvard College, Eleazer Mather, and Increase Mather, already one of the most influential figures in New England.[26]

As Pope has argued, this clerical minority played a crucial role in stoking the fires of lay resistance to the Halfway Covenant,[27] which guaranteed the failure of attempts to achieve a lay consensus. Central to the laity's objections to the innovation, Mitchell complained bitterly, was their recognition that "some of the Ministers are against it."[28] Though in sheer numbers ministerial opponents could hardly match supporters of the innovation (supporters outnumbered opponents by a seven to one ratio at the Synod of 1662),[29] they certainly did in their publications, through which they sought openly to foment lay rebellion.[30]

No less than clerical proponents of the Halfway Covenant, dissenting ministers fully understood that the laity would determine the outcome of this explosive controversy: the innovation would be implemented only in churches that achieved lay consent. Consequently, in contrast to previous discussions of church order, which ministers directed largely at English audiences or their clerical brethren, opponents directed their tracts on the Halfway Covenant squarely at ordinary churchgoers.[31] The central purpose of Chauncy's most notorious polemic, *Antisynodalia Scripta Americana*, Mitchell fumed, was not to seek biblical truths but merely "to amuse and trouble the people." Indeed, the dissenting ministers went so far as to revise and simplify the original Chauncy manuscript, which they had earlier presented to the General Court, so that it would be understandable "to many meaner [i.e., less-sophisticated] Persons" among the laity.[32]

The dissenting ministers continued to hammer upon the bald fact—obvious to any churchgoer—that the Halfway Covenant violated an understanding of baptism that, Chauncy noted in *Antisynodalia*, "hath been both the Judgment and general practice of the churches of the *Bay Patent* . . . for the space of thirty years." The innovation was just the sort of hated "humane invention" that dissenting lay people feared that it was, opposing ministers repeated, and they desired "nothing but to retain and maintain those dispensations, which we have so dearly bought, and so long enjoyed without interruption, before the pleaded for conversion of New England."[33]

As Williston Walker long ago observed, this pamphlet war was "unexampled in the history of the new world," and it would remain unparalleled in Massachusetts church history until the Great Awakening. Not surprisingly, given the stakes in the debate, passions intensified on both sides until the rhetoric grew nearly hysterical. In what must have been as amazing to the laity as it was frightening, clerical opponents at length condemned fellow ministers who approved the Halfway Covenant as nothing less than "sinners" and "the abominations of Antichrist." Not only would the Lord demand the repeal of the Halfway Covenant, but he would also demand repentance from its authors for suggesting the sin in the first place: "The leaving off, or forsaking of sin, is not sufficient to true Repentance; there must be a confessing of sin, and publick and particular confession of publick and scandalous sins, (as this [Halfway Covenant] is conceived to be)." No less strident, proponents of the measure, such as Salem's John Higginson, declared publicly that failure to implement the Halfway Covenant represented "one of the great sinnes of the country."[34]

In recounting the immediate events of the 1660s, historians have described this ministerial division, but they have devoted little attention to its consequences upon lay-clerical relations and the evolving development of church government.[35] Previously, ministers had exercised extreme caution in avoiding public criticism of one another. Numerous examples from the first years of settlement demonstrated that divisions among church authorities frequently divided the laity. The swift and severe punishment of John Wheelwright underscored the hazards that civil and church officials saw in mutual condemnation among the clergy, a danger that would become apparent again in the bitter lay divisions that accompanied clerical rifts during the Great Awakening.[36]

Facing a ministry that agreed upon little beyond the conviction that the fate of the country lay in the balance, churchgoers had no choice but to reach their own conclusions on this issue, a development that would have lasting repercussions upon the development of Congregationalism. In previous decades, as noted earlier, lay people relied on ministers to determine Congregational provisions and contributed little of their own to the process. The clerical dispute over the Halfway Covenant altered this one-sided transmission of church government. The division among the elders over baptism meant that ministers could not simply present their unanimous assessment of God's truth to the laity for ratification, as they had in winning lay approval for the *Cambridge Platform*. Rather, for the first time churchgoers would have to choose between two openly conflicting ministerial interpretations. The Halfway Covenant would be practiced in churches where the laity decided to accept the ministers' pronouncements or at least to forbear their dissent. The innovation would not be implemented if enough members resisted. Either way, the debate forced the laity more than ever before to assume a direct and formative role in the development of Congregational practices.

Just what the laity decided regarding the Halfway Covenant has been the subject of numerous interpretations and conflicting claims among both contemporaries and later historians. Governed by their unquestioned assumption that lay people and their ministers naturally fell into contending camps in colonial Massachusetts, many previous writers have asserted that, in general, the ministry supported the measure, while the laity opposed it. Miller, for instance, argued that the lay reaction to the Halfway Covenant amounted to "an uprising of the crowd" against "the majesty" of the ministers' "scholastical learning."[37]

In attempting to gauge lay resistance, however, most historians have taken for granted that a church's failure to implement the Halfway Covenant meant that a unified "laity" in that church opposed the measure, a crucial—and unproven—assumption.[38] By and large, churches still hoped for unanimous agreement in determining procedural matters during the 1650s and 1660s, and for the rest of the century they rarely imposed decisions upon significant minorities.[39] As such, a few dissenters, especially members of rank and substance, could generally create sufficient doubt to prevent an affirmative vote on significant procedural innovations, even if a majority favored change. A case in point occurred in Dorchester, when "severall yong men in the Towne" expressed their willingness "to Joyne to the Church if they might have their Confession taken in privat by wrighting and declared publickly to the church." Though "divers did declare themselves willing that it should be soe practiced," the church, in standard fashion, deferred the matter because "on[e] or two of the breatheren declared themselves to the Contrary."[40] Similarly, during several later Dorchester meetings devoted to the Halfway Covenant, "divers of the Church shewed their Consent" to the innovation but "some weer unsatisfied and therefore it was deferred." Finally, in 1665, "the major part of the Church" voted to baptize the children of Robert Spurs. Though "some breatheren weer unsatisfied," the ruling elder noted, they at last decided that they would not exercise their option to formally dissent: they "would not oppos the thing if Mr. Mather did baptiz them."[41]

Obviously, support for the Halfway Covenant in Massachusetts differed from church to church and varied over time. We will never know precisely how many members favored the measure at any given point. But evidence drawn from a number of churches besides Dorchester also suggests that the dispute over the innovation at no point pitted a largely united laity against "the clergy," as historians have often asserted. Not only was the clergy itself divided but, even at the height of the dispute in the 1660s and 1670s, many lay people, possibly even a majority, supported ministerial attempts to adopt the measure, a conclusion that should hardly be surprising, given our understanding of the nature of deference. Several churches, including Chelmsford, Ipswich, and Wakefield, adopted the measure quickly and with little fanfare. A strong majority of the First Church of Charlestown voted to approve the *Result of the Synod of 1662*; a quarter of the church opposed the *Result*, but decided not to dissent formally. Thomas Shepard, Jr., noted that many churches neglected to practice the innovation even though large majorities favored it. All too often, he complained, "two or three" worthy laymen "continue[d] to disturb the peace of an entire congregation" by opposing the Halfway Covenant. That was precisely the case in Salem, where pastor John Higginson refused to bring the matter before the church until the members were at least close to unanimous. In 1665, he finally "desir[ed] it might be voted being but 2 appearing to offer dissent." As Higginson predicted, the church voted overwhelmingly for adoption, and the dissenters deferred to the mind of the church.[42] At the Second Church in Boston, several members so strongly supported the Halfway Covenant that they refused to contribute to the maintenance of their ministers, Increase Mather and John Mayo, in light of their opposition to the measure. Finally, the civil elections of 1671 hinged largely on the question of the Halfway Covenant; as we shall see, the vast majority of towns elected deputies who favored the measure.[43]

The laity's resistance to the Halfway Covenant, in short, did not pit the members, as a united group, against their ministers. Nor did it pit the educated class of laymen against the clergy, or the remaining conservative "fathers" against the rising generation.[44] While numerous "worthy laymen" opposed the Halfway Covenant and played a significant role in postponing its adoption, this group nevertheless seems to have been just as divided as the crowd. In Dorchester, the deacons opposed extension of baptism as an old world "corruption." Both ruling elders, on the other hand, urged the church to accept its responsibilities toward the children. Similarly, while lay messengers comprised a majority of the eighty delegates to the Synod of 1662, only six voted in opposition to the Halfway Covenant. "Diverse of the [lay] Messengers," one ministerial opponent complained, "being no Logitians, and so unable to answer Syllogismes, and discern Ambiguities," were responsible for the synod's adoption of the innovation.[45]

The battle over the Halfway Covenant, then, is best understood as ideological in nature, one that tapped into numerous internal contradictions within the New England Way that the "fathers" had never sufficiently resolved. The controversy divided the laity into two contending groups who, as God's watchmen, were determined to fulfill the duties they had been taught, but discovered that in agreeing to honor one obligation, they violated another. On the one hand, ministers charged churchgoers with the duty to resist "innovations" in church government. But at the same time, clergymen taught their flocks to further the reformation of the churches. They urged their congregations to agree not to disagree in order to achieve unanimous consent. Yet they also preached that failure to dissent to the "corrupting [of] the simplicitie of Jesus Christ" in church affairs was a sin. Though churchgoers were instructed to resist ministers' "unscriptural innovations," those who did so suffered accusations of sinful "Corahism," or rebellion against the clergy. Were churchgoers to accept the conclusions of nearly all of the clergymen assembled at the Synod of 1662? Or, when faced with what was clearly an innovation, were they to obey their ministers' previous admonitions—admonitions repeated by a clerical minority—concerning the grave dangers of "humane inventions?" Just how much these conflicting duties tore at the laity became apparent during the infamous dispute in the First Church of Boston.

The controversy over the Halfway Covenant reached its peak of intensity in Massachusetts during the early 1670s, when the lower house of the General Court articulated a number of widely shared fears about the dreadful consequences of this "sinful" innovation. This "accursed thing," the deputies wrote, represented an "invasion of the rights, liberties, and privileges of churches," and threatened "a subversion of gospel order," the "utter devestation of these churches," and the "inevitable and total extirpation of the principles and pillars of the congregational way." In defending these terrifying claims, the deputies needed merely to point to events in the First Church of Boston, the "beacon" of Congregationalism, which had become so fiercely divided over the Halfway Covenant that the church experienced a fiery separation, the first of its kind in Massachusetts. The Boston separation became the focal point for lay resistance to the Halfway Covenant and eventually divided the entire colony.[46]

The virulent altercation within the First Church of Boston was not fully representative of the members' reaction to the Halfway Covenant in other churches in Massachusetts. The First Church was among the most conservative in the colony, refusing to practice the Halfway Covenant until the third decade of the eighteenth century. No other Massachusetts church suffered an outright separation between dissenters and proponents of the measure.[47] But for two related reasons, the First Church represents an ideal laboratory for studying the responses and perspectives of ordinary churchgoers to the innovation. For one, the laity was forced to address this critical issue on its own, in the absence of a minister. Secondly, the laity kept remarkably detailed accounts of their debates that illuminate their understanding of both the immediate questions surrounding the controversy and their conception of the larger significance of the Halfway Covenant.

As was the case in most churches, the extension of baptism had been a source of division in Boston in the 1650s and early 1660s. Pastor John Wilson and teacher John Norton navigated skillfully through rocky waters in addressing the topic, proceeding slowly enough to avoid a major collision with their lay opponents while gradually convincing the church to accept at least the principle of the Halfway Covenant.[48] But the church refused to go any farther, and the issue remained highly volatile, straining the delicate balance of church order to the breaking point.

Boston's elders, who fully believed in the Scripture grounds and critical necessity of the new admissions standards, could not see the members' resistance to the conclusions of the Halfway Synod for what it was: an attempt to abide by the ministers' own previous warnings to resist abuses of clerical "Awthoritie" and to oppose "Ceremonies and humane Inventions." These opponents were determined to honor the watchman obligations clergymen had taught them, in short, though in this particular case the results were hardly what the ministers hoped for.[49] For Wilson and other clergymen, lay dissent to the Halfway Covenant was simply a manifestation of a decline in respect for ministers within individual churches and for the clergy as a whole. Asked on his deathbed to list the sins that had provoked God's displeasure upon the country, Wilson singled out rebellion against the ministers, which manifested itself specifically in the laity's willful disobedience to the elders' pronouncements in the Synod of 1662 and its shameful neglect of the rising generation:

> That is, when people rise up as *Corah* against their *ministers*, as if they took too much upon them, when indeed they do but rule for Christ, and according to Christ; yet it is nothing for a brother to stand up and oppose, without scripture or reason, the word of an elder saying [I am not *satisfied!*] and hence if he do not like the administration (be it *baptism* or the like) he will turn his back upon God and his ordinances, and go away. And for our neglect of *baptising* the children of the *church*, those that some call *grand-children*, I think God is provoked by it. Another sin I take to be the making light of, and not subjecting to the authority of *Synods*, without which the churches cannot long subsist.[50]

It is especially ironic that later historians have cited Wilson's dying words as evidence of a "declension" in lay spirituality when, in fact, those words were inspired by the fierce resistance of a group of churchgoers who believed they were engaged in a desperate struggle to preserve Congregationalism and Massachusetts's status as "beloved in the Lord" from sinful innovation.[51]

For years, the Boston members' reverence for their ministers, along with the elders' continued respect for lay rights, prevented a major flare-up over the issue of baptism. But the significance of the clergy's steady hand in managing church affairs, and of the elders' influence in general, became obvious when, four years after the loss of John Norton, pastor Wilson died in 1667. For the first time in thirty-seven years, the church found itself bereft of a minister, and without clerical guidance, the conflicting duties and responsibilities facing the laity became overwhelming.

The Bostonians correctly saw theirs as the most influential church in New England. Left on their own to determine the church's stance toward the Halfway Covenant and, in their eyes, the future of Congregationalism, a majority of Boston's members decided to establish a bastion of resistance to the innovation in a last-ditch effort to shore up New England Congregationalism's "primitive" foundations. Ironically, the specific measures they employed in attempting to preserve the old order forced the churches of the Bay to reassess and, in some cases, to revise their stances toward Congregational autonomy, unanimous consent, church councils, and the rights of dissenters. The First Church effort to preserve existing practices and principles, in short, ended up changing the system forever.

The explosion in Boston was ignited by the decision over Wilson's replacement. Several months after their pastor's death, a large majority of the First Church, led by ruling elder James Penn, voted to issue a ministerial call to seventy-year-old John Davenport of New Haven, known to the Bostonians as a strong defender of lay liberties since the Anne Hutchinson church trials of 1637–1638.[52] A vote for Davenport represented a vote against the Halfway Covenant: the New Haven pastor had strongly resisted the innovation since the opening debates at the Cambridge Synod in 1646. By issuing a call to Davenport and taking steps to block the Halfway Covenant, the Bostonians hoped to initiate a counterattack to arrest a development which, they feared, threatened the entire Puritan mission.

A significant minority of over forty male church members, and nearly an equal number of wives, strongly supported the Halfway Covenant and accordingly opposed Davenport's call.[53] Here, as in other churches, the dispute obviously did not represent a division between the laity and the local minister: no clergyman was even present during the debates over Davenport. Rather, the membership itself was divided. Nor can social or economic issues explain differences between the two sides. Although, as a group, a disproportionately high economic standing and degree of involvement in town and colony politics characterized the dissenters, both sides included men of rank and substance, along with ordinary farmers. And contrary to the claims of previous writers, who have asserted that the first generation opposed the innovation and the second generation favored it, over half of these proponents of baptism extension were first-generation founders who, as full church members, stood to gain little personally through implementation of the change.[54]

The grounds of division in the Boston church, as in the colony generally, were far more ideological than sociological or economic. Davenport's opponents accepted the conclusions of the assembled clergy: the Halfway Covenant was a biblical requirement, not a sinful invention. Citing the teachings of their "faithful and able Ministers," the Boston minority explained that they considered the Halfway Covenant a "divine truth" that had been demonstrated "unto their consciences from the word of God" by a "publique and solemn declaration" in the Synod of 1662. They believed themselves under "an awfull ingagement to maintaine the travelling truth relating to duty unto the children of the church and Heb: 13: 8: to remember those [ministers] who have spoken the word of the Lord unto us." To elect a man of Davenport's persuasion would amount to "plucking downe what [the ministers] have built."[55] Given their faith in the scriptural justifications of the Halfway Covenant, the minority explained, covenant obligations left them no choice but to honor their duty as watchmen and dissent from Davenport's call, which "tend[ed] to the hindrance" of God's truth. Accordingly, they asked rhetorically,

> whither such a part of the Brethren be not bound in duty unto the improvement of the intherest of liberty which Christ hath betrusted them with all, for the regular and orderly managing of the affairs of his Church or whither they may divest themselves of that liberty, by a voluntary and designed secession or silenc or whither they may suffer themselves to be divested of

that liberty by their Brethren by a seclusion from Communion with them in Church acts, or whither to desert the intherest of liberty be not unfaithfulness and breach of Covenant.

Their duty required them to accept the synod's pronouncements, to advance Christ's church order, and to object to Davenport's call. Failure in these obligations risked nothing less than the "safety of their owne soules."[56]

Though the minority (now labeled "the dissenting brethren") followed standard practices in voicing their objections to Davenport's election, the majority "violently" rebuffed them, pointing out that in accordance with long-standing practices, dissenters were to express their opinions and objections and then to submit to the mind of the church. This much was true. But the dissenters argued, also correctly, that according to convention a minority of this size should halt virtually any significant church action, at least until the church fully examined and debated their views.[57]

The stalemate revealed, once again, the vague and sometimes contradictory nature of Congregationalism, a system whose success had relied more on spirit than upon a carefully crafted set of rules and regulations. Cooperation, mutuality, and a willingness to forgo immediate goals in the larger cause of harmony had served as the glue that held the system together. No hard rules ever specified what size minority should halt a church action or when the duty to dissent stopped and the duty to submit to "the mind of the church" began. The "tenderness" of majorities toward dissenters' views had in the past rendered such specifics unnecessary.[58] The disintegration of tenderness in Boston shocked and grieved the First Church minority, who appealed to this very distinction between love and formal rules in protesting that in "a civill Assembly the like would not have bin done, much lesse ought our brethren soe to have acted." Throughout their narrative of this trauma, the dissenters pointedly lamented how they were "sharply reproved," by the majority, "snatched up with much violence," "taken up sharply," stretched "upon the rack," and "set on the tainter-hookes," creating a portrait of congregational relationships that contrasts strikingly with accounts of church proceedings from previous decades, in which even scandalous offenders were treated with concern and compassion. Throughout the colony, protracted bitterness between supporters and opponents would stand as one of the most important legacies of the Halfway Covenant.[59]

The Boston dissenters also pointed out that even if minorities enjoyed no formal recourse within their church, divided congregations generally resorted to assistance from neighboring elders in this kind of case. Accordingly, they offered the majority a "humble request" to "shew the spirit of Jesus in patient bearing with us" and declared themselves "ready and willing to oblige ourselves to acquiesce in the advice of a Councill of Elders and Messengers." Ruling elder Penn, a strong opponent of the Halfway Covenant, at first attempted to abide by standard Congregational practices and govern the church with a degree of equanimity. He "did affectionately with tears in his eyes desire the motion of the dissenters might be hearkened unto." But the majority remained unmoved. They harshly "overruled" Penn and in July of 1667 issued Davenport an invitation to replace Wilson.[60]

The New Haven teacher could scarcely conceal his excitement at the possibility of closing out his career in Boston. Davenport accounted "the minnistration of the Gospel" in Boston as the highest honor in the land, "both in respect of those eminent lights, which have formerly shined in that Golden Candelstick, and in reference to the Generall Influence from thence through out the Country." Sharing the Boston majority's goals, Davenport hoped to establish a bastion of orthodoxy that might stem the tide of innovation before it washed away the very foundations of Congregationalism. But, fashioning himself an orthodox follower of the New England Way, he explained firmly that he expected a unanimous call. Once apprised of "the strong opposition of above 40 Brethren," he decided to defer matters until the spring, in hopes that by then there would be "noe scisme amongst you for my sake, but that you be perfectly joyned together."[61]

The Boston majority were incensed. Cursing the minority for Davenport's decision, enraged laymen cited chapter and verse from the Bible, demanding summary excommunication from "Joshu: 7:10. to 5 . . . the accursed they must be removed." Others insisted, in words that would later haunt them, "the Church shall not be a prisson to any," and insisted the dissenters apply for dismission.[62] Leading the charge against the dissenters throughout the conflict was the educated layman and wealthy merchant Anthony Stoddard, a passionate opponent of all "innovation" whose son, Solomon, would be the first minister in the Bay to practice open communion.[63]

The dissenters avoided formal censure, again appealing to elder Penn to call a council of the elders so that both sides might be heard in "a free debate in the face of the Country." This time, for reasons that remain unclear given its previous opposition, the majority complied with Penn's request. The council, comprising seven ministers and five laymen, acted quickly, deciding that in view of the irreconcilable differences dividing them, the Bostonians ought to free the dissenters to gather a new church. Twenty-nine members immediately applied to Penn for a dismission.[64]

Though virtually unnoticed by historians, the council's decision represented a landmark in the history of Congregationalism in Massachusetts.[65] For the first time in the colony's history, the elders legitimated a church division. They neither attempted to heal the breach nor denounced churchgoers on either side for their views on the Halfway Covenant: the elders vigorously defended the First Church dissenters, but they dared not condemn Davenport, the First Church majority, and, by extension, every supporter of the "old Way" in Massachusetts. In acknowledging the existence of two conflicting, yet legitimate points of view, the council in effect admitted that irreconcilable disagreements could arise within individual churches. The immediate question at hand was how to cope with these divisions. By calling for the orderly dismission of the Boston church dissenters, the elders attempted to establish the precedent of diffusing internecine struggles for the higher goal of harmony.

The council decision nonetheless brought the elders face-to-face with a fundamental contradiction in their stance toward the evolution of the Congregational Way. While acknowledging that the Reformation remained a work in progress and affirming that no platform or canon could bind individual churches, ministers had nonetheless taught that "God's truths" were "Eternal and Unchangeable." For any given question pertaining to church government, they believed, a right answer could be found in the Bible, and churchgoers were bound to accept that answer. By definition, every division over church procedures was temporary and resolvable—it was simply a matter of extracting the truth from the Bible and submitting to it. By defending the Halfway Covenant, a significant revision in church practice, and yet legitimating both sides in the division over its implementation, the elders were forced to admit, if only by implication, that there was no single, unalterable form of church order. This admission would, in time, undermine sola scriptura and the larger intellectual foundations of Congregationalism.[66]

The broader implications of the council's decisions were, for the moment, of little concern to the Boston majority, which simply ignored the elders' pronouncements. Their desperation to put an end to the Halfway Covenant had become a blinding obsession that justified virtually any behavior. In the next church meeting ruling elder Penn called upon the church to vote upon the dissenters' dismission. Penn, along with several laymen, then requested that the dissenters and their wives withdraw from the church while the vote was taken, a standard procedure. What followed, however, was anything but standard. After the dissenters departed, two church members summoned Davenport from his lodgings and sneaked him into the meetinghouse, where he received his coveted "unanimous" call to office. Then, in the following days, the church angrily denied the dissenters their dismission and, incredibly, the leaders of the majority forged a letter of release from the New Haven church that freed them to ordain their new pastor.[67]

Having secured Davenport's services, the church again attempted to initiate formal disciplinary proceedings against the opposition. The charges were ironic, for the majority had flouted either the letter or the spirit of countless Congregational provisions: demonstrating an impressive grasp of church order, the minority pointed out how letters had not been read to the church, elders had "forgotten" long-standing rules, votes had been improperly conducted, and church actions had been taken without lay consent. The dissenters were understandably shocked, then, when the majority insisted that if the minority "were suffered to goe on, it would open a doore to all licentiousness." Davenport, whose anger, single-mindedness, and ambition led him to countenance and participate in "sinful" and possibly even criminal maladministration in assuming the Boston pastorate, charged the minority with "willfullnes and obstinacy," insisting that "they had not one sillable of rule, but of will."[68]

The church was unable to substantiate any specific charge against the dissenters. But the majority did manage to hale the two deacons before the church on charges of "high contempt of the holy ordinance of god." Both had refused to partake in communion when informed that such participation would be taken to mean that they approved of Davenport's administration. The majority condemned one deacon, who somehow had an inkling of the church's wrongdoing, for professing that "he had some trouble and doubt in his mind about the regularity of Mr. Davenport's dismission." By this time the dispute had become the talk of the land. In a huge church trial that dwarfed Anne Hutchinson's far more celebrated excommunication, the Bostonians held a hearing before an audience of "neer five hundred persons," many of whom were "not of the church," and took the unusual step of dismissing the deacons from office.[69]

The dissenters, who failed in repeated attempts to convince the church to accept the council's advice and dismiss them, next attempted to call another meeting of the neighboring elders. The Boston majority exercised their option to vote down the request. Fully recognizing the gravity of the conflict and dimly aware of their frequent violations of Scripture rules, the Bostonians suffered from a siege mentality. The focus now shifted to questions of Congregational autonomy. Stiffly upholding the principle of Congregational independence, the majority not only observed that no synod or council could require a church to abide by its decisions but even averred that "to grant a Councill tends to the overthrow of the Congregational Way," a position that flatly contradicted the *Cambridge Platform.*[70]

The neighboring elders had seen enough. Congregationalism had reached an important crossroad, and only decisive action could help ensure the future success of the New England Way. John Allin of Dedham and John Eliot of Roxbury circulated a letter indicating that the Boston dissenters faced the supreme sentence of excommunication for no offense other than seeking orderly dismission in accordance with the decision of a ministerial council. Here was Congregational independence run amuck. The actions of the Boston majority forced the elders either to address formally the implications of Congregational autonomy or risk the "losse of the use and benifit of Councills" and the destruction of any semblance of interchurch supervision.[71]

More alarmingly, the elders noted, the First Church majority had staged a frontal assault upon one of Congregationalism's most cherished lay privileges: the fundamental right to dissent within a local church. Dissenting minorities, the lay majority in Boston insisted, enjoyed no rights or recourse in a Congregational church: "[T]here is no reliefe for a grieved Brother or Brethren in a church unless the Church will receive them untill the day of judgement." Ironically, it was the ministers who rushed to the defense of the members' right to speak out. How could lay people fulfill their watchmen duty if, like the Boston minority, they stood to suffer church censure for dissenting? "The consequences" of stifling dissent and refusing minorities the right to appeal for outside assistance, Allin and Eliot warned, were "like to be dangerous, not onely in the suffering of the dissenters," who were only performing their duty, but "also it will tend much to the dishonour of God and the scandall of the way of those churches as haveing noe meanes to heale breaches and other Evills in our churches." The laity had to be protected from itself, and it was "high time for the Elders to interpose."[72]

The assembled elders attempted several times in vain to secure the First Church's permission to meet in a second council. Finally, on a day when the entire Boston church "met togither to proceed against the dissenters," the elders sent seventy-four-year-old Richard Mather, by now partially blind and nearly deaf, and three lay messengers to hand-deliver a written appeal to the Bostonians. They arrived only to find "the doore was locked against them." "Upon knocking," they were coldly informed that the church refused to "take any notice" of their letter. But the sight of the elderly Mather and the other "Reverend Honored and aged Gentlemen" huddled outside in the chill of an April morning prompted some sympathy and deference: "Mr. Peter Oliver went to fetch chairs for them to sit downe at the doore."[73]

Eventually Boston's elders agreed to read the letter to the congregation. The impassioned wording of the ministers' plea underscored their conviction that this controversy represented a threat of unprecedented proportions to the Puritan experiment. "The spirit of Division," the elders warned, threatened "the common weal of our Israel . . . more and more strongly even unto the shaking of foundations." But the Boston congregation again "voted to take no notice." Following the earlier advice of Chauncy and Davenport, the Boston First Church decided "not to look to Consequents in doing our duty, but to the goodness of our cause."[74]

The council was forced to meet despite the absence of representatives from the Boston First Church, itself an unwelcome innovation, and offered another series of landmark decisions. It focused its attention on the result of the first council in the dispute. That council had been regularly called "with the consent of the Brethren, according to God." The Boston majority had repudiated the council's conclusions, even though "no reasons that we have ever heard of have bin returned from the church unto the councill for the rejection of that advice." Though, theoretically, churches retained a right to reject a council's decision, in the past churches had voluntarily submitted to the wisdom of the neighboring elders "with great reverence." By ignoring the recommendations of the first council, the Bostonians compelled the elders to confront this issue of voluntary compliance head-on. They decided that Boston's First Church must not be allowed to establish a destructive precedent: "If the Regular sentence of such a Councill may be rejected we are deprived of all meanes under God for healing of differences, errors, scandall or maladministration in churches to the great scandall of the doctrine we professe."[75]

Accordingly, because the Boston majority had called the council in the first place, and since they offered no grounds for rejecting the council's conclusions, the elders adjudged the decision of the first council to be binding upon the First Church of Boston. The council freed the dissenters to gather the new Third Church of Boston and, in another novel invention, granted them "immunity" from First Church censure. It then added nine "justifications" to these determinations, replete with dozens of scriptural references. Thirty-two ministers and laymen signed the finished document. One elder missing from the list was Richard Mather, who had fallen ill soon after being locked out of the Boston church. Three days later the man most responsible for the Halfway Covenant was dead. His grief-stricken son Increase, a bitter opponent of his father's innovation, would quickly reverse his position to become one of the most vigorous and outspoken supporters of the Halfway Covenant.[76]

In its efforts to preserve the New England Way, the First Church majority had forced the council to render several troublesome decisions, reaffirming certain Congregational principles while compromising others. By refusing to submit voluntarily to the advice of the council, the First Church left the elders no option but to affirm either the principle of Congregational autonomy or the right of churches to engage in mutual supervision. The elders confirmed the latter at the expense of the former by attributing binding status to the council's recommendations, creating a regulation to fulfill functions previously served by voluntarism. In theory, this remarkable decision stood to wrest local control from the laity and to place it in the hands of the assembled elders. But this step proved to be neither the intention nor a consequence of the council's determination. The ministers sought only to reaffirm interchurch watch and the rights of minorities to seek assistance from councils. Though the elders believed that Congregational autonomy could not be absolute, future councils would rarely follow the lead of this one by claiming binding authority or by attempting to force their decisions upon local congregations.

The council also reluctantly addressed the difficult balance between the ideal of unanimity and the rights of dissenters. In the face of doubtful church proceedings, were dissenters obliged to paralyze the church through protest or to settle for consensus and accept the majority's "sense of the meeting"? The council affirmed unequivocally the duty to speak out. Citing the founders and the *Cambridge Platform*, the ministers charged the second generation of churchgoers with maintaining the lay role as watchmen in the churches and cautioned against the sin of silence: "[T]he dissenting Brethren, if they should not make use of their Christian liberty . . . would neglect the duty incumbent upon them, (as the Renowned and Reverend Willson, Cotton, Norton) who have spoken to them the word of the Lord, in platforme of discipline touching this matter they must not onely doe nothing against it but they are to follow it."[77]

In the context of this particular controversy, the clergy celebrated lay watch, applauding the Boston dissenters for performing their sacred duty by speaking out in support of the ministers' stand. In effect, the ministers confirmed that churches must not abridge the right of lay dissent even if the goal of unanimity stood to be compromised. Their decision was of momentous importance, for unanimity in local churches would gradually disintegrate: partly as a consequence of this powerful reaffirmation of their rights, future minorities within individual churches would be far less hesitant to refute the decisions of majorities and to demand relief from councils. Moreover, new controversies would continue to arise in which churchgoers would exercise their right of dissent to defy the elders instead of supporting them, just as many had during the controversy over the Halfway Covenant. In that context, ministers would complain, condemn, and battle with their congregations. But throughout the colonial era, the ministry would never assert that the laity's duty was to keep quiet.[78]

The First Church controversy by no means remained confined to Boston: news of "[t]he divissions of our Rewben," the Boston dissenters lamented, soon traveled "through[out] the Country." Unlike previous disputes such as the Antinomian controversy, a vast, tangled web of interchurch communication and intrachurch debate accompanied the Boston First Church separation. The Boston dissenters sent long and detailed letters to "sundry other churches" relating their predicament, pleading with their neighbors "in the bowels of Jesus Christ" to ignore the many "sinister reports" that had circulated about them. The elders also sent their council conclusions to the magistrates, whereby the news spread as far as Springfield. One distant magistrate confessed to having "not that particular understanding of [Boston] affaires as some others," but felt safe in tendering approval of the councils' decisions "upon what I have heard."[79]

Lay people did not passively digest the news of the Boston controversy and the results of the councils. Churchgoers quickly recognized that the implications of the First Church dispute were not limited to Boston but concerned larger questions of Congregational theory and practice that would affect churches throughout the colony. And no less than the Halfway Covenant itself, the central issues to surface during the Boston First Church controversy—Congregational autonomy, the authority of councils, and the right to dissent—would be debated among, and to an unprecedented extent determined by, lay people.

Neighboring churchgoers considered these issues in the course of meetings devoted to the Boston church councils. Churches first encountered a dilemma in deciding whether or not to send delegates to these councils. The decision was far more perplexing than it initially seemed. Because the Boston majority opposed outside assistance, many lay people regarded the councils as violations of Congregational autonomy. Others, mirroring the position of the ministers, recognized that the Boston majority had violated an unwritten rule in refusing to grant a council to a large minority: they understood that dissenting minorities would be powerless in local churches if outside councils could be convened only with the majority's permission. According to the Salem church records, pastor Higginson "read a letter from the dissenting brethren of Boston" to his congregation in which the dissenters reviewed their predicament, swore allegiance to the "Platforme of Discipline," and pleaded with the church to send "the Elder and other messengers" to attend the second council. The Salem congregation asked Higginson to determine whether the Boston majority had "consented to such a Council." When Higginson later responded in the negative, the church refused to compromise Congregational autonomy by electing delegates. Yet after deeper analysis of the issue, the Salem laity decided that "there was and ought to be relief and remedy [for minorities] against miscarriages in particular churches in the Congregationall Way." They eventually reached a compromise, requesting representatives to attend, but in a nonvoting, advisory capacity, a solution also adopted by the First Church of Lynn.[80]

Most congregations agreed with the Salem and Lynn churches that the Boston dissenters must be heard regardless of the principle of Congregational autonomy. In Dorchester, "some express[ed] themselves as not willing to send any [council delegates], seeing the Church at Boston did not send" for help. But "after long adjetation," the "Major part of the Church did by Vote Nominate and appoint Mr. Mather" and four other representatives to attend the council. The churches of Andover, Charlestown, Watertown, Weymouth, Concord, Ipswich, and Sudbury reached the same decision, also sympathizing with the rights of the Boston dissenters.[81]

The churches of Roxbury and Dedham, on the other hand, refused to send delegates in any capacity. This fact, along with the "adjetations" in other churches, suggests that, in general, lay people were as divided over the Boston First Church controversy as they were over the Halfway Covenant. Eventually, as Cotton Mather later observed, "the whole people of God, throughout the colony, were too much distinguished into such as favored the old church, and such as favored the new church; whereof the former were against the [Halfway] synod, and the latter were for it."[82] The debates over the First Church separation eventually penetrated deeply into the political arena as well. In 1669, the deputies chose Davenport to preach the election sermon, which for several years had served as a forum for opinions on the Halfway Covenant. Davenport's sermon was nothing short of incendiary, adding fuel to the fires of lay resistance throughout the colony. The results of the Synod of 1662, he railed, were nothing but men's "Opinions, which are no part of the Faith once given to the Saints." "Popish Councils" like those in Boston served only to "bind people to receive their Superstitious Devices and Impositions as matters of Faith." Davenport excoriated the Boston dissenters and gravely censured the Court for encouraging "declension" by allowing councils to destroy Congregational autonomy. The councils in Boston reminded him of "[Theodore] *Beza* [who] saith, that such was the folly ignorance and ambition of many Bishops . . . , that you would have supposed the Devil to have been President in their Assemblies."[83]

The sermon served only to divide further the General Court, which, no less than the church members or the ministers, was split between those who despised the innovation as a sinful "invention" and those who saw a duty to support the ministry and the church covenant.[84] The deputies voted to thank Davenport for his efforts, but the magistrates, who generally supported the ministerial majority and the Halfway Covenant, vetoed the motion. The division between the two houses reached a peak when "sundry ffreemen Inhabitants" from far-off Hadley and Northampton, under the supervision of the Reverend John Russell, a known opponent of the Halfway Covenant, requested a formal investigation into the sources of God's "displeasure and departure" from New England. The deputies appointed a committee packed with opponents to look into this "great concernment." Predictably, the committee lashed out at the ministerial majority. Opponents blamed "god's displeasure" upon the "woeful declining from our primitive and foundation work" and the "innovation threatening the ruin of . . . the congregational way," while Thomas Danforth, the lone magistrate on the committee, disagreed, singling out "a practical rendering of the church covenant to be an empty, useless, and mere titular matter," and the "boldness found in many to rise up against the Lord's faithful ministers."[85]

The deputies heaped even stronger invective upon the ministry in a second report, which the Congregational historian Hamilton A. Hill described as "one of the most remarkable papers ever adopted by a legislative body." Here the deputies execrated the ministry for robbing the laity of its liberties and destroying Congregationalism, citing

> declension from the primitive foundation worke, innovation in doctrine & worship, opinion & practice, ... an usurpation of a lordly, prelatical power over God's heritage; . . . . , turning the pleasant gardens of Christ into a wildernesse; . . . these are the leven, the corrupting gangreens, the infecting spreading plague, the provoking images of jealousy set up before the Lord.[86]

According to Hill, the deputies "seem to have been strangely unconscious of the general drift of opinion among the churches and in the community." Indeed, the deputies' shocking attack upon the clergy was ill appreciated by ministers and most lay people alike. The ministers quickly embarked upon a campaign to oust the offending deputies from office.[87]

The election of 1671 turned significantly (though by no means entirely) upon the Synod of 1662. As such, it provides another yardstick for measuring lay support for the ministry and the Halfway Covenant, at least at this point. The election results suggest that a majority of lay people stood behind the ministers. Only seven of the thirty-seven towns in Massachusetts Bay elected deputies who opposed the ministry, and three of those elected a delegate from each of the two "parties." Having installed a lower house more amenable to their views, the ministers demanded and received a formal and public retraction of the previous attacks.[88] But the election of 1671 hardly ended resistance to the Halfway Covenant. In fact, considerable bitterness remained within individual churches, where lay opponents maintained "a guerilla warfare of misrepresentation and slander" in attempts to prevent implementation of the measure. The aftershocks of this clash would be felt for decades to come.[89]

As historians have pointed out, the ministers ultimately emerged "victorious" in the battle over the Halfway Covenant. By 1690, three-quarters of the churches in Massachusetts Bay practiced the innovation, and, as the election of 1671 suggests, a majority of the laity may have supported the change all along. In Pope's words, the Halfway Covenant served as a "necessary adjustment" to the unforeseen problem of declining admissions and, as Stout observes, church membership might have been limited to a "tiny and impotent fraction of the larger community" had the ministers lost in their struggle.[90]

Nonetheless, the ministers' victory was Pyrrhic at best, and historians have masked some of the most significant consequences to emerge from the controversy in their strong emphasis upon the ministers' ultimate success. Though designed to ensure Christian upbringing and to strengthen covenantal engagements within the local church, the battle over the extension of baptism divided the clergy, eroded the bonds of respect between ministers and members, and fostered sharp contention at the local level that often stretched on for years and even decades. In demonstrating how the Halfway Covenant stood as "the crowning achievement of the founders," historians have lost sight of this important, though darker, side of the story.[91]

The ministers' efforts to legitimate the Halfway Covenant initiated a process that gradually reshaped lay and clerical attitudes toward one another and toward church government generally. In justifying their own reversals on fundamental questions of church order, ministers were forced to acknowledge that Congregationalism was not the "Eternal," biblical model of church government that the founders had claimed. Ministers now asserted that all along the churches had been guilty of certain "defects in preactices," arguing that when facing questions about the baptism of the children, "we had . . . no occasion to determine what to judge or practise in that matter." Churchgoers brought up on lessons of unanimity and consensus were now told to expect further disagreement in the course of future Congregational development: "Every Stage of Truth's progress, since the first dawning of the Reformation, hath been accompanied with sharp Debates, even among the godly Professors of it," wrote John Norton.[92]

The ministers' acknowledgment of legitimately varying interpretations in matters of church order would have far-reaching consequences. How were churches to reach unanimous agreement in the face of two acceptable but mutually exclusive alternatives, such as the decision of whether or not to adopt the Halfway Covenant? The dilemma led the elders to admit that expectations of unanimity in church affairs were, in some cases, unreasonable. They fully recognized that in many churches the ideal of unanimous consent prevented the implementation of the Halfway Covenant for decades. Ministers consequently began downplaying the need for unanimity. During the later stages of the dispute over baptism, Salem's Pastor Higginson informed his congregation that while "it was desired" that the church "might all be of one judgment" on the Halfway Covenant, such unanimity could no longer be "expected." John Allin insisted that diversity of opinion was to be expected in a growing colony. He composed a letter to nearby churches pointing to the difficulty "for soe populous a congregation [as Boston's] to agree as one in their choice." Ministers on both sides of the debate over the Halfway Covenant agreed on this point. John Davenport stated in Boston that votes ought to be considered decisive "if consented to by the major part . . . . for otherwise, nothing shall pass as a Church act if the minor part dissent, which is contrary to the scripture and to Reason, and constant aproved practices of all publique societyes."[93]

These arguments struck a chord with the laity, and in the late seventeenth century the churches quietly began to move toward the majority vote. Dorchester sent representatives to the Boston Third Church council in 1669 by a majority vote; in 1678 the "major part" of the church decided to forward a petition to the General Court "against ordinarys that have not a sufficient gard over them to keepe good order."[94] Ministers understood the dangers associated with the majority vote. In Newbury, a majority voted to suspend their pastor without advice from a council.[95] But in time, the ministers recognized that the unanimous vote was simply no longer viable. By 1696, the majority vote was so entrenched that ministers offered biblical justifications that directly contradicted the councils' decisions in the Boston Third Church dispute. Though in 1669 the Boston council decided that a majority had no right to impose a minister on an unwilling minority, a council in 1696 decided that even the election of a clergyman could be decided by a majority vote: "[T]he light of nature shows that the majority Should Sway Acts. 27. 11, 12. And the Apostles settled Elders in Churches by the major votes of such Churches (manifested by lifting up of hands (keirotonesen) e i [sic] in the presence and by the order of the Apostles) Acts. 14. 23."[96]

The shift to the majority vote, once again, represented a formalization of procedures that had been governed by voluntarism. Minorities had always existed in local churches and they maintained a right to paralyze churches through their dissent. In the early years of settlement, they rarely exercised that right, instead choosing voluntarily to submit to the mind of the church. Now churches maintained the right to pass motions whether minorities chose to accept the sense of the meeting or not.

This decline of unanimity and the move toward the "major vote" would seem to represent a watershed in Massachusetts church government. But the shift was gradual, complex, and silent—and less significant than it initially appears. In the first place, unanimity in church affairs remained an ideal throughout the colonial era. The vast majority of votes in admissions, discipline, and other church procedures would continue to be unanimous well into the eighteenth century. Because ministers continued to govern by persuasion, they were reluctant to impose the will of the majority on substantial numbers of dissenters. They did not, for example, suddenly implement the Halfway Covenant in local churches by majority vote. Moreover, in cases where unanimity could not be achieved, ministers and lay people continued to value the right of dissent: even majority votes were not necessarily final. After the precedent established in Boston, minorities always maintained the option of appealing to an outside church council if they felt particularly aggrieved. Partly because minis-

ters called for majority votes only when the practice was unlikely to incur resent-
ment, and partly because minorities still maintained an effective right to dissent,
friction or even debate over the shift to the majority vote is virtually nonexistent in
the church records.[97]

Though most clergymen seem to have accepted the shift away from unanimity
and the emergence of the "major vote" as practical necessities, these developments
nonetheless seem to have troubled the ministry at a deeper level. Perhaps diversity of opinion was to be expected in "populous" churches like Boston's. But the
elders fully understood that even in smaller, more homogeneous churches like
Allin's Dedham, lay people were unable to achieve consensus. Moreover, there had
always been debate and dissent within individual churches. Why was it only within
the last ten or fifteen years that congregations were increasingly unable to overcome dissent and achieve unanimity? Most ministers did not understand the degree
to which the crystallization of inherent contradictions in the clergy's own prescriptions and in Congregationalism itself rendered lay unanimity and obedience difficult to achieve. How could lay people submit to "the ministry" when the ministry itself was divided? How could they submit to the "mind of the church" when
to do so violated their duty to dissent? Most ministers, like Wilson in Boston, could
only explain the decline of consensus in terms of an increasing lack of deference
and respect the laity paid to their elders—and nowhere was this lack of respect
more obvious than in resistance to the Halfway Covenant and the synod of elders
that endorsed it.

This understanding (or misunderstanding) began to reshape the ministers' attitudes
toward lay people, another important consequence of the struggle over the Halfway
Covenant. Clergymen resented churchgoers who frustrated their elders' will and, in
some cases, even attacked the ministry, a context that is crucial to understanding some
of the most vitriolic criticism ministers leveled at the laity in their celebrated "Jeremiads" of the 1660s and 1670s. Two of the most famous election sermons, Samuel
Danforth's *A Brief Recognition of New England's Errand into the Wilderness* and Urian
Oakes's *New England Pleaded With*, were delivered before the General Court at the
height of the "guerilla" campaign that followed the election of 1671, and both sermons
reveal the elders' bitterness over lay resistance to the Halfway Covenant.

Beyond their general descriptions of the laity's moral degeneracy, both ministers
insisted that church members no longer heeded their elders and failed to observe
the proper rules of church order. In supporting these assertions of lay "declension,"
both Danforth and Oakes pointed accusing fingers specifically at the First Church
of Boston and the opponents of the Halfway Covenant. By scorning the recommendations of the two councils, Danforth averred, the Bostonians demonstrated a lack
of reverence for the ministry unthinkable in the first years of settlement:

What readiness was there in those days to call for the help of Neighbor
Elders and Brethren, in case of any Difference or Division that could not be

healed at home? What reverence was there then of the sentence of a Council, as being *decisive* and issuing the controversie? [98]

Danforth tendered "a wholesome admonition" to ministerial opponents throughout the colony to recover their "ancient and primitive affections" to "the Lord, his Prophets, and to his Ordinances" of church government.[99]

Oakes addressed the controversy even more directly. Rather than attacking the laity in general, Oakes singled out the deputies and other worthy laymen who continued to oppose their ministers. These "designers," Oakes insisted, "are wont to make and improve false alarms of danger, that people may believe that religion and liberties are at stake, and in danger to be lost!" Taking advantage of the "credulitie and easiness of well meaning people," these church worthies misled "many good people" who "take it for granted that most of the leaders in this country are mediating a revolt from the good old principles and practises of their worthy predecessors."[100] Oakes was as interested in defending the clergy as he was in reviling the laity. Particularly threatening to him were the slanderers who accused the ministerial supporters of the Halfway Covenant of declension from the practices of the fathers:

> It hath been my observation since I came among you, that almost all the mischief in this poor country is made and carried on by lying. *Tale-bearer*, or *slanderer*, in the Hebrew, hath its origination in the word which signifies a merchant. . . . We have many such merchants, or pedlars, rather, that go up and down the country with this kind of commodity. . . . the ministers of Christ among you indefinitely have been deliberately and solemnly charged with "declension from primitive foundation work, innovation in doctrine and worship, opinion and practice, invasion of the rights, liberties and privileges of churches. . . . " I need give you no other instance of this evil spirit of jealousy and calumny than this.

To those who dismissed these "small devices" as "petty" backbiting, Oakes warned, "I look upon this course of calumnating your best men, as the very *Gunpowder-Plot* that threatens the destruction of Church and State."[101]

In addition to the sentiments expressed in their Jeremiads, ministers on both sides of the baptism question lashed out at their lay opponents as "ignorant" and "incompetent" to "Judge of the Case"—sentiments that contrasted sharply with the confident assertions of lay gifts and potentialities expressed in Thomas Hooker's *Survey of the Summe of Church Discipline* or in Cotton's early sermons before his Boston church. Clearly, the esteem in which ministers held lay people was beginning to disintegrate.[102]

And the feeling was mutual: ministers were by no means wholly off base in pointing to a decline in lay respect for the clergy and flagging commitment to the Congregational Way. Lay people, or at least many of them, did begin to recast their understanding of church government and the role of the clergy within it. Many churchgoers shared with the clergy a recognition that church government had evolved in the past and would continue to do so. But the Halfway Covenant, along with the ministers' revised stance toward Congregational autonomy, councils, and unanimity, led others to wonder whether church government was, at least in part, something that ministers had always denied and condemned: an invention of men. This bitter conclusion left many churchgoers, such as Brother Adams in Chelmsford, the Dorchester deacons, and, of course, many of the deputies, feeling betrayed. In Roxbury, a layman attributed a drought to "the sitting of the synod" of 1662, while Salemites called for a day of humiliation for "human impositions in worship." As we shall see, lay people would begin to echo the deputies' charges of clerical "tyranny," "prelacy," and, especially, ministerial "declension" with increasing frequency during the last quarter of the seventeenth century.[103] Churchgoers would also begin to question the extent to which ministers were God's unique spokesmen in matters of church government and would become far less inclined to strive for the ideal of sola scriptura.

In the final three decades of the seventeenth century churchgoers would remain devoted to spiritual pursuits. But many would examine Congregationalism and the role of their ministers in church government in a different light. Once some began to wonder whether the New England Way was really a matter of interpretation, management of church affairs became considerably more problematical for the clergy. The timing for such a development could not have been worse: in response to the disruptive social changes that would arise in the decades to come, churchgoers would look to their ministers and to church government more than ever before as sources of cohesion. Both suffered from bruised credibility when they were needed most.

6

An Uneasy Balance

"AFTER COMING OUT OF THE MEETING HOUSE" one Sunday in 1661, Lydia Dastin of Reading spotted four young men laughing and chatting. She promptly filed a complaint with the elders, charging that her brethren "laughed and jibed at the minister that then had been dispensing the word to them," and urged the officers to proceed to censure. A preliminary examination of the case, however, revealed that the foursome had not "laugh[ed] at the Minister" at all "but as they Sayd at a Senseless joke put forth" by one of them. The elders reproved Dastin for her malevolent misapplication of mutual watch, then attempted to resolve the incident quietly, convincing her to apologize to the young men in private. To the elders' dismay, the wrongfully accused angrily refused to accept Dastin's confession. Concerned that news of the incident might have leaked out, they forced the officers to acquaint the entire congregation with her "sinful rashness" and demanded that she beg forgiveness in public for damaging their personal reputations and "blemishing [their] names." The local minister condemned the entire affair as another example of the sinful "jealousy" that increasingly plagued Massachusetts churches.[1]

The late seventeenth-century church records reveal that ministerial complaints of excessive church contention reflected far more than hyperbole or rhetorical flourish. Admittedly, from the first years of settlement ministers had lamented the "Divisions and Distractions" in New England and its "hankerings after the Whoredomes of the World." But, as ministers insisted, lay disputes in the final third of the seventeenth century were unprecedented in their frequency and, especially, their nature. As the Reading case illustrates, second-generation churchgoers seemed increasingly willing to trouble their churches with trivial squabbles and to ignore traditional ideals of harmony and communitarianism. Throughout the colony, congregations ignited over an unending variety of issues, in confrontations that pitted church members against church members, members against nonmembers, neighbor against neighbor, and town against church.[2]

Some of this contention simply reflected the growing pains that afflicted New England society as a whole. As historians have documented well, larger social trends, such as explosive population growth, geographical expansion, and economic diversification combined in the second half of the seventeenth century with more immediate crises such as King Philip's War and the loss of the charter to create an atmosphere of instability in the colony. Larger cultural shifts also fueled church strife. The church records contain ample evidence pointing to both a marked decline in deference during the late seventeenth century and a rising spirit of individualism, developments that conflicted sharply with traditional covenantal ideals. Over the course of decades, these social and cultural changes would erode the spirit of communitarianism and mutuality upon which the success of Congregationalism heavily rested. Already, by the late seventeenth century, church government in Massachusetts began to show dramatic signs of strain.[3]

Though ministers and congregations alike often attributed local strife in the late seventeenth century to a larger decline in religiosity, such claims were often ironic, for much church contention issued from inevitable social changes whose consequences contemporaries interpreted in religious terms. Many scholars have described the painful expansion and division of New England towns, for example, which forced increasing numbers of "outlivers," weary of travel to the meetinghouse over rocky roads and in cold weather, to seek permission to establish their own civil and religious institutions. Members of parent churches felt sinfully betrayed when groups of families from outlying areas broke off from them to establish their own church and invariably questioned whether outlying residence justified "breach of church covenant."[4] Churchgoers interpreted these confrontations as religious crises of eternal significance, not merely as consequences of geographic growth. Until the authorities gradually established precedents and firm guidelines, bitter struggles often accompanied attempts to gather new churches out of old ones.

The gathering of the Chebacco church typified these sorts of conflicts.[5] In 1679, "250 souls" from Ipswich, "of which the nearest [lived] about 3 miles and a half from the towne," sought to establish their own church. The parent church complained to the General Court that "these people have been travelling to church for 30 years." The outlivers' "burden," they insisted, was a "pretended one." Deeply disturbed, the Ipswich church never acknowledged the legitimacy of geographic and economic issues that motivated both sides. They did not see the division mainly in terms of a reduced tax base: for them the struggle largely concerned a violation of church order and breach of covenant. When the Chebacco residents "irregularly" lined up a minister and began construction of a meetinghouse, the parent church formally censured dozens of former "brothers" and "sisters" for their sinful proceedings.[6] The sacred significance of the division greatly troubled the new church as well. Once the General Court approved their gathering, the Chebacco members quickly commissioned a committee to compose a lengthy narrative of the entire affair, hoping to convince later generations and, one senses, themselves, that they had handled an unfortunate situation in a way of God.[7]

No less than geographic expansion, social and economic diversification heightened tensions in Massachusetts, giving rise to conflict and competition among various economic groups such as merchants and farmers. Economic advancement fostered instability when individuals quickly achieved a degree of wealth and rank in society that offended the sensibilities of those accustomed to more traditional Old World patterns of hierarchy and social station. As social distinctions blurred in communities where townspeople often enjoyed little knowledge of affairs beyond their own village, people long accustomed to deferential relationships became overly jealous of their place in the local "pecking order" and flared angrily at the slightest insult from those "beneath" them.[8]

These sorts of social and cultural changes unavoidably spilled over into local churches, which, since the founding, had served as a principal forum for airing community grievances.[9] The records of Rowley, Chelmsford, Reading, and numerous other churches demonstrate the willingness of members to disrupt church harmony by pursuing local rivalries and petty jealousies that were, in pastor John Fiske's estimation, "very rash and unadvised and without any regular ground." Particularly upsetting to the godly was the growing frequency of disputes like Dastin's, in which "unbrotherly, unfaithful, and unjust" personal quarrels engulfed entire congregations; Bradford churchgoers sadly observed that such "tares of discord" had erupted "almost in every Christian society" in New England.[10]

Beyond the bickering associated with local social and economic change, larger cultural shifts also contributed to the breakdown of church harmony and the disintegration of a spirit of mutuality. Throughout Massachusetts, lay commitment to communitarian ideals clearly began to fade in the late seventeenth century as a spirit of individualism began to thrive. While a definitive study of individualism in colonial New England has yet to be written, Michael Zuckerman and other scholars have pointed to the gradual emergence in the seventeenth century of colonists who "were inclined to set their own advantage before the public good." This individualistic spirit "is not to be identified simply with acquisitiveness," as Richard Gildrie has observed, but represented "a much broader attitude" that placed a heightened emphasis upon private goals, personal autonomy, and public reputation, "even at the expense of communal interests."[11]

As Gildrie notes, we need not "regard the relationship between individualism and communalism as a simple dichotomy."[12] But in the arena of church government, rising individualism and a declining commitment to the communitarian ideals of the church covenant (or "covenantal piety") clearly reinforced one another, as lay people began to place personal aspirations ahead of the corporate goals of the church. An obsessive concern with the individual "reputation," for example, helps explain why churchgoers like the wrongfully accused in Reading refused to settle minor disturbances privately, demanding instead to clear their names in public—and often bitterly divisive—church hearings. A Rowley member sought to vindicate his "blessed reputation" by suing (unsuccessfully) his own minister. "A good name," he explained, is "desired above great riches . . . if we be charged to promote the good name of our neighbor then we are strictly commanded to help forward our own." Such priorities, Beverly pastor John Hale repined, citing a 1670 declaration of the General Court, reflected an increasingly "serfish [sic] spirit" of individualism among the laity, "minding our owne things more than the things of Christ, and of private before the publick good."[13]

Lay people further demonstrated flagging commitment to covenantal ideals through their deliberate abuse of mutual watch. The laity, ministers complained, increasingly exercised mutual watch not out of concern for their neighbor's soul, but out of a spirit of personal vengefulness and animosity. "In managing the Discipline of Christ," clergymen complained, "some (and too many) are acted by their Passions and Prejudices more than by a spirit of Love and Faithfulness towards their Brothers Soul, which things are . . . so dreadful violations of the Church Covenant."[14] Contemporary church records suggest that these charges represented neither empty exaggeration nor baseless rhetoric, as some historians have been too quick to assert. In 1670, for example, Richard Hildrich of Chelmsford[15] accused Thomas Barrett[16] of "lying" in public because in a recent town meeting Barrett had said "that his hair stood right up or on end," when in truth, "to the observation of witnesses it did not." "This thing," the exasperated pastor noted, "after scanning, was by vote" thrown out of the church. Here church discipline, an ordinance of God, was employed not to reclaim an errant brother, as in the past, but merely to humiliate a neighbor. One searches earlier disciplinary records in vain for such cases that, like the Dastin affair in Reading, point to an unmistakable decline in the sense of communitarianism and mutuality among some second-generation churchgoers.[17]

The decline in lay covenantal piety also manifested itself in churchgoers' stubborn refusal to accept church decisions—particularly in matters of discipline—with which they disagreed, demanding instead the right to air their grievances before councils of outside elders. "After thirty or forty years experience in the way of *Congregational Churches*," John Eliot wrote, lamenting this development, "[w]e finde more and more need to insist upon [councils]" to resolve specific questions that churches formerly would have settled on their own. Time and again in the 1670s, Rowley members, sometimes individually, sometimes in groups, demanded the right to advance their positions before outside councils.[18] Later in the century, two councils were called not as a consequence of division but by lone individuals who refused to accept censures administered by their local churches. In both cases, the council ruled against the offender and upheld the decision of the church.[19]

The corrosive effects of declining covenantal piety, rising individualism, and local jealousies are encapsulated in a dispute in Rowley, where a remarkably trivial argument between two neighbors spread to the church and eventually inflamed the entire congregation.[20] In the course of a routine discussion of little apparent significance, Thomas Leaver, a linen weaver, suggested to Mr. Philip Nelson, a wealthy merchant and prestigious town father, that the latter had been "deceived."[21] Nelson answered, "god is not in heaven if I be deceived." Leaver cautioned Nelson to watch his language, which tended toward blasphemy. Nelson refused to tolerate this "insult," especially from a lesser figure like Leaver. Far more concerned with his wounded pride than corporate ideals, the infuriated merchant decided to put his neighbor in his place and lodged a civil suit against him for "slander."

As had been the custom since the first years of settlement, the local pastor, Samuel Phillips, attempted to mediate the dispute quietly in a private conference. But, as was increasingly the case in other communities, the minister was unable to resolve the quarrel:[22] though Leaver formally apologized to Nelson three times in private, the indignant merchant refused to drop his lawsuit. Pastor Phillips then attempted coercive measures to achieve results that in previous decades he likely would have attained voluntarily. He brought the case before his church, announcing that Leaver had offered "three confessions, two to[o] many" and convinced the membership to censure Nelson for persisting in his lawsuit instead of voluntarily accepting the apology.

In the course of these remarks, the pastor offered some vague comments that, several members concluded, impugned the authority of the civil arm. Offering their minister little chance to explain himself, they tattled on Phillips, who found himself tendering satisfaction at the next meeting of the Quarterly Court. The Rowley minister might have extinguished the smoldering dispute himself at this point. But instead he chose to throw fuel on the fire, promptly climbing into the pulpit to denounce publicly Nelson's allies, who, he insisted, misinterpreted his earlier comments and raised false charges against him. Perhaps impressed by Nelson's example, several members responded by filing a lawsuit, accusing their own minister of slander and damaging their reputations. The affair embroiled the entire church; eventually over thirty members ended up in court to testify for one side or the other.

The elders' inability to resolve these kinds of disputes at the local level points to another cultural change that increasingly undermined Congregational church order. Numerous historians have pointed to a general decline in deference in virtually all social relationships during this period and, as principal authority figures within local communities, ministers suffered deeply from this development. Throughout the colony, clergymen began to complain of the laity's disorderly conduct during church meetings, decried the general lack of respect for ministerial authority in matters of government, and condemned churchgoers' "bold carrage to aged leaders."[23]

The records indicate that, indeed, lay people became increasingly rambunctious during church meetings. The Boston church trials in 1640 were models of lay-clerical cooperation in comparison to the unruly hearings often described later in the century. In 1665, the Chelmsford church spent an entire day bickering over whether one Thomas Chamberlain had broken a promise in "refusing to herd his cattle." The hearing quickly broke down into pandemonium,

> some saying ther was no covenant [i.e., promise to herd his cattle], others there was. Some saying that what he promised was to their understanding absolute, others conditional. Some saying that in case of the condition that a

cow keeper might have been had, others not. And so testimonies coming point blank each as others, yea some of them in writing.

Struggling to moderate the proceedings, pastor John Fiske grew especially vexed with brother Robert Proctor, who signed petitions of support "to the writing[s] on both sides" of the argument.[24] Matters grew so confused that Fiske and the church failed to issue the dispute, deciding simply to "leave the matter to God," hardly a standard or appropriate outcome for a formal disciplinary case.[25]

The erosion of ministerial authority in local churches reflected a number of developments beyond a general decline of deference. As David D. Hall has observed, second-generation ministers seemed lacking to churchgoers in comparison with the heroic founders of the 1630s and 1640s. Ministers were keenly aware of the laity's tendency to regard recent Harvard graduates in a harsher light than their first-generation predecessors. Rowley's Phillips, among others, openly chided his congregation for refusing to accord him the respect that founding pastor Ezekiel Rogers had enjoyed. Internal disagreements within the clerical community over issues of church order also compromised the authority of local ministers. The Halfway Covenant, in particular, persisted as a topic of debate in many late seventeenth-century churches and continued to remind churchgoers of the clergy's inability to provide decisive answers to important questions of church government.[26]

What contributed most to the decline of ministerial authority in church affairs, however, was the increasingly profound understanding of Congregational practices and principles attained by the members—and what they did with it. After studying the *Cambridge Platform* at its ratification and assisting in government for years (and, in many cases, even decades), lay people believed that their mastery of the Congregational Way easily matched their ministers'. Though ministers had always relied upon deference in governing their churches, they had also preached many anti-deferential messages, and in the second half of the seventeenth century churchgoers began to elevate Congregationalism's antiauthoritarian themes, while glossing over traditional calls for restraint and order. Hypersensitive to any perceived encroachment on their "rights," they held their officers tenaciously to the standard of sola scriptura, constantly demanded defenses of their ministers' biblical interpretations, and openly challenged their elders over simple matters of opinion.

The reciprocal relationship between the laity's mastery of Congregational practices, the erosion of ministerial authority, and the general decline of deference in Massachusetts is nowhere more obvious than in the *Notebook of John Fiske*. Though pastor Fiske easily qualifies as a first-generation "founder" (he arrived in Salem in 1630), he suffered a gradual but unmistakable loss of status over the decades, as his Chelmsford congregation grew increasingly uncooperative, disrespectful, and contentious. Fiske's career thus calls into question efforts to explain the decline of ministerial prestige mainly with reference to the laity's lack of respect for Harvard-educated, second-generation newcomers. Fiske's difficulties also cast doubt on suggestions that ministers themselves fostered lay insurgence by trespassing upon the members' turf in church affairs, an offense virtually guaranteed to incite defiance. The Chelmsford pastor carefully adhered to Congregational provisions throughout his lengthy tenure.[27]

What changed in Chelmsford was the laity's sense of its own authority in church affairs. From the outset, the Chelmsford members had defended their liberties, refusing to approve of church actions simply on the minister's say so. But by the 1660s, the members began constantly to throw their pastor on the defensive. Well versed in Congregationalism and virtually obsessed with their watchmen duties, the laity seemed to relish playing devil's advocate with their minister, calling Fiske's authority into question every step of the way as he attempted to define and defend church procedures.

Typical of this lay combativeness was a controversy over the effort to appoint William Fletcher[28] to the office of deacon.[29] At the gathering of the Chelmsford church in 1656, the members had offered Fletcher, formerly of Concord, the deaconate. When the church requested a conversion testimonial of Fletcher, the latter refused, arguing that as a member of the Concord church he maintained a right simply to transfer his membership to Chelmsford. He apparently turned down the deaconate during this confrontation. Six years later, two members complained to Fiske that Fletcher had recently groused in public that the church had unfairly "laid him by (his place of deaconship)."

On a November morning in 1662, pastor Fiske convened a meeting to determine whether Fletcher had unjustly accused the church of wrongdoing. The debate quickly turned to the related topic of "second relations": had the church proceeded scripturally in requiring a second conversion testimonial of neighboring communicants who sought to transfer their membership to Chelmsford? The minister clearly supported second relations, but, anticipating debate, he offered "liberty to all" Chelmsford members to express their views on the matter. In the exchanges that followed, the laity demonstrated that its commitment to larger Congregational provisions—particularly the limits imposed on churches by the higher laws of the Bible—far outweighed any deference owed to pastor Fiske. Thomas Barrett opened the debate by demanding "to know whether there were any rule out of scripture to compel any to second relations." Richard Hildrich announced that "he had nothing against it and that twas practiced in Cambridge." Robert Proctor joined in. "What is not of faith," or Scripture rule, he reminded the congregation, "is sin." He would "consent to it" only "if this making of second relation be fundamental of faith and may appear" in the Bible.[30]

Fiske insisted that the preservation of purity, or the "well being" of the church, compelled them to require second relations. Thomas Adams, the local cooper, leaped up in protest to his pastor's justification. The larger issue, Adams lectured his minister, regarded the relationship between "fundamentals, substantials, and circumstantials" of church order. The particular question of relations concerned "substantials," he noted, "for what members can be admitted with us but in this way[?]" Now, "in point of instituted worship," he asked, rhetorically, "is there anything to be owned which can be proved only by necessary consequences," such as the "well being" of the church, since "under the law everything to the least was expressly prescribed" in the Bible? The layman's argument was irrefutable, prompting Fiske to review the Scripture justifications for relations. Adams quickly objected. The question at hand, he reminded his minister, concerned *second* relations: "[W]e find not that they [that] have passed under the rod and measuring rod should pass it a second time." The weary pastor provided Scripture grounds for second relations.[31]

Fiske then raised the question of whether Fletcher had in fact been unfairly "laid by" in the matter of the deaconate. The minister insisted that Fletcher had simply withdrawn from consideration. Thomas Chamberlain[32] and Adams disagreed, countering that the church had subtly forced Fletcher's hand. They wrangled with their pastor toe to toe. Chamberlain questioned the original vote on procedural grounds; Fiske defended the vote. Adams insisted that "no person so employed in the work of deacon by the vote or anointing of the church should be laid aside but for sin." Fiske responded that "this touched not the question but takes for granted that the church laid by Brother Fletcher." Shifting gears, Adams explained to the congregation,

> A father having two children or a man two servants, one he hath employed several years and found him faithful in his business, the other which he hath had the trial of for but a few weeks, he engages to attend the second business with his brother but he excepts against it unless his brother yield to such condition which he cannot. The father fosters the younger in the work and gives him his breakfast, the other is neglected and so attends not the business as before. He looks, and who would not look, that the father laid by the elder.[33]

Fletcher should not have been passed over merely because he "scrupled" a second relation, Adams repeated, citing "I Tim. 3:10, being found blameless, let him use the office." Brother Chamberlain chimed in again, condemning the church for failing to labor sufficiently with Fletcher in an effort to convince him to assume the office: "[T]he church dealt not with Brother Fletcher and quickened him not up to his work." Fiske responded that the church had been unable to agree upon a Scripture "rule" that Fletcher had broken by refusing the deaconate and therefore had not pressed the matter.

Fiske eventually produced "four arguments" to "prove Brother Fletcher laid by himself." After debating much of the day, the majority finally agreed that the church had not acted unscripturally in the Fletcher affair. The members also demonstrated that they were no less concerned with church purity than they had been years earlier—they voted to reaffirm the practice of second relations. But the entire episode had been an exhausting ordeal for pastor Fiske. Though he achieved the votes he hoped for, few spoke up during the debates in support of their minister. Indeed, the church seems to have reaffirmed second relations despite the pastor's advocacy rather than because of it.

In general, as Robert Pope has noted, "nothing in John Fiske's career distinguished him from the majority of his clerical contemporaries."[34] The struggles of other ministers certainly mirrored those of Fiske. As in Chelmsford, lay people in Rowley were far more interested in enforcing limitations on their pastor's authority than in acknowledging restrictions upon their own prerogatives. "What care I though God commands this or that[?]" pastor Samuel Phillips complained, mocking the laity's attitude. "I will not be limited or restrained."[35] One particularly thorny case for the pastor involved the admission of Mr. Nehemiah Jewett,[36] who appeared before the church to offer a conversion relation in 1677. Several churchgoers cited Phillips's handling of this routine procedure to trump up charges of clerical "tyranny," even though it was the dissenting members themselves who in fact violated standard Congregational procedures. The confrontation erupted when brother Richard Holmes, a millwright,[37] vetoed the admission, stating that "he had matters of offence" against Jewett. Philip Nelson also "declared against his admission," and Samuel Highill[38] "desired [Phillips] would not thrust a member upon the Church." Phillips reminded Highill that "he was not the Church," angrily deferred the admission, and informed the assembly that the dissenters stood guilty of breach of covenant, for they had forwarded no complaints about Jewett during the entire *year* that the candidate stood propounded.[39]

In the days that followed, Nelson went about the town "in a factious way" circulating a petition to "get as many as he could to oppose the Elder" and to prevent Jewett's admission. "God's house should be built without axes and hammers," the contentious Nelson pontificated, in reference to Phillips's alleged effort to "thrust" the candidate upon the church. Upon receiving the petition, an outraged Phillips tore into the dissenters for their efforts at undermining church unity. Especially galling, the minister fumed, was Nelson's hypocritical "complain[ing] of hammers and axes, jarring in the house of God when it is himself firstly and chiefly that lifts up the hammers and has been the chief instrument to break the peace of the church."[40]

Nelson responded by accusing his minister, once again, of violating lay liberties: "if two or three have been dissatisfied" with a candidate, he informed Phillips, "the Church in such cases has forborne." Phillips acknowledged that "if one dissented we ought not to proceed" but only if "there was ground sufficient for his dissent." The pastor again castigated Nelson and his supporters for their breach of Scripture rules in failing to raise objections to Jewett earlier. He demanded to know just what Nelson and Holmes had against the candidate.[41]

Holmes at last revealed that the roots of their animosity rested in yet another petty lay squabble. Months earlier, "being together in the marsh where they have ground lying together and having words about damage recovered from each other, there were some angry words between them and Nehemiah [Jewett] threatened to cast him into the creek." Reminding Holmes that Jewett had tendered an apology, Phillips asked the dissenter "if his actions were not worse than Nehemiah's words." Had not Holmes "offered his knife to Nehemiah's breast?" during the dispute, as was rumored?

"What if I did?" Holmes snapped.

"I told him [that] to dally with such tools in a passion.———"[42]

Several days later, Nelson again objected to Jewett's admission. Because Nelson had "nothing new to allege," Phillips suggested "that the work we met about might no longer be hindered" and announced his intention to call for a church vote despite Nelson's objection. Infuriated, one brother Platts railed that other ministers such as "Mr. Shepard" were "hindered by five or six objecting" and would not run roughshod over lay dissent. When the pastor ordered him to "desist," Platts stood up and turned his back on Phillips, carping, "[W]hat part have we in David— what part have we in church privileges?" The dissenter castigated the minister as "the wilfulest man within fifty miles" and affirmed that "Nehemiah Jewett was no member."[43]

Though issues of clerical power and lay privilege emerged during this dispute, the division did not pit the laity against the clergy. The majority of the Rowley members stood firmly behind their minister, once all the facts were aired. They admitted Jewett and censured Platts for insisting that "the officer and almost all the Church would lay down their privileges that his might be attended." Platts himself apologized for employing clerical tyranny as an excuse to attack the minister, admitting "[h]is heart did check him for it as soon as he had spoken [out]" against Phillips.[44] Still, these rancorous, unseemly struggles demonstrate that some lay people had stretched the traditional concept of watchfulness to justify personal pride and contempt for clerical authority. For the clergy, the danger extended beyond the consequences of disorder within their churches and the disintegration of a spirit of cooperation. Taken together with rising local contention and declining covenantal piety, ministers saw in the behavior of people like Philip Nelson and brother Platts evidence of something far more ominous: churchgoers had simply become less religious.

As we have seen, no individual more clearly embodied the second generation's waning respect for ministerial authority and a declining commitment to covenantal ideals than Rowley's Philip Nelson. Nonetheless, when called to account for one of his countless run-ins with Pastor Phillips, Nelson responded in a way that reflected neither apathy nor a heightened, individualistic concern for his "reputation." In a scene that mirrored lay repentances in the 1630s, Nelson literally broke down in tears before his congregation:

> He humbly and with tears bewailled the many evils he had fallen into in breaking the commands of God . . . he acknowledged that he had done sinfully and broken his Covenant with God and His people to submit to the government

of Christ . . . and further added that it was his grief that he should so carry it with such contempt aginst Samuel Phillips whom God had made an instrument of his soul's good, and therefore it had been his delight to see and had prized his ministry—and also added that he had forsaken God before [God] had forsaken him and left him to fall into so many evils.[45]

The episode illuminates the transitional nature of church life during the late seventeenth century: though the records point to an unmistakable increase in church discord, they also contain considerable evidence of enduring lay commitment to the New England Way. In focusing largely upon contention and nascent individualism issuing from social, economic, and cultural change during this period, previous writers have created a distorted picture of affairs within the churches.

Though a decline in covenantal piety certainly began to plague Massachusetts churches during the second generation, this process was still in its earliest stages in the late 1660s and in the decades that followed. The church records suggest that, despite the waning commitment of some members to the ideals of the church covenant, ministers and most lay people still regarded the proper observation of church order as a central "means" of achieving grace. Clergymen continued to describe Congregational practices, or the "ordinances," as central to New England's larger identity and, though ministers often complained that churchgoers supervised their elders too aggressively, struggles over lay "rights" and ministerial "authority" indicated that church government still mattered. With much justification, ministers bemoaned misuse of discipline and mutual watch. But most churchgoers continued to honor their obligations in these areas; widespread *apathy* over these and other issues of church government would not appear until well into the next century.

For ministers and churchgoers alike, the concept of mutual watchfulness remained at the center of covenant obligations. In 1682, pastor John Higginson of Salem reminded his congregation to "watch over such as were reported to be given to drinking and company keeping and to deal with them in a regular way" through private admonitions followed by reports to the church elders. The Salem members had followed this advice all along. The previous year "Abigail Kippin [had been] complained of to the Church by her neighbors Brother Grafton, Thomas Giggles, Jo Ingerson, Elizabeth Gardener that she had gone on in a way of excess of drinking and fuddling, and they had often admonished her one alone, and 2 or 3 of them together, and yet she had gone on therein." Kippins presented a "paper full of poenitent expressions," but the members decided that "Poenitential words without works meet for repentance" ought not be accepted, and the offender was admonished. Seven months later the church restored her to full communion.[46]

The long arm of mutual watch even extended from church to church. In 1689 the Dorchester church discovered that Experience Holiar, who had recently been dismissed to Charlestown, had "Lapsed by the sin of fornication with her Husband" before marriage. The Dorchester elders promptly wrote to Charlestown, noting that "She by her Letters having signifyed to us, her sens of and sorrow" for the offense, they judged it "Expedient she should show her Repentance eminently there." These sorts of episodes were hardly unusual; virtually all church records dating from the final third of the seventeenth century point to a continued commitment to the practice and principles of mutual watch.[47]

That same general level of commitment to collective watchfulness and church discipline extended to the rising generation, or halfway "children of the church," who have been mistakenly described as "indifferent" in previous studies. In 1668, for instance, three Salem children were brought before the church on charges of fornication. Despite the fact that they faced censures, they professed "their willingness to submit themselves to the ordinance of Christ." The church admonished all three. Pastor Higginson then gave notice "unto all other Children of the Covenant amongst us that they must expect to be under the watch and discipline of the church." Many churches, such as those in Bradford, Charlestown, Dorchester, and Salem, requested that the "children of the church" formally submit themselves to church discipline. Of 104 "children" in the Dorchester church, 100 openly declared in 1677 "ther willingness and subjection to the government and discepline of Christ in and by his church." Only four halfway members refused to submit to the discipline of the church. Later, in 1682, Patience Blake of Dorchester "refused to owne the covenant and submit to the Government of Christ in his Church," but later "she did make confession and acknowledgment of her great sin in soe doeing and this she did Vollentarily."[48]

The Dorchester records provide further evidence that these halfway members were anything but apathetic in their attitudes toward spiritual concerns. The children who submitted themselves to church discipline were also asked to submit to a test of their "knowledge." Of the one hundred, ninety-nine passed the test. Only Nathaniel Mather was brought before the church for "falling short of what he should have attained" in "knowledge." He promised "to doe his best to attain more."[49] Descriptions of the halfway members' indifferent attitudes toward church discipline and covenant obligations are difficult to reconcile with the confession of Dorchester's Mercy Modesly, who in 1681

> was called before the Church (though not in full Comunion but (under government Obligations) by her submitting to the Government of Christ in his Church) she was Called to answer for her sine of fornication. She did appeare but being put to it to speak by way of accknowledgement of the sin, she gave noe answer but weept.[50]

Notwithstanding the increasing misuse of censures by vengeful churchgoers, most lay people still regarded church discipline as a sacred ordinance of God. Though in the eighteenth century censures and repentances would become something of a formality,[51] the second generation maintained the central concerns of the founders in disciplinary matters. Church purity and reclamation of the sinner's soul remained far more important goals than revenge or mere "punishment." Churches thus continued to struggle with offenders by whatever means to "reclaim" them. The Dorchester church demonstrated remarkable perseverance with one Consider Atherton, whom they called to account no less than five times before they finally admonished him for drunkenness. Though "he was found asleep in the high way under thee wall beyond Hawkins brook and could not be awakened" by those who discovered him, Atherton first refused to appear before the church and then two weeks later flatly refused to repent. Summoned by the church a third time, Atherton still "did not give Satisfaction," but the church decided to defer the matter to see what "his Lif and Conversation would be." Atherton's response was less than exemplary: he went on a veritable binge and was discovered drunk, the deacon lamented, "the second day and the therd day and the fifth day" in one week. Goodman Andrews "saw him first reell and then fall off from his hors and Judged that he lay ther an hower before the Elder came." Ruling elder Blake confirmed that he "found him lying on the ground fast asleep with his hat off and hors feeding in the way but he could hardly wake him and when he was wakened could not give a Rational answer he was soe drunk and reeled and staggered as he went." Atherton refused to appear at two more meetings, exhausting the church's patience. Considering his "frequent drunkeness and Idleness and breach of former promises to the Church the horrible refractorynes to and Contempt and rebellion against the Church," they formally declared "in the name of Christ that the said Consider Atherton to be a obstinat ofendor and a incoridgable drunkard." Yet for all his repeated offenses and refusals to hear the church, the members exercised remarkable charity, deciding to give Atherton only an admonition, the minimum disciplinary sentence, in hopes that given more time he might repent and return to the fold.[52]

Just as concern for the offender's soul outweighed a desire for punishment in disciplinary decisions, so the maintenance of church purity still superseded the members' heightened concern with individual privacy or "reputation." Church discipline maintained its unique status as the only institution that in public assembly probed into the most personal details of a member's life. A case in point occurred in 1668, when the Chelmsford officers summoned one Joshua Fletcher to appear before the church. A member had spotted Fletcher using a ladder late one night to climb into the upstairs bedroom of a neighbor's home. Suspecting foul play, this vigilant watchman apparently stayed up all night until Fletcher emerged from the same window at dawn. When the witness later discovered that the bedroom in question belonged to Fletcher's romantic interest, he convinced the church to call the youth to account for fornication. Despite the overwhelming circumstantial evidence against him, Fletcher stubbornly denied any wrongdoing, forcing pastor Fiske to recount publicly all of the sordid details of the case, which he spiked with his own pungent commentary.

The time: his coming to her under such pretense both in the night, in the dark of the night, speaking it a deed or work of darkness which we should have no fellowship with Eph. 5:11 And even in the dead of the night, a time when persons are usually in their sound sleep.

The place: her bedchamber where she was either in or upon her bed, an act of shameless impudency.

The space of his abode with her: his continuance with her in this place at such a time for several hours together (from 11, 12, or 1 at night to the morning and this at such a season . . . when frost and snow was on the ground.) And thus rationally conceived it hardly can be seen how it should be tolerable to have sat and abode with her without fire or other help of warmth, in a modest way.

The manner of coming into that place: (climbing up the house and entering in at the window.)[53]

Fiske castigated Fletcher for "turning our Bethels into Bethavens, the bringing in devils, satyrs, and Ziim [wild beast of the desert] and Ijim [wild beast of the island]." The members agreed with their minister and solemnly voted to excommunicate the offender.[54]

Fletcher carried himself before the Chelmsford church "boldly as without shame." But ministers, members, and offenders usually regarded church disciplinary censures with grave seriousness. Church admonition sparked protest and even rage from humiliated offenders, who increasingly sought relief from outside councils. But apathy rarely characterized the lay response to church censure. Church discipline reduced even obstinate, unrepentant offenders to humility. In 1683 the Braintree church called upon Isaac Theer to repent for several counts of theft. Though he never satisfied the congregation, Theer agreed to appear before the church and was clearly humbled by the experience. Moving "pathetically to acknowledge his sin and publish his repentance," the pastor noted, Theer initially lost his nerve, but was "prevented (by our shutting the east door) from going out." He then "stood impudently, and said indeed he owned his sin of stealing, was heartily sorry for it, begged pardon of God and men, and hoped he should do so no more, which was all he could be brought unto, saying his sin was already known, and that there was no need to mention it in particular, all with a remiss voice, so that but few could hear him." When the church judged his efforts unacceptable, Theer "flung out of doors with an insolent manner, though silent."[55]

The Braintree church met with greater success fourteen years later in reclaiming Samuel Tompson, who, for reasons that remain obscure, had grown so angry with his minister that he "absent[ed] himself from the Publike worshipe, unlesse when any stranger preached." Pastor Moses Fiske described the youthful offender as a "prodigie of pride, malice, and arrogance," his manner "being before the church proud and insolent, reviling and vilifying their Pastor, at an horrible rate, and stileing him their priest, and them a nest of wasps." The "nest" admonished Tompson unanimously. Fiske noted sympathetically that though "warned to repent . . . this poor man goes to the tavern to drink it down immediately, as he said." One night, several weeks later, the troubled youth appeared unexpectedly at Fiske's home and quietly humbled himself before his pastor. Initially, the church insisted "his conversation did not agree therewith," but over the following months, Tompson added and enlarged upon his confession until "the major part of the church voted his absolution."[56]

Many second-generation offenders, to be sure, refused to confess their sins. But disciplinary measures had never been wholly successful in inspiring repentance. Only about half of those disciplined in Boston in the early decades of settlement successfully repented, and some of those fell back into sin. Though the nature of the church records make firm conclusions impossible, fragmentary evidence suggests that the second-generation churches witnessed similar levels of contrition and repentance as the first. In Boston, for example, a majority of offenders confessed their sins in the 1670s, while in Charlestown around half repented. Even in the fractious First Church of Rowley, nearly every transgression recorded resulted in an acknowledgment of wrongdoing before the church.[57]

The sincerity of second-generation repentances is difficult to assess, given that few statements of confession remain for analysis. But one rare example gleaned from the Charlestown church records suggests that members' repentances—though often written out instead of delivered orally—were based upon the same assumptions as in previous decades. In 1678 the church convinced Solomon Phips to repent for "sinful contention" with John Fowle. Phips admitted to engaging in "an open Scandalous Quarrel in the High way" where his "behavior was very unchristian and unfit both in Words and Deeds to the Just offense of Sober and Godly persons."[58]

While Phips did not rehearse every step in the morphology of repentance as Richard Wayte had in 1640,[59] his statement nonetheless contained the same two essential components of repentance: the notions that sin was offensive because it offended God and that true repentance sprang from God's grace. Phips thus requested prayers "that I may Adorn that Holy Gospel which I feare may have suffered by my former foolish and sinful Demeanour" and asked the congregation to "pray to God that of his Infinite mercy, he will, for the sake of Jesus Christ pardon my Iniquity and purge away my Sinn, And Give me grace for the future Soe to watch over my Spirit, my Tongue, and Actions."[60]

The disrespect that some churchgoers might show for their neighbors or their superiors, in sum, should not be confused with a general lay disregard for Congregational church practices, which most churchgoers continued to regard as ordinances of God. Similarly, squabbles with the local minister should not be confused with contempt for the ministry generally. While many lay people were less hesitant to challenge their own minister on questions of church government, most believed that their local elder, more so than the ministry as a whole, could be mistaken on points of church order. In Rowley, an offender refused to submit to his church in 1677, affirming that "as to both of his offences he was not convinced of any evil in them, but if he might have five Elders to give their judgments if they said he offended he should submit." Nine years earlier, a significant minority in Rowley had dissented from a vote to admit several candidates who had announced their intention to leave town within a few months. According to pastor Samuel Phillips, three neighboring ministers, who, "by God's providence were there at the time," offered "their judgment that we ought not for the forementioned reason to keep them out of church fellowship" and "upon this concurrent judgment of the Elders the Church did yield that [the candidates] should come upon trial for their admission."[61]

Relative to the eighteenth century, congregations rarely refused to heed the advice of neighboring elders and ministerial councils. In the wake of the division of the Boston First Church, ministers were virtually unanimous in the need for local congregations to accept voluntarily council decisions. And with but a few prominent exceptions, congregations complied, willing to accept from a council what they would not accept from the local minister. The first decades of the eighteenth century, as we shall see, witnessed an erosion of the authority of councils, and the ministry in general, because councils contradicted one another, or were clearly mistaken, or suffered internal divisions. Such disagreement further eroded the understanding that church government in all its particulars flowed inevitably from the Bible.[62]

Though local ministers suffered from a general decline of deference in governing their churches, the significance of this development thus remained limited during the seventeenth century. Previous historians have suggested, in contrast, that mutual suspicions between some churchgoers and their ministers motivated clergymen to separate themselves from their degenerate flocks by emphasizing a sacerdotal conception of the clergy, looking to apostolic succession, rather than the call of the church, as the source of their authority. The creation of the Boston Association in 1690—a regular ministerial assembly that discussed questions of doctrine and discipline—represented one outcome of this trend. Other manifestations were evident in the decline of lay ordinations and the demise of the office of lay elder within individual churches.[63]

Though a sacerdotal conception of the ministry and a cultural separation between ministers and lay people did begin to emerge during this period, previous accounts have overstated the significance and influence of these changes in the second generation. The cultural separation between ministers and lay people was a gradual process. The emergence of a genuine division between elite and popular religious culture—a division that was never "complete" in colonial New England—would not become significant until the first decades of the next century. While in the 1720s, for instance, some ministers were reluctant to share the government of their churches with lay elders,[64] Salem's second-generation minister refused to rule the church *without* a lay elder. Second-generation ministers also demanded the election of ruling elders in Roxbury, and in Dorchester the minister allowed himself to be outnumbered when the church elected two ruling elders in 1701. In Newbury, a council of ministers and lay representatives recommended that the church elect two lay elders to help stabilize church affairs.[65] Several other large and prestigious churches continued to employ ruling elders; even in those churches where the office fell into disuse other "worthy laymen" played a prominent role in assisting the minister in government.[66]

Ministers also continued to insist that worthy laymen accompany them as church representatives to synods and councils. In Rowley, several councils contained as many lay delegates as ministers. At the Reforming Synod of 1679, ministers refused to commence deliberations until every church was represented by lay delegates. Ministerial efforts to separate themselves from the laity into their own classis, in short, remained largely insignificant until the eighteenth century.[67]

Though mutual suspicions between ministers and members continued to rise in the late seventeenth century, it bears repeating that much church contention was fueled by individual and community conflict, and was not lay-clerical in nature. Local church divisions often arose even in the absence of a minister. Ministerial candidate Peter Thatcher informed the lay people of Milton that their internal squabbling had discouraged ministers from settling there: "[T]hose Lamentable animosityes and divisions which hath been in the place . . . hath occasioned your unsettlement until now."[68] The Taunton church experienced a bitter fight over admissions procedures in 1665, a date when the church did not have a minister; likewise, the Danvers church was notoriously strife-ridden prior to the pastorate of Samuel Parris.[69]

Even when ministers suffered direct congregational attacks over issues of church government, the battle lines were almost never drawn along a strict lay-clerical axis. Many of the worst lay-clerical squabbles saw lay majorities side with the minister. In both Rowley and Chelmsford, as we have seen, several members accused the minister of usurping lay privileges, but in both cases, majorities rejected the accusations.[70] Scattered cries of ministerial "tyranny" accompanied the debates over the Halfway Covenant, and there is little question but that similar fears continued to develop in the second generation. But lay concerns over ministerial encroachment, though more frequent, did not become widespread or fully articulated among critics until the early 1700s and beyond, when ministers overtly threatened lay privileges.

Finally, it is important to remember that the decline of ministerial prestige in local church affairs applied largely to church government. The vast majority of lay attacks upon the ministry during the late seventeenth century concerned procedural issues, not theology: in the pulpit, ministers still reigned supreme.[71] Notwithstanding the emergence of Quakers and Baptists, few "radicals" emerged from within Massachusetts churches. Arguably, the elders suffered fewer major theological divisions in the second half of the seventeenth century than their counterparts had in the first generation. Ministers who came under fire over issues of church order still commanded respect and affection from their congregations. At the height of lay-clerical squabbling in Rowley, Samuel Phillips received an invitation to assume another pastorate, providing the church with a perfect opportunity to unload the embattled minister in an amicable fashion. But the congregation—including Phillips's most bitter adversaries—adamantly refused to part with their minister.[72]

While rising individualism, a decline in deference, and diminished covenantal piety were clearly evident in the second half of the seventeenth century, it is important to maintain a measure of proportion and balance in assessing the significance of these changes. Churches certainly suffered from more quarreling and a wider variety of conflict in the last third of the seventeenth century than in the founding period. But Clifford K. Shipton has estimated that the period from 1721–1740 witnessed more than three times the number of serious church divisions than the period from 1680–1720. Some churches, like the First Church of Beverly, gathered in 1667, kept careful church records that contain little evidence of conflict; many other churches enjoyed a relative calm in comparison to the storms that would strike prior to and during the Great Awakening. As Increase Mather observed, churchgoers continued to regard the "ordinances" as a principal means of attaining grace in the later seventeenth century; for all its difficulties, Massachusetts still owned "both the faith and order of the Gospel."[73] Nevertheless, ministers still saw a need to restore lay confidence in the clergy and to reaffirm the role of church government in maintaining harmony. They found that source of cohesion and higher authority in the founders' crowning achievement: the *Cambridge Platform*.

7

Declension and Reform

WRITING IN 1679, Increase Mather reminded readers that a number of "precious souls" remained "in every Congregation" in Massachusetts. Given the alarming changes apparent in the late seventeenth century, most ministers took little heart in the remnants of godliness that Mather detected. The new generation of churchgoers was obviously less respectful and more contentious than the founders, developments that could be explained, ministers insisted, only by a decline in popular religiosity. In less confident moments, even Mather acknowledged bluntly that "the present Generation in New England is lamentably degenerate."[1] In general, ministers observed, the laity profited so little from the means of grace as to appear "sermon proof." In 1683, Samuel Torrey of Weymouth mournfully observed that "there is little or nothing of the Life of Religion to be seen or appearing either in the Frame or Way, Hearts, or Lives of the generality of the professors of it. And that which remains thereof, *ready to die!*"[2]

Like the seventeenth-century clergy, numerous historians have attempted to explain the developments we have seen in this period—community conflict, church squabbling, declining deference, and rising individualism—by asserting that second-generation churchgoers were simply less religious than their predecessors. Described most eloquently by Perry Miller, the related processes of a "declension" in lay spirituality and a secularization of New England's religious culture have been analyzed by scholars for decades. Though certainly weather-beaten after nearly a half century of debate, the topic still commands a surprising amount of attention from historians: Stephen Foster, Virginia DeJohn Anderson, Michael G. Hall, Theodore Dwight Bozeman, Jack P. Greene, and David D. Hall have all addressed questions of declension and lay religiosity in recent years.[3]

The topic is central to the subject of church government in that historians have pointed to this purported decline in lay religiosity as the root cause of waning commitment to the ideals of the church covenant, an explanation that differs little from the seventeenth-century clergy's. This argument is by nature circular: historians explain the decline in covenantal piety with reference to declining lay religiosity; they "prove" this declining religiosity, in turn, by pointing to waning commitment to covenant ideals.

A closer analysis of most of the symptoms that ministers and later historians have seized upon to advance this concept of a decline in lay piety suggests that the thesis vastly oversimplifies developments influencing church life during this era. Such an examination points not to a sudden decline in lay religiosity but to a gradual shift in its locus. What historians have often identified as a secularization of the culture in fact constituted only the first symptoms of a century-long shift toward the privatization of religion, as churchgoers gradually became more focused on the individual religious experience and less concerned with communitarianism, covenantal ideals, and, by the time of the Great Awakening, Congregationalism itself.[4] Historians have mistakenly confused a decline of covenantal piety, in short, with a decline in personal religious commitment that, the records suggest, in fact wavered little throughout most of the colonial era.

Perhaps the linchpin of the standard declension argument rests with the simple fact that fewer churchgoers in the second generation joined their churches in full communion. Miller, Darrett B. Rutman, and numerous other historians have asserted that declining admissions and the need for the Halfway Covenant represented irrefutable proof that the second generation was less "gracious" than the first, but historians have never been unanimous on this issue. Edmund S. Morgan speculated that the Halfway Covenant and the decline in full membership rates need not necessarily be interpreted as evidence of a declension in personal piety. "The very fact that the half-way covenant was needed," he argued, "may be testimony, not to the decline of religion, but to the rise of an extraordinary religious scrupulosity. . . . The second generation of Puritans may have become so sophisticated in the morphology of conversion that they rejected, as inconclusive, religious experiences that would have driven their parents unhesitatingly into church membership."[5]

In a later overview of the debate, James Hoopes supported Miller's view. Historians will never be able to prove quantitatively that the second generation was as "pious" as the first. Hoopes pointed out that "the religiosity of an age is exceedingly difficult to measure . . . participation in communion was external behavior which, though quantifiable . . . does not necessarily indicate an identical subjective state (pietistical emotion) in every communicant." Miller's view, at least, "has the strength of being based on verbal evidence," such as the ministers' jeremiads and complaints of lay contention.[6] On the other hand, Rutman and others have asserted that "there is little in the extant material of the mid-seventeenth century to support the musings about 'scrupulosity' and religious sophistication from which Morgan derives his idea of a heightened interest," a position Bozeman supported over twenty-five years later.[7]

In claiming that virtually no records remain to dispute their declension thesis or to support notions of an enduring piety, historians have repeated the same errors they have committed in discussing church government generally: they have ignored sources pertaining to the laity and popular religion, and they have relied instead solely upon selectively chosen comments drawn from the ministerial community. None of these historians has based speculations of waning lay religiosity upon an examination of extant church records or lay religion itself. Contrary to the assertions of several writers, sufficient "verbal evidence" remains from both lay and clerical sources to suggest that significant numbers of nonmembers were not so much "degenerate" as they were holding back from full communion—and the ministers knew it.

Hall has presented convincing evidence to indicate that by the first decades of the eighteenth century ministers fully accepted the concept of lay scrupulousness. Evidence drawn from the voices of both ministers and lay people suggests that this phenomenon can be traced even farther back, into the last third of the seventeenth century at the very least. Writing in 1696, John Danforth described halfway members as those "that *pretend* not to be able to examine and prove themselves and discern the Lords body." Earlier, Cotton Mather noted that "Doubts and Fears" prevented churchgoers from seeking full communion. He later cited the public testimony of grace as central to the problem, describing the test as "a *Scare-Crow* to keep men out of the *Temple*." Meanwhile, Samuel Parris preached several sermons in Danvers in which he identified and condemned lay scrupulousness.[8]

The church records contain many lay voices bearing upon the spiritual estates of both halfway members and members in full communion; previously ignored, these voices support the observations of Danforth and Mather. As far back as 1668, for example, a Dorchester mother brought her child to the church for baptism but because she judged herself not "worthy," she decided she "durst not adventure" upon the Lord's Supper. The same year, several lay people informed Beverly pastor John Hale that they wished to hold back from full communion "upon sence of their present unfitness." Beverly's Thomas Patch owned the covenant in 1668, but "upon fears of his own unfitness proceeded no further." Patch became a full member a year later.[9]

Several churchgoers in Beverly refused to participate in the Lord's Supper even though they had qualified to join the church *in full communion,* providing powerful evidence of the prevalence and strength of lay scrupulousness. In 1687, one Mrs. Thorndick made "profession publickly of her faith and repentance," but "not beeing clear in her owne spirit did not at Present proceed to the Lords Supper." Mark Haskall, who qualified for full communion in 1686, stood back from the Lord's Supper for nearly five years, "being not clear in his owne spirit." He "first came to the Lords Supper" in 1691. That same year Mary Trow "came to the Lords Supper having before made profession of faith and repentance" three years earlier, in 1688. In 1692, pastor Hale noted that Mary Ellenwood was "baptized upon the profession of her faith and repentance; yet desiers to waite a while before she comes to the Lords Supper."[10]

Similar doubts afflicted one George Barborn of Dedham. In relating his conversion experience to the church in 1710, Barborn explained that he

> had many thoughts of joining to the church of Christ in this place, and to draw near to God in special ordinances: but was discouraged in the consideration of that text of scripture 1 Cor. 11. 29. I thought in the consideration thereof that if I should come unworthily to the Lords Table it would be far worse for me in the day of judgement than if I had never come, and therefore I dare not venture it.

The actions of these churchgoers in Beverly and Dedham strongly suggest that scrupulousness, not declining personal piety, prevented many candidates from joining their churches in full communion.[11]

Upon recognizing that churchgoers capable of achieving membership were refusing to come forward, ministers took procedural steps to cajole recalcitrants. In 1684, the Salem minister acknowledged that churchgoers had refused to seek full membership even though they were undoubtedly qualified. He reminded the members of "their duty of observing and Encouraging such as they knew to be Godly to joyn the Church." Suspecting that a number of applicants for halfway membership were in fact converted, the Bradford minister recommended that all candidates first take a test for full membership "to see whether [their] questions and objections might not be answered, their fears removed and their spirits encourged" and, that failing, accept admission on a halfway basis.[12]

Some ministers no longer waited upon candidates to come to them in private but instead tracked down likely prospects and interviewed candidates in their own homes.[13] An extraordinary entry in the Chelmsford church records details the actual results of this sort of examination, furnishing another striking piece of evidence pertaining to the religiosity of the second generation. In 1663, the church voted "that from this time forth the pastor taking one of the said brethren with him (at least) shall take some opportunity to inquire into the spiritual estate of the children of the church grown up to years of discretion . . . and examine them touching their knowledge of the doctrine of faith, touching their experiences." Fiske recorded brief summaries of these meetings, providing a rare glimpse of the spiritual condition of the "unconverted" youth. The Chelmsford minister discovered that some of the children were already converted, and even those who had not achieved grace were far from simply "degenerate." Of the thirteen examined, Fiske described only Jonathan Bates as "very ignorant." He judged seven competent in "understanding" and five either converted or on the verge of "closure with Christ." Of the five, only one had recently approached Fiske to seek admission. The other four—including Fiske's own son—had neglected even to begin the process of seeking admission by coming before the elders. A similar case appeared in Salem. In 1665, a woman approached the elders for a test of her "understanding," so that she might have her daughter baptized. During the test, the elders discovered that the woman was converted and propounded her for full communion.[14]

A related symptom of lay scrupulosity appeared in the increasing unwillingness of members and nonmembers to speak before the church. This shyness required the elders and their churches to alter the procedural requirements in admissions and repentances. On several occasions, young men indicated that they would join their church in full communion only on condition that the elders would write down their relations in private and then read them to the church. A Chelmsford candidate refused to go even that far. He told pastor Fiske that he would join the church only if the minister wrote down his relation not only in private but in the absence of any lay representatives. In Salem, the minister was forced to read a candidate's relation because the man had "not an audible voyce." By the 1680s, most churches began to allow men and women alike to deliver their relations to the elders in private, who then read them to the congregation.[15]

Foster has advanced a useful hypothesis to explain these developments, suggesting that the easing of admissions procedures reflected a larger effort on the part of the second generation to maintain a proper balance between the maintenance of church purity and the need for an inclusive church. These issues of inclusiveness and sectarianism did not neatly divide laity and clergy, and any changes in admissions procedures appeared with the consent—if not at the demand—of the members. Notwithstanding continued lay grousing over the Halfway Covenant, for example, ministers had convinced three-fourths of churches to practice the measure by the 1690s, and both clergy and laity made clear that in making their churches more inclusive they did not intend to sacrifice purity. Halfway members, as we have seen, did bring themselves under church watch, and churches were careful to subject them to church discipline.[16]

Though churches refused to compromise purity in adopting the Halfway Covenant, they recognized that an overemphasis upon sectarianism had created an obstacle that continued to discourage diffident but otherwise pious candidates from seeking admission. Public testimonials, which some churches had already eased in the 1660s, consequently came under even more careful scrutiny. The First Church of Charlestown shifted admissions requirements by mutual consent of the laity and elders. In 1685, the church "voted and concurred" that "*men's relations*" would be "for the future read." The church's justification for the reform, the minister noted, was that the candidates' "own pronouncing" had been "constantly found inconvenient." Apparently little debate accompanied the change; the vote passed unanimously or, as ministers were fond of writing, "nemine contradicente." At Boston's Old South Church, the laity took a decisive step on its own to alter church procedures. Convinced that requirements for public testimony discouraged prospective candidates from seeking full communion, the laity quickly passed a formal church act upon Pastor Thomas Thatcher's death in 1678, stipulating that henceforth all conversion testimonials would be written and read to the congregation. They then requested that their new minister, Samuel Willard, assent to the clause prior to his ordination.[17]

Anticipating an innovation that would become widespread in the eighteenth century, the members and elders of the First Church of Salem jointly agreed to jettison public testimonials after a candidate openly disputed the scriptural grounds for the practice. Again, the move appears to have been initiated by the laity. In 1665, one Bartholmew Gidney "propounded his desire of partaking of the Lords Supper: saying he had submitted unto Examination of the Pastor and publikely professed his Faith and owning of the Covenant, he saw not that anything more was required of him from Scripture." After the issue was "spoken to by the Pastors and severall brethren," the church consented to Gidney's motion, "though with respect to others it was left to future consideration." A month later the pastor introduced four candidates who hoped to participate in the Lord's Supper without offering an oral public confession: "The Pastor expressed that after his examination of them, he did approve of them, as able to examine themselves and discern the Lords body . . . he knew not of any Church-barre according to the Scriptures that might hinder them from partaking of the Lords Supper." Several lay people "did speak for it," two "peaceably expressed their dissent" but indicated "that they would not oppose" the mind of the church, and the rest "professed their consent" to the change.[18]

The members' shyness similarly forced churches to alter disciplinary procedures, permitting written testimonials of repentance to replace spoken ones. The Chelmsford church adopted this change in 1662, Salem in 1664, Dorchester in 1679, and Topsfield in 1686. Again, churches altered the procedure to accommodate the laity. In Salem, the church was forced to readmit two women charged with "uncleanness" largely on the testimony of "several brethren" because the offenders "could speak little themselves." Similarly, Samuell Blake, also charged with the "sin of fornecation before marredg," admitted his offense and "made some kind of acknowledgment but his voice was soe low that scarce any herd that litle which he spake except a few which stood Clos by him."[19]

Though even in the 1630s some members found it difficult to speak before the church in admissions and disciplinary cases, the problem was far more serious in the second generation. The records offer little hard evidence to explain this development. Most likely, members no longer feared questions from the audience, which had become infrequent by the second half of the seventeenth century. Moreover, some members scheduled to face the church requested the exclusion of nonmembers from admissions and disciplinary hearings, even though nonmembers were not entitled to speak during or after the proceedings.[20] The second generation faced a new challenge in that many appealed for admission or forgiveness before an audience that included their parents, a requirement that many of the founders never faced. Consequently younger members had less sense of their speaking before spiritual equals. Historians have also demonstrated that even after their parents died, second-generation churchgoers perfected the art of "ancestor worship" and the myth of their parents' heroic past, exaggerating out of all proportion the first generation's standards of godliness and absence of scandal.[21] Ministers unwittingly exacerbated the problems of scrupulosity in offering public statements purporting that "the present Generation in New-England, as to the body of it, in respect of the practice and power of Godliness, is far short of those whom God saw meet to improve in laying the foundations of his Temple here."[22]

In fact, there is little reason to believe that the second generation fell "far short" of the first in either the practice or power of godliness. Though some churchgoers demonstrated waning commitment to the church covenant, most continued to hold the Congregational Way sacred. And while covenantal piety may have declined, little evidence remains to support the concept of a general decline in personal piety. To the contrary, churchgoers remained deeply concerned with questions of salvation and the soul—so concerned that, as Morgan hypothesized long ago, many refused to seek membership in order to avoid the dire consequences of "partaking unworthily."

Notwithstanding the evidence of lay scrupulousness and enduring piety, ministers clearly perceived a decline in religiosity among ordinary churchgoers. This perception, historians have suggested, led clergymen to redefine the balance of church power in the late seventeenth century in order to reduce lay authority in the local decision-making process.[23] Certainly, rumblings could be heard within the clerical community concerning the need for more order within Massachusetts Bay churches. Again and again ministers lambasted lay people for their failure to submit to the elders. "Look into the congregations," Samuel Willard complained, "and there you shall see . . . Ministers despised, their Office questioned, their Authority cast off."[24] For some, the solution to this problem lay in coercion. "Men will simply not obey the Gospel," William Hubbard wrote in 1684, "[w]ithout some strength from the civil arm."[25] A decade later, sentiments began to surface again in the clerical community to bind individual churches to the conclusions of synods. "*Synods*," Cotton Mather declared,

> being of *Apostolical example*, recommended as a necessary Ordinance, it is
> but reasonable, that their Judgment be acknowledged DECISIVE, in the Affairs
> for which they are ordained; and to deny them the Power of such a Judgment,
> is to render a necessary Ordinance *of non effect*.[26]

Mather also claimed new powers for the ministry in local church affairs: "The Pastor of a church may by himself *Authoritatively* suspend from the *Lords-Table* a Brother accused of suspected *Scandall*, till the Matter, may and should be regularly examined." Moreover, Mather insisted, in a dramatic claim of ministerial authority, "the *Elders* of the church have a *Negative* on the *Votes* of the *Brethren*."[27]

Like that of most of his colleagues, Cotton Mather's bark was worse than his bite when it came to issues of church government and lay liberties. Despite his fulminations on ministerial authority, Mather was almost deferential to the laity in governing his own church. Though he favored the Halfway Covenant, for example, he refused to implement the measure in his Second Church of Boston because *two* members scrupled.[28] The example is instructive of the caution required in assessing the ministers' stance: historians have indeed demonstrated that some second-generation ministers like Mather *claimed* increasing powers for themselves.[29] But relying upon scattered ministerial assertions rather than analysis of actual practices within the churches, they have provided little evidence to indicate whether ministers even attempted to implement the measures they discussed in their writings and in their private meetings; nor have they demonstrated that the "authoritarian" sentiments expressed by a handful of ministers were widely shared among the clergy.

The crises of the 1670s and 1680s—rising community contention, church disorder, King Philip's War, the loss of the charter—did indeed force New Englanders to take stock in their larger mission and identity, and they included church government in this reexamination.[30] But although some ministers responded to these developments by supporting institutional reforms in the New England Way, most recognized that lay people would likely resist unwelcome changes; they anticipated opposition from their fellow clergymen as well. Making a virtue of necessity, most ministers ultimately attempted to ease tensions within their churches not by pushing for novel coercive measures but by reaffirming their commitment to the Congregational Way.

In their public proclamations on the topic, ministers continued to invest the ordinances with a sacred significance, urging hearers to recommit themselves to the Congregational system that stood at the center of New England's national identity. While railing at the laity's declension, John Wilson urged his listeners to remember that Congregationalism stood as the foundation stone of the Puritan mission:

> [C]onsider, what came you into this wilderness for? did you come to gaze upon one another? No, you came to see, and hear the great Prophet, even the Lord Jesus in his Ministers, that you might have the Ordinances of God in his Churches rightly gathered, and the holy Sacraments rightly administered.[31]

Similarly, in 1670, Samuel Danforth described New England's "errand into the wilderness" as the perpetuation of the "Liberty to walk in the Faith of the Gospel with all good Conscience according to the Order of the Gospel." The Congregational Way, he added, continued to define New England: "What is it that *distinguisheth New-England* from other Colonies and Plantations in *America*?" he asked. "Not our transportation over the *Atlantick* Ocean, but the *Ministry* of God's faithful Prophets, and the fruition of his holy *Ordinances*."[32] Urian Oakes affirmed that the Reformation had been brought to its "highest step" in the Congregational Way, reminding listeners of their duty to perpetuate the one true church:

You have been *as a City upon an hill* (though in a remote and obscure Wilderness) *as a Candle in the Candlestick that gives light to the whole House* (world I mean) as to the pattern of God's House, the Form and Fashion and Outgoings and Incomings thereof: served as an example to many but was ignored by others.[33]

The loss of the Massachusetts charter served only to enhance the significance of the "ordinances," as ministers quickly reminded listeners that the Puritans had ventured to the New World not to establish a new form of civil government but to reform further Christ's true church. After the restoration of the charter, Cotton Mather averred, "If any one ask, unto what the Sudden Matchless thriving of *New-England* may be ascribed? It is the Blessing of God upon the *Church-Order,* for the sake whereof . . . this Plantation was first Erected." The mutual condemnation that lay people and ministers heaped upon one another for "decline" from this sacred "pattern of God's house" demonstrated that the Congregational Way remained at the very core of the Puritans' self-awareness and sense of mission.[34]

Notwithstanding these spoken proclamations, the real test of clerical intent came at the Reforming Synod of 1679: if the ministers hoped to modify the Congregational Way, here was their forum. Convinced that a number of "evils" and the general "dying interest in religion" had brought King Philip's War and other "judgements on New England," Increase Mather called upon the elders to isolate the specific offenses that had "changed the tenour of [God's] Dispensations" toward the colony and to consider "what is to be donn so that those evills may be reformed." That the General Court and the ministers readily agreed to assemble a formal synod testifies to the crisis atmosphere of the times. Previous synods convened only for matters of utmost concern: the Antinomian controversy, the *Cambridge Platform,* and the Halfway Covenant.[35]

Though little appreciated by previous historians, the topic of church government and the erosion of lay-clerical relations stood at the center of the Reforming Synod's agenda. Well before the synod, the First Church of Dorchester had acknowledged that neglect in "watching over one another" and a want of "church dissapline" represented New England's "provoking sins." The General Court suggested institutional redress for church discord, specifically urging the elders to consider "the revisall of the platforme of discipline agreed upon by the churches, 1647."[36]

The elders summarily rejected the Court's recommendation. Far from attempting to abridge lay rights, the ministers, once they came together to speak as a whole, accepted Increase Mather's charge to extend an olive branch to the laity. Sensing that ministerial descriptions of the laity's "dying interest in religion" were just as overblown as lay charges of clerical "prelacy," the elders utilized the Reforming Synod to clear the air and to ease the atmosphere of mutual condemnation.

The elders' first formal action at the Reforming Synod hinted at their larger strategy in attempting to cope with an increasingly uncooperative laity. Mirroring their response to the Antinomian affair in the 1630s, the ministers began the proceedings by offering a powerful reaffirmation of the members' rights, in an effort to rekindle the spirit of mutuality and lay-clerical cooperation that served as the foundation of Congregational church government. Upon assembling the delegates, the clergy discovered that "several Churches had only sent Elders [i.e., ministers] and not brethren with them" as representatives. They immediately halted all proceedings. "Noe Vote should passe," they declared, until each church sent lay delegates. The ministers then composed a strong defense of lay participation in synods, which they wrote into the preface of their *Result* of the proceedings, and in turn read before every congregation.[37]

> That which is expressed in the Platform of Discipline, concerning this particular, was assented unto [by the Synod], *viz.* that not only the Elders but other Messengers ought to be delegated by the churches, and so to have their Suffrages in such Assemblyes. . . . the interest of the People in such Conventions is strongly asserted and evinced by our *Juel, Whitaker, Parker,* and others against Papists and Prelates, who maintain that *Laicks* (as they call them) are not fit matter for a Synod.[38]

Once the churches were properly represented, the elders began serious deliberations, detailing the provoking evils and offering elaborate measures for reformation. Their reform program was not based on a forward-looking attempt to alter New England worship and practice. Rather, the elders proposed an ingenious strategy to develop innovative methods to recreate for the present generation the spiritual experiences of the venerated founders and to restore the churches to their primitive foundations. "If New-England remember whence she is fallen, and doe the first works," Increase Mather wrote, "there is reason to hope that it shall be better with us then at our beginnings." Ministers addressed declining covenantal piety by calling upon churches to read their covenants aloud and to reaffirm their covenant obligations publicly. This practice of "covenant renewal," in effect, recreated the founding experience of the church, an exercise that the second generation had never enjoyed. As Charles E. Hambricke-Stowe has pointed out, covenant renewal also served as a vehicle for spiritual reformation and a tonic for the perceived "devotional crisis" within the churches.[39]

While historians have amply described the second prong in the elders' assault on sin at the Reforming Synod—the implementation of strict sumptuary legislation—they have ignored a third component that closely mirrored covenant renewal.[40] Acknowledging that much church turmoil issued from misunderstandings over church government, the elders attempted to ease tensions by reaffirming their commitment to the *Cambridge Platform.* Increase Mather sensed that lay people were more suspicious of their local ministers than of the clergy as a whole. They might therefore accept from the collected assembly what they would not accept from their own pastor. "Coming from a *Synod* as their joint concurring Testimony," Mather wrote, the elders' declaration of support for the *Platform* "will carry more Authority with it, than if one man only, or many in their single capacityes, should speak the same things." After reading and discussing the *Platform*, "each Paragraph being duely and distinctly weighed," the elders announced that they "unanimously approve of the said Platform, for the substance of it, desiring that the churches may continue stedfast in the order of the Gospel according to what is therin declared from the Word of God."[41]

Mather urged the elders to go beyond a simple ministerial assent to the *Cambridge Platform*. Church government remained, after all, a joint venture shared by ministers and members, and the current generation, he observed, had never "made any public confession or profession of the faith and order of the Gospel" as the founders had in the late 1640s. Nor had the new generation enjoyed the benefit of their ministers' biblical justification of the Congregational Way. Mather consequently recommended that the laity read and endorse the document as well. That way, Mather wrote, "both Churches and Elders may have a more right and full understanding one of another." The General Court subsequently ordered a reprinting of the *Cambridge Platform* "for the benefit of these churches in present and after times," and ministers agreed that every church should formally declare its "adherence unto the Faith and order of the Gospel according to . . . the Platform of Discipline."[42]

The assumption behind the clergy's plan was that churchgoers would overlook their suspicions of their current ministers while honoring the legacy of the heroic founders. This assumption proved correct. Lay people throughout the colony recognized the *Platform* as the crowning achievement of the fathers, not the creation of a crop of second-generation clergymen who seemed all too prone to "defection." As such they viewed the founders' statements on church order in a way they refused to view the conclusions of their own ministers: as tantamount to "the Word of God."

Accordingly, congregations assembled throughout the Bay to consider the ecclesiastical "constitution." Late in 1679, Josiah Flynt gathered his Dorchester church in a special meeting "to read the platforme of Church dissepline to see how farre the Church did agree with it in their practice at which time ther weer 8 or nine Chapters read over and the rest left till another time." In Reading, the elders presented the church with a printed copy of the *Platform* and set aside several days for "perusing the Booke." The minister then "distinctly read" the *Platform* "in their hearing," and the laity unanimously "approved of it for the substance of it to be according to the word of God." Throughout the colony, churches similarly endorsed the *Platform* and the *Result* of the Reforming Synod unanimously and with little debate.[43]

Designed in part to "clear" the elders from "the suspicion and scandal of defection" from the standards of the fathers, the "*Platform* renewal" was a brilliantly conceived and well-executed exercise in public relations. At a point when clerical disagreements and scattered threats upon lay liberties forced jittery churchgoers to question the clergy's motives regarding church government, the elders' strong show of support for Congregationalism helped assure the members that both individually and collectively the clergy entertained no plans of encroaching upon lay rights or advancing sinful innovations. Virtually every elder in the Bay formally endorsed the *Platform* as a product drawn "from the Word of God." Those differences that existed among ministers, they insisted, only concerned particulars.[44]

The importance of the public *Platform* renewal extended beyond its utility in reacquainting the laity with Congregational provisions. Congregational reratification of the *Platform* reinforced for a new generation of churchgoers the understanding that church government was based upon their own free consent. Churchgoers were further reminded that the *Platform* served as a guarantee of their ecclesiastical rights and a set of higher laws that strictly limited the authority of their elders. Drawn from the Bible, ratified by the fathers, and steeped in tradition, the *Cambridge Platform* became reinvested with a sacred significance as the laity's ecclesiastical constitution, Bill of Rights, and last line of defense against any possible ministerial encroachment.

Beyond its importance in easing tensions among lay people and refocusing the attention of ministers and churchgoers upon New England's larger mission, the Reforming Synod established Increase Mather as Massachusetts's most influential religious leader. Just as John Cotton embodied the foundation process for the fathers, Mather assumed the mantle as Congregationalism's staunchest and most influential defender during the second generation. In the face of repeated ministerial cries for Congregational reform in the late seventeenth and early eighteenth centuries, Mather held tenaciously to the *Cambridge Platform*, strongly defended limitations on clerical authority, and upheld the rights of the laity. Firmly committed to the founders' vision of a system of government grounded upon mutuality and trust among ministers and their flocks, Mather torpedoed numerous threats to that understanding, including, as we shall see, his own son's *Proposals* to "reform" the Congregational Way.[45]

Though ministers offered a strong public defense of lay liberties at the Reforming Synod of 1679, previous writers have dismissed their actions as subterfuge and rhetoric. Pointing to the fact that the elders assented to only the "substance" of the *Cambridge Platform*, for example, Hall suggested that the clergy's commitment to that document was "strangely equivocal." In actual practice, we have been informed, ministers attempted to curb their unmanageable congregations by restricting important liberties such as the right to add consent to clerical decisions. "It is clear," Hall concluded, "that the brethren were right in accusing the ministers of 'presbyterian' intentions."[46] A question remains, then, whether in actual practice clergymen sought to redefine the balance of church order at the local level and, importantly, whether lay people continued to participate actively in church government as they had for the previous half century.

The church records demonstrate unequivocally that, while some ministers groused at lay unruliness and at least contemplated institutional solutions, Massachusetts Bay churches adopted few changes in the second half of the seventeenth century that served to alter significantly lay participation in church government. The ministers assented to only "the substance" of the *Platform* in 1679 not because their commitment to it was "equivocal" but because by 1679 church practices varied from the exact language of the document in several particulars: ministers now deemed it permissible to administer the sacraments in neighboring churches, ordinations were more often performed by fellow ministers than by laymen, fewer churches employed ruling elders, and public professions of faith for church admission were usually delivered to the elders in private and then read to the church.[47]

These practices, which had evolved gradually over the decades, evoked little protest or even debate from the laity, for they did not represent a meaningful abridgement of the members' liberties. In general, the church records indicate that lay people continued to prevent ministers from practicing undesirable "innovations" that stood to compromise their rights. As one Massachusetts Presbyterian complained in 1670, the churches continued to be "such a heavy stone at the ministers legs that they cannot fly their own course."[48]

Nowhere did the laity more dramatically illustrate to the elders the explosive consequences of clerical efforts to "fly their own course" than in Newbury, where renewed friction stemming from the Presbyterian sympathies of the ministers and the stiff resolve of many lay people finally ignited a conflagration that eventually became the talk of land.[49] The Newbury elders, James Noyes and Thomas Parker, had leaned toward Presbyterianism since the church was gathered in the 1635, condemning Congregationalism as "an epidemical disease . . . a democratical government." But after a series of confrontations with their congregation and the Bay elders during the 1640s, the Newbury ministers apparently suppressed their desire to "assume the power [of government] wholly to themselves" and managed to oversee church affairs without "any *considerable* trouble" for over twenty years.[50]

By 1665, John Woodbridge, also a Presbyterian sympathizer, had begun to assist Parker, filling in for Noyes, who had died nearly a decade earlier. Not surprisingly, the church never ordained Woodbridge; indeed, given his disdain for Congregationalism, it is difficult to determine why the church hired him even temporarily. Apparently Woodbridge and Parker sought to avoid confrontation over issues of church authority until the newcomer had been well entrenched: Woodbridge's opponents later described the minister as "an intruder, brought in by craft and subtilty, and so kept in, notwithstanding he was voated out twice."[51]

Encouraged by his new ally, Parker began in the late 1660s to argue once again for clerical supremacy in local church affairs. In the absence of the early church records, it is impossible to determine precisely how Parker's sentiments translated into church practices. But court records reveal two areas of lay concern. First, Parker boldly "resolved nothing shall be brought into the church, but it shall be brought first to me, and if I approve of it, it shall be brought in, if I do not approve it, it shall not be brought in." Second, many Newbury members objected to Parker's specific manner of calling for votes, insisting that the minister manipulated silent consent to his own advantage.[52]

Lay dissatisfaction over these practices and the ministers' generally autocratic sentiments left the church deeply divided. As usual, the rift was not purely lay-clerical. Approximately half the church, some of whom had prior connections with Parker in England, supported the minister, pointing out that clergymen had employed silent consent since the founding, just as they had always determined whether controversial cases were sufficiently "ripe" for church consideration. The dissenters, on the other hand, recognized that other ministers in Massachusetts had begun to permit the members to assist them in the resolution of doubtful cases. They insisted upon the same privilege in Newbury and also demanded implementation of the "handy" vote.[53]

As was so often the case in major church divisions, the lay uprising in Newbury was led by an informed and articulate "worthy layman," Mr. Edward Woodman, a merchant, mercer, deputy, town officer, and vendor of "wine and strong water." But the dissenters in Newbury did not consist of an unusually powerful or educated group. Dozens of ordinary churchgoers stood behind Woodman, even though defense of their liberties forced them to defy their ministers, two councils of neighboring elders, and numerous court decisions. Woodman's supporters included ordinary farmers such as William Moody and William Titcomb, the weaver Thomas Browne, the cordwainer Steven Swett, the shoemaker William Ilsley, and Edmund Moores, of whom little is known. Several second-generation "children" such as Benjamin Lowell, Abraham Merrill, and John Bartlet, Jr., also defied the authorities in defense of traditional lay liberties. Only two of the forty-one dissenters merited the title "Mister."[54]

Woodman fired the opening salvo in defense of lay rights, confronting pastor Parker in a public meeting and cursing him as

> an apostate and backslider from the truth, that he would set up a prelacy, and have more power than the pope, for the pope had his council of cardinals, that his practice or actings did not tend to peace or salvation, that he was the cause of all our contention and misery. That you are an apostate and backslider.

For good measure, Woodman added that Parker's principal lay ally, Captain William Gerrish, "was no lover of that truth [and] his gray hairs would stand where captain Gerrish his bald pate would."[55]

The quarterly court admonished Woodman for his outburst. But two magistrates, Samuel Symonds and William Hathorne, dissented from the majority. They justified Woodman, condemning Parker's fundamental assault on lay privileges and the Congregational Way:

> We perceive that a great part (if not a greater part) of that church doe stand for the congregational way of church government and discipline to be exer-

cised amongst them (which is the way the churches here doe professe to the whole world to be the way and the only way according to the gospel of Christ,) and that it is and hath been for a long time a very great burthen and grievance to them, that they have not freedom in that respect, (where there is occasion of actings) as by the word of God they ought to have, and other churches have in this country, and at the beginning their own church also quietly did enjoy for some space of time.[56]

Parker's supporters insisted that the case was not so simple. They protested efforts to "raise an odium" on them as "sacrilegious robbers of the church," and, in a response to the court composed by six laymen, they insisted that the Woodman faction was simply hypersensitive to issues of lay liberty. "Mr. Parker hath been blamed for bringing things of too meane a nature to the churches examination," they claimed, "[a]nd strangers have taken notice of the over much liberty of some in church actings." The difference between the two sides largely concerned "the manner of testifying the assent or dissent of the church, not from any substantial disagreement." Parker's supporters then cited the *Cambridge Platform* in defending the silent vote.[57]

Perhaps emboldened by the support from the two magistrates, Woodman and his supporters decided that they were sufficiently experienced and informed to conduct church business entirely on their own. They proceeded to "meet in a church assembly, act as a church themselves, voting these or those church orders of theirs, send messengers to call any other member before them to give satisfaction to the church for matters offensive to them"—and all this "against the consent and prohibition of their pastor."[58]

Faced with a crisis spinning out of control, the elders convened a council on the third of November, 1669. They admitted that both sides had legitimate grievances, and confessed to "the difficulty and intricacy of the matters before us [and] our own insufficiency to reach the narrows comprehended in your questions and case." They then quickly concluded that the dissenters had acted "irregularly" in acting "as if they were the church." The elders further declared "that all these former irregulars done by them as church acts are null," and naively urged both sides to "study to be quiet" and "become one in the Lord" by adhering to Scripture.[59]

Exulting in his vindication, Parker promptly passed a church censure on Woodman and his assembly. But the dissenters understood Congregational procedures and their rights within them: they protested that the minister had made no effort to seek their repentance, nor had he attempted "any due or regular means to convict" them in a church hearing. Parker therefore stood guilty of breach of covenant, having passed "sentence before judgement, the coarsest proceeding among men." The neighboring elders would eventually uphold the laity's charge.[60]

Several days later, the dissenters, again claiming to be the church, convened to consider formally Parker's offenses. They delivered a "suspension" to the startled pastor on March 16:

[W]e cannot but judge you worthy of blame, and do hereby blame you, and for the restoring of peace to the church we are enforced, though with great grief of heart, to suspend you from acting any thing that doth appertain to your office, in administering seals and sacraments, or matters of government as an officer, until you have given the church satisfaction therewith.

The dissenters did grant Parker the right to "lay prophecize" or preach "as a gifted brother." Two laymen signed the document "in behalf of the church," which then elected ruling elders to supervise further church meetings.[61]

Parker's suspension once again drew the anxious attention of the neighboring elders, who again huddled in council. In their plea for relief, the Newbury dissenters again expressed in unmistakable terms that their actions were rooted in their familiarity with and profound commitment to the Congregational Way.

As concerning church order or discipline[,] we know not what may be against us, for we wholly own that, which the New Testament doth clearly hold forth as the mind of Christ to his church, that which the general court hath established for the synod book, we hold the substance of it. We own Mr. Hooker's Polity, Mr. Mather's catechisme, Mr. Cotton's Keys, for the substance of it. That, which the churches have practised in general with a joint consent as far as we know. Yea that, which hath been New England's glory, in which God hath come nearer to them than to any other people.

"We abide constant to those principles," they vowed, "[a]nd will not turn presbyterians." The "controversy," they repeated "is whether God hath placed the power in the elder, or in the whole church . . . It is denied that the fraternity have anything to do with it, but the minister only" and "such as do not consent hereto are Corahites . . . decliners to levellism . . . a people that nothing will satisfy."[62]

The elders labored to convince both sides to submit to the *Cambridge Platform*, but the truce proved short-lived. The Newbury church encountered a problem that nearly all churches would soon begin to face: the *Platform*, like the Bible itself, was simply too vague to serve as a set of rules for people not committed to getting along. "The platform of discipline," Parker's supporters complained, which the dissenters "agreed should be their rule," nonetheless "proves nothing to them, unless they may be the judges and interpreters of it."[63] Church meetings again broke down in chaos. Parker called four of Woodman's supporters before the church to answer for "irregularities," but

instead of answering, they fell to contradicting their pastor, endeavouring what they could that their charges, which were in writing, might not be read or heard. But when the resolution was that they should be read, instead of hearkening to them, whereby they might understand what they were charged with, that they might give satisfaction[,] they raised an hubbub, knocking, stamping, hemming, gaping, to drown the reading.[64]

Having become the "talk of the country" (one Edward Lumas of Ipswich was haled before the civil authorities for professing that "Mr. Parker of Newbury had sent a letter to the lord arch bishop of Canterbury for help and relief about their troubles"), the case at last wound its way to the General Court. The Court was careful to condemn Woodman's followers for suspending Parker (whose advanced age, at this point, prevented him from further participation in the affair), noting that while "the whole church agreeing may censure an officer," only "a major part" had supported Parker's suspension in Newbury "and that by a very few." But ultimately the civil authorities sided with the dissenters. The Court acknowledged that "the peace and edification of the church of Christ is much promoted and depends upon the amicable close of spirit and united judgment, between the officers and the brethren, the speaker and the hearers." In light of the "distance in judgment in reference to discipline and of affections" the court ordered Woodbridge "not to impose himself or his ministry" upon the First Church of Newbury. The Court further advised the church "to choose a ruling elder or two . . . for the healing of this great breach." Finally, the court strongly affirmed that "our lord Jesus Christ hath given [the members] liberty in voting in all their own concerns" and urged the Newbury church henceforth to take votes as the dissenters demanded, by "the lifting up of hands." Woodbridge quickly resigned and the church hired another minister, whom they kept on trial for nearly two years before deciding to proceed to ordination.[65]

The Newbury affair demonstrated in unmistakable terms the messy consequences of ministerial tampering with lay privileges. Few other ministers, if any, repeated the mistakes of Parker and Woodbridge. In general, lay people exercised as much initiative in church affairs in the late seventeenth century as they ever had. When John Higginson, Jr., took office in Salem in 1660, for example, the first church action required the elders to erase anything in the past church records for which a vote was not explicitly recorded. Lay participation is evident in nearly every entry in the church record book, and throughout Higginson's lengthy tenure, virtually no changes in church procedure were attempted without a church vote.[66]

Topsfield minister Joseph Capen maintained a similar relationship with his members. In 1688, Capen disagreed with his congregation's decision to accept a statement of repentance, but nonetheless kept his silence and allowed the members' judgment to stand. The case involved one William Averell, Jr., who had "fallen under Scandall by irreverent carriage in Ipswich meeting house on a Lecture day in the time of worship . . . [the] people thought he was drunk because he Vomited and strong Liquor came up." Capen protested that Averell "did not own that he was drunk." Rather, he apologized because he "did sinfully to give people such occassion to think so of him, as if he had ben drunk." The subtlety of Averell's carefully worded confession was not lost upon the Topsfield minister, but because the church "generally manifested their satisfaction" Capen restored the offender to communion.[67] Two years earlier, Capen reaffirmed the lay right to consent in matters involving admission. In 1686, lay dissenters vetoed two candidates for admission who, Capen said, "should have come in." As had been customary, the candidates' entrance to the church was "deferred."[68] Some ministers began to claim a right to a "negative vote" or veto power over church decisions in cases such as these. But ministers almost never attempted to implement this new power until the eighteenth century, and even then they employed the measure only at great risk of church division.[69]

In Chelmsford, John Fiske continued to manage his church in careful accordance with Congregational provisions until the day he died in 1675. During one church debate Fiske informed the congregation that "he was determined not to speak much at present," but would give the brethren "full scope" to discuss the issues and "only order should be seen by [Fiske] to be observed." In spite of the difficulties his opponents heaped upon him, Fiske allowed and encouraged a great deal of lay participation and continued to speak scornfully of Presbyterianism.[70] In Dorchester, Rowley, and Salem, members did not merely add consent to the ministers' decisions in disciplinary cases. Rather, the members made the decisions regarding both the offenders' guilt and appropriate sentences.[71]

In 1678, a Rowley offender approached the pastor with two witnesses and asked "whether he should come to the sacrament next sabbath." The pastor replied, simply, that "it was not in my power to give him liberty . . . I could not take off the censure nor admit him." That decision belonged to "the body of the Church." Whether in larger churches or smaller ones, rural villages like Chelmsford or "urban" areas like Boston, surviving records make clear that the fundamental balance between clerical "authority" and lay "liberty" shifted little during the late seventeenth century in the actual operation of church government.[72]

Though second-generation ministers and church members ultimately agreed to adhere to the balanced system of order practiced by the founders and codified in the *Cambridge Platform*, the truce was an uneasy one. Reliance upon the *Platform* alone could not insure the success of Congregationalism. The *Platform* was simply too vague to provide definitive answers to every question of government. The *Platform* certainly provided a skeleton for a successful system of church order, but the flesh and blood came in a spirit of mutuality and harmony that continued to disintegrate in the face of social and cultural forces set into motion in the latter half of the seventeenth century. As more churchgoers sought deliberately to exploit the *Platform*'s vagueness and fewer demonstrated interest in the tradition of agreeing not to disagree, ministerial and lay attitudes toward one another would continue gradually to drift apart. During the next century, many members of a new and increasingly divided generation of clergymen would attempt to adopt the sorts of coercive measures in church government that their predecessors had only contemplated. The challenge would lead to a another, more serious round of conflict between "innovators" and defenders of Congregationalism, and would eventually give birth to new conceptions of the nature and significance of the Congregational Way.

8

Clerical Conflict and the Decline of Sola Scriptura

IN 1726, PASTOR SAMUEL DEXTER informed his Dedham congregation that a "Generall Meeting of Ministers" in Boston had decided to initiate rotating fast days in local churches. Several lay people, wary of "innovation" and angered that congregations had not voted on the matter, "made some objection" that "Ministers were about to deprive the Church[es] of their power." Instead of citing Congregational precedent or offering Scripture grounds for the ministers' decision, Dexter merely dismissed the charge as "frivolous" and proceeded with his plan to invite several neighboring ministers to Dedham to conduct a fast.[1]

The pastor's reply hardly eased the members' indignation. In a scene repeated throughout Massachusetts in the first decades of the eighteenth century, church worship and practice in Dedham, though designed to serve as an essential means of grace, instead became the focus of bitter contention. In response to the phalanx of clerical authority that later assembled to supervise the Dedham fast, many angry churchgoers stayed home and "went about their worldly Occasions," while others "Usid the Utmost Endeavour to prevent other peoples attending" the services. Pastor Dexter was shocked to discover that one enraged member informed his wife "he had reather she should got to hear Mass and if she did [attend the fast] he desired not to See her in his house more." The charge, again, was ministerial "innovation," that "God never required it and was weary of it." For most Dedham churchgoers, the minister lamented, these issues of church order obscured the clergy's larger message of spiritual revival. "Peoples heads and hearts Seem to be fillid with this Noise," Dexter sadly observed, "[a]nd very little Said of any Impressions from that days Services."[2]

Though Dexter was quick to trumpet his own noble intentions in convening the fast, he was no less caught up in tensions over church authority than the membership. The minister escalated the conflict several days after the service, lashing out from the pulpit at the "Invectives of the Railers and Neglecters and dispisers" among the laity who "said that we were serving the Devill." Dexter then accused the dissenters of sheer ignorance, praying bitterly for the Lord to "forgive them they know not what they did." Though many members sided with Dexter throughout the affair, the dissenters were hardly in a mood to consent silently to this deliberate insult. In an unseemly exchange, one member stood up and shot back that Dexter "told a Devilish Lye" while others hurled an "abundance of reproach" at the embattled minister.[3]

The Dedham imbroglio reflected the widespread divisions over government that had begun to erupt in local churches during the late seventeenth and early eighteenth centuries. A welter of internal and transatlantic developments heightened tensions between ministers and their flocks, including the Salem witchcraft hysteria, the imposition of religious toleration, and increasing social fragmentation. But most important, ministers themselves undermined the Congregational Way and their own preeminence within their churches by falling victim to bitter internal disagreements over church government. Some ministers, weary of the laity's disrespectful attitudes toward the clergy, sought to adopt institutional changes in order to strengthen their authority in church affairs. Others agreed with the need to modify the "ordinances" but sought mainly to help clergymen police one another. Ministers were by no means united in their stance toward the laity; fiery clerical dissenters such as John Wise and Increase Mather adamantly and publicly opposed any attempts by their colleagues to violate the traditional balance of power between churchgoers and the elders, warning that any innovations that smacked of coercion would only alienate the laity and exacerbate church disorder.

The clergy's divided approach to church government at the turn of the century contrasted sharply with the united stance it had adopted during the Reforming Synod. The divisions not only weakened ministerial leadership at the local level but heightened concerns among ordinary churchgoers about the nature of Congregationalism itself. Did the New England Way follow inevitably from Scripture, as ministers had taught for over a century, or was it merely a "humane invention" after all? Varying clerical opinions about Congregational practices furthered doubts about the legitimacy of sola scriptura—the long-standing belief that the New England Way represented the only biblical form of church order—that had first surfaced during the controversy over the Halfway Covenant. In the inevitable confusion that followed, church government increasingly became an arena for "confusion" and lay-clerical contention rather than a means of attaining grace.

While late seventeenth-century ministers inherited a number of difficulties familiar to their predecessors—a "backsliding" laity, rising individualism, and the usual charges and countercharges of spiritual "declension"—clergymen recognized that many of the challenges facing their churches were unique to the new generation. Nowhere was this concern more obvious than in the shifting nature of church "disorder." Though, as we have seen, lay misconduct had long been the subject of clerical condemnation, previous complaints among the ministers had centered primarily around trivial squabbles between churchgoers who refused to live up to communitarian ideals of harmony and cooperation. Even during the worst periods of this petty "contention," churchgoers had generally respected the clergy as an institution and had honored the sanctity of the ordinances.

By the turn of the eighteenth century, lay people began to direct their resentments squarely at the ministry itself. Throughout the colony, ministers complained that disrespect for clerical authority had reached new and alarming heights. Disputes between ministers and congregations over clerical salaries grew endemic, to the point where they were virtually expected. Ordinary churchgoers reviled their pastors during disagreements, ministers complained, and lay people further insulted them by falling asleep during sermons. Ministers did not exaggerate when lamenting the "vilest *Ingratitude*" and "heaps of Indignities" from which they suffered. Evidence of lay anticlericalism appears in church records, in court records, in lay testimonies, and in sermons. Never had the "messengers" God sent to a people, lamented William Williams, felt so "despised and rejected."[4]

Ministers expressed further dismay at the growing doubts that lay people began to display about the sanctity of church government itself. Church offenders flatly ignored the decisions and recommendations of their local congregations in disciplinary cases, boldly demanding instead to be heard before councils of outside elders. If council decisions displeased them, churchgoers dismissed them as mere matters of interpretation. Eventually, lay people would come to question whether the larger provisions of Congregationalism represented simple opinions, rather than sacred commandments of church government drawn from the Bible.[5]

The laity's increasing lack of confidence in the ministry and its rising uncertainty toward Congregational church government grew out of a number of internal and imperial challenges that undermined belief in the New England Way. In 1684, England annulled the Massachusetts charter, sweeping away the civil government that had served, in theory at least, as a "nursing father" for the churches. England restored a measure of local control to the colony in 1689, but not before adopting legislation that forced the Puritans to grant religious toleration to rival denominations within Massachusetts. Two years later, Increase Mather successfully brought English Congregationalists and Presbyterians together under the compromise known as the Heads of Agreement, reflecting a willingness among Massachusetts ministers to legitimate former opponents whom for generations they had castigated as sinful "innovators." As Robert Middlekauf has argued, these developments signaled to some clergymen that the "era of Congregational dominance had passed." A number of ministers began to tinker with "a fresh understanding of the meaning of New England"; some even suggested that "the essentials of religion did not lie in the forms of church organization." Religious toleration, along with the ministers' increasing acceptance of their Presbyterian "brethren," implied to many churchgoers that Congregationalism represented Massachusetts's preference rather than God's holy commandment.[6]

Though the imposition of toleration and the adoption of the Heads of Agreement undoubtedly helped to erode the concept of sola scriptura, the impact of these developments upon the Congregational Way was nevertheless neither decisive nor immediate. As Harry S. Stout has observed, ministers were quick to point out that religious toleration protected the cherished church liberties that distinguished Massachusetts from the world. Ministers further noted that the Heads of Agreement were essentially Congregational in nature, particularly in their affirmation of lay privileges. As Williston Walker noted, the Heads were more influential in shaping church order in Connecticut than in Massachusetts, where they occasioned little or no local church debate.[7]

Even more than events initiated overseas, internal affairs in Massachusetts threatened Congregational traditions and frayed the bonds between clergymen and churchgoers during the third generation. The 1692–1693 witchcraft crisis in Danvers (or "Salem Village"), for example, served to undermine church discipline even as, ironically, it helped to bring much neighborly contention in local churches and villages to a sudden and explosive conclusion. Historians may never settle upon a firm "cause" of the witchcraft tragedy, but virtually all agree that rivalries among local families, within the church, and between town and church contributed heavily to the atmosphere of recrimination in Danvers that helped fuel the outbreak and spread of the hysteria. Though few other towns shared the specific geographical and intrachurch factionalism from which Danvers suffered, many, as we have seen, suffered from the general epidemic of social and community tensions in the late seventeenth century. It should come as no surprise, then, that several neighboring villages also proved receptive the witchcraft hysteria. Andover saw more churchgoers jailed on suspicion of witchcraft than Salem and Danvers put together, and townspeople from many other villages contributed to the hundreds of witchcraft accusations. Though some historians have emphasized the atypicality of the witchcraft affair, in short, the contention that gave rise to it was anything but unusual; where towns ordinarily saw conflict confined to frivolous lawsuits or bitter church squabbles, Danvers saw witchcraft, an extreme response to which contention might lead.[8]

Lay people in Danvers later referred to the nightmarish events as "the sorest afflictions, not to this village only, but to this whole country, that ever did befall them," while Robert Calef pointed to the "Malice of Ill Neighbors" in sparking the calamity.[9] In wrestling with the consequences of the disaster, many churchgoers seemed finally to accept the ministers' admonitions that the witchcraft crisis, along with catastrophes such as King Philip's War and the loss of the charter, represented God's "Judgement" upon New England for its degeneracy. The process of coming to grips with these events—particularly the tragedy in Danvers—contributed to an evaporation of local squabbling and helped to usher in the "reformation of manners" at the end of the century observed by Richard C. Gildrie. As ministers pleaded for calm and healing, churches witnessed an unmistakable decline in the number of disciplinary hearings and a marked shift away from cases of petty contention that had required so much of their attention in previous decades. The First Church of Salem censured members routinely in the years leading up to the witchcraft episode; its records describe eighteen different admonitions or excommunications from 1674 to 1690, including many cases that involved routine contention. The witchcraft affair brought church censures to an abrupt halt: after Giles Corey's excommunication in 1692, petty squabbling and formal censures virtually disappear from the Salem records for the next forty years.[10] The First Church of Dorchester, which had censured some twenty members for a variety of contentious offenses from 1682 to 1693, disciplined only five from 1694 to 1705; none of these five cases involved the kind of trivial disputes that had racked communities in previous decades.[11] Similar patterns appeared in Topsfield, Beverly, Milton, and nearly all of the other churches whose disciplinary records appear to be complete.[12]

While clergymen and lay people undoubtedly welcomed the decline in church censures, this development was not entirely positive, for it also reflected uncertainties that the witchcraft tragedy had fostered concerning both ministerial judgment and the entire system of church discipline.[13] Lay people fully understood that many innocent victims had unjustly suffered the terrible sentence of excommunication during the witchcraft controversy, a fact the First Church of Salem finally acknowledged formally in 1712 when it reversed the excommunications of Rebecca Nurse and Giles Corey, both of whom had been put to death. The reversals were probably unprecedented in Massachusetts church history, insofar as they owed neither to procedural error nor the victims' repentance, but to the church's "Darkness and Temptation," and its "Sin, Error or Mistake" in the "Application of that Censure." A similar vote passed in the Danvers church. These reversals reminded churchgoers that, no less than court decisions, church censures were rendered by fallible human beings, a conclusion that undermined the sacred character of church discipline.[14]

In the aftermath of the Salem affair, churches thus began quietly to modify the kinds of penalties they would impose upon offenders. Henceforth they exercised extreme caution in passing upon sinners the grave sentence of excommunication. The witchcraft victims in Salem and Danvers were, in fact, among the last individuals to suffer excommunication in their respective churches during the colonial era, and throughout the colony churches began simply to "suspend" offenders from communion until they demonstrated suitable repentance. A council of elders in Woburn articulated openly what many churches had long since concluded silently, cautioning churches in 1706 to avoid excommunications except in "very weighty and very Clear cases." Moreover, though churches by no means ceased exercising church discipline, they began to focus largely upon more obvious violations for which questions of guilt were matters of little controversy. In church after church, the overwhelming majority of disciplinary cases throughout the first three decades of the eighteenth century concerned either fornication or excessive drinking. Unsurprisingly, churchgoers who suffered admonition in more controversial matters often refused to regard their censures as tantamount to the word and will of God; many became even more emboldened to challenge their censures by appealing to ministerial councils. Eventually, many churches would shy away from any disciplinary case that threatened to foster division.[15]

As we might expect, several developments beyond the Salem witchcraft controversy also contributed to this general shift in the laity's stance toward discipline and ministerial leadership in church government. Though, for the clergy, the laity's increasing skepticism continued to provide proof of declining spirituality among churchgoers, lay disrespect had little to do with waning piety and much to do with the ministers themselves, who continued to gradually undermine Congregationalism through their own disagreements over church order and, in many instances, their personal misbehavior.

Clergymen openly acknowledged the rising tendency among ministers to heap contempt upon themselves, and church government generally, through their own misdeeds. The proportion of ministerial misdemeanors may not have risen dramatically in the third generation. But with the gathering of some 219 churches between 1692 and 1755, and the attendant rise in the ministerial population, both the number of clerical offenses and, importantly, the publicization of these transgressions, increased dramatically.[16]

Ministers complained angrily of colleagues "who are not Conscientious in their Aims and views,"[17] citing examples like the Reverend Peter Thatcher, who in 1720 chose to break covenant with his Weymouth church to assume the pulpit of the more prestigious Fifth Church of Boston. Thatcher's quest for fame and fortune angered a sizable minority of the Fifth Church membership, and the vast majority of ministers agreed that Thatcher's career move represented a gross violation of his clerical obligations. An outrageous brawl punctuated Thatcher's ordination in Boston ("I dont believe the like was ever heard of or seen before" an astonished layman reported. "No bear garden certainly was ever like it"), and eventually the Fifth Church endured an acrimonious separation over the controversy, which became a topic of widespread debate in Massachusetts.[18]

Meanwhile, an entire series of highly public sexual misadventures, all involving Cape Cod ministers, scandalized the churches throughout the colony. In 1718, the Eastham church ordained one Samuel Osborn, who "had been publicly recorded as the father of a bastard child at Edgartown." (Pastor Osborn angrily denied paternity, insisting that he had been merely guilty of fornication.) Later, Billingsgate churchgoers declared their call to pastor Josiah Oakes "utterly void and of none Effect," after discovering that the minister's wife had been "with Childe" months before their marriage. While several ministerial councils struggled to sort out the Oakes affair, news leaked out that the bride of Sandwich pastor Benjamin Fessendon had gone underground within weeks of their marriage. She returned months later to face charges "for Concealing herself while Suspected with child." Brewster pastor Nathaniel Stone lamented the eviscerating effects of clerical misbehavior upon church discipline, observing that lay people would hardly take seriously his denunciations of fornication when neighboring ministers not only committed the same offense but went unpunished for it. "I am apprahensive," the pastor announced to his flock, "that the comonness of the sin of uncleanness, together with the publick countenance that has been given to that sin by toe many ministers and churches both, may tend to render it lightly accounted off."[19]

Stone specifically denounced "the countenance that has of late been given by many ministers and churches to the openly scandalous sin of uncleanness in a neighbouring Pastor, viz: Mr Osborn," pointing to the mounting problems fostered by the ministers' unwillingness to discipline their own in cases of "sinful immorality." Such laxness damaged the clergy's credibility almost as much as the offenses themselves. The leniency with which the clergy treated pastor Joseph Morse of Dorchester Village, whom a council charged with a litany of offenses including "false speaking," "Criminal Lying," "Neglect of Family prayer," forgery, and drunkenness, became the talk of the colony, as representatives of disciplinary councils reported back to their churches on the sordid nature of their findings. Pastor Samuel Dexter of Dedham, who sat on the Morse council, affirmed that while "the preacher of truth should be a man of truth," some members in Dorchester Village "would as soon trust a Punkepaccy Indian as Mr. Morse." The council eventually declared Morse "unworthy of the Ministry," but Dexter complained angrily of some ministers' indulgence: despite the "Enormities of his Life," Morse fell just one vote shy of receiving a "dismission," which would have freed him to assume another pulpit.[20]

The elders' split decision in the Morse case reflected their recognition of the bind created by efforts to enforce strict rules of clerical behavior. Each time ministers chastised a colleague, they unwittingly encouraged lay people to question the authority of local ministers in church affairs.[21] In an effort to avoid bringing the ministry into contempt in the eyes of the laity, ministers often sought to avoid public condemnation of one another. During one controversy, Marblehead's John Barnard, a veteran of numerous councils, noted that the Boston elders planned to censure a minister who had convinced his church unjustly to excommunicate a member. Barnard warned that if the ministers condemned the pastor in front of his own people, they would cripple their colleague's pastorate and encourage lay people to challenge disciplinary decisions. Barnard labored all night before successfully mediating a reconciliation that avoided public condemnation of any party.[22]

For all the cynicism fostered by clerical misbehavior, the single greatest threat to ministerial authority—and to the credibility of Congregationalism itself—was the increasing division within the clergy over "innovations" in church procedures, some of which, churchgoers protested, stood to trample upon lay liberties. Ministers had always quarreled among themselves over church order to some extent; issues as basic as membership requirements and the scriptural basis of church covenants had long been the subjects of spirited clerical debate. But in the first decades of the eighteenth century, the lack of unanimity among the ministers became so great and so widely publicized that it reinforced emerging doubts in the minds of churchgoers as to whether the Bible indeed offered clear prescriptions for church procedures.

Perhaps the most celebrated of the clerical innovators was Northampton's Solomon Stoddard, who addressed problems of declining membership and lay disorder by openly rejecting a number of traditional Congregational practices. In response to lay scrupulousness and fears of "partaking unworthily," Stoddard dispensed with the test of grace as a condition of church admission, arguing that the Lord's Supper itself served as a converting ordinance. Similarly, Stoddard urged his colleagues to address rising disorder in the churches by granting binding status to the decisions of ministerial synods and councils.[23]

Sentiments similar to Stoddard's had been expressed by Massachusetts Presbyterians as far back as the 1640s. But the context of such attacks upon the Congregational Way had shifted dramatically by the end of the century. With the imposition of toleration, Stoddard's views, at least theoretically, seemed far more threatening to the standing Congregational churches than previous challenges. Moreover, unlike many earlier critics who emerged from within Massachusetts, the Northampton pastor refused to adopt a low profile. Stoddard openly engaged the Mathers in a pamphlet war, publishing a number of highly critical works that attacked the sanctity of the *Cambridge Platform* as they defended his own practices.[24]

On the heels of the Stoddardean controversy, another assault upon Congregationalism arose with the gathering of Boston's "Brattle Square" or "Manifesto" church in 1698. Led by Harvard tutors John Leverett and William Brattle, a group of Boston merchants gathered the church in order to address the "Trouble that many have conceived (perhaps not unjustly) against Relations . . . a particular church covenant exclusive of Universal communions and the like." In 1699, the church ordained Benjamin Colman, a student of Brattle, as its first pastor, and shortly thereafter released its infamous *Manifesto*, which, while affirming allegiance to the *Westminster Confession of Faith* of 1680, defined and defended a number of dramatic innovations in worship and practice.[25]

The Brattle Square Church broke from standard Congregational practices by dispensing with formal admissions relations, reading portions of the Scripture aloud during worship in the absence of any explanation (a practice opponents called "dumb reading"), and opening baptism to the children of any professing Christian. The *Manifesto* also diminished the role of the laity in church affairs, affirming that "admissions to Sacraments is to be left wholly to the prudence and Conscience of the Minister," the "Brethren are to have no voice in ecclesiastical Councils," and the "Essence of a Minister's call is not in the Election of the People but in the Ceremony of Imposing hands."[26]

The written defense of orthodox Congregational practice fell upon the Mathers, who expressed the fears of many that the gathering of the Brattle Square Church portended the demise of the New England Way. Upon reading the *Manifesto*, Increase Mather declared that "if we Espouse principles as these, ... we then give away *the whole Congregational course* at once." His son Cotton agreed, describing the gathering of the church as "a day of temptation upon the town and land," one that threatened to "utterly subvert our churches." The Mathers opened up another front in their pamphlet war, this time engaging Colman and his associates Simon Bradstreet and John Woodbridge. The Mathers called for a reprinting of the Synod of 1662's principles relating to the consociation of churches, in hopes of discouraging "the irregular Proceedings of any People hereafter contrary to that advice," and castigated the Brattle Square Church for its unscriptural innovations.[27]

The Mathers' spirited objections to Stoddardeanism and the *Manifesto* were nonetheless somewhat misleading insofar as they masked several fundamental assumptions that many ministers soon came to share with the innovators. First, like Stoddard and the *Manifesto* men, who made at best token efforts to justify their innovations through Scripture, the Mathers (and many of their allies) had similarly begun to drift away from sola scriptura. Increase Mather, who had earlier sealed the Heads of Agreement, was hardly in a position to attack his Massachusetts adversaries by insisting that Congregationalism represented the only "true" form of church order; that position, as we have seen, was also undermined by the clergy's forced acceptance of religious toleration. Secondly, many clergymen had come to agree with the "innovators'" belief that lay disorder threatened Congregationalism far more than modest procedural modifications in a handful of local churches. Indeed, within a few years, many ministers dismissed the Manifesto Church's procedural changes and violations of sola scriptura as largely insignificant, and joined with Colman and Brattle in an effort to seek institutional changes designed to strengthen clerical authority.[28]

Clerical attitudes had been gradually evolving in more authoritarian directions for decades. As several historians have documented, many third-generation ministers, partly in response to their perceived loss of prestige, began a movement toward "professionalization," through which they sought to elevate themselves into a distinct and unified clerical leadership class.[29] In the process, many became nearly obsessed with the topics of popular insubordination, their own authority in church government and, as Samuel Willard preached in 1694, "Orders of Superiority and Inferiority among men." Touting the clergy as "*The Lights of the World*" in church affairs, ministers like Samuel Wigglesworth warned churchgoers to neither "oppose" nor "resist" local ministers or the "Authority which Christ hath put into their hands." Instead, ministers commanded, "Obey them that have rule over you, and submit yourselves," for as Thomas Paine bluntly informed the Weymouth congregation, "Ministers are rulers of Christ's Church."[30]

Though previous ministers had also groused about their unruly congregations while celebrating their own preeminence, third-generation clergymen went beyond idle complaints: they agreed to push for actual institutional changes in government to bolster their position in church affairs, even if it meant reducing lay initiatives in the decision-making process. This strategy broke dramatically from that of their second-generation predecessors, who, at the Reforming Synod of 1679, eschewed coercion and sought to nurture lay support by emphasizing common goals shared by shepherds and their flocks. The ministers' new efforts to organize themselves and to restore "order" in Congregational practice began formally with the establishment of clerical associations in Massachusetts Bay. The first of these, the Cambridge-Boston Association, described its goals in 1690 as

1. To debate any matter referring to ourselves.
2. To hear and consider any cases that shall be proposed unto us, from churches or private persons.
3. To answer any letters directed unto us, from any other associations or persons.
4. To discourse of any question proposed at the former meeting.[31]

The topics discussed in association meetings reflected the ministers' hopes to standardize practices within individual churches and to strengthen both the gathered clergy and the authority of local ministers. Those topics included the right of ministers to officiate in churches other than their own, the power of councils, pastoral inquiry into scandals, ruling elders, and the powers of ministers in their churches. In 1704, the Cambridge-Boston Association earnestly appealed to ministers throughout Massachusetts to organize themselves into similar associations and to establish lines of communication with one another. The clergy eventually established five such organizations.[32]

While the ministers acknowledged that association decisions remained nonbinding upon individual churches, some clergymen grew weary of addressing disorder with mere advice. All too often local churches simply ignored the pronouncements of councils, since congregational autonomy rendered the assembled elders powerless to enforce compliance with their wishes. The ministers consequently attempted to put some teeth into council decisions, a process that culminated in their efforts to adopt Cotton Mather's *Proposals*.[33] In 1705, ministerial delegates from five Massachusetts associations convened in Boston to determine "what further Steps are to be taken, that Councils may have due Constitution and Efficacy in supporting, preserving, and well ordering the Interest of the Churches." The ministers proposed a number of significant innovations in church government, the most dramatic of which stood to create a standing council of ministers and delegates to consider and pass judgement upon local church disputes. Ministers would look upon the decisions of this proposed council as "final and decisive," and the council reserved a right to declare any church that refused to abide by its rulings "no longer fit for communion with the churches of the Faithful." Obviously, this council stood to reduce the decision-making liberties of lay people in their local churches. Ministers accused of scandal, for instance, would be tried by the standing council rather than by their own congregations.[34]

The proposed standing council would include lay delegates, but the ministers manifested their increasing dissatisfaction with the role of the brethren in church government by attempting to reduce the authority of lay representatives. In previous years, lay delegates often outnumbered ministers in synods and in councils, often by wide margins.[35] Though councils rendered decisions by simple majority vote, enabling lay delegates to outvote the clergy, this arrangement rarely fostered difficulties because lay delegates usually voted in agreement with their ministers. Apparently, by 1705, ministers feared that councils might become divided along lay-clerical lines, for they included a startling provision in the *Proposals* that decreed, "[N]o act of the [standing] councils are to be reckoned as concluded and decisive, for which there has not been the concurrence of the Major part of the Pastors."[36] In years to come, churches would write to their neighbors inviting one minister and one delegate to attend ecclesiastical councils, rather than the usual contingent of one minister and two to four "worthy laymen." Disputes would also arise over the method of counting council votes—whether by simple majority of delegates, as had been the past practice, or by numbers of churches. All of these developments, like the *Proposals* and certain provisions of Stoddardeanism and the *Manifesto*, bore testimony to the widening rift in lay and clerical attitudes toward church government and one another.[37]

The *Proposals* also demonstrated the clergy's flagging commitment to the principle of sola scriptura. In sharp contrast to their predecessors who, for example, carefully defended procedural modifications with Scripture warrants during the controversy over the Halfway Covenant, the authors of the *Proposals* offered virtually nothing in the way of biblical justification for their innovations. They even acknowledged that many specific practices of government within local churches were based upon interpretation, insisting that councils ought not pester churches whose differing practices represented "meer tolerable differences in Opinion." Predictably, this desacralization of church order left lay people less willing to accept the ministers' word as law and even less apt to submit to church censures.[38]

The ministers' rising spirit of authoritarianism might have fundamentally shifted the delicate balance of Congregational church government—and deeply ruptured lay-clerical relations—had the elders stood united in their efforts to impose their will upon their flocks. But vehement criticism of this authoritarian approach quickly emerged from within the ranks of the ministers themselves. Several clerical "traditionalists" helped to galvanize lay opposition to ministerial innovation and ultimately rendered impossible any efforts to adopt significant institutional changes. The church records affirm, for example, that clergymen largely debated the *Proposals* among themselves; few ministers, if any, even bothered to bring them before the membership for consideration.[39] In acknowledging the failure of his reform program, Cotton Mather noted that "some very considerable Persons among the *Ministers*, as well as of the *Brethren*," feared "the *Liberties of particular Churches* to be in danger of being too much *limited* and *infringed*" by his initiatives, and "in Deference to these Good Men, the *Proposals* were never prosecuted, beyond the Bounds of *meer Proposals*."[40]

The "considerable persons" who helped torpedo the *Proposals* included Governor Dudley, an Anglican who refused to assist in a strengthening of the Congregational clergy, and Cotton Mather's own father, Increase. As J. W. T. Youngs has observed, Increase Mather held to the traditional belief that ministers enjoyed no more authority in ecclesiastical councils than lay delegates. Still a powerful figure among the clergy, Increase harshly criticized his son's *Proposals* for their usurpation of lay rights. The *Proposals* "took the very same path the church of Rome walked in," he noted, insofar as "their beginning was a taking the power of privilege from the brethren."[41]

An even more significant and celebrated opponent of the *Proposals* was John Wise of the First Church of Essex, then known as Chebacco Parish.[42] Wise, who gained provincial renown for his chaplainship during the siege of Quebec and for his resistance to arbitrary taxation during the Andros regime, penned two lengthy pamphlets in the second decade of the eighteenth century, *The Churches' Quarrell Espoused* and *A Vindication of the Government of New-England Churches*, both of which castigated the Massachusetts ministers for their encroachments upon lay rights and assaults upon the Congregational Way.[43] As is commonly known, Wise's analysis and defense of New England church government in *A Vindication* eventually carried him to an exploration and celebration of democracy, earning him the reputation among later historians as "America's first democrat." But although patriots reprinted both of Wise's pamphlets during the Revolutionary crisis in 1772, his significance among contemporaries rested less upon his political thought than in the divisions in the clerical community that he both fostered and reflected through his vigorous opposition to the *Proposals* and the autocratic ministerial sentiments that gave birth to them.

Wise's initial effort, *The Churches' Quarrell Espoused*, which sought to alert readers to the hidden dangers that Cotton Mather's *Proposals* posed to the Congregational Way, might justly be described as one of the earliest examples of American muckraking. Regardless of ministerial claims to the contrary, Wise cautioned his readers, the sinister forces behind the *Proposals* ultimately sought nothing less than the destruction of lay liberties and the subversion of New England's "venerable Constitution," the *Cambridge Platform*. Ministers approached the *Platform* with a "trowel" in one hand, he wrote, promising only "to plaister over a chink or two, where the old work by length of time, is somewhat Weather-beaten, to pacify the Jealousies of the Inhabitants." But in "reality," he warned, "they have in the other hand a formidable *Maul*... to break down the Building; for they are *all hands at work banging the Platform in pieces, upon which the old Fabrick is Built*."[44] Wise dissected the *Proposals* one by one to demonstrate precisely how they threatened to erode lay liberties and minced no words in vilifying ministers for the authoritarian attitudes upon which this movement for "reform" rested.

Wise acknowledged in his writings that disorder plagued some churches, but he angrily refuted claims that linked lay unruliness to weaknesses in the *Cambridge Platform*. To the contrary, Wise averred, the ministers had no one but themselves to blame for disorder. Anticipating a major theme of the Great Awakening, during which ministers heaped blame upon one another for the general decline of religion, Wise asserted that ministerial authoritarianism, not lay "declension" or deficiencies in the *Cambridge Platform*, fostered disruptive behavior among churchgoers: "any such embroilments as have lately happened in the churches," he wrote, "have been more the Folly of the Administrators in not keeping to the Rules of Government" than "from any Defect in the Constitution." Ministers concerned with such disorder, he continued, would serve themselves best by adhering to the *Platform*, which contained more than adequate provisions for healing internal church difficulties.[45]

According to historians, Wise's defenses of the *Platform* and traditional practices represented a landmark in Congregational theory partly because they lacked "any reference to revelation." Such assertions exaggerate the degree to which Wise broke from biblical justification and attribute to the early eighteenth century a complete break from sola scriptura that did not characterize Congregationalism until the 1730s and beyond.[46] In fact, Wise mirrored his times and his culture: though he clearly understood that belief in sola scriptura was waning, he never made the leap followed by later eighteenth-century writers, who boldly asserted that the Scriptures contained no specific form of church government and flatly denied any direct connection between the Bible and the *Cambridge Platform*. To the contrary, Wise (no stranger to irony) quoted his rival Cotton Mather to advance his own position that "[w]e have a Platform left us that is according to the Word of our Gracious Lord, and the pattern in the Mount." Echoing the vocabulary of the founders, Wise described the proposed Standing Council as a "Humane Invention," demanded justifications "from the Canon of Scripture," and ridiculed ministers who had "Out King'd all Kings on Earth," "*Out Bishop't all Bishops*" of Great Britain, and "Out Pope't the Pope."[47]

The Chebacco pastor nevertheless recognized that the continued emergence of subtle variations in church procedures, increasing division among the clergy, and the implications of toleration left many churchgoers less inclined to accept the notion that the New England Way reflected perfectly a system of church order contained in the Bible. Consequently, he buttressed his defense of Congregationalism by drawing connections between New England church practices and traditional principles of constitutionalism, free consent, and accountability. Though the *Cambridge Platform* continued to represent a sacred constitution for him, Wise clearly placed less emphasis on the "sacred" and more on the "constitution." While the *Platform* ("the Constitution of Church Government") could be scripturally justified, the document drew increasing legitimacy in Wise's analysis from its ratification by the churches and from the principle of free consent. Lay people could rightfully be "dispossessed" of the liberties granted in the *Platform* only by "some superior

power" that ministers did not enjoy or the members' own "voluntary Act." It was
an act of "great Boldness," he insisted, for the ministers to "invade" the "Government of these churches, without [the laity's] consent." Lay people, he averred, long
known for their "Eagle-eyed watch," ought to "leave . . . at home" ministers who
attempted to institute innovations in the absence of a ratifying "Certificate, Order,
or Vote from the Churches."[48]

Wise was no less forceful in defending the traditional concepts of limited authority
and higher law, and in tying these principles to church government. "All *English* Men
are priviledged by, and strictly Bound to the Law," he reminded readers. Just as "all
men keep to commission" in civil government, he continued, echoing John Cotton's
comments from a century earlier, so in the churches "our Platform is our settlement"
and ministers must recognize that its "laws are their boundaries." Whether in church
or state, he repeated, men are limited by "the Precept of Law." These arguments are
especially significant because they demonstrate that, even during this period of rising clerical authoritarianism, churchgoers continued to receive traditional messages
concerning lay rights and limitations on authority.[49]

In 1717, Wise extended his thought in *A Vindication of the Government of New
England Churches*, which includes another spirited defense of the *Cambridge Platform* and the New England Way. No specific event seems to have motivated Wise to
write his second pamphlet; rather, he was motivated by the increasingly autocratic
sentiments shared by some Massachusetts clergymen. And again, much of Wise's
argument rested on traditional grounds: Congregational church order, he argued,
differed little from the practices of the "ancients" during the first three centuries of
Christianity, before the church had been corrupted. Like the first Christians, New
Englanders elected and deposed their ministers, held the keys to admissions, and
censured fellow members. Wise insisted that the *Cambridge Platform* was drawn from
the "Divine Original" form of church government, cited the writings of Thomas
Hooker and Increase Mather, and devoted an entire section of *A Vindication* to Scripture justifications of the New England Way.[50]

Wise finally broke from traditional defenses of the New England Way in explor-
ing several new secular lines of justification, emphasizing the harmony between
Congregationalism and current conceptions of reason, natural rights, and English
constitutional government. In discussing the origins of the *Cambridge Platform*, Wise
thus averred that the "Effect of Christ's goodness, care, and creating power" enabled
the founders to utilize "the Light of Reason as a Law and Rule of Right" in constructing the document. The *Proposals*, in contrast, could be justified neither by
"reason" nor "Divine wisdom instampt on human nature."[51]

Wise's discussion of reason and natural rights led him to his remarkable defense
of democracy, a facet of church government that, for Wise, was to be celebrated,
not merely tolerated. In light of democratic principles, the supposedly "disorderly"
developments so objectionable to other ministers in fact represented welcome and
needed changes. New Englanders ought not lament the majority vote as a regret-

table response to the loss of unanimity, Wise insisted, they should celebrate it as central to democracy. Wise further praised the New England Way for its balance of powers, and its emphasis upon free consent and accountability, all of which were central components of a democratic system.[52]

As Perry Miller pointed out, these secular justifications of church practices obviously contributed to the ongoing desacralization of the New England Way. Less appreciated is the extent to which Wise's writings demonstrate that church government remained as one important avenue through which new political concepts infused New England culture. The clergy still represented a central means of the dissemination of political principles for churchgoers, and church government continued to serve as an important arena in which those ideas were both introduced to and used by lay listeners. Just as Wise used controversy over church order to explore for lay readers concepts of reason and natural rights, those concepts would in time enter into the vocabulary of actual debate in church meetings, which continued to serve as a training ground for their use by ordinary people. By the early 1730s, for example, lay dissenters in a bitter controversy that split the First Church of Salem based their objections to clerical maladministration as much on "natural rights" and "reason" as they did the Scriptures or even the *Cambridge Platform*.[53]

While Wise undoubtedly served as a conduit through which secular conceptions of government infused church order, a far more difficult question concerns the converse: to what extent did Congregational precepts infuse civil politics? Though ministers regularly discussed practices and principles of "secular" politics in their Sunday sermons and, especially, in election sermons, Wise was one of the very few writers since John Cotton to specifically intertwine analyses of church and civil government.[54] However brief, his discussions of the relationships between Congregationalism, democracy, and English constitutionalism at the very least forced readers to consider the nexus between principles of civil and church politics, even if Wise's primary intention was merely to defend the New England Way. At one point Wise directly addressed the issue of the "democratizing" influence of church government upon secular institutions, and the relationship between the English constitution and the *Cambridge Platform*. He regarded that relationship as reciprocal and considered questions of which gave rise to which as something of a chicken-egg argument: "Considering the affinity in these two Constitutions, one would be ready to Query, Whether the Heroick true English Spirit is not Parent to both? Or whether they are not equal Debtors to the Gospel, for their Original?"[55]

Obviously, little evidence remains in the church records bearing directly upon the influence of church government on eighteenth-century civil or "secular" politics. But insofar as New England's political culture and national identity remained tied to Congregationalism, it would seem safe to propose that any development that "secularized" or democratized church government also broadened, secularized, and democratized the larger political culture as well. And Wise made clear his belief that Massachusetts's wider culture indeed remained significantly religious and that "politics" still meant church politics. While Massachusetts's civil rights and civil government were significant, Wise bluntly reminded readers that church government and church liberties were ultimately far more important. The former, he averred, concerned mere "outward Fortunes," while the latter pertained to matters of the "immortal soul."[56]

Wise further asserted that Massachusetts's national identity remained intimately tied to Congregationalism, announcing that he labored in "Service of my Country" in defending the *Cambridge Platform*. Assaults upon the "constitution" of church government represented nothing less than an attack upon the nation to which the *Platform* was so central; Wise consequently described the fomenters of the *Proposals* not merely as sacrilegious "robbers" of church privileges but as "Traytors." He later condemned the ministers for their "Treason" against their country. While Massachusetts could certainly celebrate its "liberties," Wise reminded his readers, the specific rights and privileges that distinguished Massachusetts from other nations were the lay rights ensconced in the *Cambridge Platform*. In tying Massachusetts's national identity to concepts of the rights and privileges of ordinary people, Wise drew a connection that would remain vital in Massachusetts long after Congregationalism ceased to shape political culture.[57]

In 1729, Stoneham pastor James Osgood recorded a list of his "Books That have Ben Read." At the top of the list appears "John Wise Churches Quarrell Espoused." Though we know precious little about his career, Wise appears to have been influential in the clerical community and in local church affairs. In 1703, he delivered the right hand of fellowship at the ordination of Gloucester's John White, who went on to become his friend and disciple. Later, at another ordination, Wise offered a public address on the *Cambridge Platform*, "much applauding the N. English venerable Constitution."[58] In 1717, Wise headed an ecclesiastical council in Wenham that attempted to settle a controversy surrounding the excommunication of one William Rogers. Under Wise's leadership, the council of elders exonerated the accused, then chastised the Wenham church: "[T]he said church seems to us either obstinately bent on a design to subvert the ancient constitution of these churches, or through the prevelency of some temptation are rushing upon their own confusion."[59]

These episodes suggest that Wise swayed many clerical allies to his traditional views toward lay liberties—or perhaps they indicate that Wise's writings reflected clerical attitudes that were commonplace among the ministry in the first place.[60] In their haste to discuss ministerial authoritarianism in the first decades of the eighteenth century, historians have not sufficiently emphasized the significance of clergymen who shared with Wise a rejection of ministers' efforts to separate themselves from popular culture.[61] Despite the emphasis that some placed upon professionalization, sacerdotalism, and the need for lay submission, many ministers remained fully committed to traditional Congregational principles and practices. As a consequence, the clergy never succeeded in diluting long-held notions on limitations on authority, accountability, and the need for an informed, watchful laity. Indeed, many ministers continued to emphasize lay rights and responsibilities no less forcefully than their predecessors had.

Ministers frequently expressed these traditional sentiments in their sermons. Preaching in 1718 before an audience that included no less than twenty clergymen, Increase Mather acknowledged the authoritarian tendencies of some ministers and offered a simple admonition for colleagues who exaggerated their own importance in church affairs: "God did not make churches for ministers, he made ministers for churches."[62] Numerous clergymen had maintained this stance all along, and continued to urge lay people and ministers alike to recognize limitations on clerical authority. John Tufts of Newbury reminded a lay and clerical audience in 1729 that churchgoers must continue to hold ministers to their duties and obligations. "It is sometimes necessary that Christ's Ministers should be put in mind to fulfil their ministry . . . when it is so, those Brethren, which are under their pastoral care, should exhort them to Take heed that they fulfil their Ministry." Weymouth's Thomas Paine asserted that "Ministers are Rulers of Christ's Church," but nonetheless affirmed that clergymen "are no less obliged to the Rules of strict piety and Holiness" than "other Christians are."[63]

Even the deferentially minded William Brattle—from whom we might least expect compromise on issues of clerical control—affirmed the traditional tenets of free consent, higher law, and accountability in church government. Notwithstanding the procedural innovations of their church, the "*Manifesto* men" had never denied the importance of free consent; to the contrary, they acknowledged, as Miller observed, that "a church should be founded upon mutual agreement."[64] And Brattle, though notorious for his aristocratic, "Anglicized" manners, repeatedly invoked the *Cambridge Platform* in 1697 when speaking before a group of students on the topic of church government. A pastor must govern "not dispotically, arbitrarily, or by his own humour and will," Brattle instructed, repeating principles that ministers had shared since the days of John Cotton. "We ought not thus to Lord it over God's people. Nor ought we to Rule and govern the flock by laws and rules of mans Invention." Brattle found it inappropriate for "a church, much more a private Brother, to attempt to teach and guide the minister," a sentiment with which Cotton would have sympathized. But, Brattle asked, "must a church then be Tyrannized over? God forbid." The Cambridge teacher cautioned that "it is a thing possible for a gospel minister to be scandalous." In such cases ministers "may, nay ought" to be disciplined and even "removed" by the laity. "Ministers are accountable here on earth," Brattle reminded the future clergymen, "as well as other men."[65]

Despite rising uncertainties over the validity of sola scriptura, many ministers still taught that the only "higher law" or absolute rule to guide the lives of Christians was Scripture rule. Hatfield pastor William Williams, a son-in-law and close ally of

Solomon Stoddard, strongly supported principles of sola scriptura and practices of lay watch in an ordination sermon delivered before the laity and neighboring ministers in Waltham. Notwithstanding his father-in-law's insistence upon the binding authority of councils, Williams warned churchgoers in 1723 that "to submit their faith and consciences in matters of Religion to any humane authority whatsoever, whether *Popes* or *Councils*, is to rob Christ of his Prerogative." "Nothing ought to be admitted, that is *contradicted* by Scripture," he continued, "nor anything imposed that is not prescribed therein . . . Christians may not give up themselves to the conduct of any man's judgement as a rule to determine his faith." Churchgoers must think independently, Williams continued, and maintain their duty of watchfulness. Because "many things" have been "imposed upon the World by those who pretended to authority," churchgoers and ministers must together "search into the mind of Christ" and "keep themselves exactly to it, as to all *Officers, and Ordinances and Rites* in Worship." Roxbury pastor Ebenezer Thayer reflected ministerial concerns with the decline of deference but nonetheless echoed Williams's sentiments in a powerful exhortation on sola scriptura and the limits of clerical authority. Ministers should be "treated" with "that Deference, Regard, and Honour, which is due to their Character," he preached, before solemnly warning the laity that ministers "may not dare to urge any thing upon their people, but what they can Preface with a, *Thus saith the Lord.*"[66]

Despite deepening antagonisms that plagued lay-clerical relations at the turn of the century, some ministers actually *expanded* the lay duty of watchfulness beyond the scope of church government, offering unprecedented admonitions to their listeners to reject ministers who preached unsound doctrine. Such watchfulness depended on the maintenance of an informed laity. "Private Christians" must be "well established" in the "truth," William Williams reminded his audience, "that they may not be *toss'd with every wind of doctrine, through the slight and cunning craftiness of men.*" Churchgoers must "labor to understand the truth . . . that they are not *lead* blindly." Even Solomon Stoddard vigorously warned churchgoers to think independently and to avoid blind obedience to authority. Stoddard acknowledged that an informed laity was necessary to prevent the spread of unsound doctrine and practice among God's people. "A knowing People," he warned, "may in time become an ignorant People." It was the ministers' solemn duty to prepare the laity through careful, even painstaking instruction: ministers must instruct the laity in the "Principles of Religion, and the Rules of God's Word," Stoddard preached. "They must take pains to make them understand."[67]

Though some ministers continued to justify the New England Way biblically and others employed more secular defenses such as the light of "reason," Congregationalism's important messages of higher law, accountability, and lay participation remained central to Massachusetts religious culture during the opening decades of the eighteenth century. Nevertheless, the emergence of those clergymen who sought openly to enhance ministerial prerogatives, and the ministers' general lack of unity on important issues of government, forced churchgoers to choose between competing voices. As we shall see, most elected to defend their traditional rights and liberties when participating in church government. But the divisions among the ministers, the decline of sola scriptura, and continuing social and cultural change would force increasing numbers to question the larger relevance of Congregationalism, even as they continued to defend most of its central political principles.

9

Perpetuation and Disintegration

THE NIGHT OF MARCH 9, 1733, found Longmeadow pastor Stephen Williams adding a daily entry to a diary he would keep for over sixty-five years. Much of the previous evening, he began, had been devoted to "discourse with Deacon E. and T. N. about church government." Abruptly, Williams broke into earnest supplication: "[T]he Lord grant we may not be so taken up about church government so to neglect the practice of Christianity—but oh Lord grant vitall religion . . . prevent feuds and contentions among us." Williams later complained that "several ministers" had refused to attend a meeting of the Hampshire Association, deplored the emergence of "divisions" among the clergy, and prayed for the Lord to "help in this day of difficulty to prevent further confusion and disorder." The "feuds and contentions" that Williams lamented had perplexed local churches for several decades. But by the 1730s, conflict over church government had become so intense throughout Massachusetts that ministers prayed regularly for relief from the "spreading leprosy" of church disorder.[1]

The disintegration of church of church order was a gradual process, as we shall see, and influenced different churches at different times. Despite the ongoing shift toward individualism and the decline in covenantal piety, most ministers and congregations struggled during the first three decades of the eighteenth century in an effort to reach accord over principles and practices of church government. Many ministers still instructed lay listeners in the Congregational Way, and members continued to participate actively in the decision-making process. Clergymen who sought to stem church disorder by compromising lay liberties generally saw little success during this period; indeed, most Congregational provisions pertaining to lay rights would remain vital throughout the colonial era.

Yet ongoing disagreement over church government—both within the clerical community and among lay people themselves—eventually proved too difficult an obstacle for many congregations to overcome. Lay people and many ministers remained committed to principles of free consent, limited authority, and higher law, but by the 1730s they often found it impossible to isolate a specific set of higher laws upon which they could generally agree, and according to which they would hold themselves accountable. As churchgoers witnessed the continuing desacralization of the Congregational Way, and suffered an erosion of their sense of certainty and inviolability of Congregational practices, they became more likely than ever to fight over issues of church government. The Massachusetts clergy was far too divided over specifics of church order to provide definitive answers in the face of an explosion of church disorder.

Many churches that managed to avoid this intensifying conflict saw lay people adopt a stance toward Congregationalism that ministers deemed even more ominous than contentiousness: they began to lose enthusiasm altogether for covenant obligations and the ordinances. The eve of the Great Awakening thus found many congregations either fighting over issues of church government or simply ignoring them. Churchgoers would defend traditional lay liberties and exercise the ordinances on their terms—if they could agree upon them—or not at all. Either way, by 1740 nearly everyone agreed that Congregationalism stood at the very brink of destruction, and ministers prayed fervently for "revival."

The authoritarian posture adopted by a number of clergymen during the first half of the eighteenth century should not be taken to mean that ministers actually assumed a more aristocratic control over local church affairs at this time. Neither the rise of clerical associations nor attempts to adopt the "innovations" advanced in the *Manifesto* or the *Proposals* tell us anything of substance about actual practices of government within local churches.[2] As was the case in their analyses of seventeenth-century Congregationalism, scholars have based assumptions of clerical supremacy in eighteenth-century church affairs largely upon the *desires* of some ministers to abridge lay liberties. No historian has even attempted to document the extent to which ministers succeeded in modifying church practices in accordance with their whims. And, unsurprisingly, the lay response to these clerical overtures has been almost completely ignored.[3]

The church records dating from the first decades of the eighteenth century suggest that despite the self-aggrandizing bluster some clergymen expressed in their sermons or associational meetings, ministerial prerogatives remained strictly limited in local church meetings. While churches came to vary in certain specific procedures, the decision-making process at the local level did not shift fundamentally. Churchgoers continued to enjoy liberties they had possessed for nearly a century; to some extent they even enhanced their authority in church affairs. The fundamental changes in church government from the late seventeenth century to the Great Awakening, in short, involved neither a decline in lay rights nor the ascendancy of clerical control in church government, but growing disagreements over principles, a gradual divergence of practices, and the eventual demise of the laity's commitment to Congregationalism itself.

One principle over which churchgoers rarely disagreed was the ongoing need to limit the authority of ministers and members by higher laws. Virtually all churches gathered through the 1730s and beyond included clauses in their covenants in which members and officers agreed to govern themselves according to Scripture rule. In Grafton, the church vowed to "use the holy Scriptures, as our Platform where we may Discern the mind and will of Christ, and not the new found Inventions of Men," while the First Church of Harvard pledged "Obedience . . . in all of the Ordinances of the Gospel." The First Church of Abington promised simply to adopt practices "agreeable to the prescriptions of [God's] holy Word."[4]

While professing devotion to the Bible, churchgoers fully understood that conflicting scriptural interpretations had emerged within the clerical community, particularly over matters of church government. As uncertainties over the relationship between Congregational practice and the principle of sola scriptura continued to grow, churches relied increasingly upon the *Cambridge Platform* to guide them in church affairs. Often churches insisted upon allegiance to the *Platform* as a condition of gathering or brought up the subject at the ordination of new officers. In response to a lay request in Wenham,

> The Pastor Elect promised to feed and rule this Church of Christ, over which the Holy Ghost had made him overseer, by Divine direction and assistance agreeable to the mind and will of God revealed in the Holy Scriptures[,] particularly that in points of Discipline, Hee should conform to that Holy Word of God as explained in the Platform of Church Discipline formerly agreed upon and assented to by these Churches in their Synod.[5]

Lay people in other churches required similar resolutions. Prior to the selection of a minister in the Ninth Church of Boston, the laity resolved in 1736 to "adhere to the Faith and Order of the Gospel, as exhibited by these Churches in their confesion of Faith and Platform of Church Discipline." One James Odell of the First Church of Salem even signed his church covenant with the added affirmation, "as to Discipline I take the Platform as to the Substance for any ruling." Long settled churches sometimes reviewed the document and reaffirmed their commitment to it.[6]

This emphasis on the *Cambridge Platform* demonstrated churchgoers' continued commitment to principles of constitutionalism and higher law as their faith in sola scriptura waned. But it also reflected heightened practical concerns over the rising amount of conflict surrounding church government in eighteenth-century Massachusetts. As churches gradually came to acknowledge the absence of specific biblical warrants, church practices increasingly diverged, often opening a door to controversy. In an effort to head off conflict, ministers and their flocks attempted to resolve controversial topics before they emerged as sources of unrest; assent to the *Platform* represented one means of advancing stability.

Agreement upon the *Cambridge Platform* alone, however, could hardly guarantee order and harmony within local churches, because the prescriptions of the *Platform* itself were so often the subject of varying interpretations. Ministers and their flocks consequently sought to soften potential points of friction by addressing and resolving more specific points of church order, especially prior to church gatherings and ordinations. The process of hammering out agreements on particular procedures forced churches to choose among various practices circulating in Massachusetts, particularly in the area of admissions requirements. Shortly after the 1698 ordination of the Reverend Joseph Green in Danvers, the pastor and congregation together approved the *Platform*, and then debated and approved no less than nine detailed steps for admission to full communion.[7] Other congregations chose from a number of alternatives: while many continued to require spoken "relations" as a condition for full membership,[8] some allowed relations in writing, and others, like the First Church of Harvard, voted "to Receive Persons to full Communion without any Relation written or verball." Significantly, many churches that dispensed with public testimony still limited full membership to regenerates, and required the pastor to summarize private meetings between candidates and the officers.[9]

The specific procedural choices churches made were generally less revealing than the process by which they reached these decisions.[10] Whether churches elected to affirm long-standing Congregational practices or adopted modest revisions, lay people, as much or more than ever before, made the choices themselves, establishing their own provisions of government. In a reversal of the seventeenth-century flow of power, in which ministers set the rules of government and then requested lay consent, the First Church of Beverly set the rules for incoming pastor Thomas Blower in 1701 and demanded his consent as a condition of ordination. The Beverly church records reveal how the members first requested that Blower "Give his Company with the Church at ther present meeting to Confer with him in matters Refering to church disepline in order to his beeing Called to office by said Church" and then forwarded demands "that in the admission of members there bee a publick Relation and major Vote of the Church," among other requirements. The First Church of Danvers ordered pastoral candidate Joseph Green to read the church records "to inform himself of the foundation of their church here, and of their method and order in their church discipline" prior to his ordination. The Ninth Church of Boston took similar precautions in 1737, even passing a resolution ordering pastor-elect William Hooper to call a church meeting if seven members requested it. The church required Hooper to assent to this and five other measures prior to his ordination. The laity in Gloucester and Upton adopted similar safeguards.[11]

Eighteenth-century lay people continued to participate actively in church affairs not only during the gathering process or when hiring ministers, but when reaching routine decisions as well. Much church voting remained perfunctory in nature; in a process that often differed little from the mid-seventeenth century, eighteenth-century ministers generally raised questions before their churches and, as the Sturbridge pastor noted, invited "discourse and debate" in order to achieve a sense of the meeting. That achieved, the ministers generally called for, and received, the church's unanimous and silent consent. In more serious cases, or for those in which a sense of the meeting was uncertain, ministers called for a hand vote.[12]

A hearing located in the records of the First Church of South Andover, extraordinarily rare in its detail, illustrates these continuities, both in the decision-making process, and in practices of admissions and discipline.[13] The case concerned "differences" between two brothers, Samuel and Jonathan Blanchard, who in 1719 became embroiled in a dispute over their inheritance. Pastor Samuel Phillips assembled the members to see whether the church required peaceful resolution of the matter as a condition for admitting Samuel Blanchard to full membership. After "some discourses" that revealed the specifics of the disagreement, the pastor raised the question in the positive: "[I]f you will overlook that Difference so that [it] shall not hinder your consenting to the admission of S. Blanchard to full communion, signify it by Lifting up the Hand." "Whereupon," the pastor noted, "Few or none of the Brethren Lifted up the Hand." The pastor then placed the question in the negative:

> If the brethren Refuse to Consent to the admission of Samuel Blanchard to full communion, till it appear to the Church that said Blanchard does his utmost in Reason for setting peace between him and his Brother Jonathan signify it by Lifting up the Hand, whereupon the Major part (by far) Lifted up the Hand.

There is little reason to believe that this vote merely represented an affirmation of the pastor's recommendation, as had sometimes been the case in the early seventeenth century; apparently the minister never voiced an opinion on the matter.

At the next church meeting, the pastor brought candidate Samuel Blanchard and a witness before the church to "Enquire whither [Blanchard had] done his utmost in Reason, for healing the breach." The procedures revealed in the exchanges between the pastor and the laymen differ little from similar examples drawn from in the seventeenth century.

QU: Have you been Endeavoring for peace?

SAMUEL BLANCHARD: Yes sir.

QU: Have you Told your Brother privately wherefore you are offended with him; And have you privately made propositions to him reasonable in your account?

SAMUEL BLANCHARD: Yes sir.

QU: Were they accepted?

SAMUEL BLANCHARD: No sir.

QU: Did you tell him that you would observe the Gospel Rule to take one or two with you and so talk with him?

SAMUEL BLANCHARD: Yes sir. I did, setting a day for it.

QU: And have you done accordingly?

SAMUEL BLANCHARD: Yes sir.

QU: Who were the men that went with you?

SAMUEL BLANCHARD: My Brother Mr. Thomas Blanchard, and my Brother Stephen Osgood.

Mr. Thomas Blanchard, please to tell the church what propositions your Brother Samuell made to his Brother Jonathan.

T.B.: The Sum of what he said is this; He offered Jonathan to give him Ten pounds only to fulfill his promises made before witness To him; Or: He would accept of Ten pounds, and so aquitt him from his promises.

QU: Well, and did Jonathan accept of Either proposition?

SAMUEL BLANCHARD: No sir. Tho since He offers to give 8 pounds to Brother Samuel to acquit him from his promises.

QU: Mr. Samuel Blanchard cant you take up with 8 pounds?

SAMUEL BLANCHARD: Having seriously considered the matter I declare before the church that I will accept of what my Brother Jonathan will freely Give me, be it more or less (in Lieu of the Promises he made me of moneys and Lands soon after our Father's death) Hoping and Believing it will be more for peace to do so, than to Bind my Brother to a Certain sum.

Mr. Samuel Blanchard, you speak well, and like a Christian, I thank you for Discovering such a peaceable [Condescending?] spirit rather, I thank God who has given you such a Spirit. I believe you will be no Looser [loser] by it.

The decision on admission could not have been less in doubt. The pastor therefore called for a silent consent: "And now, Brethren, that I proceed (in a short time) to the admission of Samuel Blanchard to full communion. I shall take your Silence for consent; whereat all were Silent."

Because the members in South Andover were united throughout the Blanchard case, little debate and few lay contributions accompanied the voting. Many decisions, however, found ministers less successful in achieving a sense of the meeting. In these kinds of cases, lay people did not hesitate to speak out. In 1729, the East Barnstable church attempted to decide whether one Joseph Davis had adequately addressed objections that one Captain Lothrop had raised against Davis's candidacy for admission. The account in the church records suggests that, while the minister kept order during the proceedings, lay people discussed the issues and reached their own decisions with little coaching. The record also reveals the painstaking efforts that clergymen employed in their efforts to demonstrate that votes reflected the "mind of the church" rather than the will of the minister.

The pastor first read Davis's "answers" to Lothrop to the members "twice or three times," and then "desired them to consider about the matter." Captain Lothrop suddenly "desired the matter might be for some reasons suspended." The pastor reported that after "some Debate"

> the Pastor then told them he was desirous to know the minds of all them present and that he should therefore ask them all one by one, which he did beginning with the youngest, praying all to speak with freedom. And it appeared there was a majority for neither—upon which one stood up and said it was his mind if there was not a large *majority* for either, it would be best to suspend.

The pastor called for a vote, and the congregation decided to suspend the matter, the vote taken "by the Lifting of hands."

Several weeks later the pastor "stopt" the members after lecture "to know of them whether they were ready for a *vote* either way" on Davis's admission and indicated that "it [was] proper now to proceed upon the affair." Accordingly, he asked

> all *singly* what their mind was and all generally were [inclined?] to proceed forthwith upon the affair. And the *objector* was asked whether he had anything further to *object* against it—and he replied he should submitt to the church as a *member* of the *church*. Then the *Pastor* desired them to Consider of the matter a little which was whether the objections against *Joseph Davis* considered with his answers unto them were a sufficient bar to his *reception* among us, yea or no.

After "some pause" the matter was put to vote by a "Lifting of hands" whether the objections "were sufficient to bar" Davis from membership. "Not one [hand]," the pastor noted, "was lifted up." He then asked "if they thot the *objections* were not *sufficient*," and "the hand of almost every brother was lifted up." Having clearly demonstrated the mind of the church, the pastor proceeded to admission.

Ministers did not always achieve the kind of agreement evident in South Andover and in East Barnstable, and, in general, churches by no means enjoyed the degree of unanimity that characterized most voting in the early seventeenth century. When faced with divided opinions, eighteenth-century churches generally relied upon simple majority rule. In 1722, the Reading church received a letter from an "agrieved party" in Worcester requesting their elders' presence at a council. The pastor "Read their Letter to this Church and desird them to Signify their minds." While some favored compliance, several laymen "Spake to oppose" attendance at the council. One noted the great distance, or "the length of the way," while another pointed out that a previous council had already issued a ruling on the matter. One Kendal Parker, obviously familiar with Congregational procedures, pointed out that only one side of the Worcester church had sent for help; "there fore he thout it was not best for us to send." The final decision was rendered entirely by the laity: the entire passage contains nothing to indicate that the minister even offered an opinion. He called for a vote in the affirmative, "but few hands were held up for it." He then "desird the negative" and declared that because "more voted against it than for it where-fore I goe not." Though minorities usually accepted the will of the majority in these sorts of routine decisions, they reserved the right in extraordinary cases to seek the advice of outside councils. As we shall see, minorities would begin to exercise this right with such frequency during the third and fourth decades of the eigh-teenth century that church order would be thrown into disarray. Nevertheless, though harmony and unanimity would become less characteristic of church meet-ings than in the previous century, lay authority in the decision-making process would remain undiminished.[14]

Lay people also continued to observe their watchmen role and to hold their churches and their officers accountable to Congregational provisions. As was the case in previous generations, effective watch required an informed laity; the records suggest that churchgoers continued to learn the details of Congregational practice through attendance upon the sermon and public church procedures. In Westfield, the preacher-poet Edward Taylor responded to a dispute with his congregation by constructing two remarkably detailed sermons on church government, which he employed to review and to biblically justify nearly all of the central principles and procedures of Congregationalism. In what must have taken hours of instruction, Taylor discussed details of admission, discipline, and the respective rights and du-ties of members and clergymen. Similarly, pastor John Brown delivered a sermon to his Haverhill congregation in 1731 in which he discussed and recommended the elec-tion of ruling elders to assist him in disciplinary matters, while South Andover pas-tor Phillips cited chapter and verse from the *Cambridge Platform* in instructing his congregation on "their Duty with respect to the Children of the Church." As was the case in the seventeenth century, ministers delivered these lessons on church order before their entire congregations—not just members—providing nonmembers with an opportunity to learn the details of the Congregational Way.[15]

Ministers also publicly discussed church order and the duties of their office dur-ing ordination proceedings, particularly when delivering the "charge" to newly ordained officers. During the ordination of pastor James Chandler in Georgetown, Reverend Moses Hale of Byfield spelled out for ministers and lay people alike the awesome responsibilities incumbent upon members of the clergy. As the church's "overseer," Hale observed in 1732, the able minister must be prepared to "Reprove, rebuke, exhort," but always "with all long suffering," for ministers must "Give none offense in anything that the ministry be not blamed." In governing the church, cler-gymen must "Wisely and impartially discuss the holy discipline with which the house of God is to be ordered and governed" with the laity, and serve as examples "in word[,] in conversation, in charity, in spirit, in faith and in purity." Gloucester pastor John White, in a preface to a volume of ordination sermons, tied the ceremony of the "charge" directly to the principle of accountability: "At the ordination of Minis-ters, (where there are crouded Assemblies of Ministers and people) the Preacher, with an abundance of freedom, sets forthe the Duties of ministers in the full extent of it: leaving to the people to judge, whether their ministers are defective, or no, in their Holy ministrations."[16]

Ministers also passed on principles and practices of government to new generations through the performance of church procedures. Admissions and disciplinary hearings remained public; usually churches encouraged both members and nonmembers to witness repentances and the varying sorts of testimonies employed in admitting new members. Newly established churches reinforced the principle of free consent by reading their covenants aloud and then adding their assent publicly, while older churches accomplished the same end through the practice of covenant renewal. As we have seen, the hiring of new ministers represented prime opportunities for congregations to discuss and review provisions of church order.[17]

Ministers continued to read council results to the laity as well, from which churchgoers learned Congregational principles and practices, and acquired information about new developments in other churches. In 1722, Dorchester pastor John Danforth read the result of a Norton council to his congregation and used the opportunity to instruct his flock on the specific issues of government the council had addressed. The council had been assembled at the behest of one John Skinner, who had been suspended by the Norton church before he had a chance to appear before the members to defend himself. The council sided with Skinner, and, in justifying that result, Danforth reminded his own Dorchester listeners that "Our Churches being in Peace do usually before they Censure offenders Cite them to appear before the Church to show Cause (if they can) why they should not be Censured." Danforth acknowledged that the Norton church had failed to follow that procedure for fear that if the offender appeared "with a party to agitate the matter in a time of Contention it might have Broken the Church all to pieces." Still, the council affirmed that any church facing such a controversial case "should not proceed to a censure without the Presence and Advise of a Council of Churches." The elders, the minister added in his report, also reviewed several other procedural matters such as methods of voting and the specific means by which disciplinary cases ought to be brought before the church.[18]

Churchgoers clearly benefited from this instruction. The records suggest that, no less than their predecessors, early eighteenth-century lay people understood church procedures and the respective roles of members and officers. In 1726, for example, the membership of the First Church of Bradford received word from an offender who "desired to be restored" from suspension after dropping a written confession in the mail. Bradford pastor Thomas Symmes had recently died, forcing the church to address the issue in the absence of any ministerial assistance. The laity's response demonstrated not only their knowledge of Congregational provisions but their grasp of the logic behind them. They refused to accept any confession in the absence of the offender's physical presence, arguing that "as a Confession is designed for the humiliation of the Penitent" and to serve as an example for others in the congregation, "neither of these ends" would be "so well answered when it was made" by means of a letter. The church also surmised that other penitents forced to confess before the congregation "would complain of partiality" if the church allowed this member to repent in absentia.[19]

Until the 1730s, when signs of apathy began to surface, members generally took their obligation to render responsible church decisions no less seriously than their predecessors, and they continued to speak out when faced with questionable proceedings. In Abington, "a number of brethren" lodged a protest in 1723, after the church disciplined a deacon for "irregularities" because they "did not fully understand the proceedings," and demanded a second vote. Similarly, in Groton, the members forced the minister to call for a new election when several churchgoers expressed themselves dissatisfied with the means by which the church elevated John Farnesworth to the deaconship. In both cases, the churches affirmed the initial decision—but the laity rested in the knowledge that the votes had been properly conducted. In North Andover, a watchful laity vetoed the admission of a candidate to full communion in 1728; apparently several members were aware of a grievance maintained by a member who was unable to attend that day. The church deferred the admission until the matter was cleared up. Similarly, several members of the First Church of Hopkinton withdrew from communion in 1733 partly because of the church's "receiving [several] members from Framingham without a dismission."[20]

Church members continued to exercise their right to speak out even when dissent required them to overrule their ministers. In 1728, Ichabod Boynton, a member of the Bradford church, acknowledged his sin of drunkenness, prompting pastor Joseph Parsons to recommend his restoration to full communion. The laity refused to allow it, because Boynton had not confessed before the entire congregation. The members' instructions to their recently elected pastor demonstrated not only a familiarity with and a commitment to local practices but a recognition that disciplinary procedures had come to vary somewhat from church to church. They informed pastor Parsons that while some churches required offenders to repent only before the full church members, it had been "the Practice of this church to require a publick acknowledgement of Penitents before the whole Congregation" of members and nonmembers, a practice the church intended to continue. Even after Boynton confessed before the full congregation, not one member voted to readmit him. The flustered minister demanded "that some reason might be given" for the church's resistance to his wishes. After the church requested and received a second reading of the confession, one Captain Kimball informed the pastor that in the opinion of the members, the offender's statement was vague and insincere: the acknowledgement "was not satisfactory because though several times of his excessive drinking had been proved upon him, he had not confessed himself guilty of a one of these times." Similarly, in 1730, Brewster pastor Nathaniel Stone strongly opposed a disciplinary vote of his church but did nothing about it beyond scolding the members and urging them to be "more thoughtfull and ponderus" in the future. The Topsfield church voted in 1702 against dismissing several members; the minister and three local luminaries favored dismission, but the church's decision stood as final and decisive.[21]

These cases demonstrate that ministers could not exercise increased control in local churches by simply claiming the right to do so. Regardless of the local minister's opinion, offenders could not be restored to the church without the consent of the laity, nor could candidates for membership be admitted. Despite ministerial pronouncements on their own authority and the attempts of some to govern their churches in a more autocratic fashion, in sum, the right of lay consent continued to prevent ministers or clerical associations from forcing their wills upon reluctant congregations.

While most ministers continued to honor the members' liberties, some clergymen, as we have seen, were certainly less committed than others to the preservation of lay privileges, Congregational tradition, and the sanctity of the *Cambridge Platform*. Figures such as Solomon Stoddard, the "*Manifesto* men," and a number of authoritarian members of the mainstream Congregational clergy did hope to put their pretensions into practice at the local level. But although these ministers helped to undermine sola scriptura and the New England Way by raising doubts and sparking divisions within the clerical community, they enjoyed limited success in subverting the decision-making process within local churches—even their own.

Notwithstanding the attention that the Brattle Square Church has received from historians, for example, Increase Mather reported that "not above two ministers" in all of New England approved of the *Manifesto*. Unsurprisingly, lay people showed even less interest than the clergy in surrendering the church liberties the *Manifesto* stood to take from them. The First Church of Boston went so far as to pass a formal resolution to denounce the *Manifesto* and the ministers who proclaimed it; the church further agreed to fund a reprinting of the *Cambridge Platform*. A survey of contemporary church records suggests that most congregations simply ignored any Brattle Square practices that stood to abridge lay privileges.[22]

Even within the Manifesto Church, lay people apparently enjoyed some decision-making authority. As Robert Middlekauf noted, the Brattle Street Church regarded its covenant as "one contrived through the laws of nature" more than a "divinely ordered instrument." Anticipating cultural developments that would eventually influence most churches in Massachusetts, in short, the Brattle Square Church stripped its government of connections with sola scriptura. But scanty as they are, the Brattle Square Church records clearly point to the local elders' commitment to voluntarism. The *Manifesto* noted, for example, that members must vote in disciplinary hearings, and the ministers cited the principle of free consent in justifying their decision to modify their terms of admission. "That which pertains to all is not valid," they observed, in justifying broader church membership, "if some sorts have not a consent in it." Though some *Manifesto* practices restricted lay liberties, this "liberalization" or relaxing of admission requirements—a long-standing development that continued to spread to many churches in the eighteenth century—stood to increase the proportion of churchgoers eligible to participate in church government.[23]

The larger influence of Stoddard upon the evolution of Congregational practice in Massachusetts is equally problematical. There is little doubt but that Stoddard, through his theological writings, commanded considerable attention from his fellow ministers. As Perry Miller noted, Stoddard's *Safety of Appearing at the Day of Judgment*, which justified open communion, circulated widely in the clerical community and represented "the only speculative treatise since the founders and before Edwards that makes any constructive contribution to New England theology." Furthermore, as we have seen, increasing numbers of clergymen agreed with Stoddard's stance on consociationalism and his calls upon the ministry to strengthen church order.[24]

Stoddard's reputation among his ministerial colleagues, however, must be distinguished carefully from his influence upon the decision-making process within local churches. Historians have yet to produce evidence that significant numbers of ministers in Massachusetts (even on "the frontier") began to exercise the more autocratic powers of local church government that Stoddard advocated in his publications. To the contrary, in his study of church life in western Massachusetts, Paul Lucas argued that many if not most neighboring churches rejected Stoddard's teachings on church government; as Harry S. Stout noted, "Stoddard's views were not accepted even by many of his fellow ministers in the Connecticut River Valley, and within the churches lay people generally resisted his 'presbyterian' sentiments."[25] Few church records from the area remain for analysis, but those that do survive, such as the records of Westfield and later, fragmentary evidence drawn from Enfield, Hadley, Longmeadow, Somers, Springfield, and Suffield, suggest that, at the very least, many western Massachusetts churches reached decisions by popular consent.[26]

It remains questionable whether the "Pope" of the Connecticut Valley governed even his own church with the "dictatorial powers" he supposedly sought to put "into the hands of ministers." Like most Congregational ministers, Stoddard shared government with lay officers. Stoddard not only employed deacons throughout his lengthy tenure, his church even elevated lay people to the ruling eldership, an office most ministers rejected in their efforts to separate themselves into a distinct governing classis. A lay elder even assisted in Stoddard's ordination.[27] And for all Stoddard's fulminations in his writings that "[t]he community are not fit to rule and judge in the Church,"[28] the Northampton church records—though fragmentary—clearly indicate that the laity did enjoy the right to "judge" and to vote in church affairs before, during, and after the tenure of Stoddard. Membership requirements, they reveal, were "Voted and consented to by the Elders and Brethren of this Church" in 1672, the year Stoddard was ordained. In 1715, years after Stoddard had advocated a more Presbyterian form of church organization in print, the Northampton church did finally acknowledge the authority of outside councils—but this acknowledgment was reached with the consent of the laity. Stoddard carefully noted in the records that his "Proposals" were "Read in the Church of Northampton" and "after some discourse" with the membership, the church "voted in the Affirmative."[29] Based upon their examination of Stoddard's printed works, historians have strongly emphasized the Northampton minister's rejection of the "congregational principle of obligatory consent." But they have yet to provide strong evidence (much less unequivocal proof) that any Congregational church in Massachusetts—including Stoddard's own—reached important church decisions without the consent of the members.[30]

That lay people enjoyed at least some decision-making authority in Northampton is less surprising in light of the rationale Stoddard employed in justifying his "Superior Council" to his congregation. Stoddard's comments in the manuscript church records suggest once again that, regardless of the autocratic sentiments he expressed among other ministers, the Northampton minister sang another tune when faced with the practical realities of governing his own congregation. A desire to impose bald clerical "tyranny" upon lay people seems to have been less at the heart of his efforts than a desire to strengthen the gathered ministry; Stoddard hoped to reinforce stability in a system of church order that was rapidly disintegrating, partly because of divisions among the ministers themselves. Considering the frequency with which churches and ministers ignored councils, Stoddard explained to his congregation, existing Congregational provision offered "no remedy" in cases of clerical "mal-administration." The only "effectual means for addressing grievances," he asserted, was to grant councils binding authority.[31] Like many of his colleagues, then, Stoddard sought to strengthen associations and councils mainly to help ministers and congregations police one another.[32]

For all of the (deserved) attention Stoddard had received for revivalism, in short, his ecclesiological influence was limited. Other "innovators" were even less successful than the Northampton pastor in forcing procedural changes upon local churches, particularly in cases where lay liberties seemed to be at stake. In Cambridge, William Brattle attempted to revise admissions practices in accordance with the *Manifesto*, announcing that although future candidates for admission would have to submit to private meetings with the elders, the church would no longer require them to make a formal public testimony of grace, a practice that increasing numbers of lay people were coming to oppose. But the congregation would not allow Brattle to establish church policy on his own: the proposal sparked an immediate church division. Facing the angry opposition of numerous members who remained concerned with issues of church purity, Brattle agreed to "let something be communicated to the church by my self or the Elder, wherein I received satisfaction from those who ask communion with us as to their spiritual fitness for it," a compromise to which the laity assented. As was so often the case, a significant difference existed between what the "liberals" preached on the subject of clerical prerogatives and what they were able to practice on the local level.[33]

Lay resistance to clerical innovations and pretensions of greater authority was even better exemplified by events in the Third Church of Boston under the ministry of Ebenezer Pemberton. The son of James Pemberton, a principal founder of the Boston Third (or "Old South") Church during the quarrel over the Halfway Covenant, Pemberton had been earmarked to succeed pastor Samuel Willard in the early 1690s. The church backed off when Pemberton's close ties to Brattle Square Church became apparent and periodically debated his status for several years: though clearly impressed with Pemberton's preaching abilities, some members remained leery of his "liberal" orientation. Eventually the church managed to "lay aside their differences" and ordained Pemberton in 1700.[34]

Pemberton's opponents quickly saw their worst fears realized. The new minister's Anglicized manners and leanings toward the practices of the Manifesto Church soon offended many members of the congregation, initiating a steady stream of protest and recrimination. In 1703, the church considered hiring another minister, in hopes that he might "repair some one of our many breaches." The source of these breaches, more often than not, was Pemberton. In 1704, the pastor cut his hair and entered the pulpit sporting a neatly coiffed wig, much to the disgust of Samuel Sewall and other members of the congregation. Some churchgoers began to wear their hats during Pemberton's sermons. Members grew so sensitive to Pemberton's elite manners that an angry confrontation resulted from something as seemingly inconspicuous as the minister's method of addressing the congregation. In giving notice for a church meeting in 1707, Pemberton addressed the members not as "brethren" but as "Gentlemen of the Church and Congregation." On the appointed day, Pemberton entered the meeting house only to find the pews nearly empty. The following morning the members stiffly informed the pastor that "they were not gentlemen" and "therefore were not warned to come" to the meeting. Later, the membership protested Pemberton's usage of "Saint Luke, Saint John," sarcastically reminding their minister that they never used the term "Saint" in that context.[35]

Most of Pemberton's offenses remained matters of insult rather than genuine "mal-administration." But the Boston minister crossed that line in 1709, when he announced that a member had sinned and then, in the absence of any discussion over specifics, produced a written confession and requested the offender's readmission. Pemberton's bold violation of standard Congregational procedures shocked the membership. Speaking on behalf of the congregation, Sewall angrily protested that the church knew nothing of the case and was hardly in a position to consent to a readmission. "An ignorant consent," Sewall explained, affirming a principle Congregationalists had shared for generations, "is no consent." Pemberton backpedaled quickly to reveal the specifics of the offense, but the members refused to let the matter rest. They forced a formal apology from Pemberton and a solemn pledge never to repeat a similar breach of Congregational liberty in the future.[36]

After thirteen years of these sorts of squabbles, the Boston Third Church laity finally ran out of patience and took decisive action. The church believed that none of the minister's various offenses constituted formal grounds for dismission, so they decided to elect a co-pastor. The membership nominated Joseph Sewall, son of Judge Samuel Sewall, who had dogged Pemberton's every step on the road of "innovation." In the face of Pemberton's vigorous opposition, the church elected the younger Sewall by a two-to-one margin. One layman, elated by the result, explained that he finally anticipated the end of the "controversies which prevailed during the greater part of Mr. Pemberton's ministry." Sewall acted as a counterbalance to Pemberton's "liberal" views, affirming, for example, the scriptural bases of lay elders, which Pemberton had denied. Pemberton, like the other innovators, found it impossible to "fly [his] own course" without careful regard to lay privileges and Congregational traditions.[37]

Many churches certainly enjoyed relatively peaceful lay-clerical relations in the early decades of the eighteenth century, and, notwithstanding the effort of the innovators, churchgoers and clerical traditionalists managed to preserve the rights and liberties lay people had enjoyed for a century. Nevertheless, by the 1720s and the 1730s the amount and intensity of church conflict once again began to reach disruptive levels. "Unhappy [is the] state of the world with respect to Ecclesiastical Controversies, respecting government," lamented Longmeadow pastor Stephen Williams, reflecting on the discord that plagued Massachusetts churches. "I have been considering what a state we are in," he continued, "and [am] obliged to mourn our Broken state." Essex pastor Theophilus Pickering agreed, warning that these "jarres and contests, into Which-like our churches have been so Lamentably Involved," increasingly distracted the faithful from spiritual concerns.[38]

Earlier, at the turn of the century, church conflict was often tinged with anticlericalism. Even ministers like Samuel Dexter of Dedham, who generally abided by standard practices, struggled with church members hypersensitive to ministerial professionalization and any hint of innovation. But during the two decades prior to the Great Awakening, clerical attempts to abridge lay rights and resistance to church officers who sympathized with "liberals" like Brattle and Pemberton were less frequently at the center of church controversy. Though ongoing lay-clerical disputes certainly contributed to the breakdown of church government, it bears repeating that ministers and lay people were too divided among themselves to justify generalizations that see this kind of conflict as the singular or root cause of Congregational disintegration. Many divisions had little or no direct connection with issues of clerical authority, and most did not break down neatly along a lay-clerical axis. As had been the case throughout the colonial era, most disputes pitted members against members, or the minister and a significant number of his allies against the rest of the church.

The squabbles of the 1720s and 1730s cannot be traced to the neighborly contention so often thrust into the churches in the 1680s and 1690s any more than they can be reduced to simple anticlericalism. Instead, far more than in the previous century, most church disputes fell under the broad category of church government itself. Churches divided internally over an unending variety of procedural issues during the 1720s and 1730s, ranging from psalm singing to the election of deacons, from disciplinary cases to methods of handling controversies among neighboring churches. A host of specific questions centering around church order, including the use of the silent and "handy" vote, opened a rift in the Norton church in 1722; disagreements over church procedures also contributed heavily to a formal separation in Marblehead in 1716. In 1723, conflict erupted in North Reading when several members "greatly departed from the Platform." In 1725, the First Church of Ipswich suffered "unhappy discord" over whether its pastor maintained a right to remove; that same year "malancholly Divisions and Animosities" struck the First Church of Reading. Routine disciplinary cases divided the First Church of Framingham and twice split the First Church of Abington. In 1729, dissenters charged Leicester pastor Parsons and his supporters with "Male-Administration"; when Parsons in turn portrayed his opponents as a "mob" and described their meeting as a "cabal," the dissenters brought the minister up for slander. The First Church of Hopkinton battled over admissions requirements in 1735. Several churches wrangled with one another in 1736 over whether the First Church of Salem ought to ordain John Sparhawk.[39]

Churches found the choice of a minister an especially arduous task, one compounded by the decision to grant members of the town a voice in the selection process. Events in Dedham typified the difficulties ministers faced in seeking unanimous calls and then in attempting to govern a laity whose support was often far from complete. The Dedham church suffered a division in 1725, even before it had ordained Samuel Dexter; apparently, a number of churchgoers were unhappy with the decision to offer the pastorate on the basis of a majority vote. Dexter accepted the pastorate despite the split verdict, observing that churches were generally so divided that ministers could no longer expect unanimous calls: he agreed to the Dedham offer because he had "as Clear a vote for Settlement as can be well looked for in this Day."[40]

Dexter began his labors enthusiastically, but within a few months his tone began to change, as a stream of church divisions gradually drove the minister to distraction. First the new minister expressed concerns that in general "the people are not so easy and agreeable as might be wished for." Within a year, Dexter prayed regularly to God to "Deliver me from unreasonable men—Some such I have to do with . . . they seem to be under a Hellish impetus—when all the while they charge it upon conscience." The records do not reveal the specific difficulties within the Dedham church, but, predictably, certain "procedures" of church government stood at the heart of the problems, a conclusion reinforced by the findings of an ecclesiastical council.[41]

The squabbles among churchgoers over government in the 1720s and 1730s represented the culmination of several developments that had long been set into motion.

First, declining commitment to and confusion over the meaning and significance of sola scriptura, along with the continuing divisions among ministers over church practices, meant that, far more than ever before, no set of absolute standards of church government remained for churches to draw upon. As we have seen, churches attempted to abide by the *Cambridge Platform*, but churchgoers long recognized the vague and subjective nature of Massachusetts's "constitution." "Men can make a nose of wax of the Platform," one group of churchgoers observed, "[a]nd bend it as they please."[42]

Second, and perhaps more important, churches witnessed a continued decline in "covenantal piety," as lay people gradually lost commitment to the goals and obligations of the church covenant in the face of rising individualism. This development manifested itself in many ways, such as in churchgoers' refusal to submit to or to participate in mutual watch, or to accept decisions of their local churches as final. Churchgoers often stood aloof from church discipline, which increasingly they dismissed as arbitrary or a simple matter of opinion. Eventually, as we shall see, many churchgoers would come to question the larger relevance of Congregational church government to their spiritual lives.[43]

A growing reliance upon ecclesiastical councils emerged as both a symptom and a cause of this continuing decline in covenantal piety. Suffering increasingly from a development that had begun in the previous century, local ministers found themselves unable to heal internal controversies on their own. Lay people refused to accept censures from their local congregations, believing that, if they looked hard enough, they might find other churches or elders that might interpret matters more sympathetically. Church members consequently began to demand relief from councils at even the slightest provocation. In the First Church of Abington, for example, dissenters twice refused to accept the majority's "advice" in disciplinary decisions, each time demanding an outside council to adjudicate. In both cases the council vindicated the church majority. A lone member forced the Norton church to call a council over a routine disciplinary case in 1722; similar episodes occurred in North Reading in 1725 and in North Andover in 1728. Over the protests of the majority, a minority of nine Reading laymen demanded a council in 1723, charging their pastor with "partiality in administration," while in Kingston, a churchgoer who had bitterly vilified his pastor as a preacher of "profane trash" refused to accept a unanimous censure, insisting instead to be heard before a council.[44]

In the past, as we have seen, divided churches and aggrieved individuals usually abided by council decisions, as long as ministers seemed to judge the case honestly and objectively. It always helped when the council's decision was unanimous. But in the eighteenth century, councils themselves grew divided, rendering nearly useless Congregationalism's most important means of conflict resolution. Ministers publicly repudiated a previous council's decision before "a Cloud of Witnesses in the Church" in Wenham, disagreed mightily over a verdict rendered in Dorchester Village, and engaged in an angry pamphlet war over the Reverend Peter Thacher's move from Weymouth to the Fifth Church of Boston. Lay and clerical delegates from ten churches were up all night, stalemated, attempting to render a decision in a Reading division in 1725. Bitter disagreements among the elders over the right of the First Church of Springfield to ordain one Robert Breck inflamed churches in western Massachusetts in 1734; the Boston press publicized the affair in eastern Massachusetts as well. At about the same time, as we shall see, delegates from dozens of churches struggled with divided opinions over a highly public controversy in the First Church of Salem.[45]

Disputants began to exploit divisions within the clerical community by packing councils with delegates likely to offer favorable rulings. After representatives of three churches arrived to offer counsel in a quarrel in Dorchester Village, a dissenter, Elhanon Lion, demanded "liberty to call in 3 other Churches of His own Choice," which would likely support his minority position. It was hardly coincidence that Wenham's William Rogers appealed to John Wise in a case that allegedly involved church "tyranny," nor was it surprising that Wise condemned the Wenham church. Wenham pastor Joseph Gerrish responded by convening a council of his own ministerial allies, who predictably refuted Wise's allegations. Eventually churchgoers coined the term "anticouncils" to describe this practice of handpicking councils for the express purpose of reversing previous council decisions. Stoddard complained about the practice as early as 1715; anticouncils would later become routine during and after the Great Awakening.[46]

Such developments further eroded churchgoers' faith in the ministry and in the Congregational Way, as lay people began to recognize that, as was the case in local disciplinary hearings, there was nothing remotely "absolute" about a council decision. Council findings represented the opinions and interpretations of learned men, not the Word of God. Churchgoers consequently became increasingly prone simply to ignoring councils whose decisions they found disagreeable. Dissenters in the First Church of Canton rejected the advice of a council in 1725, in Leicester in 1728, in the First Church of Sandwich in 1727, and in the Second Church of Beverly in 1735. In 1723, a council of elders at the Second Church of Reading became so frustrated with the churches' practice of ignoring "advice" that they resolved that "unlesse the Pastor and Church, and also the Aggrieved Brethren . . . would first Resolve, and bind themselves by verbal Promise" to obey the council in advance of a decision, the elders and messengers would simply "Return to their Several Places of Abode." All sides agreed, but when the elders vindicated the Reading pastor, the dissenters ignored the council and continued to raise opposition for years.[47]

By the 1730s, in sum, turmoil within the Congregational churches had clearly reached crisis proportions. A divergence in practices, along with the divided state of the clergy, undermined faith in sola scriptura and in the Congregational Way. The ministers' strongest attempt to take decisive and united action—the *Proposals* of 1705—had not only failed, it had sparked jealousy and distrust among lay people and ministers alike. Church disputes threatened to become unresolvable as councils and anticouncils repudiated one another. Neither ministers nor church members were oblivious to these developments, but most were not yet willing to accept the disintegration of Congregationalism as either insignificant or inevitable. Consequently, when the crisis of the eighteenth century culminated in a cataclysmic division in the First Church of Salem, the elders decided to take a final stand to demonstrate that some sort of orthodoxy remained to hold the Congregationalists together.

Just as the Antinomian controversy exposed the dangerous theological inconsistencies among ministers in the 1630s, and just as the rupture in the First Church of Boston revealed the depth of animosity fostered by the Halfway Covenant, so the Samuel Fiske affair in Salem laid bare the shattered state of Congregationalism by the 1730s. Dozens of ministers entered the fray hoping to prove that, in spite of overwhelming evidence to the contrary, substantial agreement remained among the clergy and Congregationalism still possessed effective tools to maintain order and to discipline wayward churches and officers. They left the battle exhausted and beaten, demoralized by the "destitute" condition of the churches, and more convinced than ever that Congregationalism was failing in its larger mission of serving as a means of grace.

The central figure in the dispute was pastor Samuel Fiske, a Harvard graduate of the class of 1708, who preached in a number of towns in Maine, New Hampshire, and Massachusetts before receiving a unanimous call to the Salem pulpit in 1718.[48] Shortly after his ordination, Fiske terminated weekday lecture sermons in Salem. Apprised of the laity's unhappiness with this move, Fiske agreed to offer the lectures on an informal basis, but he discontinued them for good within a few years. The minister cited lax attendance, but, in fact, he was motivated by displeasure with his salary. The matter rested for years, until Fiske abruptly shocked his congregation in 1728 by upbraiding them from the pulpit for neglecting to follow through on a vote that had passed years earlier. In 1718, Fiske announced, the church had agreed to pay its pastor to revive weekday lecture sermons but then had done nothing further. In passing a vote and then ignoring it, Fiske intoned, the congregation stood guilty of two church offenses of the utmost gravity: "sacrilege and perjury."

The seriousness of the minister's charges left the congregation profoundly shaken. The members did recall that Fiske had broached the subject of reviving the lectures, but several distinctly remembered that the meeting had adjourned before the matter was even debated, much less voted upon. Indeed, "not a single person" in the entire congregation "remember[ed] it passing into a Vote." When the members turned to the church record book to examine the minutes from the church meeting in question, they discovered that an account of the controversial vote had been written "in a different ink, and a great Pen, and interlined," and "crowded between two votes." Fiske insisted that he had merely written the vote down on a separate slip of paper and later entered it into the records. He attributed the different colored ink to the fact that "he had two ink Cases." This explanation satisfied only half the church.

The other half, led by worthy laymen John Nutting, Judge Benjamin Lynde, and Benjamin Lynde, Jr., insisted that Fiske "*interpolate[d]* in the church records" a vote that had never passed.[49] The dissenters sent formal written charges to Fiske, and then withdrew from communion. But a majority of the church (just over one half) sided with the minister and would defend him vigorously throughout the entire affair. The nature of the division reveals once again that few church divisions neatly divided a united laity against their minister.

The debates during the early stages of the altercation demonstrate how eroded and transformed Congregationalism's theoretical underpinnings had become by the 1730s. Neither side based their complaints or their actions primarily upon appeals to lay duties, the *Cambridge Platform*, or the traditional practices of the New England Way. To the contrary, the majority at one point offered the remarkable assertion that "the brethren" of the church "have no right to judge the pastor," an explicit denial of Congregational principles of dissent and watchfulness. References to the *Cambridge Platform* were surprisingly uncommon throughout the affair. The dissenters based their position on reason and natural rights as much as biblical precedent or Congregational tradition, suggesting that by the 1730s the laity had begun to share the more secularized understanding of the basis of church government that Wise and others had introduced in previous decades. In a new "enlightened" vocabulary that in some respects echoed the writings of Wise, the dissenters thus demanded "Satisfactions" from Fiske that "Rational Creatures" might "justly claim" and later insisted that they maintained a "natural Right" to choose "the most suitable method" to issue the dispute.[50]

The dissenters formally appealed for assistance to several Boston churches. Their petition to the Second Church of Boston underscored the laity's recognition of the alarming increase in church divisions, the ineffectiveness of ecclesiastical councils in disciplining offending ministers and churches, and the "Contempt of the Discipline and good order of the churches in this Land" that threatened not only the New England Way but religion in general. Unless the elders united their efforts to enforce some standards, the dissenting laymen wrote, "We shall be in the Utmost hazard of Sinking into Such indifferency and Liberliness [sic] in Religious Matters as will in a little time altogether Destroy the Power if not the Very form of Godliness from amongst us."[51]

The elders agreed. They believed that the Fiske affair represented an ideal case upon which to take a firm stand. The controversy was of great symbolic significance, for it involved one of the oldest and most prominent churches in the colony. And most elders seem to have accepted that Fiske's guilt—at the very least in his mishandling of the dissenters' complaints—was a cut-and-dried matter. In addition to strengthening councils, they hoped to preserve their own credibility by serving notice that the clergy would not tolerate this sort of ministerial behavior.

Benjamin Colman accordingly wrote to Fiske and announced his decision to intervene. "What a Division and rent is this in your Body, or rather in Christ's!" an aggrieved Colman wrote. "Nigh one Half (as we hear) of the Brethren so near to an utter Breaking off and Separation from you!" A council, he affirmed, was the dissenters' "acknowledged Right according to the Profession and Practice of these Churches." Fiske exploded. Insisting that he had "no Occasion for a Council," he warned Colman to observe strict rules of Congregational independence and ordered him not to "intermeddle with my affairs."[52]

Colman ignored Fiske's warnings and organized a council of delegates from four churches that met in Salem on July 17, 1733. The elders quickly confirmed that considerable evidence of forgery existed, that Fiske had denied the dissenters' "reasonable and just requests" to attain satisfaction, and granted permission to the dissenters to take communion with neighboring churches. Fiske and his supporters immediately wrapped themselves in the mantle of Congregational independence. They refused to heed or even countenance the council's decision and dared the elders to do something about their intransigence.[53]

The elders picked up the gauntlet. The four churches on the first Salem council, Boston's Second and Third, Gloucester, and Revere, formally admonished the Salem church and then invited no less than twenty-seven other churches to "unite our Endeavors" against Salem's obstinacy in a last-ditch effort to demonstrate that local churches were answerable to higher laws and would pay a price for ignoring ecclesiastical councils. In response to the invitation, an enormous council—undoubtedly the largest in the history of colonial Massachusetts—convened in Salem in 1734.

The great size of the council testified to the elders' unity and determination to issue a forceful statement in resolving the Salem dispute. But in the final analysis, their actions served only to underscore the divided state of the ministry and the ultimate powerlessness of the elders to take any concerted action of genuine consequence. In a revealing illustration of the fractured state of church government in Massachusetts, laymen within the council fought with laymen, ministers battled with ministers, and lay delegates and clergymen cast jealous eyes at one another.

First, nine of the twenty-seven churches invited refused to attend because they could not agree upon the legitimacy of sending delegates to a council that had been repudiated by the Salem majority. Then, even before the council began deliberations, the lay-clerical tensions that so often troubled Massachusetts churches nearly shattered the whole endeavor. Two churches sent only lay delegates to Salem. The ministers from these churches had refused to attend, but their members had nonetheless insisted upon representation. The example once again illustrates the complexity of lay-clerical divisions. Historians have suggested that ministers sought to enhance their control over the laity by violating the Congregational autonomy of local churches. That was sometimes the case. Yet here neighboring *lay* delegates deliberately violated the autonomy of the Salem church—which had utterly refused to countenance the council—for the purpose of combating Fiske's ministerial "tyranny," while their ministers defended principles of Congregational independence.[54]

Bitter arguments quickly erupted in the council chambers over the presence of these lay delegates and whether they maintained a right to participate in the absence of their ministers. After some debate, the council voted in the affirmative, a conclusion that angered a number of clergymen: several ministers refused to vote, while others "entered their dissent" to the decision. The ministers then raised larger questions over the general "manner of voting," in light of the "disproportionate number of [lay] delegates from Some of the Churches." These concerns reflected fears among some ministers that the council might divide along lay-clerical lines, a striking contrast to the spirit of lay-clerical cooperation evident in councils during previous decades. The clergy's response to the voting issue only heightened those sorts of suspicions. Though usually councils accepted majority votes "by persons," they decided to vote by churches, which stood to minimize lay influence.[55]

These preliminary skirmishes hardly ended the council's difficulties; indeed, the delegates were just getting warmed up. Upon questioning Fiske's adherents, the elders discovered that, in the opinion of the Salem majority, the pastor had long ago offered "very reasonable and Christian" written proposals to the dissenters for reconciliation. Several ministers insisted that these proposals "Should be brought into the Council." Others opposed, arguing that the proposals had little to do with Fiske's alleged forgery or his outrageous response to the injunctions of the first council. Nor had the Salem church advanced them—Fiske had written them on his own. After a lengthy and acrimonious debate, the council's vote to bring in the proposals "passed in the negative," a "very grievous" result to "a great number." Five ministers summarily withdrew from the council and returned home, while six more announced that they "declined to give over Judgement pro or Con" on any of the proceedings to follow. Several lay delegates "were of the same mind," though most disagreed and elected to stay and vote.[56]

The irony of these developments was not lost upon the participants, especially pastor Nathaniel Appleton, a delegate from the First Church of Cambridge. At the very moment when the elders had come together to bolster the sagging authority of councils by taking a firm, united stand, the divisions among and between the ministers and the lay delegates over sundry procedural issues paralyzed them from taking decisive action. Little wonder that in similar cases throughout the province local churches ignored the decisions of the assembled elders and that church government gradually lost much of its force in the eighteenth century. "I would only observe," Appleton lamented, "how Unhappy it is, that when those who come together to heal division among others Should be divided among themselves, a Melancholy token that the Churches then convened had not so much presence of great head of the Church att the convention."[57]

The remaining delegates voted to condemn Fiske and his supporters, and expressed their intention to withdraw communion from them and to censure the church formally. But the ministers' last stand had been an abject failure, and they knew it. Appleton maintained "little Expectation" that this admonition would meet with success, "considering how the matter [had] been driven on." The Cambridge minister was correct. Fiske and his followers simply ignored the council and, when the dissenters demanded a separation, the Salem majority built another meeting-house.[58]

Appleton predicted that "[t]hese proceedings are like to occasion a greate deal of debate in the Country." Again, he was correct. Massachusetts culture, it bears re-peating, remained religious; few controversies in civil government or secular affairs during the 1730s captured public attention like events in Salem, which forced minis-ters and lay people throughout the colony to confront, if often belatedly, the unmis-takable erosion of their church government. The controversy became "the poblick Talk of the Country," as churchgoers and their elders eagerly debated the specifics of the case. In accordance with Congregational provisions, ministers explained the controversy to all twenty-seven churches invited to the council, and, in the after-math, the results spread as far as Hatfield in western Massachusetts and even to Newington, Connecticut.[59]

The various antagonists in the Fiske controversy wrote and published six pam-phlets pertaining to the affair, totaling nearly 300 pages.[60] The council appointed a committee to prepare a narrative of their proceedings for publication and "when printed," to send copies to all of the "Congregational Churches in the Province." The result, entitled *A Faithful Narrative of the Proceedings of the Ecclesiastical Coun-cil Convened at Salem in 1734*, totaled ninety-two pages. The First Church of Boston received its copy in March 1735, "superscribed to the Pastor, to be Communicated," or read to the entire church. The significance of the Salem affair and concerns with the state of church government were evident in the decision of the Boston members to stage a public reading of the pamphlet. They gathered in the meetinghouse on a cold winter night and listened for hours as the elders detailed the vastly tangled coun-cil proceedings. "One of the Pastors read out of it one Hour," the minister noted, "[a]nd the other for another Hour. The Weather being very cold, a Motion was made that we should adjourn to Mr. Jonathan Williams's House, which was voted. And the Brethren immediately repairing thither, we finished reading of the Book abovesaid."[61]

The First Church of Beverly also demanded a complete disclosure of events in Salem. In 1735, the church voted that *A Just and Impartial narrative of the contro-versy between the Rev. Samuel Fiske . . . and a number of brethren*, a 115-page collec-tion of testimony, letters, and other relevant documents, "might be laid before the Church and read in their Presence and Hearing." Some opposed the motion on tech-nical grounds, because this particular pamphlet "was neither directed to the Pastor nor the Church directly or indirectly," but the minister noted that the laity "gener-ally insisted upon it, that this Book should be read in (or att) a Church Meeting." A later entry in the Beverly church records refers to "the reading of *both* the above said Books," suggesting that the church read *A Faithful Narrative* as well.[62] That neigh-boring churches would spend hours reading hundreds of pages on the Salem dispute testifies to the controversy's sobering effect upon churchgoers. With clerical authority waning, councils increasingly ineffectual or ignored, and divisions rampant among the laity and ministers, the New England Way seemed on the verge of self-destruction.

Gloucester pastor John White and Benjamin Prescott of the Third Church in Salem employed the Salem dispute as a point of departure for published explorations of both the contemporary state of church government in Massachusetts and the theoretical bases of the *Cambridge Platform.* A disciple of John Wise, White appropriately subtitled his 1734 pamphlet *New-England's Lamentations,* "The Declining State of our Church Order, government, and discipline." White summarized most of the problems that beset Massachusetts churches in this publication. Councils, he noted, were "ineffectual" largely because of the implementation of "*Anti-Councils,* whereby contrary Results are given on the same Case, to the great Reproach of *Councils,* and Blemish of Our *Church-Government.*" Echoing Wise's sentiments, White blamed the ministry for church disorder. Too often ministers wandered from the biblical "Rule" and governed in an "Arbitrary" fashion. Worse, ministers violated higher laws or "professed *Principles,* making our *Wills* the Rule," which amounted to "*Tyranny.*" When the laity in Massachusetts, "a people fairly possessed of *Liberties* and *Privileges* are thus dealt with, this leads directly to contention and confusion."[63]

White offered a two-pronged solution to the problems facing the churches. First, he issued a call for the revival and implementation of ruling elders. Lay elders were critical to achieving a balance of power, White believed, when serving as watchmen over their ministers. Had Salem employed ruling elders to assist and supervise Fiske, White argued, the entire controversy would have been avoided.[64] The function of ruling elders, at least as White conceived them, contrasted sharply with their role in earlier generations, when they served as clerical allies in church government. Advocates of the office now considered lay elders as representatives of the people in church government, an institutional recognition of the divisions that now increasingly pushed lay people and ministers into two contending camps.[65]

A number of churches debated the reinstitution of ruling elders in the 1730s and several elected them. As soon as the Salem church formally divided, the dissenters elected two ruling elders to counterbalance the ministry. The church continued to employ ruling elders until well into the nineteenth century. The First Church of Revere and the Fifth Church of Boston, both of which were intimately acquainted with the Fiske affair, ordained lay elders in 1735 and 1736, respectively. In Beverly, pastor Joseph Champney explicitly refuted the biblical basis of lay elders. Nonetheless, considerable sentiment in the church favored their election. Three times the matter came to a vote, though the measure never passed. Similar debates on ruling elders arose in other churches as well.[66]

The second and most important part of White's plan for Congregational reformation centered around a plea for churchgoers to recommit themselves to the *Cam-*

bridge Platform: "Study the Principles of your *Faith* and *Order*, be heartily recon-
ciled to, and be Zealous in the Defence and Practice of them." What White could
not recognize, of course, was that ministerial unity, communitarianism, and voluntarism had been keys to the success of Congregationalism, not simple adherence to
the *Platform*, a vague and even contradictory document. Whether accepting or refusing invitations to attend the Salem council, ministers cited the *Platform* in justifying their decisions, and Fiske cited traditional Congregational liberties whenever
convenient, especially in refusing to heed the councils' admonitions.

Particularly striking in *New England's Lamentations* was White's affirmation that
the *Cambridge Platform* was nothing more than a "humane composure." White
quickly pointed out that "sermons, catechisms, confessions of faith, and the like"
were also human inventions, and excoriated ministers who seized upon the recognition of the *Platform*'s human origins as a justification to flout it. But the crucial
fact remained that by the 1730s, the strongest supporters of the *Cambridge Platform*
no longer regarded the New England Way as a product of revelation that followed
the Bible in every particular. This recognition, as we have seen, was gradual. Wise
took an important step earlier in the century by justifying Congregationalism on the
basis of natural law in addition to Scripture rules. White carried his mentor's thought
a step further in asserting that the *Platform* was what for a century ministers had
denied—simply an invention of men.[67]

Considering that *New-England's Lamentations* also contained the first public accusations condemning certain Massachusetts clergymen for their links to Arminianism,
White's views on church government were all the more significant: his condemnations of Arminian principles suggest that as the focus and justification for church
government became increasingly secularized and divorced from revelation, most
ministers nevertheless remained steadfast in the pulpit, preaching in an orthodox
and conversion-oriented manner. While church government became less informed
by the Bible and things of the spirit, in short, the same should not be concluded of
the culture in general. This dichotomization would culminate in the aftermath of
the Great Awakening, when many congregations would insist upon evangelical
preaching while maintaining a skeletal system of church order that many came to
regard as a civil agreement rather than a product of Scripture.[68]

Another important reconsideration of church government and the *Platform* appeared in Benjamin Prescott's *Letter to a Friend*, published in 1735.[69] Prescott, pastor
of the South Peabody church, sat on the council during the Fiske affair and published his *Letter* to vindicate the council's decisions.[70] Like White, Prescott jettisoned
sola scriptura as a justification for the Congregational Way and emphasized instead
the concept of the consent of the governed. While "Church Government, Church
Communion, Watch etc. are in Scripture most strictly enjoined," he noted, "there
is in Scripture no Form of Church Government laid out in such concise and express
Terms, but that it is necessary for churches to agree as the methods and modes

thereof." The specifics were "in Scripture very much left to Humane Prudence and Descretion."[71]

The *Platform* was "highly reasonable," Prescott averred, and agreed with Scripture. But what bound churchgoers to abide by the *Platform* was neither the Scriptures nor even reason, but their own voluntary consent, a political concept that churchgoers increasingly vested with sacred significance once they no longer looked mainly to sola scriptura to justify Congregationalism. When a group of Christians consent to "this or that Form of Church government for their mutual edification," Prescott wrote, "then that form so agreed to, becomes in a manner Sacred." Voluntary consent required all that "have agreed or consented to the Government" to abide by it; Prescott thus justified the *Platform* like a constitution, a term which, especially since the writings of Wise, had became synonymous with the *Platform*. Similarly, no individual church that voluntarily joined in a consociation maintained a "liberty to practice" whatever it pleased. Both Prescott and White venerated the *Cambridge Platform*, in short, but, anticipating developments in political thought over the next several decades, they defended the traditional liberties and responsibilities of the brethren not primarily on the Bible but on the basis of natural rights, reason, free consent, and limitations on authority.[72]

That churchgoers still fought over issues of church government suggests that in general they continued to value Congregationalism as an important facet of their spiritual lives. But by the mid-1730s, the signs of disinterest in covenant obligations that had begun to surface in previous decades became widespread and unmistakable. Reflecting upon the general state of church government in the aftermath of the Salem affair, several local congregations joined with their ministers to acknowledged the failure of mutual watch, the demise of church discipline, a decline in familiarity with Congregational provisions, and a general lack of interest in church order.

As we have seen, many churches exercised church discipline only in the most obvious of cases in the 1720s and 1730s, a development that in part reflected a decline in commitment to mutual watch. The First Church of Cambridge acknowledged "a great many disorderly walkers" among both full members and children of the church. This "Sinful disorder," they decided, was "very much owing to our not Exercising the faithful and friendly watch over one another." The church "Solemnly promise[d]" to resume mutual watch.[73]

But a lack of commitment to mutual watch represented only part of the problem. Churches also became reticent about disciplinary concerns because they recognized that so many cases proved impossible to resolve. All too often disciplinary cases—and issues of church government generally—seemed to result only in divisions, followed by councils and anti-councils, and so many churches silently chose to ignore them.[74] From time to time churches vowed to revive strict discipline, but little came of these efforts. In Cambridge, the effort to restore discipline and mutual watchfulness met with little success; twice the church openly acknowledged their failure.[75]

The First Church of Beverly responded to growing apathy by undertaking a complete reexamination of their covenant, the foundations of their church, and church government in general. They concluded by acknowledging "the Platform as the Rule of Church Government and Discipline and That this Church will observe it as their Rule for the future." But surprisingly, the vote "passed by a very small margin." Upon further discussion, the church members admitted that the reason for the "small margin" was the members' lack of familiarity with the *Cambridge Platform*. Accordingly, they appointed a committee of worthy laymen to "peruse" the document, which recommended acceptance.[76]

Other obvious signs of disinterest in church government began to surface as elders began to note that members refused to bother themselves with church meetings. Officers in Beverly, Brewster, Boston's First and Third Churches, Framingham, Haverhill, Longmeadow, Wakefield, and other churches complained of "very thin" attendance at church meetings during the 1730s. In 1736, only six members turned out for a disciplinary hearing at the Seventh Church of Boston. The elders simply dropped the case. Churches even lost interest in the Fiske affair. As the months passed and the Salem dispute dragged on to include quarrels over the titles of the two churches and the location of the respective meetinghouses, the Beverly and Boston First Churches, both of which had spent hours considering the case, finally gave up, deciding to drop the matter from all consideration.[77]

Heavy storm clouds had clearly gathered in the years preceding the Great Awakening. As the Salem dispute demonstrated, churchgoers remained committed to principles of accountability, free consent, and other lay rights. Nevertheless, by 1740, Congregationalism had lost much of its force and had ceased to serve many of its functions, often standing as an obstacle on the path toward salvation rather than a means to grace. At last acknowledging, as Benjamin Colman observed, the degree to which church government had "hindered the growth of the Church and the Success of the Gospel among them," ministers finally understood that problems of contention and apathy could not be addressed simply through institutional change. Instead, they would seek to restore harmony in the churches by rekindling the power of the spirit among their followers. While the elders would exceed all expectations in reviving spiritual vigor in Massachusetts, they would also come to question whether the Congregational Way of their forefathers could continue to occupy a central place in the religious life of Massachusetts.[78]

10

The Great Awakening and the Privatization of Piety

Three years after the great awakening of 1741–1742, the First Church of Byfield received notice from several members who sought to justify perhaps the most serious of Congregational violations: formal separation from the church. One Benjamin Plumer explained his breach of covenant by questioning Byfield pastor Moses Parsons's qualifications as a genuinely "faithful experienced minister of Jesus Christ." Plumer accused the clergyman of failing to "bear a proper Testimony against such as oppose" the Awakening, a clear "Work of Gods Grace." "I don't remember Sir," he informed his pastor, "that you ever so much as gave Thanks for Such an Unspeakable Favor to the World as Mr. Whitefield." Another dissenter, Samuel Adams, explained that "it does not please the great God to edify my Soul" under Parsons's ministry. A third, one Joshua Boynton, objected to the church's reservations toward itinerant preachers, whom he "look[ed] upon as Ministers of Christ Authorized by his Spirit to preach the Everlasting Gospel of his Grace."[1]

Missing from the members' list of grievances were any complaints concerning violations of the *Cambridge Platform*, abuses of clerical authority, or the means by which the Byfield church reached decisions. The absence of any objections pertaining directly to church government as distinct from clerical qualifications raises some thorny questions since, traditionally, the Great Awakening has been described as a major turning point in the evolution of both the Congregational Way and New England's larger political culture. Scholars have stressed the laity's rebellion against clerical "tyranny" and their clarion demand for "strict Congregational" practices; they single out an insistence upon increased lay participation in the decision-making process which, they argue, not only popularized government within the churches but linked the Great Awakening with the American Revolution.[2] Many scholars, as Jon Butler summarizes, have described a "weakened position of the clergy produced by the Awakening as symptomatic of growing disrespect for all forms of authority in the colonies and as an important catalyst, even cause," of the events that led to independence.[3]

In fact, relationships between the Great Awakening, the evolution of Congregationalism, and lay attitudes toward "all forms of authority" were considerably more
complex than this simple democratizing model suggests. This broad survey of the
church records confirms that although the revival certainly occasioned a cloudburst
of controversy within local congregations, most churches in Massachusetts did *not*
find issues of church government, lay power, or "democracy" at the center of the
storm, or even in the cloudy periphery. Church divisions instead generally revolved
around the degree to which local ministers emphasized the necessity of grace and
the "New Birth" from the pulpit, and their willingness or refusal to embrace the
revival. As the Byfield example suggests, even radical "Separates," who withdrew from
their congregations and sometimes formed their own churches, generally acted in
response to these issues rather than fundamental questions of lay authority in the
local decision-making process that had sometimes dominated Congregational discourse in the past.

Rather than the democratizing turning point that historians have described,
Massachusetts's Great Awakening is better understood as an event whose onset reflected ongoing tensions within the colony's religious life and whose consequences
accelerated changes in both Congregationalism and the larger culture that had long
been under way. Though New Light and Separate practices heightened individualism and contributed to declining deference, for example, neither of these developments commenced with the Great Awakening. Similarly, many congregations chose
to maintain only a skeletal system of church order in the aftermath of the Awakening. But the erosion of church government hardly stood as a sudden lay victory in
the cause of "democracy." Rather, it represented the fruition of developments that
had begun decades earlier. Many features of the New England Way had clearly become desacralized well before 1740, and numerous ministers and their congregations
had long before decided to ignore issues like discipline and mutual watch rather than
fight over them. Alongside the ongoing developments in church order that were
decades old came the new, distracting, and ultimately transforming issue of revivalism. The emphasis upon evangelism and the New Birth that fueled the Great Awakening underscored the diminished relevance of corporate ties and Congregational
procedures as churchgoers focused increasingly on issues of personal piety, the individual "conscience," and novel means of seeking salvation. The divisions that accompanied the revival reflected the shift away from Congregational practices as a
central "means of grace" far more than a democratization of church government.

Writing in 1742, Pastor Nathaniel Leonard recalled the languishing state of religion
in Plymouth before the Great Awakening:

> Religion was then under a great decay; most people seemed to be taken up
> principally about the world and the lusts of this life; though there appeared
> some serious Christians among us that had the things of God at heart, who

greatly bewailed the growth of impiety, profaneness, and other evils, which threatened to bear down all that is good and sacred before them. We were sensible of an awful degeneracy.[4]

Like the Reverend Leonard, most ministers believed that a "decay" in lay spirituality explained not only "worldliness" but declining respect for the clergy and the "General Lukewarmness" toward covenantal obligations and church government.[5] As we have seen, the Massachusetts clergy attempted to address the problems of flagging commitment to church order through institutional change, but lay resistance, combined with the divided sentiments among ministers themselves, frustrated their efforts. At last accepting their own internal disagreements as central to their external difficulties, the clergy stopped bickering over church order and began praying "year after year, that God would pour out his Spirit" to spark a "Revival of decaying Religion."[6]

Alerted to the great success of the English evangelist George Whitefield in stirring up popular religious enthusiasm in the southern colonies, the Massachusetts clergy concluded that a similar religious "awakening" might help reverse the decline of personal and covenantal piety among lay people in New England. This design was, in fact, far more realistic than previous efforts to curtail church disorder and reduce apathy through the creation of standing ministerial councils or enforcement of the third way of communion upon offending churches. The New England Way had always served best as a means toward grace when ministers motivated their flocks to honor voluntarily their covenant duties and to submit to the Word of God.[7]

In deciding to invite the controversial Whitefield to New England, the elders apparently overrode their fears that disorder within the churches might accompany an upsurge in religious interest.[8] Because the clergy regarded disrespect for the ministry, lay disorder, and declining piety as mutually reinforcing variables, a rekindling of religious interest stood only to revive respect for the ministers and to reinvigorate church order. Previous revivals, such as those initiated by Jonathan Edwards in the Connecticut Valley in the early 1730s, had met with just these results.[9]

Whitefield's success in "awakening" large numbers of churchgoers throughout New England in 1740 and 1741 surpassed all expectations. In addition to dramatic increases in full church membership, many ministers described a sudden infusion of lay interest in religious subjects, a healthy moral reformation within the community and, at least initially, a restoration of harmony among churchgoers. In Plymouth, pastor Leonard wrote, "[T]he Gospel made a wonderful impression on the minds of all Sorts of people and Men Women and children were much awakened & some (we believe) were converted . . . great additions were made to the Church of Such as we hope will be Saved."[10]

Though the Awakening was experienced as a novelty, this study has shown how many churchgoers in Massachusetts had been predisposed to respond to the messages of Whitefield and the other native itinerant preachers who followed him. In response to the ongoing problem of lay scrupulousness, ministers had begun to blur the lines of distinction between salvation and damnation. Whitefield (like Jonathan Edwards before him) served an "awakening" function in warning lay people that many labored under a false sense of security. If not clearly reborn, churchgoers were damned. Those especially uncertain of their salvation, such as youthful or halfway members, found this reminder of the necessity of the "New Birth" particularly threatening and responded to the evangelicals with the greatest numbers of conversions.[11]

The itinerant preachers' status as outside observers reinforced their messages, for the authority of local ministers had reached a nadir. Eventually, some evangelicals began to exploit the weakened state of the standing clergy by blaming the ministers for New England's spiritual apathy in an effort to kindle lay "enthusiasm." The clerical community had weathered reproach from ministerial critics in the past; John White and his allies had condemned their colleagues in the 1730s for their "pretensions" and usurpation of lay rights, just as John Wise had done earlier in the century.[12] But the itinerant preachers extended this criticism during the 1740s, took it directly to the people, and, most importantly, placed it in terms of salvation and damnation. Echoing the first Puritan criticisms of the Church of England, evangelists such as Whitefield, Gilbert Tennent, and, most notoriously, James Davenport, went beyond their emphasis upon the New Birth to charge that ministers had misled their churches with lax admissions requirements and cold, dead preaching, symptoms of the chilling fact that the clergymen themselves were unconverted.[13]

These grave warnings proved successful in eliciting conversions, but carried with them dangerous implications. Though Whitefield, an Anglican, scarcely preached a word on church order or debates over lay rights and clerical prerogatives, the terrifying specter of unconverted ministers sundered lay-clerical relations within many churches. Ministers thus witnessed the rise in religious affections that they sought, but with precisely the opposite effect they had hoped for in strengthening harmonious covenantal bonds and church order.[14]

The ministry itself grew bitterly divided over the revival, heaping yet more fuel upon the fires of contention within local congregations, as churchgoers became divided into camps of Old Lights, who opposed the revival, and New Lights, who supported it. Numerous congregations demanded of their ministers the new style of evangelical preaching popularized by Whitefield, insisting particularly upon spontaneity in delivery and an emphasis on the New Birth. Some ministers who refused to comply resigned or suffered dismission at the hands of their congregations. Some groups of lay New Lights broke off from their parent churches to form illegal "Separate" organizations. Other lay groups initiated Old Light separations from New Light ministers. Perhaps a majority of both lay people and their ministers fell somewhere in between these extremes, praising the positive effects of the religious awakening, while decrying excesses such as lay separations and church disorder. Regardless, the unhinging effects of the revival touched nearly every church. The turmoil within the churches gradually died down to reveal unmistakable changes in Congregationalism and lay-clerical relationships. Precisely how the Great Awakening contributed to the evolution of the New England Way and lay attitudes toward church authority remains to be explored.[15]

What, if any, were the lasting effects of the Great Awakening on church government? Any consideration of this question must begin not with events in the standing churches but with an examination of the rise and subsequent development of the Separate movement. The reason for this emphasis is twofold. Of all the various religious groups that emerged during the Great Awakening, we have been told, none were more concerned with church order, popular participation, and "liberty" than these "strict Congregational" New Lights. In contrast to moderate New Lights, who usually supported the revival, decried its excesses, but demanded few institutional changes, the Separates turned their backs on standing churches and gathered their own (often illegal) organizations. Some adopted church covenants that limited clerical authority, including reinstating the office of ruling elder. The Separate movement eventually withered and died, scholars have suggested, largely because standing ministers embraced an evangelical style of preaching and revamped church order to reflect Separate demands for greater lay participation. If we are to find forces that democratized church government, in short, we are most likely to locate them among the Separates, who, according to historians, exerted an influence far beyond their numbers and as a group became a primary engine of cultural transformation in eighteenth-century New England.[16]

We should not overlook the importance, however, of the fact that historians have based their accounts of the development and significance of the Separate movement on evidence mainly drawn from Connecticut rather than Massachusetts. While a large number of Separate petitions and church records are available for Connecticut,[17] only a handful of Massachusetts Separate organizations left accounts of church meetings and votes, and just a few of their Separate petitions and brief published justifications for separation remain.[18] Because relatively few sources pertaining to the Massachusetts radicals remain, historians have generally lumped the Separates from the two colonies together when analyzing them.[19] An examination that focuses specifically upon the Massachusetts Separates and considers distinctions between them and the Connecticut group casts new light on the goals, process, and lasting democratizing influence of both the Separate movement and the Great Awakening.

Connecticut Separates shared with their Massachusetts brethren a desire for a more heartfelt, "experiential" religion and evangelical preaching—both were, in fact, central to the movement. But in the early stages of the Great Awakening, many Connecticut radicals complained about excessive clerical control, whereas most across the border did not. This difference between the two groups reflects, in part, varying ecclesiastical developments and institutional settings in the two colonies.

In Connecticut, many churches had for decades chafed under the yoke of the *Saybrook Platform* of 1708, which removed decision-making authority from the laity by granting ministerial synods and associations binding powers over local congregations. A significant proportion of the laity never accepted the authority of the document and many churches simply ignored it.[20] During the convulsive lay rebellions in the early 1740s, many Connecticut lay people lashed out at the "unscriptural" nature of the *Saybrook Platform* and demanded instead adherence to the "ancient constitution," the *Cambridge Platform*.[21]

In Scotland, Connecticut, a group of Separates protested the standing church's acceptance of "the *Saybrook* Platform," which they considered "disagreeable to the Word of God." Pastor Solomon Paine of Canterbury indicated that his Separate church refused to accept "their being yoaked together, or incorporated into a corrupt Constitution [i.e., the *Saybrook Platform*] under the Government of another supream Head, than Christ, and governed by the precepts of men." The Canterbury Separates voted to govern themselves according to the *Cambridge Platform*. Killingly's Separate pastor Eliphalet Wright also condemned the *Saybrook Platform*, adding that in general his church objected to "the ministers, or ministry, ingrossing into their hands, the power of church government."[22]

Although Massachusetts churches also suffered lay-clerical tensions in the years preceding the Awakening, mutual resentments apparently did not approach the level of those suffered in Connecticut churches[23] and were far less focused upon issues of ministerial authoritarianism.[24] As we have seen, the vast majority of churches in Massachusetts still recognized the *Cambridge Platform* as their official "constitution" of church government, and earlier ministerial efforts to impose the kinds of ecclesiastical changes accomplished in Connecticut had completely failed. As a consequence, Massachusetts congregations were less concerned with questions of clerical control during the Great Awakening; adherence to the *Cambridge Platform* helps explain why Massachusetts provided somewhat less fertile ground for Separatism than Connecticut.

Though less sensitive to issues of clerical authority than their Connecticut neighbors, Massachusetts churchgoers still occasionally included accusations of ministerial "tyranny" in justifying their separations from standing churches during the 1740s. In 1744, for example, Chebacco pastor Theophilus Pickering angered a considerable number of New Lights in his congregation by condemning the revival. The aggrieved brethren demanded a church meeting to discuss the issues, but Pickering refused to comply. The dissenters consequently cited their minister's abuse of office as one of several justifications in forming a Separate church.[25]

Such protests were hardly unique to New Light Separates in Massachusetts, however, and they were largely incidental to the Great Awakening. In the First Church of Concord a group of Separates advanced nearly identical charges of clerical abuse against pastor Daniel Bliss, who, like Pickering, refused to convene a church meeting or to call a council to address disagreements within the church. But in Concord, the minister was a New Light, the Separates Old Light.[26] In general, the church records do not reveal that Old Light ministers governed their churches with a heavy hand or that New Light and Separate ministers allowed for a unique degree of lay participation. An examination of the decision-making process within an individual church sheds little light on whether that particular church harbored Old or New Light sympathies; similarly, strict adherence to Congregational governance rarely stood as a central factor in precipitating either Old or New Light separations.[27]

The complexity of the relationship between church government and the Great Awakening in Massachusetts is signaled in lay-clerical developments in Boston and Framingham. Samuel Mather, pastor of Boston's Second Church, was, in matters of church government, as strict a Congregationalist as Massachusetts ever produced.[28] Yet despite his firm commitment to lay rights, he fell into disfavor with New Lights in his congregation and eventually led an Old Light separation from Second Church.[29] In Framingham, pastor Matthew Bridge's method of government represented the antithesis of strict clerical control. He studied the *Cambridge Platform* and publicly affirmed his allegiance to this "Constitution spiritual and political" prior to his 1746 ordination. Virtually all church decisions during Bridge's thirty-year pastorate were reached by popular consent. The Framingham pastor was so solicitous of lay liberties as to refer to himself as merely the "moderator" of church meetings, whose function was more to preside over meetings than to add the weight of office to the decision-making process. Nevertheless, Bridge, an Old Light, suffered a New Light separation shortly after assuming office; his detractors denounced him as a "Socinian" who failed to preach the doctrine of original sin.[30]

Perhaps the most telling case occurred in Salem, where the Great Awakening served as the backdrop for the final act in the Samuel Fiske drama. Here, not only did a crisis in ministerial authority precede the Awakening by a decade[31] but the expected association between revivalism and lay rights was actually reversed. After the autocratic Fiske and his supporters broke off to form the Salem Third (or Tabernacle) Church in 1735, the original church recovenanted on principles of lay liberty and strict observation of standard Congregational practices. One of the congregation's first actions was to elect two lay elders who would help assure that ministers did not seize control of church affairs. Thus the First Church of Salem would seem to fit the profile of an emerging New Light congregation. But, in fact, the church became Old Light during the Great Awakening. Meanwhile, Fiske's supporters at the Salem Third Church, who upheld their pastor's demand for strict ministerial control in their 1735 separation, fired their minister and hired Dudley Leavitt, a New Light. A number of Old Lights from Fiske's Third Church, in turn, separated and returned to the First Church, joining the enemies from whom they had separated earlier. Clearly, the Awakening made for strange bedfellows, and a congregation's attitude toward church government, lay rights, and clerical pretensions did not necessarily correlate neatly with its attitude toward the revival.[32]

Separate petitions make clear that issues of church order were not irrelevant to the movement. Dissenters in both Sturbridge and Milford lodged the common Separate protest that their standing churches practiced lax admissions standards and consequently suffered from impurity: "we don't look upon this Church to be a visible church of Christ," the Milford Separates wrote, for "the Lord hath made us to see that this Church are thieves and robbers, because they come not in by the door; we mean, by Christ, by love to God and towards another, and according to the Scriptures; we mean by faith." Still, it is critical to distinguish the Separates' demands for strict admissions from the more abstract issue of democracy: in virtually every case their grievances centered on claims that the churches were insufficiently pure, not insufficiently democratic. Neither the Sturbridge nor the Milford Separates complained that the minister refused to allow them to participate in admissions hearings. The Massachusetts Separates rarely raised these kinds of issues. Rather, they complained that the church as a whole suffered because individuals had been admitted who had not experienced the Separates' version of the New Birth.[33]

Whether in Abington, Barnstable, Boxford, Brewster, Duxbury, Framingham, Georgetown, Methuen, Newbury, Rehoboth, Sturbridge, or Wakefield, nearly every complaint left on record by Massachusetts New Light Separates points to the preeminence of theological issues over questions concerning ecclesiology, democracy, and lay participation in church government.[34] In 1749, for instance, the church of Milford gathered to hear "the Reasons of Samuel Warren, Daniel Corbett, Jr., and Eunice Lathome for their withdraw from us." In striking contrast to Connecticut petitions, the Milford Separates' list of grievances do not contain a single reference pertaining to lay liberties in church government or clerical "tyranny." The most important of their complaints concerned the absence of "that food for our souls by the word that was preached here which we have found in the word of God and elsewhere."[35] Eleven Sturbridge Separates offered slightly less specific statements in 1749, but once again indicated that questions of clerical power and lay participation were of little immediate significance.[36]

The circumstances surrounding New Light separations from the First Church of West Newbury and the First Church of Essex during the mid-1740s cast further doubt upon the significance of church government and clerical authority to the Separates' cause. Pastor Thomas Barnard moderated church meetings in West Newbury with great sensitivity to lay liberties, making certain that every church action met with the members' approval. Nothing in the West Newbury records even hints that issues of government contributed to the dissatisfaction of dissenters who withdrew from the church. Rather, their objections, once again, rested with the minister's doctrine. As one Samuel Sawyer explained, "[I]n his Opinion the Preaching herd and the Easiness of the Church with it were contrary to the Gospell, particularly that in some Sermons, on Revelations 22. 14. the Pastor had perverted the Text, advanced the free Will of Man too high and derogated from the free grace of God." Eventually twenty-four other Separates withdrew to join a Presbyterian church, a patently inappropriate move had issues of church government and strict clerical control motivated them. Similarly, in 1747, a number of New Light dissenters from the First Church of Essex met to discuss "an agreement Proposed Between the Prisbiterian Church in Newberry" and two Congregational churches "with respect to a Prisbitery

Being Raised out of themselves." The Separates voted "that we do Cordially agree to Conform with said Churches . . . Thinking it is likely we shall come into said agreement." That same year, a New Light dissenter withdrew from the First Church of Georgetown, renounced the Congregational Way, and announced his intention to join a Presbyterian church.[37]

Although Separates sometimes professed a deep commitment to the practices of the early New England churches, they revealed their lack of concern for issues of government through their frequent disregard for basic Congregational provisions and, especially, covenant obligations. If dissatisfied with a minister's preaching, Congregationalists had always been obliged to consult with him in private in an effort to reconcile differences. That failing, those individuals aggrieved were to bring their complaints before the entire church. Yet in Barnstable, pastor Russell affirmed that the Separates made no effort to "acquaint the pastor" with their grievances nor to convince the church of their views. Similarly, if dissatisfied with a lay conversion testimony, the member's duty to God, the church, the candidate, and himself was to voice his protest. The Barnstable Separates ignored these covenant obligations.[38]

Separate pastor Isaac Backus regretfully acknowledged his Middleboro church's neglect of "strict Congregational" practices as well. The church's failure related directly to the fact that the Separates had emerged from congregations that increasingly neglected church government. Unconcerned with church order at the moment of founding, the members were now unprepared to handle the many responsibilities and practical issues involved in managing a church. Though a recognized ideal, the mutual watchfulness that characterized churches in the seventeenth century seems to have been largely disregarded among the Middleboro Separates. More surprisingly, in light of the Separates' supposed commitment to the pure church,[39] the congregation often failed to discipline its members. In 1749, Backus noted "a great want of disapline here in this church." One Phobe Fobes was known for two years to have been guilty of fornication, yet the church did not reprimand her.[40]

In general, many Separates refused to countenance standard covenant duties as well as long-standing, shared interpretations of the biblical foundations of church practices if those interpretations contradicted their own understanding of biblical truth and communication with the spirit. As the layman Edward Goddard of Framingham averred, "Every man" possessed a liberty of "Worshipping according to his Apprehensions of the meaning" of Scripture.[41] Seen in this context, the Separates' emphasis upon spiritual experience to the near exclusion of covenantal obligations and church government represents one radical result of developments in lay-clerical relations dating back to the 1720s and 1730s, rather than a new departure in lay assertiveness that emerged as a consequence of the Great Awakening.

While the Separate movement did not reflect desires to restore or to democratize Congregationalism in Massachusetts, many radical and New Light practices did reflect ongoing cultural shifts that affected all churches: rising individualism and declining deference. Though ministers had complained of a loss of respect since the middle of the seventeenth century, their concerns centered principally around issues such as salary and lay disorderliness in church government. New Light Separates broke new ground in defying ministerial authority not only in their boldly stepping "out of place" to practice lay exhortation but in their willingness to challenge ministers on theological grounds. Separates in Milford, Barnstable, and many other churches did not hesitate to dismiss their pastor's doctrines and develop their own theological conclusions, apparently agreeing with a Newbury Separate who wrote, "[W]e lookt upon it as the natural right of every Man to enquire and judge for himself in matters of Religion and that without Check or Control from any Man. He is bound to act according to the Dictates of his own Conscience."[42]

The Separates' willingness to break covenant on the grounds of their personal theological conclusions (or "conscience"), along with the general decline of mutuality evident in both Separate and standing churches, also reflected growing individualism in the eighteenth century. Powerful forces of localism and communitarianism remained in colonial Massachusetts; declining covenantal piety and greater emphasis upon personal religious experience do not prove that, in general, society was more individualistic than communitarian.[43] Nevertheless, historians have documented well the increasing social, political, and economic diversification during this period, and in this atmosphere of rapid social change or "fragmentation," corporate identities became less tenable.[44] As Bruce C. Daniels argues, economic growth and increasing diversity served as important factors in "replacing a spirit of community with one of individual aspiration"; scholars have also discovered that revivalism was strongest in areas where diversification and fragmentation were greatest.[45]

In the arena of church government, rising individualism and social and economic diversification rendered less effectual institutions and practices geared toward the closely knit religious communities of the early seventeenth century. These developments neither culminated in nor began abruptly with the Great Awakening; as far back as the 1670s, concern with the individual "reputation" motivated churchgoers to resist the "mind of the church" and to appeal censures to councils and (eventually) anticouncils, even at the cost of shattering harmony in the local community. As churchgoers came to place even greater value upon privacy and personal piety, church covenants and mutual watchfulness became far less relevant,[46] which further helps explain why, in churches throughout the colony, ministers suffered so much difficulty in managing their congregations. A growing emphasis upon privacy heightened the desire of churchgoers to dispense with the requirement of conversion relations during the 1720s and beyond; at the same time, many continued to insist that statements of repentance be delivered only before full church members rather than the entire congregation.[47]

The effusion of religious spirit that accompanied the Great Awakening confirmed that while churchgoers during the 1740s were no less pious than in previous generations, the rising spirit of individualism had gradually become incongruous with certain cultural and institutional realities in Congregational churches. Whitefield, an Anglican, avoided discussions of church government, mutual watch, or covenantal responsibilities; indeed, in no small measure Whitefield enjoyed success in New England because he celebrated an individualistic religious experience before audiences for whom traditional covenantal relationships were becoming largely atavistic.[48] This emphasis upon religious individualism was reflected in a number of novel practices shared by churchgoers during the revival. For example, many were now willing to cross town lines and to identify with speakers from outside the local community. These translocal revivals inevitably brought strangers together, and fulfilled a need for a religious experience that was necessarily more subjective and individualistic than it had been in the seventeenth century when members of the same community shared carefully structured forms of worship and practice.[49]

Ministers in the standing churches reflected and advanced the privatization of piety in Massachusetts both in the means by which they restored order in their congregations and in their shifting attitudes toward church government after the Great Awakening. The virulent contention or "censoriousness" of the 1740s has, perhaps understandably, obscured the equally important theme of accommodation within individual churches and within the clerical community. As Harry S. Stout has shown, both Old and New Light ministers eventually came to recognize that all sides suffered from the mutual condemnations and the lack of clerical accord that accompanied the Great Awakening. In order to retain their status as God's unique spokesmen, ministers would have to focus their energies upon issues that united churchgoers, rather than those that divided them. Most Old and New Light ministers eventually discovered that in many fundamental respects the two sides were not as far apart as they had imagined.[50]

Central to this accommodation was the isolation of several "essentials" that all orthodox ministers shared, many of which were theological. Clergymen urged all pastors and congregations to adhere to the central doctrines of Calvinism; in particular, ministers pressed their colleagues to exercise caution in advancing orthodox discussions of the relationship between faith and works.[51] Ministers also agreed that churchgoers could not enjoy absolute assurance of their own salvation or that of others, and that sanctification did provide evidence of justification.[52]

Importantly, ministers also became largely united in their determination to minimize church division and, especially, separatism. Many clergymen reached accommodation with their local churches by accepting congregational preferences, whether for evangelical or itinerant preaching, or for more traditional messages and styles of delivery. Meanwhile, in their efforts to halt separatism, ministers resolved that virtually no matter of administration justified church withdrawal. In Essex, for example, a ministerial council upheld lay charges that pastor Theophilus Pickering "had been wanting in his examining Persons Fitness for the Lord's Table." The elders also condemned Pickering for his stubborn refusal to call church meetings to discuss the issues with the aggrieved brethren, in open violation of Congregational rules. But at length, the council vindicated the minister, insisting that his offenses not only failed to justify separation but did not even constitute grounds for censure.[53]

Pickering's lay opponents correctly observed that the ministers had no interest in holding Pickering to Congregational provisions; they only intended to "bear witness against separations."[54] The episode demonstrates not only how meaningless councils had become but that ministers would now cast the ordinances to the wind in their determination to preserve order. In a remarkable (if silent) revolution, ministers now regarded most specific provisions of Congregationalism—the Puritans' very reason for coming to the New World—as mere "circumstantials": matters of opinion over which good men might disagree but ought never divide.[55]

Ministers and lay people had gradually come to accept that admissions, discipline, and decision making no longer united churches in an effort to practice God's ordinances; rather, these practices too often led churchgoers and clergymen to struggle over their own prerogatives and to argue among themselves and between one another over varying interpretations of proper church order. The inability of the elders or congregations to speak with one voice on church order became so complete by the mid-1740s and 1750s that even councils became not only ineffective but nearly farcical. In 1744, a council in Upton reached a "result" that, in the words of Grafton pastor Solomon Prentice, was "sighned by Every member of the Council; who Excepted against what particulars they pleased." Looking over the list of objections, Prentice noted "as many exceptions allmost as members of the Council." The elders read the result to "the poor people and left [it] with them to chue [chew] upon and the Council went home, Leaving the people in worse Circumstances . . . than we found them." In Northampton, the members debated endlessly with Jonathan Edwards in 1749 and 1750 in an effort to decide whether the church should convene a council whose task would be to determine whether the church was "ripe" to convene another council.[56]

As a consequence of these developments, many congregations and pastors began increasingly to dissociate themselves from the ordinances, choosing to ignore more divisive issues of church government instead of fighting over them. As we have seen, this process began in the 1730s; by the late 1750s and 1760s it intensified to a point where eventually a majority of the churches maintained only a skeletal version of the New England Way. Developments in Merrimac were typical. Pastor Paine Wingate continued to exercise government in an outwardly Congregational fashion from 1726 to 1786; the church regularly elected deacons and admitted a handful of members to full communion each year. But by the late 1740s, the church rarely engaged in the kinds of lively discussions over government that so frequently punctuated church meetings in Massachusetts over the previous century and a half. The absence of debate in Merrimac reflected concord between pastor and people only in the sense that both sides agreed to disregard church order. Aside from an occasional case of fornication and a small number of members whom they censured for "neglect of public worship" during the Great Awakening, mutual watch and church discipline were largely ignored.[57]

Practices in dozens of other congregations mirrored those in Merrimac. As early as 1746, a group of Newbury laymen condemned the "Lax State" of church government in Massachusetts and, pointing to the *Cambridge Platform* observed, "It would do much better now" if the document was actually "put in practice" by local churches.[58] The First Church of Halifax openly acknowledged that the "ancient discipline" of the church had become "decayed" by 1759; the First Church of Grafton devoted little time to church government by the 1760s after earlier admitting its decline of mutual watch; the First Church of Hopkinton apologized in 1756 for censuring several Presbyterians in the congregation, noting that details of church order were only matters of "conscience" or opinion.[59]

The Merrimac church manifested its lack of concern with church government in early November of 1746 when a meeting was so poorly attended that participants were unable to conduct votes. Lax attendance, which had begun to hamper church meetings in the 1730s, continued to plague the churches in the 1740s and beyond; reflecting upon churches throughout the colony, Jonathan Edwards noted that "when Church meetings are appointed," all too often ministers "found by Experience . . . but few [members] come." The Second Church of Beverly was unable to pursue a disciplinary case in 1746 because of slim attendance; that same year virtually no one appeared at a West Boxford meeting warned to elect a deacon. In Grafton, members became so bored and "tyrd" with their discussions of Separate complaints that "many of them beged that they might go home" while "others drew off with out Leave."[60]

Many churches reflected shifting attitudes toward church order in institutional ways. Important changes in admissions requirements reflected not only ongoing concerns with the difficulty of public relations, but fewer scruples among churchgoers over issues of church purity and, importantly, diminished sensitivity over the respective prerogatives of members and ministers. By the 1760s, most churches no longer required candidates to offer relations in order to achieve full church membership. This change did not mean that churches completely jettisoned the ideal of pure membership, practiced "open communion," or allowed any nonscandalous churchgoer to join with full privileges. The records make clear that many churches still required candidates to undergo private examination by the pastor to determine their "experiences" of grace, and members still maintained a right to veto those of questionable character.[61] But the fact remains that lay people willingly surrendered the keys to admissions—the object of many intense battles over the colonial era— and handed them almost entirely over to their ministers. The records make clear that in many cases even deacons were not allowed to witness private relations. Virtually no controversy or even debate seems to have accompanied this important procedural shift, a dramatic testament to the laity's continued (even heightened) emphasis upon personal salvation and the declining primacy of covenantal relationships and church procedures.[62]

Churches also manifested a reduced concern with church purity and a desire to distance themselves from the ordinances by electing lay committees to supervise various church affairs. Initially, these committees, which begin to appear in the records as early as 1727, consisted of six to ten "worthy laymen" (sometimes, but not always, including the deacons) who assisted the pastor in tasks such as the preparation of disciplinary cases or the church's position for an ecclesiastical council.[63] By the 1750s, lay committees often assumed complete control over matters such as discipline, performing duties formerly carried out by either the pastor or the "presbytery" of minister and lay officers. Often, with no help whatsoever from the local minister, they investigated offenses, presented disciplinary cases before the church, and then offered recommendations to the members, who usually added a perfunctory endorsement to the committee's conclusions. Pastors continued to administer censures, but typically deferred to lay committees in the actual decision-making process.[64] In unusual cases, lay committees exercised extraordinary powers; while "Destitute of a Pastor" in 1765, the First Church of Reading appointed a committee to "Examen Persons that Should offer themselves to the communion of the Church and Receve the Satisfaction that they Shall Give and propound them to the Church" for membership.[65]

As was the case when churches revised admissions procedures, remarkably little disagreement accompanied the emergence of these lay committees. Usually, the pastor simply recorded the church's decision to establish such a committee; few records shed light upon the motivation behind the move. Entries from the records of the First Churches of Haverhill and Halifax, however, do provide some important clues. They suggest that after becoming tired of internal divisions over government and, especially, discipline, clergymen and congregations agreed to adopt lay committees to distance the membership and, eventually, ministers, from controversy. Thus in 1731, Haverhill pastor John Brown proposed the establishment of a "Comittee of some of the most prudent and well respected men" to assist him in church discipline, in an effort to "prevent the trouble of laying [disciplinary cases] before the whole Brotherhood."[66]

A decade later, the Halifax church elected a lay committee to oversee discipline and to bring offenders "to a sight and sense of Sin." In a lengthy justification for his church's vote, Pastor John Cotton could hardly point to the practices of his ancestors. He recognized that lay committees represented a departure from early Congregationalism and, unsuprisingly, he never cited the *Cambridge Platform*. Moreover, although Cotton asserted the change "is not proposed to excuse others from the necessary duty of Christian watchfulness," he clearly believed that the failure of mutual watch and the divisiveness of church discipline made the innovation imperative. In a striking commentary on rising individualism and the disintegration of covenantal piety, Cotton noted that "[w]hen particular members undertake to make enquiry" into disciplinary matters, "they are charged either with prejudice, or doing what is none of their business." Many "contentions and difficulties might be removed and healed without public scandal," Cotton explained, through the implementation of lay committees designed to "prevent as much as possible all difficultyes that may arise in the church relating to [disciplinary] offenses."[67]

In arguing for the institution of a lay committee in Northampton, Jonathan Edwards made clear that the churches of western Massachusetts shared the same difficulties as those in the east. Under the old arrangements, Edwards asserted, church discipline had become destructive of its own ends—not only in Northampton, but throughout Massachusetts. "No one thing has been the occasion of so many and Great wounds," Edwards observed before his congregation, than "Our way of managing Church discipline." Between lay people "quareling with their minister" and "quarrelling one with another," discipline had "hurt the Interest of Religion . . . not only for a little while but a long Time[,] not only in one Church but all over the Land." Instead of "being that wise and excellent means of healing," he continued, "it has proved the worse disease. [W]orse than all the scandals. The Remedy has been far worse than the disease." The ongoing struggles over church government, Edwards continued, had also fostered considerable apathy. Because the churches had been "contending" over church discipline "till wore out with it," he noted, "the multitude don't undertake to watch" any longer and so lay committees "need to be appointed" to supervise community behavior.[68]

Lay committees required some members to share in responsibilities formerly held by pastors and church officers, and therefore might appear to represent an important step in the direction of democratization. But Edwards's comments do not support such an interpretation. Indeed, Edwards bluntly (and publicly) justified the need for committees of "worthy laymen" by pointing to the apathy, inability, and lack of wisdom among ordinary members (or the "mixt Multitudes").[69] Though the conclusions of lay committees were always subject to the members' approval, the level of participation in the decision-making process declined for ordinary churchgoers under these new arrangements. Churchgoers' willingness to accept this new institution reflected the desire among both pastors and members to quietly distance themselves from the ordinances rather than desire of an assertive laity to exercise more initiative in church affairs.

Predictably, though they succeeded in reducing contention, lay committees did not motivate churchgoers to practice stricter discipline. To the contrary, they seem to have provided members with an excuse to avoid disciplinary matters and mutual watch. As had been the case earlier in the century, most churches in the aftermath of the Great Awakening continued to exercise discipline only for obvious offenses like fornication and drunkenness. The First Church of North Andover failed to censure a single member between 1750 and 1759, the First Church of Topsfield between

1745 and 1760. The Halifax church censured eighteen offenders between 1740 and 1744. But fourteen of those cases involved drunkenness or fornication. Similar patterns emerged throughout the colony.[70]

In the early seventeenth century, an absence of disciplinary cases on the records sometimes reflected the members' success in resolving conflict privately. But by the mid-eighteenth century, the paucity of cases was generally rooted in the churches' unwillingness to bother with discipline. In 1763, a Methuen member complained that his church failed to take notice even when members withdrew from communion, while members in Scituate lambasted the church for a "criminal neglect of Discipline with respect to offending members." Several laymen in Newburyport observed that within the churches "slander and other immoralities are past over without restraint."[71]

The Wenham church took extraordinary pains to avoid disciplinary concerns. In 1751, pastor Joseph Swain read a paper from one Mr. Josiah Fairfield to the church "containing certain articles of complaint against Mess: John Gott and Richard Kimball." The church rejected the complaint because the paper lacked a date. Fairfield dated and resubmitted his accusations but three weeks later the church again "voted to take no notice" of the case, "inasmuch as said Fairfield does not positively affirm what he complains of, but setts them forth as his apprehensions." Fairfield rewrote his allegations to refine the disputed terminology, but the church still refused to countenance the matter at the next church meeting, this time "because some of the Articles of complaint were now depending in Law." Fairfield requested a council; the church refused. After lobbying the church for seven months, Fairfield convened a council on his own, which recommended that the church take up the case. Following the council's advice, the church listened to Fairfield's charges, quickly dismissed his "Evidences" as "insufficient," and then suspended him from Communion for "offering to the Church such Complaints as he has not proved." Fairfield sought refuge at the First Church of Beverly, which wrote to Wenham desiring any "Objections they had against Mr. Fairfield's Request to sit down with them at the Lord's Table." In an outright breach of covenantal obligations, the Wenham church voted to ignore the letter and let Fairfield go his way.[72]

Diminished enthusiasm for church government as the sine qua non of New England identity among ministers and lay people alike is evident not only in procedural changes and neglect of discipline but in the nature of the physical records themselves. Even records that appear to be regular and detailed leave little impression that churches devoted much time in the 1750s and 1760s to debate or discussion of Congregational theory or practice; councils became less frequent,[73] and lengthy church divisions involving abstract concepts of lay rights and ministerial tyranny—such as the Salem dispute in 1734—were rare, though not unheard of.[74]

The records of church meetings also display a dramatic decrease in volume. Joseph Champney, who served as pastor in the First Church of Beverly from 1729 to 1773, kept church records regularly until 1738. From January 1, 1738, to March of 1752,

Champney added only seven perfunctory entries to the records of church meetings. The Revere First Church record book, which contains thirty-one pages of entries covering church meetings during the 1720s and twenty-one pages covering the 1730s, includes a scant two and a half pages for the 1760s. Similar patterns are evident in the records of many other churches. The records of the Fourth Church of Haverhill include only five entries from 1745 to 1757. While in some instances the paucity of church records was undoubtedly a function of poor record keeping, the Haverhill records clearly indicate that the church convened only five meetings over the entire twelve-year span.[75]

The relative disregard that many ministers and congregations held for church government after the Great Awakening reflected their changing priorities: far more than ever before, the concerns of most ministers and churchgoers by the 1750s and 1760s had shifted away from procedural matters toward issues of personal salvation and doctrine. These priorities opened up a new battleground upon which lay people would once again affirm their authority. Since the founding, ordinary churchgoers, or at least some of them, felt sufficiently confident in their understanding of church government to question and resist not only the local minister but even the conclusions of the assembled elders. Yet ministers rarely saw people within their congregations cast doubt upon their doctrine unless it was flagrantly heretical—by and large, whatever may have been the case in church government, the ministers' role as God's prophets went unchallenged.

This understanding would come to an abrupt halt during and after the Great Awakening. At first, doctrinal challenges, as we have seen, emanated mainly from the radical New Lights: "Every Man," the layman Edward Goddard of Framingham averred, "has a Right of judging for himself, of trying Doctrines by the inspired Scriptures."[76] As ministers divided more clearly into "rationalist" and "evangelical" preaching orientations, lay people of all stripes would have little choice but to step into the theological arena, often for the first time. Increasingly, the subject of clerical councils during the 1750s and 1760s involved "Uneasiness" among lay people "at the Doctrines delivered by the Pastor."[77] Ministers unable to abide by the wishes of their congregations suffered censure or dismissal, actions that congregations took with unprecedented frequency during the Great Awakening and its aftermath.[78]

Though the Great Awakening certainly rekindled lay interest in things of the spirit, it did not reverse the ongoing disintegration of Congregationalism: the revival neither revived covenantal piety nor restored church government to a central place in the religious life of Massachusetts. In a process that took decades, churchgoers no longer defined themselves according to the specifics of the New England Way, nor did they look to the ordinances as a central means of attaining grace. Moreover, while it would certainly represent a more exciting conclusion to suggest that lay people rebelled against clerical tyranny during the revival, seized control of government from their ministers, and completed a revolution within the churches that helped pave the way for 1776, the records suggest that the Awakening did little to democratize church government. Free consent, limitations on authority, and popular participation had characterized Congregational churches for well over a century. As we shall see, these principles survived the Great Awakening, but they stood as neither unique goals nor consequences of the revival.

At the same time, we should not be too hasty in dismissing the larger significance of the Great Awakening. Though we can tie neither "strictly Congregational" nor increasingly democratic church practices directly to the revival,[79] we have also seen that in more abstract ways it hastened changes in the laity's stance toward church authority. During the upheavals of the 1740s, dissatisfied churchgoers began to express individualism and rising concern for personal piety not by squabbling over procedural details but by breaking covenant with their churches on the grounds of individual "conscience." They manifested declining deference by questioning openly their minister's theology and, most important, by firing pastors who defied their wishes, whether in matters of church order, preaching style, or doctrine. The Great Awakening provided lay people with an opportunity to demonstrate unequivocally that, to whatever degree they chose to exercise it, church authority ultimately resided entirely in their hands. It forced ministers to acknowledge that for their audiences communitarianism and covenantal obligations—even Congregationalism itself—paled in importance to matters of the individual soul. And it served as a powerful reminder to the clergy that, in Increase Mather's earlier words, "God did not make churches for ministers, he made ministers for churches."[80]

Afterword

In 1750, the first church of Northampton faced the momentous decision of whether to fire its pastor, Jonathan Edwards. When the issue finally came before the church for a vote, a contemporary recounted, the members' arms flew up collectively in the affirmative, "as if they went with Springs." The Northampton church did not dismiss its minister for preaching heresy. Nor did Edwards stand accused of sinful "maladministration." Most important, no one charged Edwards with violating the Scriptures. The church's outward justification for firing its pastor was Edwards's refusal to accept the people's preferences in determining requirements for church admissions.[1]

Edwards's dismissal reflected not only a transformation in the Massachusetts laity's stance toward church authority, but the effects of social, economic, and cultural change upon Congregationalism. Edwards's response to rising individualism, an emerging (if nascent) "capitalistic" outlook, and declining covenantal piety— developments that affected congregational life in most Massachusetts communities— clashed sharply with the views of most of his church members. Edwards became, in many (though by no means all) respects, a genuine "strict Congregationalist," who condemned the effects of these changes upon church life, and sought to restore more traditional patterns of lay-clerical relations, covenantal obligations, and church government. His congregation would have none of it.[2]

The circumstances of Edwards's dismissal also confirm that while over the course of a half century most lay people had come to regard admissions requirements and other specific Congregational practices as matters of interpretation or preference, they did not reach the same conclusions about larger principles of free consent, accountability, or their own rights. Indeed, the actions of the Northampton church point to a fundamental shift in lay attitudes toward larger conceptions of authority that had evolved gradually over the course of the colonial era. In matters of theology, doctrine, or government, by the 1750s churchgoers held their ministers far more accountable to their own collective will than to the Bible.

Just what congregations demanded from their pastors in matters of church government varied considerably in the aftermath of the Great Awakening. A minority of congregations chose to govern themselves in accordance with procedures that differed little from those practiced prior to the revival. Government in many smaller, rural congregations sometimes seemed a throwback to earlier generations; practices also changed little in some congregations that enjoyed unusually lengthy pastorates.[3] Lay people in other congregations, as we have seen, chose to surrender their authority in many areas, passing the keys to admissions to the ministers and turning "watch" over to committees of their peers, in order to avoid church government.

The degree to which any given church decided to observe or to ignore particular practices of government was determined entirely by the laity, and all Congregational churches in Massachusetts continued to rest upon and operate according to principles of free consent. Even when Congregationalism assumed a diminished importance, churchgoers still continued to vote on some significant issues, such as the election and dismission of officers and occasional disciplinary cases, and on countless sundry, if seemingly petty, procedural details: the members of the First Church of Medford decided to restore the hand vote in 1744, reversing an earlier church vote of 1714; the First Church of Weston determined in 1753 that "the Books properly belonging to the church should be covered at the Church's cost"; the First Church of Sturbridge, upon the death of its minister, voted in February 1760 to seek a neighboring clergyman to administer the sacraments.[4]

As several historians have noted, pastors increasingly adopted an evangelical definition of the function of the ministry. The kinds of clerical pretensions to power evident in the early decades of the eighteenth century are almost wholly absent from the church records dating from the 1750s and 1760s.[5] For the rest of the eighteenth century at least, the clergy arguably became a service class largely bereft of its apostolic aura, its responsibilities prescribed by the laity. This changing clerical role reflected the privatization of religion in the years approaching the American Revolution: churchgoers were far more interested in pursuing personal salvation and less interested in church government, which they regarded as a matter of personal preference or "conscience" more than an arena of broader public concern. And with the shift, "politics" clearly no longer primarily meant church politics.

While questions of lay liberty and clerical authority in church government would rarely consume congregations in the 1760s and 1770s, ministers would soon find themselves preaching once again on topics of free consent, popular participation, and limitations on authority, though now in a civil context. Such themes carried with them a special resonance in a religious culture so deeply steeped in these traditions. Few would disagree with Cambridge Second Church pastor Samuel Cooke, who, in the aftermath of the Boston Massacre, observed, "[T]hose in authority, in the whole of their public conduct, are accountable to the society that gave them their political existence." Even deferentially minded churchgoers and ministers recognized traditions of accountability and resistance to arbitrary authority. Charles Chauncy, a strong spokesman for clerical control during the Great Awakening, nevertheless understood the dangers of unlimited power. He had always governed his own church in accordance with standard Congregational provisions of free consent and did not reverse himself in supporting Revolutionary principles any more than John Cotton had contradicted himself a century and a half earlier while simultaneously advancing the powers of church officers and pointing to the need to limit carefully their authority.[6]

Writing in 1858, the Congregational historian Joseph S. Clark assured readers that American democracy "owes its origin, not to Greece nor Rome, nor to the immortal George Washington, even; it sprang up spontaneously from that system of church polity which our New England fathers deduced from the Bible; and it was in practical operation, so far as colonial dependence would allow, a hundred and fifty years" before the American Revolution. Hyperbole and parochial conceit aside, we can now see in Clark's claims a fundamental truth of no small moment for the development of New England's Revolutionary ideology. As Benjamin Prescott had observed, Massachusetts ministers and churchgoers came to attach a significance "in a manner Sacred" to principles of free consent, limited authority, and popular participation over the course of a century and a half of experience with church government and the Congregational Way.[7]

Notes

Introduction

1. John Cotton, *An Exposition Upon the Thirteenth Chapter of the Revelation* (London, 1655), 71–73.

2. See, for example, John Cotton's *A Briefe Exposition . . . Upon the Whole Book of Ecclesiastes* (London, 1654), 75, 167, 179–180; *A Brief Exposition on the Book on Canticles* (London, 1654), 130, 139–142; *The Powring Out of the Seven Vialls* (London, 1642), I, 16. Similar discussions appear frequently in the merchant Robert Keayne's 584-page manuscript Notebook of John Cotton Sermons and Boston First Church Proceeedings, dating from 1639 to 1642, located at the Massachusetts Historical Society. A transcription of the first one-third of this notebook appears in Hell M. Alpert, ed., "Robert Keayne: Notes of Sermons by John Cotton and Proceedings of the First Church of Boston from 23 November 1639 to 1 June 1640" (Ph.D. diss., Tufts University, 1974). All nonsermonic portions of the Keayne manuscript, along with those of a second Keayne notebook, have been transcribed by Merja Kytö of the University of Helsinki. I wish to extend my thanks to Ms. Kytö for allowing me the use of her transcriptions. The Albert dissertation is hereafter cited as Albert, "Keayne Notebook of Cotton Sermons and Boston First Church Proceedings." References to the Keayne manuscripts are hereafter cited as Keayne Notebook of Cotton Sermons and Boston First Church Proceedings.

3. Joshua Coffin, ed., *A Sketch of the History of Newbury, Newburyport, and West Newbury* (Boston, 1845), 87, 82; "Diary of Cotton Mather," Massachusetts Historical Society, *Collections*, 7th ser., (1911), 8, 54.

4. See, for example, Joseph S. Clark, *A Historical Sketch of the Congregational Churches in Massachusetts, from 1620 to 1858* (Boston, 1858), 12–13. Henry Martin Dexter also regarded Congregational developments as central to the formation of democratic sentiments, though his specific formulation differed from Clark's. See his *The Congregationalism of the Last Three Hundred Years* (New York, 1880).

5. Perry Miller, "Thomas Hooker and Connecticut Democracy," in *Errand into the Wilderness* (Cambridge, Mass., 1956), 21–23, 30–31, 47; *The New England Mind: The Seventeenth Century* (New York, 1939), 441, 452. See also Miller, *Orthodoxy in Massachusetts* (Cambridge, Mass., 1933), 172–186.

6. A number of studies described a loss of confidence among clergymen in their stance toward churchgoers in the late 1630s and 1640s that spilled over into attitudes toward church

government and fostered lay feelings of anticlericalism. See Hall, *The Faithful Shepherd: A History of the New England Ministry in the Seventeenth Century* (Chapel Hill, 1972), 90–94, 110–111; Darrett B. Rutman, *Winthrop's Boston: A Portrait of a Puritan Town* (New York, 1965), 126–129; Larzer Ziff, *The Career of John Cotton: Puritanism and the American Experience* (Princeton, 1962), 208; Emory Elliot, *Power and the Pulpit in Puritan New England* (Princeton, 1975), 23. A more complete review of the earlier literature appears in James F. Cooper, Jr., "'A Mixed Form': The Establishment of Church Government in Massachusetts Bay, 1629–1645," Essex Institute, *Historical Collections* (July 1987), 233–259.

7. See, for example, Robert E. Brown, *Middle-Class Democracy and the Revolution in Massachusetts, 1691–1780* (Ithaca, 1955); B. Katherine Brown, "A Note on the Puritan Concept of Aristocracy," *Mississippi Valley Historical Review*, 41 (June 1954), 105–112; Roy N. Lokken, "The Concept of Democracy in Colonial Political Thought," *William and Mary Quarterly*, 3rd series, 16 (October 1959), 568–580; Michael Zuckerman, "The Social Context of Democracy in Massachusetts," *William and Mary Quarterly*, 3rd series, 25 (October 1968), 523–544.

8. Kenneth A. Lockridge, *A New England Town: The First Hundred Years* (New York, 1970), chapters 1 through 4. Michael Zuckerman argued on the basis of his analysis of eighteenth-century town records that serious political debate rarely occurred in town meetings; he also suggested that while most adult males could vote in town meetings, pressures for consensus meant that they rarely entertained legitimate choices. He describes civil society in New England as "a society dedicated to concord and devoid of legitimate difference, dissent, and conflict . . . a democracy without democrats." As we shall see, church government varied remarkably from civil or town government. See Zuckerman, *Peaceable Kingdoms: New England Towns in the Eighteenth Century* (New York, 1970), 185, 188.

9. John Cotton, "Copy of a Letter from Mr. Cotton to Lord Say and Seal in the Year 1636," in Perry Miller and Thomas H. Johnson, eds., *The Puritans: A Sourcebook of Their Writings*, 2 vols. (New York, 1938), vol. 1, 209.

10. As Harry S. Stout noted, after a period of decline, "by the 1680s church membership rates in Massachusetts, Plymouth, and Connecticut would rival those of the first decades of New World settlement." See Stout, *The New England Soul: Preaching and Religious Culture in Colonial New England* (New York, 1986), 98; Gerald F. Moran, "The Puritan Saint: Religious Experience, Church Membership, and Piety in Connecticut, 1636–1776" (Ph.D. diss., Rutgers University, 1974); Robert Pope, *The Half-Way Covenant: Church Membership in Puritan New England* (Princeton, 1969), 206–238; E. Brooks Holifield, *The Covenant Sealed: The Development of Puritan Sacramental Theory in Old and New England, 1570–1720* (New Haven, 1974).

11. For efforts to define democracy and discussions of the difficulty of the task, see David Held, *Models of Democracy* (Stanford, 1987), introduction and chapter 1; Jack Lively, *Democracy* (Oxford, 1975), 30; E. E. Schattschneider, *The Semi-Sovereign People: A Realist's View of Democracy in America* (Hinsdale, Ill., 1960), 129–142; Giovanni Sartori, *Democratic Theory* (New York, 1965), chapters 1 and 2.

12. Patricia U. Bonomi, *Under the Cope of Heaven: Religion, Society, and Politics in Colonial America* (New York, 1986), 186.

13. See, for examples, the studies cited in notes 5 and 6. In his outstanding *Worlds of Wonder, Days of Judgement: Popular Religious Belief in Early New England* (New York, 1989), 12 ff. and 68–69, David D. Hall acknowledges that ministers and members shared church government. He nonetheless lumps the laity together in opposition to the ministry, suggesting, "[N]ever did church members consent to major changes in the system of church gov-

ernment." As we shall see, few controversies over church government neatly divided the laity and the clergy. Substantial numbers of lay people often supported ministerial initiatives, such as the Halfway Covenant, and later changes in church government proposed by the ministers divided the clergy itself.

14. See George Selement, "The Meeting of Elite and Popular Minds at Cambridge, New England, 1638–1645," *William and Mary Quarterly*, 3rd ser., 41 (1984), 32–48; David D. Hall, "Toward a History of Popular Religion in Early New England," *William and Mary Quarterly*, 3rd ser., 41 (1984), 49–55; Avihu Zakai, *Exile and Kingdom: History and Apocalypse in the Puritan Migration to America* (Cambridge, 1992), chapter 5. See also Hall, *Worlds of Wonder*; Charles Hambricke-Stowe, *The Practice of Piety: Puritan Devotional Disciplines in Seventeenth-Century New England* (Chapel Hill, 1982); Andrew Delbanco, *The Puritan Ordeal* (Cambridge, Mass., 1989); Charles Lloyd Cohen, *God's Caress: The Psychology of Puritan Religious Experience* (New York, 1986); and David D. Hall's overview, "On Common Ground: The Coherence of American Puritan Studies," *William and Mary Quarterly*, 3rd ser., 44 (April 1987), 193–229.

15. Miller and Johnson, in *The Puritans*, vol. 1, 207–209, 212–213, and Edmund S. Morgan, in *Puritan Political Ideas* (New York, 1965), 173–175, excerpt Cotton's sermon, but in introducing the document discuss only the context of theory; neither points out that the comments were offered to the laity.

16. See David D. Hall's introduction to *The Works of Jonathan Edwards*, vol. 12, *Ecclesiastical Writings* (New Haven, 1994), 3.

17. Harold F. Worthley, "An Inventory of the Records of the Particular (Congregational) Churches of Massachusetts Gathered 1620–1805," *Proceedings of the Unitarian Historical Society*, 16 (1966–1969).

18. See, for example, Richard D. Pierce, ed., *The Records of the First Church of Boston, 1630–1868* (Colonial Society of Massachusetts, *Collections*, 39 [Boston, 1961]), 78, hereafter cited as Pierce, *Boston First Church Records*; James F. Hunnewell, ed., *Records of the First Church in Charlestown, Massachusetts, 1632–1789* (Boston, 1880), 7n., hereafter cited as Hunnewell, *Charlestown First Church Records*; and Wenham First Church Records, Wellington Poole manuscript copy, located at the First Congregational Church of Wenham, hereafter cited as Wenham First Church Records, msc.

19. See Alpert, "Keayne Notebook of Cotton Sermons and Boston First Church Proceedings," and the church trials of Richard Wayte and Anne Hibbons, discussed in chapter 3 in this book.

20. One prominent exception occurred in 1730, when some members of the First Church of Salem accused their pastor, Samuel Fiske, of inserting into the records a vote that had never been taken. See chapter 9.

21. Richard Mather, *Church-Government and Church-Covenant Discussed* (London, 1643), 82. Mather wrote the tract in 1639.

1. The Implementation of the Congregational Way

1. Thomas Shepard and Thomas Allin, *Defense of the Answer Made unto the Nine Questions or Positions Sent from New England . . .* (London, 1648), 2; Roger Clap, *Memoirs of Captain Roger Clap* (Boston, 1731), 14.

2. Perry Miller and Thomas H. Johnson, eds., *The Puritans: A Sourcebook of Their Writings*, 2 vols. (New York, 1938), vol. 1, 85–86; Miller, "Errand into the Wilderness," in *Errand into the Wilderness* (Cambridge, Mass., 1956); Avihu Zakai, *Exile and King-*

dom: History and Apocalypse in the Puritan Migration to America (Cambridge, 1992), chapters 2, 5.

3. John Cotton, *An Exposition Upon the Thirteenth Chapter of the Revelation* (London, 1655), 241–242.

4. John Cotton, *God's Promise to His Plantation* (1630; reprinted Boston, 1686), 17–18; Thomas Hooker, *The Danger of Desertion,* in *Thomas Hooker: Writings in England and Holland, 1626–1633,* ed. George H. Williams, Norman Petit, Winfried Herget, and Sargent Bush, Jr. (Cambridge, 1975), 236–237.

5. John Cotton, "Copy of a Letter from Mr. Cotton to Lord Say and Seal in the Year 1636," in Miller and Johnson, *The Puritans,* vol. 1, 209.

6. Among the best discussions of early Congregational development in England and Massachusetts are Henry Martin Dexter, *The Congregationalism of the Last Three Hundred Years* (New York, 1880); William Haller, *The Rise of Puritanism* (New York, 1938); David D. Hall, *The Faithful Shepherd: A History of the New England Ministry in the Seventeenth Century* (Chapel Hill, 1972), chapters 1 and 2; Perry Miller, *Orthodoxy in Massachusetts* (Cambridge, Mass., 1933), chapters 1–4; Edmund S. Morgan, *Visible Saints: The History of a Puritan Idea* (Ithaca, N.Y., 1963), chapters 1 and 2, J. William T. Youngs, *The Congregationalists* (New York, 1990), and Stephen Foster, *The Long Argument: English Puritanism and the Shaping of New England Culture, 1570–1700* (Chapel Hill, 1991). As Marion Starkey noted, the Puritans originally did not use the term "Congregational church." John Cotton coined the term "Congregational Way" in the course of defending the system in the 1640s; the term only "gained currency after 1648." See Starkey, *The Congregational Way: The Role of the Pilgrims and Their Heirs in Shaping America* (Garden City, N.Y., 1966), 2–3.

7. William Ames, *The Marrow of Sacred Divinity,* in *Works* (London, 1643), 150; Robert Browne, *Book Which Sheweth the Life and Manners of All True Christians . . .* (Middelburg, 1582), reprinted in Williston Walker, *The Creeds and Platforms of Congregationalism* (New York, 1893), 18–19. See Morgan, *Visible Saints,* chapter 1, who notes that significant disagreements between English Presbyterians and Congregationalists or "Independents" did not crystallize until the 1640s.

8. Morgan, *Visible Saints,* 15. Morgan noted that "the Reformation had generated a powerful impulse toward free consent as the basis of both state and church. And while most reformers stopped short of full acceptance of this principle, Puritans were committed to it, at least in broad terms" (29).

9. Henry Jacob, quoted in Champlin Burrage, *The Early English Dissenters in the Light of Recent Research,* 2 vols. (Cambridge, 1912), vol. 2, 157; Browne, *Life and Manners of True Christians,* in Walker, *Creeds and Platforms,* 19–20.

10. William Bradshaw, "Protestation of the King's supremacie" (1605), in *Several treatises of worship and ceremonies* (1660), 91–92; Robert Browne, *A Treatise of Reformation without Tarying for anie . . .* (London, 1582), 12.

11. Henry Ainsworth and Francis Johnson, *A True Confession of Faith* (Amsterdam, 1596), in Walker, *Creeds and Platforms,* 66.

12. Morgan, *Visible Saints,* 24; Thomas Hooker, "Answer to the XX Questions by John Paget; October, 1631," reprinted in Williams et al., *Hooker: Writings in England and Holland,* 271–291. Miller noted that the Separates "were few and inconspicuous" and that earlier, in Calvin's Geneva, few specifics of church order had been ironed out: "Calvin was remarkably indifferent to many minutiae of ceremony and government," *Orthodoxy in Massachusetts,* 66, 16. See also Raymond P. Stearns, *Congregationalism in the Dutch Netherlands* (Chicago, 1940).

13. Cotton Mather, *Magnalia Christi Americana*, 2 vols. (Hartford, 1820), vol. 1, book 6.

14. John Cotton sermon, March 16, 1640, in Helle M. Alpert, ed. "Robert Keayne: Notes of Sermons by John Cotton and Proceedings of the First Church of Boston from 23 November 1939 to 1 June 1640" (Ph.D. diss., Tufts University, 1974), 242.

15. Ibid.

16. George Selement, "The Meeting of Elite and Popular Minds at Cambridge, New England, 1638–1645," *William and Mary Quarterly*, 3rd ser., 41 (1984), 32–48; David D. Hall, "Toward a History of Popular Religion in Early New England," *William and Mary Quarterly*, 3rd ser., 41 (1984), 49–55; Hall, *Worlds of Wonder, Days of Judgement: Popular Religious Belief in Early New England* (New York, 1989).

17. Richard D. Pierce, ed., *The Records of the First Church in Salem, Massachusetts, 1629–1736* (Salem, Mass., 1974), 3; hereafter cited as Pierce, *Salem First Church Records*. Charles Henry Pope, ed., *Records of the First Church of Dorchester in New England, 1636–1734* (Boston, 1891), 1; hereafter cited as Pope, *Dorchester First Church Records*. See also Don Gleason Hill, ed., *The Record of the Baptisms, Marriages, and Deaths and Admissions to the Church and Dismissals Therefrom, Transcribed from the Town of Dedham, Massachusetts, 1638–1845* (Dedham, Mass., 1888), 12; hereafter cited as Hill, *Dedham First Church Records*.

18. J. Hammond Trumbull, ed., "Conference of the Elders of Massachusetts with the Rev. Robert Lenthall, of Weymouth, Held at Dorchester, Feb. 10, 1639," *Congregational Quarterly*, 19 (1877), 236–239.

19. Thomas Hooker, "Abstracts of Two Sermons by Rev. Thomas Hooker, From the Shorthand Notes of Mr. Henry Wolcott," transcribed by J. Hammond Trumbull, in *Collections of the Connecticut Historical Society* (Hartford, 1860), vol. 1, 20.

20. George Moxon, "Sermon on Romans 7:9," April 1, 1649, in Gratz Collection, box 9, vol. 21, Pennsylvania Historical Society.

21. The following is based on Hill, *Dedham First Church Records*, 1–8, 11–13. See Kenneth Lockridge, *A New England Town: The First Hundred Years* (New York, 1970), 24–30.

22. Hill, *Dedham First Church Records*, 15.

23. *Ibid.*, 3, 13.

24. *Ibid.*, 1.

25. William Hubbard, *A General History of New England from the Discovery to MDCLXXX* (Boston, 1848), 117–118; James K. Hosmer, ed., *Winthrop's Journal "History of New England," 1636–1649*, 2 vols. (New York, 1908), vol. 1, 179. The Separatists in Plymouth had apparently established a Congregational church in 1620, and accounts of Plymouth deacon Samuel Fuller's consultations with the Salem founders on the "outward forme of God's worshippe" demonstrate that the Plymouth church provided some assistance to the Salem settlers. But the Plymouth church records are lost, and their specific practices remain obscure. Plymouth did not enjoy the services of a minister for a decade and, as Miller has argued in *Orthodoxy in Massachusetts*, it is unlikely that they were on the cutting edge of Congregational development. A dissenting view appears in Larzer Ziff, "The Salem Puritans in the 'Free Aire of a New World,'" *Huntington Library Quarterly*, 20 (1956–1957), 573–584. See William Bradford, *History of Plymouth Plantation*, W. C. Ford, ed., 2 vols. (Boston, 1912), vol. 2, 90, and Robert E. Moody's overview in his introduction to Pierce, *Salem First Church Records*, xi–xvi.

26. Cotton's early statements concerning baptism, along with several other major discussions of polity, appear in Larzer Ziff, ed., *John Cotton on the Churches of New England* (Cambridge, Mass., 1968). See also Joseph B. Felt, *The Ecclesiastical History of New England; Comprising not only Religious, but also Moral, and other Relations*, 2 vols. (Boston, 1855), vol. 1, 143, and Ziff, *The Career of John Cotton: Puritanism and the American Experience*

(Princeton, 1962), chapter 3. As Felt observed, Cotton also initially expressed opposition to the view that "no man may be admitted to the sacrament, though a member of the catholic church, unless he be a member of some particular reformed church." Cotton later reversed himself and came to accept this view. Richard Mather's difficulties are detailed in Hosmer, *Winthrop's Journal*, vol. 1, 177–178. Dorchester ministers John Warham and John Maverick were also divided over admissions requirements; see B. R. Burg, *Richard Mather of Dorchester* (Lexington, 1976), 28, and chapter 2.

27. Hubbard, *History of New England*, 117–118. Miller, in *Orthodoxy in Massachusetts*, 148, agrees that the settlers' "conceptions of polity had hitherto been largely theoretical"; see also Moody in his introduction to Pierce, *Salem First Church Records*, xiii. For contrasting views, see Ziff, "Free Aire," and Starkey, *The Congregational Way*, 4.

28. Daniel A. White, ed., *New England Congregationalism in its Origin and Purity; Illustrated by the Foundation and Early Records of the First Church in Salem* (Salem, Mass., 1861), 10; Hill, *Dedham First Church Records*, 11.

29. Starkey, *The Congregational Way*, 4.

30. As we shall see, ministers and lay people alike struggled with the implications of Congregational autonomy throughout the colonial period. As events in Dorchester demonstrated, church and civil authorities quickly claimed the right to supervise church gatherings and on occasion clerical councils would over-rule decisions of local churches (see chapter 5). But such actions on the part of church or civil authorities were rare, and participants on all sides considered them of dubious legality.

31. Miller, *Orthodoxy in Massachusetts*, 160; Nathaniel Morton, *New Englands Memorial; Or, A brief Relation of the Most Memorable and Remarkable Passages of the Providence of God, Manifested to the Planters of New-England in America; With special Reference to the first Colony thereof, Called New-Plimouth* (Boston, 1669), quoted in White, *New England Congregationalism in its Origins and Purity*, 3; Hubbard, *History of New England*, 119.

32. Hubbard, *History of New England*, 119; Hosmer, *Winthrop's Journal*, vol. 1, 107, 116. See also Trumbull, "Conference of the Elders with Robert Lenthall," 232–248. Another dispute arose when Boston pastor John Wilson and Pastor Thomas James of Charlestown expressed their belief that their ordination in New England did not mean that they renounced their ordination in England; George Phillips assumed an opposite stance in Watertown. For this and other examples of disagreement among the ministers over particulars see Felt, *Ecclesiastical History of New England*, 121, 141, 163, 235, and Hosmer, *Winthrop's Journal*, vol. 1, 83, 121.

33. See, for example, Emory Elliot, *Power and the Pulpit in Puritan New England* (Princeton, 1975), 23, who asserted that while ministers "instructed" and "advised" their flocks, "the laymen defined the laws of the congregation and imposed church discipline upon themselves."

34. Hosmer, *Winthrop's Journal*, vol. 1, 173, 177. A word about the term "elder" is in order here. Throughout most of the colonial period, Congregationalists usually used the term "elder" to mean "minister." Particularly during the first decades of settlement, however, the term also incorporated lay or "ruling" elders. "Meetings of the elders" consequently sometimes referred to the assembled clergy, and other times referred to meetings that included both ministers and ruling elders; the specific meaning of the term can best be inferred from context. Ruling elders, whose functions are described in chapter 2, probably did assist ministers in defining specific church procedures.

35. *Ibid.*, vol. 1, 112–113. For another example, see Felt, *Ecclesiastical History of New England*, 136. The elders also discussed church government at the Synod of 1637, which was called during the Antinomian controversy. See chapter 3.

36. The objections are described in Hosmer, *Winthrop's Journal*, vol. 1, 113. See Robert F. Scholtz, "'The Reverend Elders': Faith, Fellowship, and Politics in the Ministerial Community of Massachusetts Bay, 1630–1710" (Ph.D. diss., University of Minnesota, 1966), chapter 3.

37. Hosmer, *Winthrop's Journal*, vol. 1, 83; Felt, *Ecclesiastical History of New England*, vol. 1, 333. The discussion over baptism in Plymouth appears at the end of the Keayne Notebook of Cotton Sermons and Boston First Church Proceedings, Massachusetts Historical Society, unpaginated but dated June 4, 1640, and is discussed further in chapter 2, below. The communication with the Plymouth churches here is significant, suggesting that by this time Plymouth and Massachusetts Bay shared the same general practices of church government. Felt reached this same conclusion in his *Ecclesiastical History of New England*, vol. 1, 255. Other examples of interchurch communication over questions of church order dating from the early years of settlement appear in Hosmer, *Winthrop's Journal*, vol. 1, 179; Keayne Notebook of Cotton Sermons and Boston First Church Proceedings, March 23, 1640; Robert G. Pope, ed., *The Notebook of the Reverend John Fiske, 1644–1675* (Colonial Society of Massachusetts, *Collections* 47 [Boston, 1974]), 242–243, hereafter cited as Pope, *John Fiske Notebook*; Hill, *Dedham Church Records*, 13–17; Felt, *Ecclesiastical History of New England*, vol. 1, 203.

38. Hubbard, *History of New England*, 182. Frank Shuffelton, in *Thomas Hooker, 1586–1647* (Princeton, N.J., 1977), 166–167, agrees that few ministers with actual experience with Congregationalism arrived in New England before Cotton.

39. Hosmer, *Winthrop's Journal*, vol. 1, 179.

40. Hosmer, *Winthrop's Journal*, vol. 1, 107, 116. Pierce, *Boston First Church Records*, 18, 25, 28, 35, 51, 52. The amount of time these ministers served as members varied from several months (Davenport, Mather, Norris, Symmes) to over a year (Allin, Knowles). John Eliot served as acting pastor in Boston in 1631 and 1632; he departed for Roxbury prior to Cotton's arrival in 1633. See Charles Henry Pope, *The Pioneers of Massachusetts* (Boston, 1900), 15, 131, 275, 305, 330, 444.

41. See Miller, *Orthodoxy in Massachusetts*, 121–122. Only five ministers among all who arrived during the first twenty years of settlement were Presbyterians, and only two churches emerged that actually flirted with Presbyterianism: that of Thomas Parker and James Noyes in Newbury and that of Peter Hobart in Hingham. Morgan has argued that by 1637 nearly all of the churches required a test of "grace" or conversion for church admission. Michael Ditmore recently disputed this claim, arguing instead that the clergy "imposed [relations] on lay members" in response to the Antinomian controversy, and did so approximately a year later than Morgan suggested. As Ditmore acknowledges, "no document remains that would settle rival claims" definitively. Nevertheless, as early as 1636 Richard Mather wrote that candidates for admission must "bee able to discerne the lord's body" in order to "clayme his right to the lords supper," which supports Morgan's earlier dating. See Morgan, *Visible Saints*, chapter 3; Michael G. Ditmore, "Preparation and Confession: Reconsidering Edmund S. Morgan's *Visible Saints*," *New England Quarterly*, 62 (June 1994), 298–319; B. Richard Burg, "A Letter of Richard Mather to a Cleric in Old England," *William and Mary Quarterly*, 3rd Ser., 29 (1972), 81–98.

42. Felt, *Ecclesiastical History of New England*, 208–209.

2. "A Mixed Form"

1. Richard Mather, *Church-Government and Church-Covenant Discussed* (London, 1643), 51.

2. See, for example, Thomas Lechford, *Plain Dealing: or, News from New England*, ed. Darrett B. Rutman (New York, 1969); John Paget, *A Defence of Church-Government Exer-*

cised in Presbyteriall, Classical, and Synodall Assemblies; According to the practice of the Reformed Churches ... (London, 1641); Peter Noyes, *The Temple Measured* (London, 1647), 21; John Owen, *A Defence of Mr. John Cotton from the Imputation ... Charged on Him by Mr. Dan: Cawdrey* (Oxford, 1658). See also Larzer Ziff, *The Career of John Cotton: Puritanism and the American Experience* (Princeton, 1962), chapters 6 and 7.

3. Thomas Hooker, *A Survey of the Summe of Church Discipline* (London, 1648; reprinted New York, 1972), vol. 2, 2; for Cotton's similar definition of "the essential forme" of a church, see David D. Hall, ed., "John Cotton's Letter to Samuel Skelton," *William and Mary Quarterly*, 3rd. ser., 22 (1965), 483.

4. Williston Walker, *The Creeds and Platforms of Congregationalism* (New York, 1893), 211, 226; Frank Shuffelton, *Thomas Hooker, 1586–1647* (Princeton, N.J., 1977), 178–179. For further analysis of the office of teacher, see Robert W. Henderson, *The Teaching Office in the Reformed Tradition: A History of the Doctoral Ministry* (Philadelphia, 1962), especially chapter 7. See also Albert E. Dunning, *The Congregationalists in America* (New York, 1894).

5. Walker, *Creeds and Platforms*, 219. Most of the *Platform*'s wording here is extracted from Mather, *Church-Government Discussed*, and John Cotton, *The Keyes of the Kingdom of Heaven* (London, 1644).

6. Once a congregation elected a minister, it was expected to maintain his services except in cases of serious violations involving theology, ethics, or administration. As was the case in Chelmsford during the 1660s and 1670s (see chapter 5), churches generally did not attempt to dismiss ministers for reasons of simple personality conflict. Churches rarely dismissed ministers until the Great Awakening, and when they did, they received assistance from neighboring elders.

7. The role of ruling elders and deacons in church government is discussed in Harold F. Worthley, "The Lay Officers of the Particular (Congregational) Churches of Massachusetts, 1620–1755: An Investigation of Practice and Theory" (Th.D. diss., Harvard University, 1970).

8. In *Winthrop's Boston: A Portrait of a Puritan Town* (New York, 1965), 128–134, Darrett B. Rutman discusses the importance of the presbytery but incorrectly attributes its origins to a ministerial reaction to the Antinomian affair. David Hall quickly dismissed the significance of the presbytery in *The Faithful Shepherd: A History of the New England Ministry in the Seventeenth Century* (Chapel Hill, 1972), 95. Though practices varied among churches and within the histories of individual churches, these ruling committees did not simply cease to exist within a few years, as Hall implied. The First Churches of Boston and Dorchester maintained a presbytery of one or two ministers and one or two ruling elders through the first decade of the eighteenth century, and the First Church of Roxbury did so until the nineteenth century. By the eighteenth century, few churches had complete presbyteries, but, as we shall see, deacons and other worthy laymen assisted ministers in administration in the many churches that chose not to elect ruling elders.

9. For examples of ruling elders exercising "managing" authority, see Pierce, *Boston First Church Records*, 42, 44, 46, 48, and the account of the 1669 division of the Boston First Church in Hamilton A. Hill, ed., *History of the Old South Church, Boston: 1669–1884*, 2 vols. (Cambridge, Mass., 1890). Hill's volumes include virtually all extant Boston Third Church Records through 1821 and documents relevant to the split between the Boston First and Boston Third churches. These documents make clear that ruling elder James Penn managed Boston's church meetings after the death of pastor John Wilson in 1667. Hereafter references to the Third Church records will be cited as Boston Third Church Records in Hill, *Old South Church*; Hill's historical commentary will be cited simply as Hill, *Old South Church*.

Though Plymouth's early church records have been lost, meetings there were obviously managed by ruling elder William Brewster. For examples of deacons assisting in church administration, see George Selement and Bruce C. Woolley, eds., *Thomas Shepard's Confessions* (Colonial Society of Massachusetts, *Collections*, 58 [1981]), 18, 152, 197; Pope, *John Fiske Notebook*, 4, 15, 17.

10. The best discussion of the office of ruling elder appears in Worthley, "The Lay Officers of the Particular (Congregational) Churches of Massachusetts." Worthley's 824–page effort far surpasses lesser published articles such as Increase N. Tarbox, "Ruling Elders in the Early New England Churches," *Congregational Quarterly*, 14 (1872), 401–416.

11. The only ruling elder on record to have been paid was Michael Powell of the Second Church of Boston. See Henry Martin Dexter, *The Congregationalism of the Last Three Hundred Years* (New York, 1880), 448n.

12. Walker, *Creeds and Platforms*, 212–213.

13. John Cotton, *The Way of the Churches of Christ in New England* (London, 1645), 14, 25; Richard Mather, *Church-Government and Church-Covenant Discussed* (London, 1643), 76; Worthley, "The Lay Officers," 272; Pope, *John Fiske Notebook*, 239–247; Keayne Notebook of Cotton Sermons and Boston First Church Proceedings, Massachusetts Historical Society, March 23, 1640.

14. Even in the 1630s, all churches did not elect ruling elders, and by the late seventeenth century a majority of churches did not employ them. Nonetheless, there was probably no point at which all churches lacked them. Size of congregation seems to have been one significant factor in a church's decision to employ a ruling elder. Questions of biblical prescription arose later in the seventeenth century. See James F. Cooper, "'A Mixed Form': Church Government in Massachusetts Bay, 1629–1645" (M.A. thesis, University of Connecticut, 1982).

15. John Cotton, sermon preached November 6, 1639, in Helle M. Alpert, ed., "Robert Keayne: Notes of Sermons by John Cotton and Proceedings of the First Church of Boston from 23 November 1639 to 1 June 1640" (Ph.D. diss., Tufts University, 1974), 154–155.

16. John Cotton, *The Powring Out of the Seven Vialls* (London, 1642), vol. 2, "Fourth Viall," 15; Richard Mather, *Church-Government Discussed*, 48.

17. Richard Mather, *Church-Government Discussed*, 57, 60–61.

18. Hill, *Dedham First Church Records*, 11–14. Roger Williams rebuked the Boston elders in 1635 for violating lay liberties by refusing to read a letter to the Boston congregation. See Samuel L. Caldwell, ed., *The Complete Writings of Roger Williams*, 7 vols. (New York, 1963), vol. 6, 73.

19. The following exchange appears at the end of the Keayne Notebook of Cotton Sermons and Boston First Church Proceedings, unpaginated, but dated March 23, 1640.

20. *Ibid.*, June 21, 1640.

21. Many examples of this kind of interchurch communication appear in the later chapters of this study; see, in particular, the Samuel Fiske controversy, discussed in chapter 9.

22. In *The Long Argument: English Puritanism and the Shaping of New England Culture, 1570–1700* (Chapel Hill, 1991), 160–161, Stephen Foster similarly observes that the process of resolving procedural tensions in the New England Way "did force a greater degree of uniformity on the churches of the Bay" and required ministers to explain to churchgoers and each other "what the New England Way was all about and where it was headed."

23. Probably Robert Cotty, a tailor who became a freeman in 1635 and apparently later moved on to Gloucester. See Pope, *The Pioneers of Massachusetts* (Boston, 1900), 119.

24. Pope, *John Fiske Notebook*, 241. Before assuming the pastorate of the Wenham church, Fiske assisted the elders in Salem; he recorded seven Salem disciplinary trials in 1637 that appear at the end of his own book of the Wenham and Chelmsford church records.

25. John Cotton, *A Briefe Exposition . . . upon the Whole Book of Ecclesiastes*, 76, 167, 180. See also Alpert, "Keayne Notebook of Cotton Sermons and Boston First Church Proceedings," 106–110, 129, 162–163, 202, 211, 214, 242–243. In *The Career of John Cotton*, Larzer Ziff offers educated guesses in attempting to date several of Cotton's most important sermon series and states his belief that the Boston teacher's printed expositions on Ecclesiastes and Canticles both dated from his English ministry. This is not necessarily the case. The copy of *A Briefe Exposition of the Whole Book of Canticles* held at the Beinecke Rare Book Library, Yale University, 213, contains the following passage: "Time was when it was thus with New England Churches: but now we cannot bear wrongs." The date of composition of many of Cotton's published sermons remains a matter of conjecture.

26. Particularly during the second generation, ministers also employed occasional sermons to discuss the Congregational Way; see John Norton, *Sion the Outcast Healed of Her Wounds* (Cambridge, 1661); William Stoughton, *New Englands True Interest; Not to Lie* (Cambridge, 1668); Samuel Danforth, *A Brief Recognition of New Englands Errand into the Wilderness* (Cambridge, 1670); and Urian Oakes, *New-England Pleaded With* (Cambridge, 1673).

27. For a skillful exploration of the spiritual lives of nonmembers, see David D. Hall, *Worlds of Wonder, Days of Judgement: Popular Religious Belief in Early New England* (New York, 1989), chapter 3.

28. Rutman, *Winthrop's Boston*, 126–129; Hall, *Faithful Shepherd*, 109. Many historians besides Rutman and Hall have overestimated lay authority in the early 1630s; some have even accepted as common knowledge that the laity ruled the churches. In *The Career of John Cotton*, 228, Ziff described church government in the 1630s as "basically a democratic system." Emory Elliott agrees in *Power and the Pulpit in Puritan New England* (Princeton, 1975), 23. See also John J. Waters, "Hingham, Massachusetts, 1631–1661: An East Anglican Oligarchy in the New World," *Journal of Social History*, 1 (1968), 362.

29. John Cotton, Copy of a Letter from Mr. Cotton to Lord Say and Seal in the Year 1636," in Perry Miller and Thomas H. Johnson, eds., *The Puritans: A Sourcebook of Their Writings*, 2 vols. (New York, 1938), vol. 1, 211.

30. *Ibid.*, 209–210.

31. Perry Miller, *Orthodoxy in Massachusetts* (Cambridge, Mass., 1933), 146.

32. Daniel A. White, ed., *New England Congregationalism in its Origin and Purity; Illustrated by the Foundation and Early Records of the First Church in Salem* (Salem, Mass., 1861), 3.

33. *Ibid.*, 2; Hill, *Dedham First Church Records*, 16.

34. White, *Salem Church Records*, 2; Hill, *Dedham First Church Records*, 17; Edmund S. Morgan, ed., *Puritan Political Ideas* (New York, 1965), 97.

35. The Browne case is drawn from Hosmer, *Winthrop's Journal*, vol. 1, 66, 71, 95. Undoubtedly, lay support for these views can be explained by the fact that Phillips initially supported Browne; the former quickly reversed his position.

36. *Ibid.*, 95.

37. Richard Mather, *Church-Government Discussed*, 60; James K. Hosmer, ed., *Winthrop's Journal "History of New England," 1636–1649*, 2 vols. (New York, 1908), vol. 1, 95.

38. Edmund S. Morgan, *Visible Saints: The History of a Puritan Idea* (Ithaca, N.Y., 1963), 99ff. The institutionalization of a test of grace remains a topic of discussion and debate among historians. Stephen Foster has recently argued, for instance, that the test was rooted

in a lay desire for purity and thus represented a ministerial "indulgence of lay initiatives." As noted earlier in chapter 1, 41n., another recent study asserts that the test was not widespread until the later 1630s and was initiated as a reaction to the Antinomian controversy. Foster, *The Long Argument*, 166; Michael G. Ditmore, "Preparation and Confession: Reconsidering Edmund S. Morgan's *Visible Saints*," *New England Quarterly*, 62 (June 1994), 248–318.

39. Lechford, *Plain Dealing*, 97; Pope, *John Fiske Notebook*, 17. References to lay witnesses in these private meetings also appear in Selement and Woolley, *Shepard's Confessions*, 18, 197.

40. Walker, *Creeds and Platforms*, 227.

41. Thomas Shepard, *The Parable of the Ten Virgins* (London, 1660), vol. 2, 200. *The Parable* was based upon sermons that Shepard delivered from 1636 to 1640.

42. Cotton Mather, *Magnalia: Christi Americana*, 2 vols. (Hartford, 1820), vol. 2, book 5, 244. The specific wording of Mather's statement suggests that initially conversion testimonials were not made public.

43. The earliest description we have of Plymouth's admissions procedures, written in 1679, about thirty years after Lechford's account, mirrors Massachusetts Bay practices precisely. See Morgan, *Visible Saints*, 61–62.

44. Selement and Woolley, *Shepard's Confessions*; Bruce C. Woolley, "Reverend Thomas Shepard's Cambridge Church Members 1636–1649: A Socio-Economic Analysis" (Ph.D. diss., University of Rochester, 1973), 24; Shepard, *The Parable of the Ten Virgins*, vol. 2, 200.

45. Hosmer, *Winthrop's Journal*, vol. 1, 84; *A Report of the Record Commissioners, Containing the Roxbury Land and Church Records* (Boston, 1884), hereafter cited as *Roxbury First Church Records*, 18; Hill, *Dedham First Church Records*, 21; Massachusetts Historical Society, *Winthrop Papers*, 5 vols. (Boston, 1929–1947), vol. 3, 390.

46. There are, of course, exceptions; Antinomians were known to object to candidates as being under a "covenant of works"; similarly, Separates objected to the content of some candidates' conversion testimonials during the Great Awakening, though it is unclear whether they did so during the actual procedure.

47. Michael Walzer, *The Revolution of the Saints* (Cambridge, Mass., 1971), 221. For general discussions of church discipline and deviance in colonial New England, see Charles E. Park, "Excommunication in Colonial Churches," Colonial Society of Massachusetts *Proceedings*, vol. 12, *Transactions* (1908–1909), 321–332; Emil Oberholzer, *Delinquent Saints: Disciplinary Action in the Early Churches of Massachusetts* (New York, 1956); and Kai T. Erikson, *Wayward Puritans: A Study in the Sociology of Deviance* (New York, 1966). Specific procedures are detailed further in James F. Cooper, Jr., "A Participatory Theocracy: Church Government in Colonial Massachusetts, 1629–1760" (Ph.D. diss., University of Connecticut, 1987), chapter 1, and David C. Brown, "The Keyes of the Kingdom: Excommunication in Colonial Massachusetts," *New England Quarterly*, 68 (December 1994), 531–564.

48. Hosmer, *Winthrop's Journal*, vol. 1, 83.

49. Amos Otis, ed., "Scituate and Barnstable Church Records," in *New England Historical and Genealogical Register*, 10 (1856), 42.

50. References to private meetings held in the 1630s appear in Bernard Bailyn, ed., *The Apologia of Robert Keayne* (Cambridge, Mass., 1964), 56–57, and Hill, *Dedham First Church Records*, 8, containing a case in which a churchgoer from a neighboring town traveled to Dedham to reconcile some difficulties with a candidate for church admission. The disciplinary notes at the end of the John Fiske Notebook include a number of examples dating from

1637 in which Salem church officers reminded members of their duty to deal privately with offenders; for references to private watch in Salem and Wenham, see Pope, *John Fiske Notebook*, 28, 240, 242, 243, 245. See also Pierce, *Boston First Church Records*, 22, 27, 30–31, 33, 49, 53, and James F. Cooper, Jr., "The Confession and Trial of Richard Wayte, Boston, 1640," *William and Mary Quarterly*, 3rd ser., 44 (April 1987), 312.

51. Bailyn, *The Apologia of Robert Keayne*, 55, 60, 61. Prior to the church trial, the General Court imposed a stiff fine upon the merchant. This rendered the case notorious and public, and no doubt contributed to the elders' decision to proceed against Keayne in a church trial.

52. *A Platform of Church Discipline Gathered Out of the Word of God ans Agreed Upon by the Elders and Messengers of the Churches. . . .* (Cambridge, 1649), in Walker, *Creeds and Platforms*, 227. Cited hereafter as the *Cambridge Platform*.

53. The hearings appear in Pope, *John Fiske Notebook*, 239–247.

54. Probably Isaac Walker, a shopkeeper who later moved to Boston in 1646. Pope, *Pioneers of Massachusetts*, 474–475.

55. Hosmer, *Winthrop's Journal*, vol. 1, 315–318.

56. As always, there are exceptions to this generalization. In 1645, the First Church of Wenham held a meeting to determine the guilt or innocence of a member charged with scandal. Because the charges were public, the church decided that it was obliged to hold a church trial in the event that the accused might be publicly cleared. He was. See Pope, *John Fiske Notebook*, 25.

57. Disciplinary procedures were quite flexible and probably varied somewhat from church to church. Depending on the offense, for example, the elders might recommend an immediate excommunication. Likewise, they might recommend two or three formal admonitions before casting a member out.

58. The best example of this argument is found in Miller, *Orthodoxy in Massachusetts*, 182.

59. Richard Mather, *Church-Government Discussed*, 61.

60. Similarly, historians have made much of the fact that some ministers later claimed to have a veto power or "negative voice" over church decisions. Such claims notwithstanding, ministers in practice almost never employed this tactic. See Hall, *Faithful Shepherd*, 112.

61. For an exception, see the case of Lynn pastor Stephen Bachiller, who attempted to excommunicate an entire group that opposed his administration. As noted later in this chapter, the elders thwarted Bachiller's plan and his church later dismissed him from office.

62. This is not to suggest that the elders welcomed any and all dissent, as the celebrated cases of Anne Hutchinson and Roger Williams demonstrate. But churchgoers were expected to speak out if they believed their church was proceeding unscripturally. Hutchinson and Williams were not tried for speaking out, but for what they spoke.

63. John Humphries, Esquire, became a freeman in 1636. Though he later served as a magistrate and was appointed sergeant major general in 1641, he "died poor" in 1653. Brother Tomkins possibly refers to one John Tomkins, who lived in Salem in 1636. Little else is known of Tomkins, beyond the fact that he fathered seven children, all of them daughters. Pope, *Pioneers of Massachusetts*, 247, 457.

64. Pope, *John Fiske Notebook*, 242–243. Richard Mather, *Church-Government Discussed*, 59, 55. Samuel Whiting and Thomas Cobbett served as ministers in Lynn in 1637. Little else can be determined concerning this case; the Lynn church records antedating 1792 do not exist.

65. Probably Francis Weston, who became an active religious dissenter. Weston became a freeman in 1633 and served as a Salem deputy and town officer in 1635 and 1636, respec-

tively. The colony banished him after the Antinomian controversy in 1638 and imprisoned him in 1643 during the Gortonite controversy. Pope, *Pioneers of Massachusetts,* 487–488.

66. Pope, *John Fiske Notebook,* 243–245.

67. Hosmer, *Winthrop's Journal,* vol. 1, 148.

68. Hill, *Dedham Church Records,* 13–17.

69. See Hosmer, *Winthrop's Journal,* vol. 1, 83, 148, 121, 173, 176, 244–45; vol. 2, 234–35, 244–245, 288; *John Fiske Notebook,* 243.

70. The following is based upon entries found at the end of the Keayne Notebook of Cotton Sermons and Boston First Church Proceedings. The first church meeting is undated; the second is dated March 23, 1640.

71. For a similar early example in which lay reservations halted church action, see Pope, *John Fiske Notebook,* 17. The most significant example of lay dissent surfaced during the effort to adopt the Halfway Covenant; lay protests delayed implementation of that measure in dozens of churches. See chapter 5.

72. Hill, *Dedham First Church Records,* 15.

3. Lay "Rebellion" and Clerical Reaction

1. John Winthrop, *A Short Story of the Rise, reign, and ruine of the Antinomians, Familists & Libertines* (London, 1644), reprinted in David D. Hall, ed., *The Antinomian Controversy, 1626–1638: A Documentary History* (Middletown, Conn., 1968), 211. Hereafter cited as Winthrop, *Short Story,* in Hall, *Antinomian Controversy.*

2. David D. Hall, *The Faithful Shepherd: A History of the New England Ministry in the Seventeenth Century* (Chapel Hill, 1972), 91; Darrett B. Rutman, *Winthrop's Boston: A Portrait of a Puritan Town* (New York, 1965), 126; B. R. Burg, *Richard Mather of Dorchester* (Lexington, 1976), 93; Larzer Ziff, *Puritanism in America: New Culture in a New World* (New York, 1973), 68. See also Stephen Foster, "New England and the Challenge of Heresy, 1630 to 1660," *William and Mary Quarterly,* 3rd ser., 38 (1981), 647–649.

3. The following discussion of the events surrounding the controversy is based in part upon Edmund S. Morgan, *The Puritan Dilemma* (Boston, 1958), chapter 10, and Francis D. Bremer, *The Puritan Experiment* (New York, 1976), 67–72.

4. Perry Miller, "'Preparation for Salvation' in Seventeenth-Century New England," *Journal of the History of Ideas,* 4 (1943), 253–286.

5. Williams quoted in Morgan, *The Puritan Dilemma,* 88.

6. James K. Hosmer, ed., *Winthrop's Journal "History of New England,"* 1636–1649, 2 vols., vol. 1, 205.

7. *Ibid.* Italics added.

8. *Ibid.*

9. *Ibid.,* 206.

10. Emory Battis, *Saints and Sectaries: Anne Hutchinson and the Antinomian Controversy in the Massachusetts Bay Colony* (Chapel Hill, 1962).

11. The Roxbury church records suggest that the Newbury Antinomians had recently moved to that town from Roxbury. See *Roxbury First Church Records,* 77.

12. Battis, *Saints and Sectaries,* chapter 17; Winthrop, *Short Story,* in Hall, *Antinomian Controversy,* 201, 208. By "support group," Battis refers to warm adherents of Hutchinson's doctrines who did not "follow through with their commitment" and recanted. "Core" group members left the colony with Hutchinson or Wheelwright, "support" group members did not.

We will never know the absolute number of Hutchinsonians. Battis found it impossible to identify the women. Still, eight towns had no core or support members. One town had one, another two, and a third town three. It seems unlikely that the addition of female Hutchinsonians would change the conclusion that the vast majority of the Hutchinsonians were centered in Boston where the church officers were sympathetic. Winthrop noted that out of the entire colony, only "nine or ten" church members—including women—were excommunicated. Seven or eight of these hailed from Boston or Roxbury. Hosmer, *Winthrop's Journal*, vol. 1, 217, 280.

13. For contrasting views that suggest the Antinomians created a crisis in confidence in the ministerial community, see Larzer Ziff, *The Career of John Cotton: Puritanism and the American Experience* (Princeton, 1962), 130, and Hall, *Faithful Shepherd*, 110–111.

14. Shepard in Michael McGiffert, ed., *God's Plot: The Paradoxes of Puritan Piety, Being the Autobiography of Thomas Shepard* (Amherst, Mass., 1972), 65.

15. As of October 1636, the elders were still discussing the issues privately with Cotton. Hosmer, *Winthrop's Journal*, vol. 1, 206–207. Ziff states that the elders submitted the sixteen questions to Cotton in November, and Winthrop reports that they were made public. Ziff, *Career of John Cotton*, 119, 125.

16. Hosmer, *Winthrop's Journal*, vol. 1, 215.

17. Samuel Seward to Edward Calamy, Jan. 24, 1704, Massachusetts Historical Society, *Collections*, 6th ser., vol. 1, 295.

18. Shepard in McGiffert, *God's Plot*, 66.

19. Morgan, *Puritan Dilemma*, 144–147; Ziff, *Career of John Cotton*, 135–136.

20. Ziff, *Career of John Cotton*, 107, 118, 123, 131.

21. Roger Clap, *Memoirs of Captain Roger Clap* (Boston, 1731), 33.

22. Hosmer, *Winthrop's Journal*, vol. 1, 259; Winthrop, *Short Story*, in Hall, *Antinomian Controversy*, 214. Stephen Foster expressed the standard view of the demise of the Hutchinsonians: "[T]he artificial unity of the Hutchinsonians was not broken until a number of them were banished." But as Winthrop indicated, Hutchinson's opinions continued to spread "long after" her sentencing and had largely disappeared before she left for Rhode Island. Foster, "Heresy in New England," 653.

23. Hosmer, *Winthrop's Journal*, vol. 1, 259.

24. "A Report of the Trial of Mrs. Anne Hutchinson before the Church in Boston," reprinted in Hall, ed., *Antinomian Controversy*, 367.

25. *Ibid.*

26. *Ibid.*

27. *Ibid.*, 358, 367. The proceedings in the church would have ground to a halt had a majority or even a significant minority opposed them. The civil arm could not have punished the membership for supporting Hutchinson in the church trial. Voting against a censure violated no law. It should also be remembered that the elders rarely disposed of dissenters by nullifying their votes through admonition. The two cases of nullification during the Hutchinson trial are among the few during the entire colonial period. See the case of Richard Wayte, discussed later in this chapter.

28. Ronald D. Cohen, "Church and State in Seventeenth-Century Massachusetts: Another Look at the Antinomian Controversy," in Alden T. Vaughn and Francis J. Bremer, eds., *Puritan New England: Essays on Religion, Society, and Culture* (New York, 1977), 179.

29. Winthrop, *Short Story*, in Hall, *Antinomian Controversy*, 216. This is not to suggest that every Antinomian was persuaded to recant. Battis reported that at least thirty-eight male Antinomians left the colony with Hutchinson or Wheelwright. *Saints and Sectaries*, 257, 259.

Historians such as Battis and Darrett Rutman have suggested that Wheelwright's Antinomian followers went into self-imposed exile after and as a consequence of Hutchinson's banishment. But as Rutman himself noted, the Boston First Church had previously agreed in October 1636 on the need to establish Wheelwright in a new church in Mount Wollaston. It should not be assumed, therefore, that dissatisfaction with the Boston church motivated all of Wheelwright's supporters to remove. See Darrett B. Rutman, *Winthrop's Boston: A Portrait of a Puritan Town* (New York, 1965), 95, 123.

30. "The Trial of Mrs. Hutchinson," in Hall, *Antinomian Controversy*, 371.

31. Shepard in McGiffert, *God's Plot*, 66; Hosmer, *Winthrop's Journal*, vol. 1, 329.

32. Jules Zanger quoted in Cohen, "Another Look at the Antinomian Crisis," in Vaughn and Bremer, *Puritan New England*, 181; Ziff, *Career of John Cotton*, 142. This view is also shared by Rutman in *Winthrop's Boston*, 123.

33. Nathaniel B. Shurtleff, ed., *Records of the Governor and Company of the Massachusetts Bay in New England* (Boston, 1853–1884), vol. 1, 207; Massachusetts Historical Society, *Winthrop Papers*, 5 vols. (Boston, 1929–1947), vol. 3, 512–515. In keeping with his view that the Antinomians fostered "a police problem of massive proportions," Stephen Foster asserted that the crisis required "the disarming of a significant proportion of the Bay Colony and the expulsion of a number of previously well-entrenched secular leaders." But Foster avoided citing any figures. That the fifty-eight who were disarmed represented a "significant proportion" of the entire colony seems overstated, if not hyperbolic. Similarly, only two men—William Aspinwall and John Coggeshall—were banished in addition to Hutchinson and Wheelwright. "Heresy in New England," 649, 653, 653n.

34. Shepard in McGiffert, *God's Plot*, 66.

35. John Cotton, *The Way of the Congregational Churches Cleared* (London, 1648), 282; Hosmer, *Winthrop's Journal*, vol. 1, 284.

36. Hall, *Faithful Shepherd*, 111.

37. Hosmer, *Winthrop's Journal*, vol. 1, 234; Winthrop, *Short Story*, in Hall, *Antinomian Controversy*, 267.

38. See chapter 2 of this study, above, 36–37.

39. Hosmer, *Winthrop's Journal*, vol. 1, 234–235.

40. Richard Mather, *Church-Government Discussed*, 78–79.

41. Worthley, "The Lay Officers," 297; Cotton, *The True Constitution of a Particular Visible Church Proved by Scripture* (London, 1642), 8. *The True Constitution* was written in 1634. Helle M. Alpert, ed., "Robert Keayne: Notes of Sermons by John Cotton and Proceedings of the First Church of Boston from 23 November 1639 to 1 June 1640" (Ph.D. diss., Tufts University, 1974), 164–165, 267–268, 280.

42. In chastising lay protestors during Hutchinson's church trial, Zechariah Symmes announced that he feared "the great dishonor of Jesus Christ and Reproach in these churches" if "this should be carried over into England." "Trial of Mrs. Hutchinson," in Hall, *Antinomian Controversy*, 367.

43. Williston Walker, *A History of the Congregational Churches of the United States* (Boston, 1894), 138, 156.

44. *Ibid.*, 156.

45. Robert F. Scholz, "'The Reverend Elders': Faith, Fellowship, and Politics in the Ministerial Community of Massachusetts Bay, 1630–1710" (Ph.D. diss., University of Minnesota, 1966), chapters 2 and 3. See also Foster, "Heresy in New England," 642.

46. Scholz, "The Reverend Elders," 101, 87, 129; Cotton sermon, December 14, 1639, in Alpert, "Keayne Notebook of Cotton Sermons and Boston First Church Proceedings," 126.

47. Mather, *Church-Government Discussed*, 55, 78; Cotton sermon, April 20, 1640, in Alpert, "Keayne Notebook of Cotton Sermons and Boston First Church Proceedings," 297.

48. Pierce, *Boston First Church Records*, 46. The decision to send Oliver to Rummeny Marsh, undated but c. 1640, is recorded at the back of the Keayne Notebook of Cotton Sermons and Boston First Church Proceedings and is discussed earlier in chapter 2, 43–44.

49. Richard Mather, *Church-Government Discussed*, 64, 62.

50. For examples, see Richard Mather's *Church-Government Discussed* and John Cotton's *Way of the Churches of Christ in New England* (London, 1645) and *Way of the Churches Cleared*.

51. Williston Walker, *The Creeds and Platforms of Congregationalism* (New York, 1893), 159ff.

52. Perry Miller, "Thomas Hooker and Connecticut Democracy," in *Errand into the Wilderness* (Cambridge, Mass., 1956), 30; John Cotton, *The Way of the Churches of Christ in New England*, preface. Miller agrees that historians have far exaggerated the significance of Cotton's conclusion that a congregation could not excommunicate its entire presbytery. Similarly, Stephen Foster urges caution in reaching conclusions about church practice that are based primarily upon ministerial tracts, correctly observing that "New Englanders in statements intended for English readers persistently understated their differences with Presbyterianism" and its more authoritarian form of church government. *The Long Argument: English Puritanism and the Shaping of New England Culture, 1570–1700* (Chapel Hill, 1991), 169.

53. John Cotton, *An Exposition Upon the Thirteenth Chapter of the Revelation* (London, 1655), 212–213; Cotton sermon, January 6, 1640, in Alpert, "Keayne Notebook of Cotton Sermons and Boston First Church Proceedings," 154–55.

54. Cotton sermon, January 13, 1640, in Alpert, "Keayne Notebook of Cotton Sermons and Boston First Church Proceedings," 159, 162.

55. Cotton sermons, January 19, 1640, and February 23, 1640, in *ibid.*, 170, 208.

56. Thomas Hooker, "Abstracts of Two Sermons by Rev. Thomas Hooker, From the Shorthand Notes of Mr. Henry Wolcott," transcribed by J. Hammond Trumbull, in *Collections of the Connecticut Historical Society* (Hartford, 1860), vol. 2, 20–21; John Cotton sermon, June 1, 1640, in Alpert, "Keayne Notebook of Cotton Sermons and Boston First Church Proceedings," 352; see also 284, 151.

57. See Lyle Kohler, "The Case of the American Jezebels: Anne Hutchinson and Female Agitation during the Years of Antinomian Turmoil, 1636–1640," *William and Mary Quarterly*, 3rd ser., 31 (1974), 55–78.

58. See James F. Cooper, Jr., "The Confession and Trial of Richard Wayte, Boston, 1640," *William and Mary Quarterly*, 3rd ser., 44 (April 1987).

59. Pierce, *Boston First Church Records*, 22.

60. The following is drawn from Cooper, "The Confession and Trial of Richard Wayte," 310–314.

61. For genealogical and other background information on the lay participants in these hearings, see Cooper, "The Confession and Trial of Richard Wayte,"

62. Cotton sermons, September 13, 1640, September 20, 1640, in Keayne Notebook of Cotton Sermons and Boston First Church Proceedings, Massachusetts Historical Society.

63. See the transcription of the trial of Anne Hibbons in "A Sinner Cast Out," in John Demos, ed., *Remarkable Providences, 1600–1760* (New York, 1972), 221–239.

64. Demos, *Remarkable Providences*, 228.

65. *Ibid.*, 226–227.

66. *Ibid.*, 234–236.

67. *Ibid.*, 233–234.

68. Keayne Notebook of Cotton Sermons and Boston First Church Proceedings, Massachusetts Historical Society, September 20, 1640.

69. Demos, *Remarkable Providences*, 234–246.

70. Pope, *John Fiske Notebook*.

71. *Ibid.*, vii, xxv.

72. This is not to suggest that churches did not vary in specific practices. Though not an issue of church government per se, the Halfway Covenant introduced significant differences in admissions standards to the churches; this topic is discussed in chapter 5.

73. See chapter 1.

74. Pope, *John Fiske Notebook*, 10–13.

75. *Ibid.*, 62, 14.

76. *Ibid.*, xxxi. Pope notes that Norton eventually repented.

4. The Presbyterian Challenge

1. Thomas Shepard, "Notes about Church Discipline," undated, Thomas Shepard Papers, American Antiquarian Society.

2. Baillie quoted in Joseph B. Felt, *The Ecclesiastical History of New England; Comprising not only Religious, but also Moral, and other Relations*, 2 vols. (Boston, 1855), vol. 2, 526; Thomas Lechford, *Plain Dealing: or, News from New England*, ed. Darrett B. Rutman (New York, 1969), 37. See also Lechford, 146, 123–124, and Scholz, "The Reverend Elders: Faith, Fellowship, and Politics in the Ministerial Community of Massachusetts Bay, 1630–1710" (Ph.D. diss., University of Minnesota, 1966), 109–114.

3. Williston Walker, *The Creeds and Platforms of Congregationalism* (New York, 1893), 159. See also Larzer Ziff, *The Career of John Cotton: Puritanism and the American Experience* (Princeton, 1962), 188ff; Williston Walker, *A History of the Congregational Churches of the United States* (Boston, 1894), 156–157, and Stephen Foster, *The Long Argument: English Puritanism and the Shaping of New England Culture, 1570–1700* (Chapel Hill, 1991), 166–170.

4. Peter Noyes, *The Temple Measured* (London, 1647), 21.

5. Ziff, *Career of John Cotton*, 188. Some of the principal entries in the "pamphlet war" between Congregationalists and Presbyterians include John Paget, *A Defence of Church-Government Exercised in Presbyteriall, Classicall, and Synodall Assemblies; According to the Practice of the Reformed Churches* . . . (London, 1647), and John Davenport's reply, *The Power of Congregational Churches* (London, 1672); Charles Herle, *The Independency of Scripture of the Independency of Churches* . . . (London, 1643), and the response of Richard Mather and William Tompson, *A Modest and Brotherly Answer* . . . (London, 1644); William Rathband, *A Brief Narration of Some Church Courses* . . . *in New England* (London, 1664), and Thomas Weld, *Answer to W.R.* . . . (London, 1644); Samuel Rutherford, *The Due Right of Presbyteries* . . . (London, 1647), and Richard Mather, *A Reply to Mr. Rutherford* . . . (London, 1647); Robert Ballie, *A Disuasive* . . . (London, 1646), and John Cotton's response, *The Way of the Congregational Churches Cleared* (London, 1648).

6. See Scholz, "The Reverend Elders," chapter 4.

7. *A Reply of Two Brethren to A.S.* . . . (London, 1644), in Walker, *Creeds and Platforms*, 138. See Perry Miller, *Orthodoxy in Massachusetts* (Cambridge, Mass., 1933), 121–122; Joshua Coffin, ed., *A Sketch of the History of Newbury, Newburyport, and West Newbury* (Boston,

1845); Robert Lord Goodman, "Newbury, Massachusetts, 1635–1685: The Social Foundations of Harmony and Conflict" (Ph.D. diss., Michigan State University, 1974); and Robert Emmet Wall, Jr., *Massachusetts Bay: The Crucial Decade, 1640–1650* (New Haven, 1972).

8. See Goodman, "Newbury, Massachusetts, 1635–1685."

9. Deliberations among Massachusetts clergymen were published in *Reply to A. S.,* in Walker, *Creeds and Platforms,* 138. The Massachusetts elders also cited their forbearance in the case of Parker and Noyes to counter the claims of English critics that they refused to "suffer any that differ from us," insisting that the Newbury church practiced its Presbyterianism without the "least molestation or disturbance" from the authorities. See Coffin, *History of Newbury,* 12.

10. Stephen Foster, "English Puritanism and the Progress of New England Institutions, 1630–1660," in David. D. Hall et al., eds., *Saints and Revolutionaries* (New York, 1984), 31.

11. The elders' conclusions are summarized in James K. Hosmer, ed., *Winthrop's Journal "History of New England," 1636–1649,* 2 vols. (New York, 1908), vol. 2, 139, and *Reply to A. S.,* in Walker, *Creeds and Platforms,* 138.

12. Hosmer, *Winthrop's Journal,* vol. 2, 139; Ziff, *Career of John Cotton,* 207–208; Burg, *Richard Mather,* 96–97. Stephen Foster observes that "New Englanders in statements intended for English readers persistently understated their differences with Presbyterianism." *The Long Argument,* 169.

13. Discussions of Newbury practices appear in Pope, *John Fiske Notebook,* 17, 19–23, 32–33. Presbyterianism was also publicly discussed in the First Church of Boston; see below, in this chapter.

14. Hosmer, *Winthrop's Journal,* vol. 2, 244–245. Socioeconomic issues contributed heavily to the unrest in Newbury and, especially Hingham, site of the celebrated "Hingham mutiny." But controversy over church government was a vital part of the equation in both cases. Because of the absence of early church records, we know little about the specific lay responses to Presbyterian practices in Newbury and Hingham during the 1640s. Later events in the dispute in Newbury are discussed in chapter 7.

15. Probably Thomas Edsell or Hedsall, who arrived in Boston in 1635 at age 47. Apparently he was not a church member; he was fined in 1652 for voting though not a freeman. Charles Henry Pope, *The Pioneers of Massachusetts* (Boston, 1900), 152.

16. The following is drawn from the Keayne Notebook of Cotton Sermons and Boston First Church Proceedings, Massachusetts Historical Society, December 28, 1645.

17. Probably Richard Hutchinson, a town officer, who was brother of Edward Hutchinson and brother-in-law of Anne Hutchinson.

18. Thomas Fowle, an armiger and merchant, joined the Boston Church in 1643 and was described by Pope as a "gentleman." Fowle petitioned for citizenship for nonchurch members in 1645. Pope, *Pioneers of Massachusetts,* 174.

19. An excellent example dating from 1637 appears in Pope, *John Fiske Notebook,* 244. In response to a request for the "grounds of his withdrawing from the church," Salem's Brother Weston responded in his church trial that "he had already told the elders his grounds" in private meetings. See the discussion in chapter 2.

20. The First Church of Wenham also felt threatened by the specter of Presbyterianism; their angry response to practices in Newbury is discussed later in this chapter. See also Foster, *The Long Argument,* 170: "[T]he aspect of Presbyterianism [churchgoers] feared most was impurity, not inequality." While it is impossible to demonstrate which the laity "feared most," church members were always exceedingly sensitive to perceived encroachments upon their liberties.

21. "Mr. [Peter] Bulkley to Mr. Phillips from England," undated, c. 1641, Houghton Library, Harvard University; Shepard, "Notes on Church Discipline," Thomas Shepard MSS, American Antiquarian Society, 1–2.

22. Pope, *John Fiske Notebook*, 17, 19.

23. *Ibid.*, 19.

24. *Ibid.*, 20–21.

25. *Ibid.*, 22–23, 32–33.

26. Walker, *Creeds and Platforms*, 168, 171–173.

27. The English context of the Cambridge Synod is discussed in Walker, *Creeds and Platforms*, 159–181; Perry Miller, "The Cambridge Platform in 1648," in Henry Wilder Foote, ed., *The Cambridge Platform of 1648* (Boston, 1949), 60–75, and Foster, *The Long Argument*, chapter 4.

28. Walker, *Creeds and Platforms*, 163–166; 175–179.

29. See Foster, *The Long Argument*, chapter 4.

30. "Plymouth Church Records, 1620–1859" (Colonial Society of Massachusetts, *Publications*, 2 vols., 22, 23 (1920, 1923), vol. 1, 229, hereafter cited as *Plymouth First Church Records*; Boston Third Church Records in Hill, *Old South Church*, 229; Hunnewell, *Charlestown First Church Records*, ix; Scholz, "The Reverend Elders," 98–99.

31. David D. Hall, *The Faithful Shepherd: A History of the New England Ministry in the Seventeenth Century* (Chapel Hill, 1972), 99–101; Harry S. Stout, *The New England Soul Preaching and Religious Culture in Colonial New England* (New York, 1986), 107–108.

32. See chapter 1.

33. See, for example, the Hibbons Trial in John Demos, ed., *Remarkable Providences 1600–1760* (New York, 1972), 226–227, Pope, *Dorchester First Church Records*, 45.

34. "Text of the Call to the Cambridge Synod," in Walker, *Creeds and Platforms*, 169.

35. See chapter 1, above, 21.

36. Walker, *Creeds and Platforms*, 140–141.

37. *Ibid.*, 171–173, 168; see also Pope, *John Fiske Notebook*, 77, for the case of George Norton, who angrily protested sending delegates from Wenham to the Cambridge Synod. This is not to suggest that a groundswell of lay opposition arose to the synod. As Robert Pope observed in his edition of the John Fiske Notebook, lay dissent was "scattered."

38. Hosmer, *Winthrop's Journal*, vol. 2, 323.

39. Hosmer, *Winthrop's Journal*, vol. 2, 329.

40. *Ibid.*, 329; Pierce, *Boston First Church Records*, 47.

41. See Walker, *Creeds and Platforms*, 174ff., and the text of the *Platform* in *ibid.*, 189–237.

42. *Ibid.*, 184–188; Nathaniel B. Shurtleff, ed., *Records of the Governor and Company of the Massachusetts Bay in New England* (Boston, 1853–1884), vol. 2, 285; vol. 3, 204; vol. 4, 22.

43. Brief references to votes on the *Platform* in other churches appear in Felt, *Ecclesiastical History of New England*, vol. 2, 18, 19, 29.

44. Pope, *John Fiske Notebook*, 90–91; *Cambridge Platform* in Walker, *Creeds and Platforms*, 218–219.

45. Pope, *John Fiske Notebook*, 96–98; 90–91.

46. Richard Mather, "An Answer of the Elders to Certayne doubts and objections against sundrey passages in the Platforme of Discipline," Mather papers, octavo vol. 1, American Antiquarian Society. Almost all of the document's forty pages consist of the elders' lengthy written responses to brief questions posed by the laity.

47. Richard Mather, "An Answer of the Elders," 14, 20, 39.

48. Shurtleff, ed., *Records . . . Mass. Bay*, vol. 3, 235–236, 240; vol. 4, 54–55, 57–58.

49. Henry Wilder Foote, "The Significance and Influence of the Cambridge Platform of 1648," in Foote, *The Cambridge Platform of 1648*, 29, 47, 49–50.

50. Miller, "The Cambridge Platform in 1648," in Foote, *The Cambridge Platform of 1648*, 60, 62 67.

51. For views that suggest the *Platform* contained significant institutional changes, see Hall, *Faithful Shepherd*, chapter 5; Foster, "English Puritanism and New England Institutions," 28–31; Francis D. Bremer, *The Puritan Experiment* (New York, 1976), 120–121; and Ziff, *The Career of John Cotton*, 227. Though in his more recent *Worlds of Wonder* he observed that the laity never consented to significant changes in church government, David Hall previously argued in *The Faithful Shepherd* that the ministers included a new clerical veto in the *Platform*. In fact, the *Platform* merely states that the officers and members should both agree before any church action is undertaken; lay people did not consider this a change in authoritarian directions. See also Stout, *New England Soul*, 51n.: "The concessions to synodical influence and authority" were partially motivated by "the ministers concern to consolidate and impose their authority over particular congregations."

52. John Wilson, "Of the Church and the Government of it," Mather MSS, American Antiquarian Society, 13.

53. *Cambridge Platform* in Walker, *Creeds and Platforms*, 233–234; Scholz, "The Reverend Elders," 154.

54. *Platform* chapter 10:7–8, in Walker, *Creeds and Platforms*, 219.

55. As best we can tell, the *Platform* went through an initial press run of 550 copies. See George Parker Winship, "A Document Concerning the First Anglo-American Press," *The Library*, 4th ser. 20 (1940), 51–70; Lawrence G. Starkey, "The Printing by the Cambridge press of a Platform of Church Discipline, 1649," *Studies in Bibliography: Papers of the Bibliographical Society of the University of Virginia*, vol. 2, (1949–1950), 79–93; and Winship, *The Cambridge Press, 1638–1692* (Philadelphia, 1945), 108–110.

56. In his discussion of the construction of the *Cambridge Platform*, Stephen Foster casts the laity and clergy into competing camps, arguing that in defining church government "the clergy usually spelled out the particulars for the benefit of their own side." He further observes that "the 'democracy' did not put up much of a sustained opposition to the clerical resurgence." In fact, lay people did not resist because, upon analyzing the *Platform*, they perceived no such resurgence. Foster, *The Long Argument*, 170.

57. The most detailed portrait of church practices in the aftermath of the adoption of the *Cambridge Platform* appears in Pope, *John Fiske Notebook*; lay-clerical relations in the second half of the seventeenth century are discussed in chapter 6.

58. *Cambridge Platform* in Walker, *Creeds and Platforms*, 210, 214, 218–219, 221–224, 227–229.

59. *Ibid.*, 208.

60. Norton quotes are from *Three Choice and Profitable Sermons* (Cambridge, 1664), 2–3, 37; John Cotton, "A Reply to Mr. Williams," *Publications of the Narragansett Club*, vol. 2, 187. "A Reply to Mr. Williams" was written in 1647. *Cambridge Platform* in Walker, *Creeds and Platforms*, 203–204.

61. Norton, *Three Choice and Profitable Sermons*, 12.

62. "Text of the Call to the Cambridge Synod," in Walker, *Creeds and Platforms*, 169–170.

63. *Ibid.*

64. Hill, *Dedham First Church Records*, 1; Pope, *John Fiske Notebook*, 3.

5. *Congregationalism in Crisis*

1. Boston Third Church Records in Hill, *Old South Church*, vol. 1, 22.

2. Perry Miller, *The New England Mind: From Colony to Province* (Cambridge, Mass., 1953), chapters 7 and 8; Darrett B. Rutman, "God's Bridge Falling Down: 'Another Approach' to New England Puritanism Assayed," *William and Mary Quarterly*, 3rd ser., 19 (1962), 408–421; Robert Pope, *The Half-Way Covenant: Church Membership in Puritan New England* (Princeton, 1969), 73–74; Stephen Foster, *The Long Argument: English Puritanism and the Shaping of New England Culture, 1570–1700* (Chapel Hill, 1991), chapter 5; Harry S. Stout, *The New England Soul: Preaching and Religious Culture in Colonial New England* (New York, 1986), 58–61. See also Ross Beales, "The Half-Way Covenant and Religious Scrupulosity: The First Church of Dorchester, Massachusetts as a Test Case," *William and Mary Quarterly*, 31 (1974), 465–480; and Edmund S. Morgan, "New England Puritanism: Another Approach," *William and Mary Quarterly*, 3rd ser., 18 (1961), 236–242.

3. For discussions of the theory and evolution of baptismal practices in the seventeenth and eighteenth centuries, see Edmund S. Morgan, *Visible Saints: The History of a Puritan Idea* (Ithaca, N.Y., 1963), chapters 3 and 4; Pope, *The Half-Way Covenant*; Norman Pettit, *The Heart Prepared: Grace and Conversion in Puritan Spiritual Life* (New Haven, 1966), chapter 6; Perry Miller, *From Colony to Province*, chapters 4 through 7, and Miller, "The Half-Way Covenant," *New England Quarterly*, 6 (1933), 676–715.

4. Cotton quoted in Increase Mather, *The First Principles of New-England Concerning the Subject of Baptisme and Communion of Churches, Collected out of the Printed Books, but chiefly out of the Original manuscripts of the First and chiefe Fathers in the New-English Churches* (Cambridge, 1675), 2–4; John Cotton sermon, January 13, 1640, in Helle M. Alpert, ed., "Robert Keayne Notes of Sermons by John Cotton and Proceedings of the First Church of Boston from 23 November 1639 to 1 June 1640" (Ph.D. diss., Tufts University, 1974), 163. Richard Mather initially agreed with Cotton before reversing his opinion and supporting the Halfway Covenant. See B. Richard Burg, ed., "A Letter of Richard Mather to a Cleric in Old England," *William and Mary Quarterly*, 3rd ser., 29 (January 1972), 92.

5. See Increase Mather, *First Principles*; Miller, *From Colony to Province*, chapters 7 and 8.

6. James F. Cooper, Jr., "The Confession and Trial of Richard Wayte, Boston, 1640," *William and Mary Quarterly*, 3rd ser., 44 (April 1987), and above, 66–67.

7. Jonathan Mitchell, Preface to *Propositions Concerning the Subject of Baptism and Consociation of Churches, collected and Confirmed out of the Word of God, by a Synod of Elders and Messengers . . . In the Year 1662* (Boston 1662), in Williston Walker, *The Creeds and Platforms of Congregationalism* (New York, 1893), 302–303.

8. See Foster, *The Long Argument*, 182, who notes that a remarkable proportion of Massachusetts's population—perhaps 50 percent—consisted of adolescents and young adults at this time.

9. Pope, *Dorchester First Church Records*, 35, 165; Pierce, *Salem First Church Records*, 103–104; For similar lay demands for baptism extension see Pierce, *Salem First Church Records*, 105, 114–115, and Pope, *Dorchester First Church Records*, 33, 34, 55, 165. Little is known about the layman Edward Brecke. Charles Pope indicates that he became a town officer in Lancaster in 1652, though he appears in the Dorchester church records in 1655. Apparently this is the same Brecke who argued for broader admissions standards during the debates over the *Cambridge Platform*. John Gidney, a worsted weaver in Norwich, England, arrived in Salem with his wife and family in 1637. He later became an innkeeper and vintner. Bartholmew

Gidney was apparently John Gidney's son. John Massy was born in 1631, son of Jeffry Massy, who served as a Salem town officer and constable. Little is known of Samuel Williams, beyond his occupation. Note that all of these proponents of the Halfway Covenant were essentially first-generation founders. Charles Henry Pope, *The Pioneers of Massachusetts* (Boston, 1900), 66, 184, 305.

10. For a discussion of events leading to the 1657 synod, see Joseph B. Felt, *The Ecclesiastical History of New England; Comprising not only Religious, but also Moral, and other Relations*, 2 vols. (Boston, 1855), vol. 2, 149–150; Walker, *Creeds and Platforms*, 257–262; and Pope, *Half-Way Covenant*, 26–30.

11. *A Disputation Concerning Church Members and their Children in Answer to XXI Questions* (London, 1659), 20–24; extract reprinted in Walker, *Creeds and Platforms*, 291–300.

12. See Miller, "The Half-Way Covenant," 681–682; *Colony to Province*, chapters 7 and 8; Larzer Ziff, *Puritanism in America: New Culture in a New World* (New York, 1973), Pope, *Half-Way Covenant*, 40n.

13. See in particular Pierce, *Boston First Church Records*; Pope, *Dorchester First Church Records*; Pierce, *Salem First Church Records*, 92ff.

14. Pierce, *Salem First Church Records*, 104; Pope, *Dorchester First Church Records*, 35–36. Reference to church discussions over the Halfway Covenant appear also in Pierce, *Boston First Church Records*, 55–56; Pope, *John Fiske Notebook*, 111–113; and Pierce, *Salem First Church Records*, 114–115. As noted in Pierce, Salem pastor John Higginson read passages from Cotton's *Way of the Churches* and Thomas Shepard's *Church Membership of the Children* (Cambridge, 1669) in an effort to demonstrate the founders' support for the measure.

15. Jonathan Mitchell, Preface to *Propositions Concerning Baptism*, in Walker, *Creeds and Platforms*, 302–303.

16. Pierce, *Salem First Church Records*, 103–105; Pope, *Dorchester First Church Records*, 35–36; Pierce, *Boston First Church Records*, 55–56; Pope, *Half-Way Covenant*, 19–26.

17. See Worthley, "The Lay Officers of the Particular (Congregational) Churches of Massachusetts, 1620–1755: An Investigation of Practice and Theory" (Ph.D. diss., Harvard University, 1970), 400; Pope, *Half-Way Covenant*, 23–26; Felt, *Ecclesiastical History of New England*, vol. 2, 141.

18. Walker, *Creeds and Platforms*, 262–269; Pope, *Half-Way Covenant*, chapter 2.

19. The result of the Synod of 1662 appears in Walker, *Creeds and Platforms*, 301–339.

20. The first of the synod's propositions, which is two pages long, contains nearly fifty biblical references and justifications.

21. The General Court "Judged [the *Result*] meete to commend . . . unto the consideration of all the churches and people of this jurisdiction, and for that end ordered the printing thereof"; Nathaniel B. Shurtleff, ed., *Records of the Governor and Company of the Massachusetts Bay in New England* (Boston, 1853–1884), vol. 4, part 2, 60. See Pierce, *Salem First Church Records*, 104, which indicates that the *Result of the Synod* "was published and had been read in the church," and Hunnewell, *Charlestown First Church Records*, ii, which indicates the same.

22. Mitchell, Preface to *Propositions Concerning Baptism*, in Walker, *Creeds and Platforms*, 311ff.

23. John Cotton sermon, March 16, 1640, in Alpert, "Keayne Notebook of Cotton Sermons and Boston First Church Proceedings," 242.

24. See Cotton's sermon in Larzer Ziff, ed., *John Cotton on the Churches of New England* (Cambridge, Mass., 1968), 41–68. These arguments are further analyzed by Perry Miller in *The New England Mind: The Seventeenth Century* (New York, 1939), 443, and *Colony to Province*, 87.

25. Pope, *John Fiske Notebook*, 111. Pastor Fiske addressed each of Adams's arguments and was one of the few ministers who experienced little difficulty in persuading his congregation to adopt the Halfway Covenant; see 111–113.

26. Ministerial opponents are listed and discussed in Pope, *Half-Way Covenant*, 53–70. Henry Dexter notes that most of the key Connecticut churches also opposed the Halfway Covenant. *The Congregationalism of the Last Three Hundred Years* (New York, 1880), 474n.

27. Pope, *Half-Way Covenant*, 134, 264.

28. Mitchell, Preface to Increase Mather, *First Principles*, A7.

29. Cotton Mather, *Magnalia Christi Americana*, 2 vols. (Hartford, 1820, vol. 2, book 5, 258.

30. A complete bibliography of the pamphlet war appears in Walker, *Creeds and Platforms*, 238–244.

31. See Harry S. Stout, *The New England Soul: Preaching and Religious Culture in Colonial New England* (New York, 1986), chapter 3. Stout notes that in the aftermath of the English Civil War New England ministers focused less on events overseas and instead turned their attention inward toward local issues such as the Halfway Covenant.

32. Charles Chauncy, et al., *Antisynodalia Scripta Americana* (London, 1662). Mitchell quoted in Pope, *Half-Way Covenant*, 72; Chauncy quoted in Pope, *Half-Way Covenant*, 55n.

33. Chauncy et al., *Antisynodalia*, 1, 4.

34. Walker, *Creeds and Platforms*, 269; Chanucy, et al., *Antisynodalia*, 2, 6, 3; Pierce, *Salem First Church Records*, 104.

35. Miller, *Colony to Province*, 91–104; Pope, *Half-Way Covenant*, 73.

36. See chapter 3.

37. Miller, *Colony to Province*, 105, 108; David D. Hall, *The Faithful Shepherd: A History of the New England Ministry in the Seventeenth Century* (Chapel Hill, 1972), 200; Stout, *New England Soul*, 107.

38. Miller, *Colony to Province*, 105, 108, 109. Miller described the struggle as at once primarily involving "the crowd" against the ministers, elite "worthy laymen" against the ministers, and first generation "fathers" against the second generation. In his chapter on the Halfway Covenant, Stephen Foster argues that the laity "resisted clerically inspired initiatives as 'Presbyterian' if not 'Prelatical.'" *The Long Argument*, 179.

39. The gradual shift from the unanimous vote to the majority vote in the late seventeenth century is discussed later in this chapter.

40. Pope, *Dorchester First Church Records*, 45.

41 *Ibid.*, 49. Increase Mather also believed that his father forbore implementation of the Halfway Covenant mainly because of the absence of unanimity. Increase Mather, "Life of Richard Mather," in Perry Miller and Thomas H. Johnson, eds., *The Puritans: A Sourcebook of Their Writings*, 2 vols. (New York, 1938), vol. 2, 493. Further evidence bearing upon the Dorchester church's position appears in the Boston First Church Division, discussed later, which centered on the Halfway Covenant. In 1670, at least half of the Dorchester church supported the Bostonians who favored the measure. See Pope, *Dorchester First Church Records*, 61–62.

42. Hunnewell, *Charlestown First Church Records*, ii; "Church Records of the Old Town of Reading, Massachusetts, and of the First Parish of Reading and South Reading from 1648 to 1846," typescript, Reading Public Library, 9. Hereafter cited as "Reading First Church Records"; Pierce, *Salem First Church Records*, 105–109; Shepard quoted in Miller, *Colony to Province* 109. Hamilton A. Hill, who wrote a generally reliable 800-page history of the Old

242 Notes to pages 97–100

South Church concluded that throughout the colony most lay people supported the Half-way Covenant in the late 1660s and early 1670s, a conclusion shared by Lewis M. Robinson, who asserted that slightly over half of the church members supported their ministers. Hill, *Old South Church*, vol. 1, 42; Lewis M. Robinson, "A History of the Half Way Covenant," (Ph.D. diss., University of Illinois, 1964). See also Walker, *Creeds and Platforms*, 255. Walker also concluded that in Connecticut lay opponents to the Halfway Covenant "were clearly in the minority" by the late 1660s. *Creeds and Platforms*, 263.

43. Michael G. Hall, *The Last American Puritan: The Life of Increase Mather* (Middletown, Conn., 1988), 62–63. Hall believes that most members in the Second Church of Boston op-posed the Halfway Covenant, though no direct evidence remains bearing on the majority's position. The civil elections of 1672 are discussed later in this chapter.

44. Many exceptions exist that refute the generational hypothesis advanced by Dexter, Miller, Ross Beales, and others. In Boston, as noted later in this chapter, numerous elderly members supported the Halfway Covenant, while many younger members opposed it. In Dorchester, lay opponents stated that while they disagreed, they would not dissent, which casts doubt on Beales's assertion that the innovation was accepted only after opponents died off. See Pope, *Dorchester First Church Records*, 49, and a similar example in Pierce, *Salem First Church Records*, 108. Also worthy of consideration is the fact that many churches adopted the measure at different times, again suggesting that adoption was not simply a matter of the older generation dying off. Some churches practiced extension by 1657, while others did not until the 1730s. Cotton Mather, *Magnalia*, vol. 2, 313–315; Walker, *Creeds and Platforms*, 270n. Miller asserted that the ministry was also divided along generational lines, but ignores the fact that Wilson, Norton, Richard Mather, and almost the entire Cambridge Synod favored the mea-sure. See Miller, *Colony to Province*, 95: "The minority was led [in its opposition to the Half-way Covenant] by survivors of the first generation whereas the most active of the majority (with the sole exception of Richard Mather) were of the second." This generalization also ig-nores the fact that Increase Mather and Jonathan Russell, both second-generation ministers, were strong opponents of the innovation. See also Beales, "The Half-Way Covenant and Re-ligious Scrupulosity," and Dexter *Congregationalism of the Last Three Hundred Years*, 474.

45. Pope, *Dorchester First Church Records*, 164–165, 168, 33. Pope, *Half-Way Covenant*, 43n., 44, 48, 52–53; Chauncy et al., *Antisynodalia*, 5. Note also that men of rank and substance could be found on both sides of the division over the Halfway Covenant in the First Church of Boston, discussed later in this chapter.

46. Boston Third Church Records in Hill, *Old South Church*, vol. 1, 102.

47. The First Church of Boston was one of the last churches in the colony to adopt the Halfway Covenant, postponing the matter until 1730.

48. Pierce, *Boston First Church Records*, 55–56.

49. John Cotton sermon, March 16, 1640, in Alpert, "Keayne Notebook of Cotton Ser-mons and Boston First Church Proceedings," 242.

50. Wilson quoted in Morton, *New England's Memorial; Or, A brief Relation of the Most Memorable and Remarkable Passages of the Providence of God, manifested to the Planters of New-England in America, with special Reference to the first Colony thereof, Called New-Plymouth* (Boston, 1669), 183–184.

51. Rutman, "God's Bridge Falling Down," 416, 419ff. Ross Beales also interprets the struggle over the Halfway Covenant as one involving lay "declension" in "The Half-Way Covenant and Religious Scrupulosity."

52. Based upon his examination of Robert Keayne's first sermon notebook (now miss-ing), Ezra Stiles concluded that Davenport preached in Boston with some frequency in the

mid-1630s. See Massachusetts Historical Society, *Proceedings*, 2nd ser., 4 (Boston, 1889), 159–191.

53. Boston Third Church Records in Hill, *Old South Church*, vol. 1, 21.

54. The supporters of the Halfway Covenant, for example, included first-generation luminaries such as John Hull, silversmith, mintmaster, and treasurer of the colony; Edward Raynsford, a church deacon, Jacob Eliot, a deacon, captain, and selectman; Edward Rawson, secretary of the colony; and Thomas Brattle, one of the colony's wealthiest merchants. But the supporters also included Richard Trewsdale, a servant and later a merchant; William Salter, a shoemaker, Seth Perry, a tailor; and Theodore Atkinson, a feltmaker. Hill, *Old South Church*, vol. 1, 114–119. According to Thomas Hutchinson, John Wilson, Jr., the son of Pastor Wilson, also sided with the proponents of the innovation, though his name does not appear among the founders of the Boston Third Church. Thomas Hutchinson, *History of the Colony and Province of Massachusetts-Bay*, ed. Lawrence Shaw Mayo, 3 vols. (Cambridge, Mass., 1936), vol. 1, 270.

55. Boston Third Church Records in Hill, *Old South Church*, vol. 1, 17, 39.

56. *Ibid.*

57. *Ibid.*, 16–17, 14.

58. See the discussion in chapter 3.

59. Boston Third Church records in Hill, *Old South Church*, vol. 1, 17, 47, 48, 63.

60. *Ibid.*, 14.

61. *Ibid.*, 18, 21, 22. As Robert Pope and Stephen Foster, among others, have noted, a political dimension accompanied Davenport's designs. See Pope, *Half-Way Covenant*, chapter 6, and Foster, *The Long Argument*, 198–203.

62. Boston Third Church records in Hill, *Old South Church*, vol. 1, 23.

63. *Ibid.*, 43n.

64. *Ibid.*, 25–26. The council included the ministers and lay messengers from the Dorchester, Roxbury, Dedham, and Cambridge churches.

65. One exception was Henry Martin Dexter, who argued that the council was one of the most important in the colonial era. *Congregationalism of the Last Three Hundred Years*, 474.

66. John Davenport, *A Sermon Preached at the Election of the Governor at Boston . . .* (Cambridge, 1670), 13–14.

67. Boston Third Church Records in Hill, *Old South Church*, vol. 1, 32–36. Davenport's son also seems to have been involved in the forgery of the letter of dismission. Davenport's "mystery of iniquity" was discovered in 1669 to the great dissatisfaction of neighboring congregations and many Boston First Church members. Though Davenport stiffly denied any wrongdoing, he suffered a severe and public reprimand from a large number of ministers and died several months later: see *ibid.*, 84–87.

68. *Ibid.*, 42, 52.

69. *Ibid.*, 42–49; Pierce, *Boston First Church Records*, 62. According to Harold Worthley's "Inventory of the Records of the Particular (Congregational) Churches of Massachusetts Gathered 1620–1805," *Proceedings of the Unitarian Historical Society*, 1966–1969, deacons were rarely dismissed for church offenses.

70. Boston Third Church Records in Hill, *Old South Church*, vol. 1, 52–53. The First Church majority's claims were incongruous with Congregational theory and practice in New England. The *Cambridge Platform* does include provisions for granting advisory councils, and the elders had previously ruled that minorities maintained a right to protest the decisions of the majority. See chapter 1, above.

71. *Ibid.*, 52–55, 69.

72. *Ibid.*, 52–53, 55.

73. *Ibid.*, 60.

74. *Ibid.*, 60–61; Chauncy, et al., *Antisynodalia*, 2.

75. Boston Third Church Records in Hill, *Old South Church*, vol. 1, 64–66, 69.

76. *Ibid.*, 64–67.

77. *Ibid.*, 65–66.

78. *Ibid.*, 68–69. The elders also acknowledged that minorities had just as much a right as majorities in choosing ministers.

79. *Ibid.*, 53–55, 76–78. The Third Church Records indicate that letters were sent to the churches in Cambridge, Charlestown, Dedham, Ipswich, Lynn, and Weymouth. Specific references to the Boston First Church dispute also appear in Pope, *Dorchester First Church Records*, 54, 58, 59, and Pierce, *Salem First Church Records*, 119. Hutchinson also concluded that the controversies spread throughout the colony and quoted Governor Bellingham as fearing "a sudden tumult." Davenport also sent letters explaining his side of the dispute, which were read (at least) in the Salem and Roxbury churches. See Hutchinson, "History," vol. 1, 270, and Isabel Calder, ed., *Letters of John Davenport, Puritan Divine* (New Haven, 1937), 281–282.

80. Pierce, *Salem First Church Records*, 120.

81. Pope, *Dorchester First Church Records*, 58. The second council decision and a list of elders and representatives in attendance appears in the Boston Third Church Records, in Hill, *Old South Church*, vol. 1, 64–67.

82. Hill, *Old South Church*, vol. 1, 67n., 68n.; Mather, *Magnalia*, vol. 2, book 5, 312.

83. John Davenport, *Sermon Preached at the Election*, 13–14, 12.

84. The political phase of the dispute is discussed in Miller, *Colony to Province*, 107–110; Pope, *Half-Way Covenant*, chapter 6; and Foster, *The Long Argument*, 198–203.

85. Hill, *History of the Old South Church*, 95–99.

86. *Ibid.*, 102.

87. *Ibid.*

88. The election results and a listing of the deputies appears in Hill, *Old South Church*, vol. 1, 111n. As Pope noted, the election was all the more remarkable in that deputies were rarely turned out of office. Still, the ministers' victory was far from total. Nearly a third of the deputies still opposed the ministers and voted against retraction.

89. Hill, *Old South Church*, vol. 1, 192. Miller, in *Colony to Province*, 107–110, argued that resistance to the Halfway Covenant largely ended after the election, though struggles between clergymen and elite laymen intensified over church authority.

90. Pope, *Half-Way Covenant*, 73–74; Stout, *The New England Soul*, 60.

91. Stout, *The New England Soul*, 59.

92. Walker, *Creeds and Platforms*, 302, 309–10; John Norton, *Three Choice and Profitable Sermons* (Cambridge, 1664), 8; see also 13.

93. Pierce, *Salem First Church Records*, 105; Boston Third Church records in Hill, *Old South Church*, vol.1, 68, 21.

94. Pope, *Dorchester First Church Records*, 98, 73, 78, 111. See also Pierce, *Boston First Church Records*, 59, 70, 90; and Worthley, "The Lay Officers," 466–468.

95. Robert Lord Goodman, "Newbury, Massachusetts, 1635–1685: The Social Foundations of Harmony and Conflict" (Ph.D. diss., Michigan State University, 1974), chapters 3 and 4.

96. Pope, *Dorchester First Church Records*, 111.

97. Hall suggested that majoritarianism was a consequence of second-generation lay insurgency, but in fact the gradual decline of the unanimous vote and the attendant rise of the majority vote was a far more complex process. Hall, *Faithful Shepherd*, 214.

98. Samuel Danforth, *A Brief Recognition of New England's Errand into the Wilderness* (Cambridge, 1670), 12.

99. *Ibid.*, 10, 22.

100. Oakes, *New-England Pleaded With*, quoted in Hill, *Old South Church*, vol. 1, 194.

101. *Ibid.*, 194–195.

102. The quotations appear in Pope, *Half-Way Covenant*, 72. Stout and Emory Elliot, also observe a far less confident tone in ministerial preaching. See Stout, *New England Soul*, 77, 95–96, 100–101; Emory Elliot, *Power and the Pulpit in Puritan New England* (Princeton, N.J., 1975), 13–14.

103. These charges were also bandied about in the Boston First Church, and were lodged by ministers themselves in Davenport's election sermon and in the Boston Council decisions. *Roxbury First Church Records*, 45; Pierce, *Salem First Church Records*, 98.

6. An Uneasy Balance

1. Reading First Church Records, ts, 6–7. Lydia Dastin, wife of Josiah Dastin, was born in 1613. She and her husband moved from Medford to Reading in 1647 and had five children. Charles Henry Pope, *The Pioneers of Massachusetts* (Boston, 1900), 131.

2. Thomas Shepard, *Wine for Gospel Wantons* (Cambridge, 1668), 13; Harry S. Stout, *The New England Soul: Preaching and Religious Culture in Colonial New England* (New York, 1986), 108–111. Alan Simpson asserted that most of the ministers' criticism was in fact hyperbolic and suggested that the congregations should not "be judged by the condemnations which the preachers heaped on them." See *Puritanism in Old and New England* (Chicago, 1955), 36; Larzer Ziff, *Puritanism in America: New Culture in a New World* (New York, 1973), chapter 8; and Sacvan Bercovitch, "New England's Errand Revisited," in John Higham and Paul Conkin, eds., *New Directions in American Intellectual History* (Baltimore, 1979).

3. For a discussion of population growth see Daniel Scott Smith, "The Demographic History of Colonial New England," *Journal of Economic History*, 32 (1972), 165–183. Economic developments are charted in Bernard Bailyn, *The New England Merchants in the Seventeenth Century* (Boston, 1955); Carl Bridenbaugh, *Cities in the Wilderness: The First Century of Urban Life in America, 1625–1742* (New York, 1938); Richard S. Dunn, *Puritans and Yankees: The Winthrop Dynasty of New England, 1630–1717* (orig. pub., 1962; reprinted New York, 1971), 59–190; Stephen Innes, *Labor in a New Land: Economy and Society in Seventeenth-Century Springfield* (Princeton, 1983); and Christine Heyrman, *Commerce and Culture: The Maritime Communities of Colonial Massachusetts, 1690–1750* (New York, 1984), 29–51. Difficulties arising from geographical expansion and the availability of inexpensive land are described in John Murrin, "Review Essay," *History and Theory*, 11 (1972), 226–275; James Henretta, "The Morphology of New England Society in the Colonial Period," *Journal of Interdisciplinary History*, 2 (1971), 379–398.

4. See, for example, Kenneth Lockridge, *A New England Town: The First Hundred Years* (New York, 1970), 93–118; Philip J. Greven, Jr., *Four Generations: Population, Land, and Family in Colonial Andover, Massachusetts* (Ithaca, N.Y., 1970), 103–173; Paul Boyer and Stephen Nissenbaum, *Salem Possessed: The Social Origins of Witchcraft* (Cambridge, Mass., 1974), 41–43.

5. The following is drawn from Ipswich Chebacco Parish Record Book, 1676–1726, Rufus Choate msc dated 1902, Essex Institute, 8–35. Hereafter cited as Ipswich Second Church

Records, msc. See also Pope, *Dorchester First Church Records*, 111, which contain an account of a similar division in Watertown.

6. Ipswich Second Church Records, msc, 12, 15ff.

7. *Ibid.*, 29ff. The General Court briefly delayed the gathering because it questioned the Congregational orthodoxy of Jeremiah Shepard, whom the Chebacco residents proposed to ordain. The dispute also contained an economic dimension; see *ibid.*, 36–37, 39. For a similar example, see Joshua Coffin, ed., *A Brief Sketch of the History of Newbury, Newburyport, and West Newbury* (Boston, 1845), 44–46.

8. Stout, *New England Soul*, 106–107.

9. Richard Bushman described a similar trend in Connecticut dating from the turn of the century: "[T]he meetinghouse became the battleground for all of the issues dividing the town . . . . All the animosities focused on the church." *From Puritan to Yankee: Character and the Social Order in Connecticut, 1690–1765* (Cambridge, Mass., 1967), 161.

10. "Records of the Congregational Church, Rowley, Mass.," msc, Rowley First Congregational Church, entry dated November, 1673. Hereafter cited as Rowley First Church Records, msc. Worthley described this very lengthy transcription of the early Rowley church records as "incomplete." The original records, apparently extant in the early 1960s, are now described by local church officials as "missing." Pope, *John Fiske Notebook*, 201; Reading First Church Records, 3–13; Patricia Trainor O'Malley, "Rowley, Massachusetts, 1639–1730: Dissent, Division, and Delimitation in a Colonial Town" (Ph.D. diss., Boston College, 1975); Robert Lord Goodman, "Newbury, Massachusetts, 1635–1685: The Social Foundations of Harmony and Conflict" (Ph.D. diss., Michigan State University, 1974); *Articles of Faith and Covenant Adopted by the First Church of Christ in Bradford, Mass.* (Haverhill, Mass., 1886), 7.

11. Michael Zuckerman, "Identity in British America: Unease in Eden," in Nicholas Canny and Anthony Pagden, eds., *Colonial Identity in the Atlantic World, 1500–1800* (Princeton, N.J., 1987), 132; Richard P. Gildrie, *The Profane, the Civil, and the Godly: The Reformation of Manners in Orthodox New England, 1679–1749* (University Park, Penn., 1994), 7–11. Gildrie observes that individualism at this time "took at least three occasionally contradictory forms": hedonistic, characterized by wasteful, idle, profane behavior; "pietist," characterized by an "intense commitment to personal religious experience," and possessive, which included both a drive to enhance economic status and, importantly, "self-seeking benefits such as social respectability or political influence." While the behavior of many lay people does not neatly fit any of these categories (classifications that, Gildrie notes, do not exhaust the possibilities of individualistic behavior), it frequently resembled the latter in the late seventeenth century. *The Profane, the Civil, and the Godly*, 9–11. See also Jack P. Greene, *Pursuits of Happiness: The Social Development of Early Modern British Colonies and the Formation of American Culture* (Chapel Hill, 1988), chapter 3.

12. Gildrie, *The Profane, the Civil, and the Godly*, 9.

13. Rowley First Church Records, msc, April 25, 1677; see also *ibid.*, February 8, 1675; William P. Upham, ed., "Beverly First Church Records" (Essex Institute, *Collections* 35 [1899]), 191. See also the case of Rowley's Philip Nelson, discussed later in this chapter.

14. [Increase Mather], *The Necessity of Reformation, with the Expedients thereunto, asserted* (Boston, 1679), in Williston Walker, *The Creeds and Platforms of Congregationalism* (New York, 1893), 430.

15. Richard Hildrich, or Hildreth, was born in 1605 and joined the Cambridge church in 1643. He served as a town officer there in 1645. One of the original founders of Chelmsford, he died in 1688 at the age of 83. Pope, *Pioneers of Massachusetts*, 229.

16. Little is known of Thomas Barrett. He probably arrived in Massachusetts in 1635 at the age of sixteen. He died in 1668 at the age of forty-nine, leaving behind a wife and three sons. *Ibid.*, 35.

17. Pope, *John Fiske Notebook*, 201; see also *ibid.*, 172, 223, 232; Reading First Church Records, 6–7.

18. Eliot quoted in Robert F. Scholz, "'The Reverend Elders': Faith, Fellowship, and Politics in the Ministerial Community of Massachusetts Bay, 1630–1710" (Ph.D. diss., University of Minnesota, 1966), 178; Rowley First Church Records, November 29, 1674, February 8, 1675, June 18, 1675, October 18, 1675; See also Pope, *John Fiske Notebook*, 189–191. This development points to the need for an added dimension in discussions of the "persistence of localism" in New England, for local authority clearly declined in churches in favor of appeals to outside authorities—though not provincial ones. See T. H. Breen, "Persistent Localism: English Social Change and the Shaping of New England Institutions," *William and Mary Quarterly*, 32 (1975), 3–28.

19. The disciplinary cases were heard in Weymouth and Canton and are detailed in Pope, *Dorchester First Church Records*, 101–102, 105. See also Pope, *John Fiske Notebook*, 232–233, where the pastor offered to call a council over a petty dispute involving a member's statement of repentance, and Pierce, *Salem First Church Records*, 141, for an account of a council decision in Salisbury that rescinded an excommunication.

20. The following is drawn from George F. Dow, ed., *Records and Files of the Quarterly Courts of Essex, Massachusetts*, 8 vols. (Salem, 1911–1921), vol. 7, 184–186, 80.

21. Thomas Leaver, a linen weaver, had four children. He died in 1683 at the age of sixty-eight. Philip Nelson was a wealthy gentleman and a founder of Rowley. He served frequently as a town officer. Pope, *Pioneers of Massachusetts*, 283, 326.

22. For similar examples of disputes that could not be settled privately, see Reading First Church Records, 3–14; Rowley First Church Records, May 26, 1667, November, 1673; Pope, *John Fiske Notebook*, 218.

23. Stout, *New England Soul*, 76–77; Rowley First Church Records, December 19, 1667; see also January 5, 1675; Hall, *Faithful Shepherd*, 181; Greene, *Pursuits of Happiness*, 59.

24. Robert Proctor became a freeman in Salem in 1643 and apparently moved to Concord, where he married in 1645. He joined the Chelmsford church in 1656 and died in 1697. Pope, *Pioneers of Massachusetts*, 375.

25. Pope, *John Fiske Notebook*, 198–199; See also Rowley First Church Records, entry dated November, 1673, April 10, 1677.

26. See Hall, *Faithful Shepherd*, chapters 8 and 9, but especially 181–187; Stout, *New England Soul*, 76, 105–107; Pope, *Half-Way Covenant*, chapter 7.

27. Pope, introduction to *John Fiske Notebook*, xxvii–xxviii, xxxvii–xxxix.

28. Little is known of William Fletcher beyond his being instrumental in inviting Fiske to move from Wenham to Chelmsford. Fletcher married twice and had two children. Pope, *Pioneers of Massachusetts*, 170.

29. The following is drawn from Pope, *John Fiske Notebook*, 176–179.

30. *Ibid.*, 107.

31. *Ibid.*, 215, 177.

32. Little is known of Thomas Chamberlain other than that he moved to Chelmsford from Woburn. He joined the Chelmsford church in 1655. Pope, *Pioneers of Massachusetts*, 92.

33. Pope, *John Fiske Notebook*, 178.

34. Pope, *John Fiske Notebook*, xxxviii.

35. Rowley First Church Records, December 10, 1678.

36. Nehemiah Jewett was probably the son of Joseph Jewett, a yeoman farmer and cloth-ier. Nehemiah was born in 1643. Pope, *Pioneers of Massachusetts*, 259.

37. The millwright Richard Holmes served as a town officer in Rowley and died c. 1695 at the age of approximately ninety-one. Pope, *Pioneers of Massachusetts*, 237.

38. Samuel Highill is unidentified.

39. Rowley First Church Records, April 10, 1677.

40. *Ibid.*

41. *Ibid.*

42. *Ibid.*

43. *Ibid.*, April 18, 1677.

44. *Ibid.*, May 18, 1677; November 18, 1677.

45. *Ibid.*, November 11, 1677.

46. Pierce, ed., *Salem First Church Records*, 153–154.

47. Hunnewell, ed., *Charlestown First Church Records*, x; for similar cases of interchurch super-vision see *ibid.*, ix; Rowley First Church Records, msc, November 5, 1666, May 26, 1667. Refer-ences to mutual watch are similarly common; for particularly good examples, see Pope, *Dorchester First Church Records*, 86; Pope, *John Fiske Notebook*, 195; Pierce, *Salem First Church Records*, 101, 106; Rowley First Church Records, msc, June 6, 1669, June 20, 1676, November 11, 1677.

48. Pierce, *Salem First Church Records*, 106; Pope, *Dorchester First Church Records*, 73–74, 89. Previous studies have suggested that apathy characterized halfway members' spiritual life and that churches failed to discipline these members. David Hall, citing the claims of two ministers in published sermons, suggested that these churchgoers were "markedly in-different" and refused to "subject themselves to [church] discipline." Hall, *Faithful Shep-herd*, 250. Stephen Foster also asserted that churches largely ignored the "children" in church discipline. Though fragmentary, the records contain considerable evidence to suggest that, on the contrary, churches regularly disciplined halfway members during the latter half of the seventeenth century. See, for example, Pope, *Dorchester First Church Records*, 76, 83, 85, 87, 88–89; Pierce, *Salem First Church Records*, 144; Pope, *John Fiske Notebook*, 206, 235; Hunnewell, *Charlestown First Church Records*, vi; Bradford First Church Records in *Articles of Faith and Covenant Adopted by the First Church of Bradford*, 39–42, in addition to the cases cited above. Ministers did sometimes complain about the degree to which churches exer-cised watch over the "children," but such complaints should be assessed in context, for ministers complained about a failure to "watch" in general. Rowley's pastor Samuel Phillips, for instance, acknowledged his church's failure in "calling upon" the children to join in covenant "at least not all of them" and not "watching over them" to a degree "as we ought." Rowley First Church Records, msc, June 20, 1676.

49. Pope, *Dorchester First Church Records*, 73–74.

50. *Ibid.*, 87.

51. See chapters 8 and 9.

52. Pope, *Dorchester First Church Records*, 96–97.

53. Pope, *John Fiske Notebook*, 209–212.

54. Pope, *John Fiske Notebook*, 211–212.

55. "Braintree Church Records 1753 The Church Records of Braintree [sic]," May 4, 1683. Photocopy of original ms church records held by the New England Historical and Genea-logical Society, Boston. Hereafter cited as Braintree (Quincy) First Church Records, ms.

Excerpts drawn from these records appear in Charles Francis Adams, "Some Phases of Sexual Morality and Church Discipline in Colonial New England," Massachusetts Historical Society, *Proceedings*, 2nd ser., 6 (1890–1891), 477–516.

56. Braintree (Quincy) Church Records, April 17, 1698; July 28, 1697; August 27, 1697.

57. Seven of thirteen offenders repented in Boston during the 1670s, though several fell back into sin. Four of the eight members censured by the Charlestown church from 1670 to 1680 repented before the congregation. Pierce, *Boston First Church Records*, 64–78; Hunnewell, *Charlestown First Church Records*, vii–ix.

58. *Ibid.*, ix.

59. See chapter 3.

60. Hunnewell, *Charlestown First Church Records*, ix.

61. Rowley First Church Records, November 25, 1677; September, 1668.

62. For examples in which churches accepted council determinations, see Pope, *John Fiske Notebook*, 183–184; Pierce, *Salem First Church Records*, 160–162; Rowley First Church Records, January 8, 1665; July 18, 1665; September 15, 1675; April 10, 1677. A prominent exception occurred in Newbury and is discussed in chapter 7.

63. Hall, *Faithful Shepherd*, 102–104, 95.

64. The use of lay elders in the eighteenth century is further discussed in chapters 8 and 9.

65. Pierce, *Salem First Church Records*, 84–85; *Roxbury First Church Records*, 191; Pope, *Dorchester First Church Records*, 121; Coffin, *History of Newbury*, 111.

66. See Worthley, "The Lay Officers," 470. Worthley found that deacons and other worthy laymen stepped into the fore in churches that no longer employed ruling elders. Nearly all church records with any degree of completeness contain examples of the continued assistance of "worthy laymen" in church government. See, for example, Rowley First Church Records, August 28, 1667, November 29, 1674. Given the ruling elder's role as clerical assistant during the first decades of settlement, the demise of this office may well reflect increasing laicism in church government rather than sacerdotalism.

67. It is worth noting, as Stephen Foster observes, that lay ordination began to fall into disuse in the early years of settlement; the practice was not merely a function of sacerdotalism. Foster, "English Puritanism and the Progress of New England Institutions," in David D. Hall et al., eds., *Saints and Revolutionaries* (New York, 1984), 28. See Pope, *Dorchester First Church Records*, 65, for a case in which the ruling elder received an invitation to ordain the new minister but declined.

68. William B. Trask, ed., "Milton (Mass.) Church Records, 1678–1754," *New England Historical and Genealogical Register*, 22 (1868), 261.

69. The Taunton dispute appears in Pope, *Dorchester First Church Records*, 34; Boyer and Nissenbaum, *Salem Possessed*, chapters 2 and 3.

70. See Pope, *John Fiske Notebook*, 218–221, 181; the Rowley dispute is discussed earlier in this chapter. See also the division in Newbury, discussed in chapter 7, in which nearly half the church defended the ministers against charges of usurpation of lay liberties.

71. Stout, *New England Soul*, 107. Robert Scholz suggested, in contrast, that during the later seventeenth century "a divided ministry no longer had . . . the respect of the people." "The Reverend Elders," 205.

72. O'Malley, "Rowley, Massachusetts," 110. John Fiske's Chelmsford congregation similarly considered hiring an additional minister during their struggles and cited clerical maladministration as one justification. The majority rejected the move. See Pope, *John Fiske Notebook*, 214–222.

73. See Clifford K. Shipton, "The New England Clergy of the 'Glacial Age,'" Colonial Society of Massachusetts, *Publications*, 32 (*Transactions*, 1933–37), 50–51; William P. Upham, ed., "Beverly First Church Records" (Essex Institute, *Historical Collections*, 25, 41 [1899–1905]); Increase Mather, Preface, to *The Necessity of Reformation*, in Walker, *Creeds and Platforms*, 423–424. See Worthley, "The Lay Officers," 532 and 397 for a similar description of harmony in the First Church of Barnstable. John Fiske's notebook, probably the most complete account of the period, also suggests that while the 1660s and 1670s witnessed an increase in church disputes, they nevertheless remained sporadic. Similarly, while ministers suffered countless salary disputes, these quarrels preoccupied ministers and their flocks only on rare occasions.

7. Declension and Reform

1. Increase Mather, Preface to *The Necessity of Reformation*, in Williston Walker, ed., *The Creeds and Platforms of Congregationalism* (New York, 1893), 424; Increase Mather, *A Discourse Concerning the Danger of Apostacy* (Boston, 1685), 87.

2. Samuel Torrey, *Election Sermon* (Boston, 1683), 21.

3. Darrett B. Rutman, for instance, supported Miller's stance, arguing that declining rates of full church membership, the need for the Halfway Covenant, and the obvious increase in second-generation contention indicate a general decline of the religiosity of the culture—a description that differs little from that of contemporary ministers. The same view is implicit in David D. Hall's suggestion that lay declension motivated ministers' efforts to drain power from their congregations. Perry Miller, *The New England Mind: From Colony to Province* (Cambridge, Mass., 1953), 3–146; Darrett B. Rutman, "God's Bridge Falling Down 'Another Approach' to New England Puritanism Assayed," *William and Mary Quarterly*, 3rd ser., 19 (1962). David D. Hall, *The Faithful Shepherd: A History of the New England Ministry in the Seventeenth Century* (Chapel Hill, 1972), chapters 8 and 9. See also Emory Elliot, *Power and the Pulpit in Puritan New England* (Princeton, 1975), 88–135, and Ross Beales, "The Half-Way Covenant and Religious Scrupulosity: The First Church of Dorchester, Massachusetts as a Test Case," *William and Mary Quarterly*, 31 (1974). Among those who disputed the declension thesis were Edmund S. Morgan in "New England Puritanism: Another Approach," *William and Mary Quarterly*, 3rd ser., 18 (1966), and Robert Pope in "New England Versus the New England Mind: The Myth of Declension," *Journal of Social History* 3 (1969), 95–108. More recent treatments of the issue appear in Virginia DeJohn Anderson, *New England's Generation: The Great Migration and the Formation of Society and Culture in the Seventeenth Century* (New York, 1991), Theodore Dwight Bozeman, *To Live Ancient Lives: The Primitivist Dimension in Puritanism* (Chapel Hill, 1988), 360–363; Stephen Foster, *The Long Argument: English Puritanism and the Shaping of New England Culture, 1570–1700* (Chapel Hill, 1991), chapters 5 and 6; Jack P. Greene, *Pursuits of Happiness: The Social Development of Early Modern British Colonies and the Formation of American Culture* (Chapel Hill, 1988), chapter 3 ("A Declension Model: New England, 1660–1760"); David D. Hall, ed., introduction to *The Works of Jonathan Edwards*, vol. 12, *Ecclesiastical Writings* (New Haven, 1994), 12; Michael G. Hall, *The Last American Puritan: The Life of Increase Mather* (Middletown, Conn., 1966).

4. The later stages of this transformation are further discussed in chapter 10.

5. Morgan, "Another Approach to New England Puritanism." Robert Pope supports Morgan's views in *The Half-Way Covenant: Church Membership in New England* (Princeton, 1969), and in "The Myth of Declension"; Harry S. Stout similarly refutes the concept of a declension in religiosity in *The New England Soul: Preaching and Religious Culture in Colo-*

nial New England (New York, 1986), chapters 4, 5, and 6. See also Christine Heyrman, *Commerce and Culture: The Maritime Communities of Colonial Massachusetts, 1690–1750* (New York, 1984).

6. James Hoopes, "Art as History: Perry Miller's *New England Mind*," *American Quarterly* 34 (1982), 21–22.

7. Rutman, "God's Bridge Falling Down," 417; Bozeman, *To Live Ancient Lives*, 360–363.

8. David D. Hall, ed., introduction to *Edwards' Ecclesiastical Writings*; Pope, *Dorchester First Church Records*, 111, italics added; Mather quoted in Pope, *The Half-Way Covenant*, 196; Henry Dexter, *The Congregationalism of the Last Three Hundred Years* (New York, 1880), 483; James F. Cooper, Jr., and Kenneth P. Minkema, eds., *The Sermon Notebook of Samuel Parris* (Boston, 1993), 250, 283.

9. Pope, *Dorchester First Church Records*, 55; William Upham, ed., "Beverly First Church Records" (Essex Institute, *Historical Collections* 35 [July 1899]), 186, 190.

10. Upham, "Beverly First Church Records," 202, 204–206. As Edmund S. Morgan notes in *Visible Saints: The History of a Puritan Idea* (Ithica, N.Y., 1963), 147, the wording adopted by the Reforming Synod of 1679 to reaffirm the requirement of saving faith as a condition for full membership is crucial, and is relevant to the evidence drawn from the Beverly First Church records. The synod stated that "a personal and publick profession of their Faith and Repentance, either orally, or in some other way" entitled candidates to full membership. Morgan observes that this wording could be interpreted by ministers (such as Solomon Stoddard) to justify "open communion," or admission on the basis of a profession of faith in the absence of a relation of God's saving grace. Nothing in the church records, however, suggests that the majority of ministers or the First Church of Beverly interpreted the meaning of "a profession of faith and repentance" as Stoddard might have; like the vast majority of churches, the First Churh of Beverly neither jettisoned relations of grace nor practiced open communion at this time.

11. The Barborn testimonial is located at the Dedham Historical Society, MSS coll., box B.

12. Pierce, *Salem First Church Records*, 154; Bradford First Church Records in *Articles of Faith and Covenant Adopted by the First Church of Christ in Bradford, Mass.* (Haverhill, Mass., 1886), 39, 42.

13. Pierce, *Salem First Church Records*, 177; Pierce, *Boston First Church Records*, 64; and Pope, *John Fiske Notebook*, 222.

14. *Ibid.*, 186–187. The individual who had previously applied was Fiske's daughter. Pierce, *Salem First Church Records*, 107.

15. Pope, *Dorchester First Church Records*, 45, 46, 67, see also 14; Pope, *John Fiske Notebook*, 187; Pierce, *Salem First Church Records*, 142; see also 91, where the minister read an account of a halfway member's "knowledge" to the church.

16. Foster, *The Long Argument*, chapters 5 and 6.

17. Hunnewell, *Charlestown First Church Records*, ix; Boston Third Church Records in Hill, *Old South Church*, vol. 1, 229, 252. See also *Plymouth First Church Records*, vol. 1, 262–263; Watertown Historical Society, *Watertown Records, Comprising East Congregational and Precinct Affairs . . . .* (Boston, 1906), hereafter cited as *Watertown First Church Records*, 118–119; Pope, *Dorchester First Church Records*, 46, for instances in which the test of relation was eased by mutual consent. Hall argued, in contrast, that "any proposal to enlarge the doors of the church quickly came up against the opposition of members who had passed the test of a relation and who now defended their special privileges." *Faithful Shepherd*, 200.

18. Pierce, *Salem First Church Records*, 107–109.

19. Pope, *John Fiske Notebook*, 183; Pope, *Dorchester First Church Records*, 83–84; "Records of the Congregational Church in Topsfield" (Topsfield Historical Society, *Historical Collections*, 14 [1909]), 13–14, hereafter cited as "Topsfield First Church Records"; Pierce, *Salem First Church Records*, 101, 134.

20. See, for example, Boston Third Church Records in Hill, *Old South Church*, 312, and Pope, *John Fiske Notebook*, 192.

21. See Charles Hambricke-Stowe, *The Practice of Piety: Puritan Devotional Disciplines in Seventeenth-Century New England* (Chapel Hill, 1982), 246–248, and Stout, *The New England Soul*, chapter 4.

22. [Increase Mather], Preface to *The Necessity of Reformation*, in Walker, *Creeds and Platforms*, 424.

23. Hall, *Faithful Shepherd*, chapter 9.

24. Samuel Willard, *Useful Instructions for a professing People in Times of great Security and Degeneracy* (Cambridge, 1673), 75.

25. William Hubbard, *A General History of New England From the Discovery to MDCLXXX* (Boston, 1848), 551.

26. Cotton Mather, *Magnalia Christi Americana*, 2 vols. (Hartford, 1820), vol. 2, book 5, 45.

27. *Ibid.*, 46.

28. *Diary of Cotton Mather*, Massachusetts Historical Society, *Collections*, 7th ser. (1911), vol. 8, 161–162.

29. The minutes from the meetings of the Cambridge Association (in Cotton Mather, *Magnalia*, vol. 2, book 5, 248–269) show that the ministers discussed significant procedural changes but usually arrived at the standard conclusions concerning lay and ministerial roles in church government. These continuities began to change with Cotton Mather's *Proposals* in 1704. See discussion in chapter 8.

30. Michael G. Hall, *The Last American Puritan*, xiv. See also Robert Middlekauf, *The Mathers: Three Generations of Puritan Intellectuals, 1596–1728* (New York, 1971), 98, and Stout, *New England Soul*, chapter 4.

31. John Wilson, *A Seasonable Watch-Word* (Cambridge, 1677), 6,7; For similar statements see John Davenport, *A Sermon Preached* (Cambridge, 1670), 15–16; Eleazar Mather, *A Serious Exhortation* (Cambridge, 1671).

32. Samuel Danforth, *A Brief Recognition of New-England's Errand into the Wilderness* (Cambridge, 1668), 10, 17–18.

33. Urian Oakes, *New-England Pleaded With* (Cambridge, 1673), 11, 21. Oakes and other ministers also defended lay participation in their published works; Oakes reaffirmed, for example, that the "concurrence of the Brethren" was "necessarily required to the exercise of Church Authority." See *ibid.*, 46–47, and Cotton Mather, *Magnalia*, vol. 1, 552–553, vol. 2, 75–76, 95, 208.

34. Cotton Mather, *Optanda, Good Men Described and Good Things Propounded* (Boston, 1692), 87, 41, 43.

35. Walker, *Creeds and Platforms*, 434, 412–414, 416; [Increase Mather], Preface, to *The Necessity of Reformation*, in *ibid.*, 424.

36. Pope, *Dorchester First Church Records*, 69–70; Walker, *Creeds and Platforms*, 415.

37. Walker, *Creeds and Platforms*, 417. Joshua Scottow, a lay founder of the Boston Third Church, reported that the result of the Synod of 1679 was read in every church. Joshua Scottow, *Old Men's Tears for their and Declensions, Mixed with Fears of Their and Posterities Further Falling off from New-England's Primitive Constitution* (Boston, 1691), 9.

38. [Increase Mather], Preface to *The Necessity of Reformation*, in Walker, *Creeds and Platforms*, 425.

39. *Ibid.*; Pope, *Dorchester First Church Records*, 83. See also Pierce, *Salem First Church Records*, 152; Pierce, *Boston First Church Records*, 80; Hambricke-Stowe, *The Practice of Piety*, 248ff.

40. Stout, for instance, notes "two programs of action recommended by the Reforming Synod"—covenant renewal and increased moral supervision. In fact, there were three. *New England Soul*, 98.

41. [Increase Mather], Preface to *The Necessity of Reformation*, in Walker, *Creeds and Platforms*, 425. The ministers at no time considered serious revisions of the *Platform*. There was, however, some debate during the synod itself over admissions standards. As is commonly known, Solomon Stoddard advanced a system of open communion for the churches. In deference to Stoddard, the synod offered a vague statement on admissions that was easily interpreted to support a variety of procedures. The elders also endorsed stronger civil laws to punish those responsible for the growing "evils" in society: see *ibid.*, 415.

42. *Ibid.*; [Increase Mather], *The Necessity of Reformation*, in Walker, *Creeds and Platforms*, 433; *The Results of Three Synods*. . . . (Boston, 1725), 120.

43. Reading First Church Records, ts, 3. See also Scottow, *Old Men's Tears*, 9, and Pierce, *Salem First Church Records*, 148, 150.

44. Walker, *Creeds and Platforms*, 415. Increase Mather noted that one minister (undoubtedly Solomon Stoddard) did not view the *Platform* as drawn from the Word of God. Increase Mather, *Order of the Gospel and Practiced by the Churches of Christ in New England* . . . (Boston, 1700), 39.

45. See chapter 8.

46. Hall, *Faithful Shepherd*, 186, 197, 210–213. Hall observed that in Massachusetts the issues were more muddled than in Connecticut and acknowledged that the ministers' efforts in instituting a more Presbyterian form of church order met with less success in the Bay.

47. Mather, *Magnalia*, vol. 2, book 5, 237–241; Walker, *Creeds and Platforms*, 418n.; Dexter, *Congregationalism of the Last Three Hundred Years*, 481–483.

48. Raymond P. Stearns, ed., "The Correspondence of John Woodbridge, Jr., and Richard Baxter," *New England Quarterly*, 10 (1937), 582–583.

49. Though the early records of the First Church of Newbury have long been lost, considerable documentation remains pertaining to the divisions during the 1660s and 1670s. These documents, consisting largely of court records, have been brought together and published in Joshua Coffin, *A Sketch of the History of Newbury, Newburyport, and West Newbury* (Boston, 1845), especially 72–112.

50. *Ibid.*, 54, 73.

51. *Ibid.*, 74.

52. *Ibid.*

53. In 1668, the Chelmsford members passed a formal vote to bring an offender before the church. Previously, the pastor decided whether an offense merited church action, leaving only the questions of guilt and sentencing to the membership. See Pope, *John Fiske Notebook*, 209; Keayne Notebook of Cotton Sermons and Boston First Church Proceedings, December 28, 1645.

54. Charles Henry Pope, *The Pioneers of Massachusetts* (Boston, 1900), 513, 316, 456, 74–75, 442–443, 251, 293, 312, 36.

55. Coffin, *History of Newbury*, 74.

56. *Ibid.*, 75–76.

57. *Ibid.*, 76–78.

58. *Ibid.*, 79.

59. *Ibid.*, 78–80.

60. *Ibid.*, 82.

61. *Ibid.*, 82–83.

62. *Ibid.*, 87.

63. *Ibid.*, 95.

64. *Ibid.*, 94.

65. *Ibid.*, 104, 110–111.

66. Pierce, *Salem First Church Records*, 87–88. For other examples of lay participation, see 108, 112, 113, 115, 122, 133, and *passim*.

67. "Topsfield First Church Records," 13.

68. *Ibid.*, 11.

69. The negative vote is discussed in Hall, *Faithful Shepherd*, 115–117, 211–212. The seventeenth-century church records contain very few accounts of such ministerial vetoes. See Pierce, *Salem First Church Records*, 131, where Pastor John Higginson refused to attempt a veto or "negative vote."

70. Pope, *John Fiske Notebook*, 220.

71. Pope, *Dorchester First Church Records*, 90, 96–97; Rowley First Church Records, January 8, 1665; Pierce, *Salem First Church Records*, 153.

72. Rowley First Church Records, December 11, 1678; see also September 22, 1667, January 5, 1675, June 17, 1677. Virtually all extant church records dating from the latter half of the seventeenth century through the first half of the eighteenth century affirm the continued participation of the laity in the decision-making process. The topic is further discussed in chapter 9.

8. *Clerical Conflict and the Decline of* Sola Scriptura

1. Samuel Dexter Diary, ms, Dedham Historical Society, October 24, 1726.

2. *Ibid.*

3. *Ibid.*

4. Cotton Mather, *The Minister* (Boston, 1722), 41–42; William Williams, *The Honour of Christ Advanced By the Fidelity of Ministers* (Boston, 1728), 10. Eighteenth-century anticlericalism is discussed in J. William T. Youngs, Jr., *God's Messengers: Religious Leadership in Colonial New England, 1700–1750* (Baltimore, 1976), chapter 5, and Harry S. Stout, *The New England Soul: Preaching and Religious Culture in Colonial New England* (New York, 1986), 158–159.

5. These developments among the laity are traced in chapter 9.

6. Williston Walker, *The Creeds and Platforms of Congregationalism* (New York, 1893), chapter 14; Robert Middlekauf, *The Mathers: Three Generations of Puritan Intellectuals, 1596–1728* (New York, 1971), 213.

7. Stout, *New England Soul* 118–121, 148–149; Walker, *Creeds and Platforms*, 446–449.

8. See Paul Boyer and Stephen Nissenbaum, eds., *Salem-Village Witchcraft: A Documentary Record of Local Conflict in Colonial New England* (Belmont, Ca., 1972), 376–378, and Boyer and Nissenbaum, *Salem Possessed: The Social Origins of Witchcraft* (Cambridge, Mass., 1974), 190–191n.

9. Boyer and Nissenbaum, *Salem-Village Witchcraft*, 369–371; Calef quoted in Perry Miller, *The New England Mind: From Colony to Province* (Cambridge, Mass., 1953), 251.

10. Miller, *From Colony to Province*, 202–203; Richard P. Gildrie, *The Profane, the Civil, and the Godly: The Reformation of Manners in Orthodox New England, 1679–1749* (University Park, Penn., 1994); Pierce, *Salem First Church Records*, 133–297. While several members confessed to the sin of fornication as a prerequisite to achieve baptism for themselves or their children (see, for example, Pierce, *Salem First Church Records*, 175–176, 177, 185, 189), formal censures in Salem are almost nonexistent after the witch trials. In 1703, the church threatened to excommunicate one Elizabeth Allin, who had "forsaken" the church to live "in the profession and practice of Quakerism," but there is no indication in the record that the sentence was ever carried out. See Pierce, *Salem First Church Records*, 192–193. Contention broke out anew in Salem in the 1730s under the pastorate of Samuel Fiske. See chapter 9.

11. Pope, *Dorchester First Church Records*, 87–127.

12. Relative to earlier and later periods, few records remain from the 1690s that contain what appear to be complete disciplinary records. Those that do remain strongly suggest a shift in the frequency and nature of cases that came before the churches in the aftermath of the witchcraft controversy. From 1684 to 1693, the Topsfield church censured eight members for a variety of offenses, including several cases of community conflict. The same church censured only one member in the next five years, and after that virtually every case of discipline involved fornication. The Milton church censured only one member—for fornication—from 1692 to 1702. Virtually all eighteenth-century disciplinary cases in Beverly involved fornication. The church censured three members for fornication from 1705 to 1720 and censured no one else for the next twenty years. The First Church of Boston, which passed seven formal censures from 1689 to 1691, censured no one for five years after the witchcraft controversy. The First Church of Reading, which suffered numerous trivial squabbles in the 1680s, heard only eleven cases of discipline in the twenty years after the witchcraft controversy. None of these cases involved "contention." A similar pattern appears in *Records of the Brewster Congregational Church, Brewster, Massachusetts, 1700–1792* (Boston, 1911). In the First Churches of Marblehead and Bradford, the few disciplinary cases on the church record books are mainly for drinking and fornication. In Westfield, contention among churchgoers also apparently declined; the Westfield church, which heard four cases of slander and contention in the mid-1680s, suffered only one minor case of slander in the eighteen years after the controversy in Salem. "Topsfield First Church Records"; Milton First Church Records; Upham, ed., "Beverly First Church Records"; Pierce, *Boston First Church Records*; Reading First Church Records; Thomas M. Davis and Virginia L. Davis, eds., *Edward Taylor's "Church Records" and Related Sermons* (Boston, 1981), hereafter cited as Davis and Davis, *Westfield First Church Records*.

13. As Perry Miller observed, "a reaction against orthodoxy's management of the witchcraft trials" had become "general" by the late 1690s. Miller, *From Colony to Province*, 252.

14. Pierce, *Salem First Church Records*, 219; Danvers First Church Records, ms, Danvers Historical Society, 45, 47. The Salem merchant Thomas Maule published a pamphlet entitled *Truth Held Forth and Maintained* (Boston, 1695), in which he condemned the clergy for its role in the executions. Arrested for slander, the merchant was acquitted. See James E. Maule, *"Better that 100 Witches Should Live": The 1696 Aquittal of Thomas Maule* (Villanova, Pa., 1995); Chadwick Hansen, *Witchcraft at Salem* (New York, 1969), 250–251, and James W. Schmotter, "The Irony of Clerical Professionalism: New England's Congregational Ministers and the Great Awakening," *American Quarterly*, 31 (1979), 149–150.

15. In addition to Pierce, *Salem First Church Records*, and the Danvers First Church Records, see Braintree First Church Records, 28, which indicate that excommunications nearly ended there in the mid-1690s; "An account of the Acts & transactions & votes of the

church of Wenham, since I came thither, Joseph Gerrish," ms, New England Historical and Genealogical Society, Boston (hereafter cited as Wenham First Church Records, Gerrish Notebook), which indicates that the last excommunication in colonial Wenham was passed May 1, 1692; Pierce, *Boston First Church Records*, 90, 99, which indicate that the First Church of Boston, which excommunicated six members from 1689 to 1691, excommunicated only one (for excessive drinking) in the next forty years. The Woburn council is described in Pope, *Dorchester First Church Records*, 129. These developments are explored further in chapter 9 and in David C. Brown, "The Keyes of the Kingdom: Excommunication in Colonial Massachusetts," *New England Quarterly*, 68 (December 1994), 531–564.

16. Harold F. Worthley, "The Lay Officers of the Particular (Congregational) Churches of Massachusetts, 1620–1755: An Investigation of Practice and Theory" (Ph.D. diss., Harvard University, 1970), 610, notes that forty-one churches were gathered in Massachusetts and Plymouth from 1620 to 1648; forty-four more were gathered from 1649 to 1691; and 219 were gathered from 1692 to 1755. See Frank Lambert, *"Pedlar in Divinity": George Whitefield and the Transatlantic Revivals* (Princeton, 1994), 55–56, 137–139, for a review of the literature on the burgeoning world of print and literacy in the first half of the eighteenth century.

17. Samuel Dexter Diary, ms, Dedham Historical Society, September 14, 1726.

18. Massachusetts Historical Society, *Collections*, 6th ser., 5 (1892), 392–393n; see Clifford K. Shipton's continuation of John L. Sibley's multivolume biographical series entitled *Sibley's Harvard Graduates* (Boston, 1873–1975 [vols. 1–3 by Sibley; vols. 4–17 by Shipton]), vol. 4, 306–308; and Hill, *Old South Church*, vol. 1, 400. The principal primary sources on the Thatcher controversy include *An Account of the Reasons Why a Considerable Number, . . . , Belonging to the New-North . . . , Could Not Consent to Mr. Peter Thacher's Ordination* (Boston, 1720); Increase Mather, *A Further Testimony Against the Scandalous Proceedings of the New North Church* (Boston, 1720); Increase Mather, *A Seasonable Testimony to Good Order in the Churches* (Boston, 1720); Peter Thacher and John Webb, *A Brief Declaration* (Boston, 1720); Peter Thacher, *A Vindication of the New-North* (Boston, 1720).

19. Attestation of Mary Sweet, June 19, 1725, Massachusetts Archives, Boston, 11, 442–443; Sandwich First Church Records, ms, New England Historical and Genealogical Society, Boston, 61; *Brewster First Church Records*, 26–27. The events above are expertly analyzed in J. M. Bumsted, "A Caution to Erring Christians: Ecclesiastical Disorder on Cape Cod, 1717 to 1738," *William and Mary Quarterly*, 28 (1971), 411–438.

20. *Brewster First Church Records*, 37–38; Dexter Diary, September 14, 1726; Sibley, *Harvard Graduates*, vol. 4, 305. Dexter cited a number of other cases of clerical misbehavior in his diary, and further examples are common. In 1705, a clerical council voted to "withdraw the right hand of fellowship from Mr. Sherman," pastor at Sudbury, and "not to acknowledge Him any longer as a Minister of the Gospel." See Pope, *Dorchester First Church Records*, 126, and Pierce, *Salem First Church Records*, 271. In another highly publicized example of clerical misbehavior, Watertown's pastor Robert Sturgeon voluntarily left his church after publishing an apology for his misdemeanors. See Robert Sturgeon, *A Trespass-Offering, presented unto the Churches of New-England* (Boston, 1725), and Pierce, ed., *Boston First Church Records*, 236. Concord's pastor John Whiting was dismissed in 1737 for "Intemperance." See Hill, *Old South Church*, vol. 1, 482ff.

21. Three such cases are described in "Autobiography of the Rev. John Barnard," Massachusetts Historical Society, *Collections*, 3rd ser., 5 (1836), 223–225, 226, 228.

22. *Ibid.*, 223ff. For other examples, see Pierce, *Salem First Church Records*, 281; Pope, *Dorchester First Church Records*, 143; and the dispute between John Wise and Joseph Gerrish, described later in this chapter.

23. For discussions of Stoddard's career see Sibley, *Harvard Graduates*, vol. 2, 111–122; Walker, *Creeds and Platforms*, 280–282; Stout, *New England Soul*, 99–102; and Perry Miller, "Solomon Stoddard, 1643–1729," *Harvard Theological Review*, 34 (1941), 227–320.

24. The most important works in the exchange include Increase Mather, *The Order of the Gospel* (Boston, 1700); [Cotton and Increase Mather], *The Young Man's Claim Unto the Sacrament of the Lord's Supper* . . . . (Boston, 1700); Solomon Stoddard, *An Appeal to the Learned Being a Vindication of the Right of Visible Saints to the Lord's Supper, though they be Destitute of a Saving Work of God's Spirit on their Hearts: Against the Exceptions of Mr. Increase Mather* (Boston, 1709); and Solomon Stoddard, *The Doctrine of the Instituted Churches Explained and Proven from the Word of God* (London, 1700).

25. Colman Papers, Massachusetts Historical Society, vol. 1, 6. A copy of the *Manifesto* appears in *The Manifesto Church: Records of the Church in Brattle Square, Boston, with Lists of Communicants, Marriages, and Funerals, 1699–1872* (Boston, 1902), 1–2; hereafter cited as *Boston Fourth Church Records.*

26. *Ibid.* In *Creeds and Platforms*, 473, Williston Walker observed that the *Manifesto* represented "a step away . . . from the restraining hand of stronger ecclesiastical government," but in the local decision-making process, the document called for greater church authority for ministers.

27. Increase Mather, *The Order of the Gospel Professed and Practiced by the Churches of Christ in New England* . . . (Boston, 1700), 8; Cotton Mather quoted in Walker, *Creeds and Platforms*, 477, 480. The other important pamphlets concerning the *Manifesto* include Benjamin Colman, et al., *The Gospel Order Revived* (Boston, 1701); Cotton Mather, *A Collection of Some of the Many Offensive Matters* . . . (Boston, 1701); and Increase Mather, *A Disquisition Concerning Ecclesiastical Councils* (Boston, 1716).

28. Miller, *From Colony to Province*, chapter 16; George Allan Cook, *John Wise, Early American Democrat* (New York, 1952), 86–87; Increase Mather, *Order of the Gospel Professed and Practiced*, 8.

29. See David D. Hall, *The Faithful Shepherd: A History of the New England Ministry in the Seventeenth Century* (Chapel Hill, 1972), chapter 12; Youngs, *God's Messengers*, chapter 4, and Schmotter, "The Irony of Clerical Professionalism."

30. Samuel Willard, *The Character of the Good Ruler* (Boston, 1694), reprinted in Perry Miller and Thomas H. Johnson, eds., *The Puritans: A Sourcebook of Their Writings*, 2 vols. (New York, 1938), vol. 1, 251; Samuel Wigglesworth, *The Excellency of the Gospel-Message* (Boston, 1727), 23; Thomas Paine, *The Pastoral Charge* . . . *A Sermon Preached at Weymouth August 19, 1719 by Thomas Paine, at his Ordination* (Boston, 1719), 19. See also Solomon Stoddard, *The Duty of Gospel-Ministers to Preserve a People from Corruption* (Boston, 1718), 12; Cotton Mather, *Manuductio Ad Ministerium: Directions for a Candidate of the Ministry* (Boston, 1726), 78. The ministers' emphasis on order and their own superiority mirrored increasingly authoritarian sentiments toward civil government that emerged in some quarters in the aftermath of the Glorious Revolution in Massachusetts. See Stout, *New England Soul*, 118–122, and Timothy H. Breen, *The Character of the Good Ruler: A Study of Puritan Political Ideas in New England, 1630–1730* (New York, 1970), chapters 4 and 5.

31. "Records of the Cambridge Association," Massachusetts Historical Society, *Publications*, 17 (1879–1880), 263.

32. *Ibid.*, 267, 272–279.

33. The origins of the *Proposals* are discussed in Walker, *Creeds and Platforms*, 483–486; Cook, *John Wise*, chapter 8; and Walker, "Why Did Not Massachusetts Have a Saybrook Platform?" *Yale Review*, 1 (May 1892), 68–86.

34. The text of the *Proposals* appears in Walker, *Creeds and Platforms*, 486–490.

35. Note, for example, the majority percentage of lay delegates at the Halfway Synod, discussed in chapter 5.

36. Walker, *Creeds and Platforms*, 486–490.

37. See Salem's Samuel Fiske controversy, discussed in chapter 9. This is not to suggest that henceforth councils always consisted of equal numbers of lay and clerical delegates or that the elders systematically altered voting methods. But the very fact that these subjects were sometimes debated testifies to the growing rift between the clergy and laity.

38. Walker, *Creeds and Platforms*, 489.

39. Miller asserted that the *Proposals* were "undoubtedly" sent "to all established churches," while Walker reported that the *Proposals* were "actually laid before the churches." But little evidence exists to support these conclusions. In Wenham, for example, pastor Joseph Gerrish entered the results of ministerial debates over the *Proposals* in his notebook, but nothing remains in the Wenham church records to suggest that the church debated these matters. Similarly, the *Proposals* are located at the end of the Beverly First Church Records, but there is no indication that they were brought up for discussion before the church. Finally, and perhaps most tellingly, John Wise openly taunted the clergy because the *Proposals* were only "Commended to the several Associated Ministers in the several parts of the Country," demanding "why [were not the *Proposals*] Commended nextly to the several Churches?" Miller, *Colony to Province*, 288; Walker, *Creeds and Platforms*, 486n.; Wenham First Church Records, Gerrish Notebook; William A. Upham, ed., "Beverly First Church Records," Essex Institute, *Historical Collections*, 41 (1905), 223–226; John Wise, *The Churches Quarrel Espoused or a Reply In Satyre to certain Proposals made, in Answer to this question: What further Steps are to be taken, that the Councils may have due Constitution and Efficacy in Supporting, Preserving, and Well-Ordering the Interest of the Churches in the Country?* (Boston, 1715), 112.

40. Cotton Mather, *Ratio Disciplinae a Faithful Account of the Discipline Professed and Practiced in the Churches of New England* (Boston, 1726), 184–185.

41. Increase Mather quoted in Youngs, *God's Messengers*, 72.

42. The best discussions of Wise's career and the significance of his writings for New England church government appear in Cook, *John Wise*, and Miller, *Colony to Province*, 288–302.

43. Wise, *The Churches Quarrel Espoused*; Wise, *A Vindication of the Government of New-England Churches Drawn from Antiquity; the Light of Nature; Holy Scripture; its Noble Nature; and from the Dignity Divine Province had put upon it* (Boston, 1717). An earlier edition of *The Churches Quarrel* was published in New York in 1713, but apparently did not circulate in New England.

44. Wise, *The Churches Quarrel*, 33.

45. *Ibid.*, 30.

46. Miller, *Colony to Province*, 295. Miller also attributed to Wise the belief that "conceptions of social compact, natural rights, and right of revolution . . . rather than Scripture gave the raison d'etre to Congregational societies." *Ibid.*, 296. Hall, *Faithful Shepherd*, 272.

47. Wise, *The Churches Quarrel*, 31, 86, 87, 94. Wise similarly attacked Mather's *Proposals* because they lacked "the least tincture of Scripture to gaurd [sic] them from contempt," *Ibid.*, 49, 52–53.

48. Wise, *The Churches Quarterly*, 92, 88, 29, 31, 113, 88.

49. *Ibid.*, 91, 71.

50. Wise, *Vindication*, 3–29, 76, 85.

51. *Ibid.*, 31–32.

52. See Miller, *Colony to Province*, 294–299.

53. The Salem dispute is fully discussed in chapter 9.

54. New England ministers did write extensively on the subject of government during the Glorious Revolution. But as Harry S. Stout observes, they directed their writings primarily at English audiences rather than their own congregations. Stout, *New England Soul*, chapter 5.

55. Wise, *Vindication*, 43.

56. *Ibid.*, 11.

57. *Ibid.*, 6, 82.

58. Stoneham First Church Records, ms, Stoneham First Congregational Church, entry dated February 1729; Sibley, *Harvard Graduates*, vol. 4, 421; "Diary of Samuel Sewell," Massachusetts Historical Society, *Collections*, 5th ser., 7 (1882), 23. See also John White's funeral sermon for Wise, *The Gospel Treasure* (Boston, 1725).

59. Pierce, *Salem First Church Records*, 268–269 and n.

60. See "Diary of Cotton Mather," Massachusetts Historical Society, *Collections*, 1911, 54, and Bumsted, "Ecclesiastical Disorder on the Cape." Wise's treatises motivated Brewster pastor Nathaniel Stone to contact Benjamin Coleman, urging the latter to compose a written refutation.

61. See, for example, Stout, *New England Soul*, 158–160. J. W. T. Youngs correctly notes that ministers were divided into camps of "liberals" (who, in matters of church government, were more prone to supporting "innovations") and "conservatives" (who refused to support changes in traditional practices). However, Youngs offers little analysis of the many "conservatives" who adhered to standard Congregational principles. Also, as Youngs notes, a measure of caution is necessary in categorizing ministers along these lines. Ministers often held liberal stances on some issues of church government, but conservative stances on others. William Williams is often described as an autocratic liberal, but he strongly defended traditional lay rights and responsibilities. The most valid method of determining a minister's stance toward lay rights is through an examination of the local church records—i.e., the specific methods the minister in question employed in governing his church. See *God's Messengers*, chapters 4 and 5.

62. Increase Mather, *A Sermon wherein it is Shewed That the Ministers of the Gospel need . . . the Prayers of the Lord's People for them* (Boston, 1718), 15, 23.

63. John Tufts, *A humble call to Archippus* (Boston, 1729), 16; Paine, *The Pastoral Charge*, 19, 38.

64. Miller, *From Colony to Province*, 242.

65. William Brattle, "Sermon on Matthew 22: 44–45," February 28, 1697, in John Leverett, "Sermon Notes, 1696–1710," vol. 1, American Antiquarian Society.

66. William Williams, *The great Concern of Christians and especially of Ministers to Preserve the Doctrine of Christ in its Purity* (Boston, 1723), 5, 25, 8–9; Ebenezer Thayer, *Ministers of the Gospel are Christ's Ambassadours* (Boston, 1727), 26, 17; Miller, *From Colony to Province*, 299.

67. Williams, *The great Concern of Christians*, 21–22; Stoddard, *The Duty of Gospel-Ministers*, 5, 9.

9. Perpetuation and Disintegration

1. Stephen Williams Diary, March 9, 1732, March 15, 1736, Storrs Library, Longmeadow, Massachusetts; "Chelsea, Mass., First Church Records," msc, New England Historical and Genealogical Society, Boston, 29. Hereafter cited as Revere First Church Records. "Deacan E. and T. N." are unidentified; there are no Longmeadow church records antedating 1741.

2. The *Proposals* did become the basis of the *Saybrook Platform* of church government in Connecticut, though many local churches resisted this "innovation." See Williston Walker, "Why Did Not Massachusetts Have a Saybrook Platform?" *Yale Review*, 1 (May 1892), 68–86.

3. Though his focus did not rest primarily with the lay role in church government, David Harlan observed that clerical associations never governed or even attempted to govern local churches in Massachusetts. See "The Clergy and the Great Awakening in New England," (Ph.D. diss., University of California, Irvine, 1979), chapter 1.

4. Grafton First Church Records, 6, ms, Grafton First Congregational Church; Harvard First Church Records, 1, ms, Harvard Town Hall; Abington First Church Records, 1. See also L. Vernon Briggs, ed., *History and Records of the First Congregational Church, Hanover, Mass., 1727–1865.* . . . (Boston, 1895), 55, hereafter cited as Briggs, *Hanover First Church Records*.

5. Wenham First Church Records, msc, Town Hall, Wenham, 10.

6. Boston Ninth Church Records, ms, Boston Public Library, January 3, 1736; Salem First Church Records, 1736–1835, ts, Essex Institute, 4. For similar examples see William Upham, ed., "Beverly First Church Records," Essex Institute, *Historical Collections* 41 (1905), 210; Boston Fifth Church Records, ms, Boston Public Library, August 18, 1714; Bradford First Church Records, in *Articles of Faith and Covenant Adopted by the First Church of Christ in Bradford, Mass.* (Haverhill, Mass., 1886), 46; Gloucester First Church Records, msc, Cape Ann Scientific, Literary and Historical Association, Gloucester, Massachusetts, 2; Hopkinton First Church Records, msc, First Congregational Church, Hopkinton, Mass., April 9, 1731, see also references to the First Church of Upton's endorsement of the *Platform* in the Hopkinton First Church Records, January 22, 1737; Revere First Church Records, msc, 2, 22.

7. Danvers First Church Records, ms, June 7, 1698; June 4, 1699.

8. The First Church of Halifax, for example, voted in 1735 "that those who offer themselves to Communion shall make a Relation . . . as is usually practised in most of the Churches in New-England." "Halifax First Church Records," *Mayflower Descendent*, 26 (1924), 181. A nearly identical vote appears in the Boston Sixth Church Records, ms, Boston Public Library, 1.

9. See Harvard First Church Records, ms, 101; Danvers First Church Records, ms, June 4, 1699, October 16, 1702; Stephen P. Sharples, ed., *Records of the Church of Christ at Cambridge in New England, 1632–1830* . . . . (Boston, 1906), 122–123. Hereafter cited as Sharples, *Cambridge First Church Records*.

10. As David D. Hall and Robert Pope have noted, churchgoers did not necessarily flock in to full church membership once admissions requirements were altered or eased. Lay scrupulosity continued to serve as a brake upon membership in the eighteenth century, and the absence of a relations requirement in churches like Harvard should not be taken to suggest that all churchgoers quickly became full members. Even after dropping relations, the Harvard church admitted no full members in 1737, for example, and it was not until five years after the change that seventy-six-year-old Mary Atherton joined the church in full communion. The Harvard church also continued to draw careful distinctions between the "church" (that is, full members) and the congregation of members and nonmembers. See Harvard First Church Records, 4, 102; Robert Pope, *The Half-Way Covenant: Church Membership in Puritan New England* (Princeton, 1969) chapters 8 and 9; David D. Hall, *Worlds of Wonder, Days of Judgement: Popular Religious Belief in Early New England* (New York, 1989), chapter 3; and Hall's introduction to *The Works of Jonathan Edwards*, vol. 12, *Ecclesiastical Writings* (New Haven, 1994), 35–43.

11. Willaim Upham, ed., "Beverly First Church Records," Essex Institute, *Historical Collections*, 36 (1900), 142, see also 301; Danvers First Church Records, ms, 30; Boston Ninth

Church Records, ms, February 23, 1736; Gloucester First Church Records, msc, January 6, 1703, 6; Hopkinton First Church Records, msc, January 1, 1738. For similar examples, see the Beverly Second Church Records, ms, Beverly Historical Society, 1, in which the church voted at its founding that relations would be public and votes would be taken by the lifting of hands; Boston Sixth Church Records, ms, 1, in which the church decided on admissions procedures and elected a deacon prior to the ordination of its pastor; Framingham First Church Records, ts, Framingham Public Library, 120; "Halifax First Church Records," *Mayflower Descendent*, 26 (1924), 180–181; Springfield First Church Records, ms, Springfield First Congregational Church, unpaginated but entry dated 1736. See also Henry Morris, *History of the First Church in Springfield* (Springfield, 1875), 35.

12. Sturbridge First Church Records, msc, Sturbridge First Congregational Church, 2. Virtually all extant eighteenth-century church records affirm continuities in voting procedures and in the general level of lay participation in church affairs. Some particularly good examples are located in David W. Hoyt, *The Old Families of Salisbury and Amesbury, Massachusetts*, vol. 2 (Providence, 1902), 476–498, hereafter cited as Hoyt, *Amesbury First Church Records*; Boston Ninth Church Records; Georgetown First Church Records, ms, Georgetown First Congregational Church; Grafton First Church Records; "Pain Wingate his Book. Records of the Second Church of Christ in Amesbury," ms, Haverhill Public Library, hereafter cited as Merrimac First Church Records; Pierce, *Boston First Church Records*; Halifax First Church Records, ts, Town Hall, Halifax; Haverhill First Church Records, ms, Haverhill Public Library; Marblehead First Church Records, ms, Marblehead First Congregational Church; Stoneham First Church Records. Voting practices in western Massachusetts are discussed later in this chapter, 181–182.

13. The following is drawn from South Andover First Church Records, ms, Andover Historical Society, 13–14.

14. Reading First Church Records, 51–52. For a similar example, see South Andover First Church Records, 29.

15. Davis and Davis, *Westfield First Church Records*, 375–445; see also *ibid.*, 118–157; Haverhill First Church Records, ms, November 28, 1731; South Andover First Church Records, ms, 29.

16. Georgetown First Church Records, 25; John White, Preface, to John Tufts, *A humble call to Archippus* (Boston, 1729). This volume of ordination sermons contains numerous examples in which ministers offer instruction on church order and clerical responsibilities in government.

17. For examples in which the covenant "was publickly read and consented to," see Beverly Second Church Records, December 28, 1715; and South Andover Church Records, 2. Covenant renewal is discussed in Charles Hambricke-Stowe, *The Practice of Piety: Puritan Devotional Disciplines in Seventeenth-Century New England* (Chapel Hill, 1982), 127–134, 248–255.

18. The Norton dispute is discussed in Pope, *Dorchester First Church Records*, 136. Many examples of ministerial instruction through the communication of council results appear in *ibid.*, 126–138. Other excellent examples appear in the Beverly Second Church Records, 300–301; Revere First Church Records, 20–50; and Pierce, *Boston First Church Records*, 234–247.

19. Bradford First Church Records, ms, Haverhill Public Library, 18. A layman presumably kept the records at this point in time. A similar case appears in the Bradford records, 22. Lay familiarity with church procedures and issues of church order is evident in the records of many churches. Particularly good examples appear in Pierce, *Boston First Church Records*, 158–169.

20. Abington First Church Records, ms, January 3, 1723. Samuel A. Green, ed., "The Earliest Church Records in Groton," *Groton Historical Series*, vol. 1, x, (1886, published 1887), 39. Hereafter cited as Green, "Groton First Church Records." North Andover First Church Records, ms, North Andover Historical Society, August 12, 1728. Hopkinton First Church Records, msc, June 26, 1733.

21. Bradford Church Records, ms, 23, 26; *Brewster First Church Records*, 35; "Topsfield First Church Records," 19.

22. Increase Mather, Preface, to Cotton Mather, *A Collection of some of the many Offensive Matters Contained in a Pamphlet Entitled The Order of the Gospel Revived* (Boston, 1701), 2; Pierce, *Boston First Church Records*, 41.

23. Robert Middlekauf, *The Mathers: Three Generations of Puritan Intellectuals, 1596–1728* (New York, 1971), 219; Perry Miller, *The New England Mind: From Colony to Province* (Cambridge, Mass., 1953), 255. See *Boston Fourth Church Records*, 3, 11.

24. Miller, *From Colony to Province*, 232.

25. See Paul Lucas, *Valley of Discord: Church and State Along the Connecticut River, 1636–1725* (Hanover, N.H., 1976), 169–188; Harry S. Stout, *The New England Soul: Preaching and Religious Culture in Colonial New England* (New York, 1986), 99n. See also Hall, introduction to *Edwards' Ecclesiastical Writings*, 42 and n.

26. Miller, *Colony to Province*, 232, suggests that the First Church of Hadley rejected Stoddard's teachings on church government; similar opposition to Stoddard's sentiments and affirmations of standard Congregational voting procedures are evident in practices detailed in the Enfield First Church Records, microfilm copy, Connecticut State Library; Somers First Church Records, microfilm copy, Connecticut State Library (see, for example, August 20, 1727, November 2, 1739); Springfield First Church Records, ms (see especially the lone entry dated 1736); Suffield Church Records, microfilm copy, Connecticut State Library, 1; and in Longmeadow church affairs described in the Stephen Williams Diary (see, for example, November 3, 1720, June 22, 1730).

27. At least three different men served in the office of ruling elder under Stoddard's pastorate: John Strong, Preserved Clap, and Ebenezer Strong. Harold F. Worthley, "An Inventory of the Records of the Particular (Congregational) Churches of Massachusetts Gathered 1620–1805," *Proceedings of the Unitarian Historical Society*, 16 (1966–1969), 433; "1st Church Records—1661 to 1846—Old First Book," microfilm copy, Forbes Library, Northampton, September 11, 1672. Hereafter cited as Northampton First Church Records.

28. Stoddard, *The Doctrine of the Instituted Churches*, 12.

29. Northampton First Church Records, November 5, 1672; January 11, 1715; see also October 29, 1668, February 16, 1669, October 18, 1737. Stoddard acknowledged "heats of contention" in his congregation over issues of church order. But it is worth pondering that his management of internal church affairs never engendered the kinds of bitter divisions fostered by the Presbyterian elders in Newbury, who clearly attempted to restrict lay voting privileges at the local level during the seventeenth century.

30. David D. Hall, *The Faithful Shepherd: A History of the New England Ministry in the Seventeenth Century* (Chapel Hill, 1972), 274. Hall asserted that while "effective power" often resided with the laity, "many of the third generation" clergy followed Stoddard in maintaining that "the minister alone [should] direct the actions of the church in admissions and church discipline." A "great struggle," he believed, emerged over these issues. Little evidence remains in the church records to suggest that many ministers followed Stoddard and, as we shall see, most conflict in early eighteenth-century Massachusetts did not pit autocratic ministers against their congregations. *Ibid.*, 273–274.

31. *Ibid.*; Northampton First Church Records, Jan. 11, 1715, December 9, 1714.

32. Stoddard, of course, was not alone in urging ministers to strengthen clerical oversight. The *Proposals* contained provisions for ministers to "carefully and Loveingly treat each other with that watchfulness which may be of Universal Advantage" in dealing with offending clergymen. They also included provisions for supervision of ministerial candidates, who were to "undergo a due Tryal by some one or other of the Associations, concerning their qualifications for the Evangelical Ministry." Walker, *Creeds and Platforms*, 487.

33. Sharples, *Cambridge First Church Records*, 122–123.

34. See Clifford K. Shipton's continuation of John L. Sibley's multivolume biographical series entitled *Sibleys Harvard Graduates* (Boston, 1873–1975 [vols. 1–3 by Sibley; vols. 4–17 by Shipton]), vol. 4, 109–110.

35. Boston Third Church Records, in Hill, *Old South Church*, vol. 1, 377, 385, 342, 345.

36. *Ibid.*, 346, 345; "Diary of Samuel Sewell," Massachusetts Historical Society, *Collections*, 5th ser., vol. 2, 201.

37. Sibley, *Harvard Graduates*, vol. 5, 381, 384–385; Boston Third Church Records, in Hill, *Old South Church*, vol. 1, 381, 384.

38. Stephen Williams Diary, February 9, 1739, December 1, 1738; *Records of the General Association*, 8; Essex First Church Records, msc, July 12, 1725.

39. Disputes are often described in the records of neighboring churches that sent delegates to councils convened to address the issues. The controversies above are discussed in Pope, *Dorchester First Church Records*, 135–138; Revere First Church Records, 36, 47–48, 70; Marblehead Second Church Records, ms, Marblehead Historical Society, 1–6; Beverly Second Church Records, ms, October 31, 1725; December 6, 1736; Hopkinton First Church records, June 25, 1735–Sept. 16, 1736.

40. Samuel Dexter Diary, 275; see also Marblehead Second Church Records, 1–6.

41. Samuel Dexter Diary, 281; "Dedham First Church Records. Vol.II," manuscript located at the Dedham Historical Society, 4. The council decision and the dissenters' confession are recorded at the back of this volume.

42. *An Account of the Reasons Why a Considerable Number, . . . , Belonging to the New-North . . . , Could Not Consent to Mr. Peter Thacher's Ordination* (Boston, 1720), preface.

43. These developments are detailed more fully later in this chapter, and in chapter 10.

44. Abington First Church Records, ms, November 9, 1722, December 11, 1722, August 25, 1723. The Norton dispute is discussed in Pope, *Dorchester First Church Records*, 135, 137; the North Reading council is detailed in Pierce, *Boston First Church Records*, 239; North Andover First Church Records, ms, April 9, 1728; a report of the Reading division appears in the Revere First Church Records, 34; Kingston First Church Records, msc, Kingston Town Hall, 12. A later example dating from 1741 appears in "Halifax Church Records," *Mayflower Descendent*, 27 (1925), 31.

45. The Wenham councils are discussed in Pierce, *Salem First Church Records*, 268–269 and n. See also Revere First Church Records, 11–19, and Wenham First Church Records, Gerrish Notebook, which contains an account of the case toward the back of the volume. The Dorchester Village dispute is detailed in the Samuel Dexter Diary, 287–289; the Thatcher controversy is discussed in chapter 8; the Reading division is discussed in Pierce, *Salem First Church Records*, 281. See also *Diary of Cotton Mather*, Massachusetts Historical Society, *Collections*, 1911, vol. 2, 528; "Autobiography of John Barnard," 223–225; and Sibley, *Harvard Graduates*, vol. 4, 255. The Robert Breck affair is expertly analyzed in Hall, introduction to *Edwards' Ecclesiastical Writings*, 4–17. Hall notes that the Breck affair not only divided minis-

ters from eastern and western Massachusetts but created division among ministers of the local Hampshire Association as well. The Salem controversy is discussed later in this chapter.

46. Pope, *Dorchester First Church Records*, 143; Revere First Church Records, 11–19; Solomon Stoddard, Letter of the Hampshire Association to Nathaniel Collins of Enfield, July, 1715, Forbes Library, Northampton.

47. Pope, *Dorchester First Church Records*, 143. See also T. V. Huntoon, *History of the Town of Canton* (Cambridge, 1899), 93, and an account of a similar division in Newport in Pierce, *Boston First Church Records*, 240. The Leicester council is reported in the *Boston First Church Records*, 243 and n.; the Sandwich councils in the *Boston First Church Records*, 242–243 and n.; the Beverly council in Beverly Second Church Records, ms, November 3, 1735. On the Reading dispute, see Pierce, *Salem First Church Records*, 278–279 and n. See also the South Braintree dispute of 1723, discussed in Hill, *Old South Church*, vol. 1, 411.

48. A biographical sketch of Fiske and a discussion of the immediate events surrounding the Salem controversy appear in Sibley, *Harvard Graduates*, vol. 5, 413ff. See also Robert E. Moody's introduction to Pierce, *Salem First Church Records*, xxi–xxiii.

49. [Benjamin Lynde], *A Just and impartial narrative of the controversy between the Rev. Mr. Samuel Fisk, the pastor, and a number of brethren of the First Church in Salem* (Boston, 1735), 72, 84, 93, 92, 3. On page 5 Judge Benjamin Lynde is identified as the principal author of the pamphlet. It should be noted that the Fiske case thus stands among the very few in the colonial era in which lay people accused a minister of falsifying church records.

50. *Ibid.*, 3, 13.

51. Letter from the Aggrieved to the Second Church in Boston, December 26, 1733, Joseph Bowditch Papers, box 4, folder 5, miscellaneous papers, Essex Institute.

52. [Lynde], *A Just and impartial Narrative*, 18, 57–58.

53. *Ibid.*, 80–81, 104.

54. Sharples, *Cambridge First Church Records*, 197–198. David Harlan argued that since ministers rarely intervened in local disputes, lay people in fact ran the churches. The Salem case demonstrates, once again, the limitations of this sort of lay-clerical dichotomization. Harlan, "The Clergy and the Great Awakening."

55. Sharples, *Cambridge First Church Records*, 198–199.

56. *Ibid.*, 200.

57. *Ibid.*, 201; Sibley, *Harvard Graduates*, vol. 5, 416. Appleton also noted with displeasure another trend that increasingly plagued the churches in the eighteenth century: the aggrieved brethren in Salem had appealed to the Boston elders before contacting neighboring churches (as was customary) because the former were more likely to rule in their favor against Fiske. This practice stood at the center of the Robert Breck controversy that raged in western Massachusetts also in the early 1730s.

58. Sharples, *Cambridge First Church Records*, 201.

59. *Ibid.*; [Benjamin Prescott], *A Letter to a friend relating to the differences in the First Church in Salem, wherein the proceedings of the Ecclesiastical Councils concerned in that affair are vindicated, and the objections raised against them answered* (Boston, 1735), 24; John Brown, *Remarks on some contents of a Letter relating to the divisions of the First Church in Salem* (Boston, 1735), 1–3.

60. The pamphlets included [Lynde], *A Just and impartial narrative*; [Joseph Sewall, Thomas Prince, et al.], *A faithful narrative of the proceedings of the Ecclesiastical Council, convened at Salem in 1734. Occasioned by the scandalous divisions in the First Church in that town*

(Boston, 1735); [Prescott], *A Letter to a friend* ; [Benjamin Prescott], *A Letter relating to the divisions in the First Church in Salem* (Boston, 1734); John White, *New-Englands Lamentations under three heads, The decay of the power of godliness; the danger of Arminian principles; The declining state of our Church-Order, government and discipline* (Boston, 1734); John Brown, *Remarks on some contents of a Letter.*

61. Pierce, *Boston First Church Records*, 168–169.

62. William P. Upham, ed., "Beverly First Church Records," Essex Institute, *Historical Collections*, 41 (1905), 209–210.

63. White, *New-Englands Lamentations*, 30–31.

64. *Ibid.*, 42, 32–36.

65. Harold F. Worthley, "The Lay Officers of the Particular (Congregational) Churches of Massachusetts, 1620–1755): An Investigation of Practice and Theory" (Ph.D. diss., Harvard University, 1970), 411.

66. Worthley, "Inventory," 535; Revere First Church Records, msc, 69–70; Boston Fifth Church Records, ms, April 23, 1736; William P. Upham, ed., "Beverly First Church Records," Essex Institute, *Historical Collections*, 41 (1905), 213–214; Pierce, *Boston First Church Records*, 185; Hopkinton First Church Records, msc, 53–54; Worthley, "The Lay Officers," 411.

67. White, *New-Englands Lamentations*, 2.

68. Miller, *Colony to Province*, 290.

69. See n. 60.

70. For a biographical sketch of Prescott see Sibley, *Harvard Graduates*, vol. 7, 485–492. Judge Lynde, the principal spokesman for the Salem dissenters, joined Prescott's South Peabody church in the aftermath of the Fiske controversy.

71. Prescott, *Letter to a Friend*, 2.

72. *Ibid.*, 3–5.

73. Sharples, *Cambridge First Church Records*, 128–130.

74. This gradual development would culminate in the aftermath of the Great Awakening and is discussed more fully in chapter 10.

75. Sharples, *Cambridge First Church Records*, 130–131. See also Pierce, *Salem First Church Records*, 192.

76. William P. Upham, ed., "Beverly First Church Records," Essex Institute, *Historical Collections*, 41 (1905), 210–212. Six Beverly members dissented from the vote on the *Platform*. Their reasons for dissent are unknown.

77. *Ibid.*, 212; *Brewster First Church Records*, 35–37; Pierce, *Boston First Church Records*, 169–172; Boston Third Church Records, in Hill, *Old South Church*, vol. 1, 455; Framingham First Church Records, ts, 35; Haverhill First Church Records, ms, May 3, 1739; June 28, 1739; Boston Seventh Church Records, ms, New England Historical and Genealogical Society, 36; see also Boston Seventh Church Records, 24; Stephen Williams Diary, November 14, 1730; Reading First Church Records, ts, 59. See also Marblehead Second Church Records, ms, 23.

78. The Colman quote appears in Revere First Church Records, msc, 51; see also Framingham First Church Records, ts, 30.

10. The Great Awakening and the Privatization of Piety

1. Byfield First Church Records, ms, Essex Institute, March 28, 1745; April 22, 1745.

2. William G. McLoughlin, "'Enthusiasm for Liberty': The Great Awakening as the Key to the Revolution," in Jack P. Greene and William G. McLoughlin, *Preachers and Politicians:*

Two Essays on the Origins of the American Revolution (Worcester, Mass., 1977), 47–73; C. C. Goen, *Revivalism and Separatism in New England, 1740–1800: Strict Congregationalists and Separate Baptists in the Great Awakening* (New Haven, 1962); Harry S. Stout, *The New England Soul: Preaching and Religious Culture in Colonial New England* (New York, 1986), 210–211, 216–218; See also Alan Heimert, *Religion and the American Mind from the Great Awakening to the Revolution* (Cambridge, 1968), which describes the Great Awakening as a source of Calvinist political ideology that shaped Revolutionary sentiments, and Jon Butler, "Enthusiasm Described and Decried: The Great Awakening as Interpretative Fiction," *Journal of American History*, (September 1983), 305–306, which notes that similar claims for the significance of the Great Awakening have been extended from New England to the colonies in general.

3. Butler, "Enthusiasm Described," 62.

4. Thomas Prince, Jr., *The "Christian History"* (Boston, 1744–1745), 27. The best general accounts of the Great Awakening in New England include Joseph Tracy, *The Great Awakening: A History of the Revival of Religion in the Time of Edwards and Whitefield* (Boston, 1841); Edwin Scott Gaustad, *The Great Awakening in New England* (New York, 1957); and Stout, *New England Soul*, chapter 10. For useful background information, see Cedric B. Cowing, *The Great Awakening and the American Revolution: Colonial Thought in the 18th Century* (Chicago, 1971); Ola Winslow, *Meetinghouse Hill, 1630–1783* (New York, 1952); and H. B. Parkes, "New England in the Seventeen Thirties," *New England Quarterly*, 3 (1930), 397–419.

5. Sharples, *Cambridge First Church Records*, 129. See also William Shurtleff, *A Letter to those of His Brethren* (Boston, 1743), and David Harlan, "The Clergy and the Great Awakening in New England" (Ph.D. diss., University of California, Irvine, 1979), 112.

6. Prince, *Christian History*, 27; Pierce, *Boston First Church Records*, 169. See also Hill, *Old South Church*, vol. 1, 468.

7. See J. M. Bumsted and John E. Van de Wetering, *What Must I Do to Be Saved? The Great Awakening in Colonial America* (Hinsdale, Ill., 1976), 69–70, 72. The authors note that the clergy had been preparing for a spiritual "awakening" since Jonathan Edwards's revival in Northampton in 1734–35.

8. *Ibid.*, 86.

9. Patricia J. Tracy, *Jonathan Edwards, Pastor: Religion and Society in Eighteenth-Century Northampton* (New York, 1979), chapters 5 and 6.

10. *Plymouth Church Records*, 294–295.

11. Bumsted and Van de Wetering, *What Must I Do?* 128–134; Stout, *New England Soul*, 196–197.

12. See chapters 8 and 9.

13. Stout, *New England Soul*, 194–195; Gaustad, *The Great Awakening*; and Bumsted and Van de Wetering, *What Must I Do?* chapters 4 through 6.

14. See Stout, *New England Soul*, 197–202.

15. Harlan, "The Clergy and the Great Awakening," 2, 6.

16. See Goen, *Revivalism and Separatism*, 28–31, 148–149; Stout, *New England Soul*, 210–211, 216–218; Christopher Jedrey, *The World of John Cleaveland: Family and Community in Eighteenth-Century New England* (New York, 1979), 55–57.

17. See the bibliography in Richard Bushman, *From Puritan to Yankee: Character and the Social Order in Connecticut, 1690–1765* (Cambridge, Mass., 1967), for a listing of primary and secondary sources pertaining to Separatism in Connecticut.

18. According to Harold F. Worthley's inventory of Massachusetts church records, Separate organizations rarely left accounts of church meetings.

19. Considerably more local studies have been devoted to the Great Awakening and to Separatism in Connecticut than in Massachusetts. See Butler, "Enthusiasm Described," 306–307 and n.

20. Williston Walker, *The Creeds and Platforms of Congregationalism* (New York, 1893), 495–516.

21. See Goen, *Revivalism and Separatism*, 71, 77, 83, 87, 89–90.

22. *Ibid.*, 39; Solomon Paine, *A Short View of the Difference between the Church of Christ, and the Established Churches in the Colony of Connecticut* (Newport, 1752), 52–53; Albert C. Bates, ed., *Records of the Congregational Church in Canterbury, Connecticut, 1711–1884* (Hartford, 1932), 7; Eliphalet Wright, *The Difference Between Those Called Standing Churches and Those Called Strict Congregationalist Illustrated* (Norwich, 1775), 20.

23. Richard Bushman describes this widespread lay-clerical contention in Connecticut in *From Puritan to Yankee*, chapter 10.

24. See chapter 9.

25. Jedrey, *The World of John Cleaveland*, 46–55. Four pamphlets were written on the dispute: Theophilus Pickering, *A Bad Omen to the Churches of New-England* (Boston, 1747); John Cleaveland, *A Plain Narrative of the Proceedings which Caused the Separation of a Number of Brethren from the Second Church in Ipswich* (Boston, 1747); *The Pretended Plain Narrative Convicted of Fraud and Partiality; A Letter from the Second Church in Ipswich, to Their Separated Brethren* (Boston, 1748); and John Cleaveland, *The Chebacco Narrative Rescued from the Charge of Falsehood and Partiality* (Boston, 1748).

26. See Concord First Church Records, 41. Old Light Separates in Grafton similarly objected to the "arbitrary actings" of the New Lights in their church; see Grafton First Church Records, ms, 113.

27. The church records are full of examples that demonstrate that Old Lights were neither more nor less committed than New Lights to lay participation in or clerical control over the decision-making process. Considerable lay participation is evident in the records of the First Church of Bradford, the Ipswich South Church, and the First Church of Boston, all Old Light churches. Indeed, for all of the condemnation of disorder and affirmation of hierarchy offered by Old Light spokesman Charles Chauncy, decisions in the First Church of Boston continued to be reached by popular vote; there is nothing in the church records to support Harry S. Stout's contention that, in contrast to Edwards's advocacy of "lay participation," Chauncy sought to exercise "strict clerical control" over his congregation in matters of church government. Many New Lights, such as a number who withdrew from the First Church of Milford, separated from churches that maintained standard lay-clerical roles in government. Similarly, even though the First Church of Berkeley formally endorsed the *Cambridge Platform* in 1743 and elected ruling elders five years later, the church nevertheless suffered several New Light separations. Though Grafton's New Light pastor Solomon Prentice governed in standard Congregational fashion, a number of Old Lights separated from the church, charging Prentice with "preaching Damnable doctrine," among other offenses. By 1747, enough members agreed to fire Prentice, but governmental procedures changed little with the arrival of the less "enthusiastical" Aaron Hutchinson in 1750 and the return to the fold of the Old Lights who had separated. Indeed, one of the church's first acts was to vow allegiance to the *Cambridge Platform*. The Old Light First Church of Georgetown bickered angrily with the New Light First Church of Groveland over theology, but lay and clerical roles in church government differed little in the two churches. Bradford First Church Records, November 19, 1749; Ipswich South Church Records, ms, Ipswich Public Library; Framingham First Church Records; Pierce, *Boston First Church Records*; Stout, *New England*

Soul, 203; Aldin Ballou, *History of the Town of Milford, Massachusetts* (Boston, 1882), 62ff., 75ff.; Berkeley First Church Records, ms held at First Congregational Church of Taunton, December 7, 1743, June 20, 1748, December 4, 1748, January 11, 1749; Grafton First Church Records, 111, 89. Georgetown First Church Records; Groveland First Church Records, ms, Groveland First Congregational Church.

28. See Samuel Mather, *An Apology for the Liberties of the Churches in New England* (Boston, 1738).

29. See Clifford K. Shipton's continuation of John L. Sibley's multivolume biographical series entitled *Sibley's Harvard Graduates* (Boston, 1873–1975 [vols. 1–3 by Sibley; vols. 4–17 by Shipton]), vol. 7, 223–226. Mather was unfriendly to the revival and drew fire for insufficiently "pressing the necessity of regeneration by the Spirit of grace." See also Boston Second Church Records, July 23, 1741, ms, Massachusetts Historical Society.

30. Framingham First Church Records, 120–130; Harry S. Stout and James F. Cooper, Jr., "The Self-Examination of Edward Goddard," *Proceedings of the American Antiquarian Society*, 97 (1987), 90.

31. See chapter 9.

32. Harold F. Worthley, "An Inventory of the Records of the Particular (Congregational) Churches of Massachusetts Gathered 1620–1805," *Proceedings of the Unitarian Historical Society*, 16, 1966–1969, 542; Sibley, *Harvard Graduates*, V, 423.

33. Milford Separate petition in Ballou, *History of Milford*, 78–79. For similar examples see Winslow, *Meetinghouse Hill*, 232–233.

34. See Abington First Church Records, June 11, 1744; "Records of [the Church in] the West Parish of Barnstable, Massachusetts, 1668–1807," ms photocopy, Beinecke Rare Book Library, Yale University, New Haven, Conn., hereafter cited as Barnstable First Church Records; Sidney Perley, *The History of Boxford, Essex County, Massachusetts From the Earliest Settlement Known to the Present Time . . . .* (Boxford, Mass., 1880), 178–179; *Brewster First Church Records*, 98; Halifax First Church Records, 55 (which detail the Duxbury separation); Framingham First Church Records, ts, 123, Georgetown First Church Records, ms, 31, 37; Methuen First Church Records, ms, 19–20; Result of a Council . . . 31 August 1744, First Parish Newbury Papers, box 1, folder 1, vol. 1, Essex Institute; Grafton First Church Records, ms, 121 (which detail the Rehoboth separation); Reading First Church Records, ts, 92. As noted earlier in this chapter, New Lights forced an Old Light separation from the Second Church of Boston over doctrinal issues.

35. Ballou, *History of Milford*, 78–79. For further analysis of the Milford separation, see James F. Cooper, Jr., 'Enthusiasts or Democrats? Separatism, Church Government, and the Great Awakening in Massachusetts," *New England Quarterly*, 65 (June 1992), 272.

36. The excerpts from the Separate statements appear in Winslow, *Meetinghouse Hill*, 231–236. See also Cooper, "Enthusiasts or Democrats?" 272–273.

37. West Newbury First Church Records, ms, Essex Institute, February 20, 1746. The separation is further detailed in Rev. C. D. Herbert, "Historical Sketch of the First Church and Parish of West Newbury, Formerly the Second Church of Newbury," undated, unpaginated ms, Essex Institute, and Joshua Coffin, ed., *A Sketch of the History of Newbury, Newburyport, and West Newbury* (Boston, 1845), 216–217. The statements of the Essex Separates are located in the Cleaveland papers, box 2, folder 4a, Essex Institute, dated January 23, 1747. The Separates shortly ordained John Cleaveland as pastor and remained Congregational. See Worthley, "Inventory," 212–213; Georgetown First Church Records, 42. See also Leigh Eric Schmidt, "'A Second and Glorious Reformation,': The New Light Extremism of Andrew Croswell," *William and Mary Quarterly*, 3rd ser., 43 (April 1986), 226. Schmidt de-

scribes Andrew Croswell's Boston Separate church as a "bastion of ardent evangelicalism" that was "distinguished more for its religious fervor and desire to hear itinerant ministers than by its polity."

38. See "Answer to the Reasons" of the Separate withdrawal in Barnstable First Church Records, August 2, 1754. See also Cooper, "Enghusiasts or Democrats?" 274–277.

39. See Goen, *Revivalism and Separatism*, 166.

40. William G. McLoughlin, ed., *The Diary of Isaac Backus*, 3 vols. (Providence, 1979), vol. 1, 65, 65n., 137, 156. See also Cooper, "Enthusiasts or Democrats?" 277–280.

41. Edward Goddard, *A Brief Account of the Foundation of the Second Church of Framingham* (Boston, 1750), 4.

42. Quoted in Winslow, *Meetinghouse Hill*, 236. See also Cooper, "Enthusiasts or Democrats?" 271–273, 275.

43. For a discussion of enduring communitarianism in eighteenth-century New England (and in America generally), see Barry Alan Shain, *The Myth of American Individualism: The Protestant Origins of American Political Thought* (Princeton, 1994).

44. See Bruce C. Daniels, *The Fragmentation of New England: Comparative Perspectives on Economic, Political, and Social Divisions in the Eighteenth Century* (Westport, Conn., 1988), and Bushman, *From Puritan to Yankee*.

45. Daniels, *The Fragmentation of New England*, 24; Stout, *New England Soul*, 203.

46. The institutional ramifications of these developments upon church practices are further traced later in this chapter.

47. Changes in admissions procedures are discussed and documented later in this chapter. As was the case in most procedural changes, different churches altered repentance procedures at different times. For examples of churches that either dropped public confessions in favor of private statements or considered the change, see Hoyt, *Amesbury First Church Records*, May 29, 1735; Berkeley First Church Records, ms, May 2, 1750; Boston Sixth Church Records, ms, August 31, 1731; Gloucester First Church Records, msc, 45; Grafton First Church Records, ms, January 9, 1743; Haverhill First Church Records, ms, June 5, 1730, January 17, 1732; Merrimac First Church Records, ms, June 2, 1728, Methuen First Church Records, msc, date illegible but c. September 1734; Middleboro First Church Records, ms, Middleboro First Congregational Church, August 20, 1760; Newburyport First Church Records, ms, Newburyport First Congregational Church, April 12, 1761; Revere First Church Records, msc, May 20, 1759; Sandwich First Church Records, ms, August 10, 1749; Stoneham First Church Records, ms, July 27, 1739.

48. As Frank Lambert notes in *"Pedlar in Divinity": George Whitefield and the Transatlantic Revivals* (Princeton, 1994), 7, the evangelists "exploited demand for 'experimental religion,' the term that distinguished faith expressed in a conversion experience from that reflected in subscription to a particular creed" or, in this case, Congregational practices.

49. The thesis touched upon here is developed more fully in Harry S. Stout's *The Divine Dramatist: George Whitefield and the Rise of Modern Evangelicalism* (Grand Rapids, Mich., 1991).

50. Stout, *New England Soul*, 213–215.

51. Ibid., 222–232.

52. Harlan, "The Clergy and the Great Awakening," 154; Bumsted and Van de Wetering, *What Must I Do?* 117.

53. Cleaveland, *A Narrative of the Proceedings*, 4, 5, 13; Cleaveland, *Narrative Rescued*, 6.

54. Cleaveland, *A Narrative of the Proceedings*, 13, 13n., 14; Cleaveland, *Narrative Rescued*, 20.

55. The ministers' demands for order did not apply only to New Lights. A council of elders also condemned a group of Grafton Old Lights for disorderly separation. See Worthley, "Inventory," 243.

56. Grafton First Church Records, ms, 124; Jonathan Edwards, "Narrative of Communion Controversy," in David D. Hall, ed., *The Works of Jonathan Edwards*, vol. 12, *Ecclesiastical Writings* (New Haven, 1994), 518–558.

57. Merrimac First Church Records, ms. Some churches continued to emphasize mutual watch and practice a more traditional form of Congregationalism through the Revolutionary era, and the timing of decline varied from church to church. But an overview of the records suggests that by the 1760s a majority of the churches rarely discussed issues of government and had adopted a perfunctory stance toward many Congregational practices. For particularly good examples of declining concern for church government, see the records of the Second Church of Beverly and Marblehead, the Seventh Church of Boston, and those of the First Churches of Boxford, ms and msc, First Congregational Churches of Boxford, Cambridge, Methuen, South Andover, and Sturbridge; George E. Bowman, ed., "Truro, Mass., Church Records," *Mayflower Descendent*, 28 (1915), 71–79, 109–117, 155–168; Wenham; and many others. A group of laymen from Newbury agreed that "the difference between Presbyterians and Congregationalists is not essential to religion." See "Newbury, Mass. First Church Third Church papers relating to the separation of members from and organization of a new church 1743–46. mss.," Congregational Library, Boston, entry dated June 1747; hereafter cited as Newburyport Separate Church Records. The records of the First Church of Amesbury include an inventory of books held by the church in 1741; none of the publications pertain to church government. Hoyt, *Amesbury First Church Records*, 481. See also afterword, 216, and n.3, above.

58. Newburyport Separate Church Records, ms, entry dated June, 1746.

59. Halifax First Church Records, ts, 39, April 10, 1759; Grafton First Church Records, ms, 140, July 6, 1741; Hopkinton First Church Records, msc, 56, March 29, 1756.

60. Merrimac First Church Records, ms, November 12, 1746; see also August 10, 1743; Jonathan Edwards, Sermon on Deut. 1: 13–18, June 1748, L. 20r., Beinecke Rare Book Library, Yale University, New Haven, Conn.; Beverly Second Church Records, ms, November 12, 1746; West Boxford Church Records, ms, Boxford First Congregational Church, April 16, 1746; Grafton First Church Records, ms, March 28, 1746. Other examples of lax attendance are common. See Halifax First Church Records, ts, 39; Haverhill First Church Records, ms, May 3, 1739, June 28, 1739; Hopkinton Church Records, msc, November 2, 1755; Marblehead Second Church Records, ms, 21, 23, 24; West Newbury Church Records, ms, November 30, 1752.

61. See, for example, Pierce, *Boston First Church Records*, February 13, 1756, 213; Boston Sixth Church Records, ms, October 15, 1764; Oxford First Church Records, ms, Oxford First Congregational Church, June 1733; and the Cleaveland Papers, box 1, folder 3a, Essex Institute, which describes practices in the Second Church of Essex.

62. Most churches dropped public testimony between 1730 and 1765. For examples, see Pierce, *Boston First Church Records*, 213 (February 13, 1756); Bradford First Church Records, ms, July 18, 1749; *Brewster First Church Records*, April 23, 1738; Danvers First Church Records, 81 (1757); Dedham First Church Records, vol. 2, ms, March 7, 1742; Dudley First Church Records, ms, Dudley First Congregational Church, February 21, 1745; Harvard First Church Records, December 19, 1733; Haverhill North Church Records, ts, Haverhill Public Library, February 3, 1731; Hull First Church Records, msc, New England Historical and Genealogical Society, Boston, December 10, 1734; Methuen First Church Records, msc, January 2, 1730;

Oxford First Church Records, 31 (1750); Springfield First Church Records, November 14, 1736; Sturbridge First Church Records, March 17, 1737; Tewksbury First Church Records, ms, Tewksbury First Congregational Church, February 21, 1738; Town of Weston, *Births, Deaths, and Marriages, 1707–1850. 1703—Gravestones—1900. Church Records, 1709–1825* (Boston, 1901), 530. The First Church of Cambridge, which had dropped relations at the end of the seventeenth century, voted in 1757 that it would no longer even require candidates for admission to "Stand [before the church] in the front Alley or Isle." Sharples, *Cambridge First Church Records*, 215–216.

63. In 1727, the First Church of Haverhill chose a committee of eight members (none of whom were deacons) "to Assist the Pastor in order to Discipline Scandalous Persons." Haverhill First Church Records, June 4, 1727. The First Church of Taunton had established lay committees by 1729, the First Church of Groveland by 1730; the First Church of Merrimac by 1733. Taunton First Church Records, ms, Taunton First Church, October 29, 1729; Groveland First Church Records, ms, October 9, 1730; Merrimac First Church Records, ms, January 17, 1733. For other examples dating from the 1730s, see Boston Sixth Church Records, ms, November 3, 1735; Sharples, *Cambridge First Church Records*, 207; Georgetown First Church Records, ms, October 3, 1736; North Andover First Church Records, ms, North Andover Historical Society, August 30, 1732.

64. See, for example, Merrimac First Church Records, ms, March 10, 1742, November 10, 1743; Framingham First Church Records, ms, August 25, 1764, October 5, 1766; Grafton First Church Records, ms, November 25, 1742; Ipswich South Church Records, ms, January 21, 1764.

65. Reading First Church Records, ts, September 2, 1765. Other references to lay committees are common; see Berkeley First Church Records, ms, July 25, 1750; Boylston First Church Records, ms, New England Historical and Genealogical Society, Boston, November 21, 1763; *Brewster First Church Records*, 123; Middleboro First Church Records, ms, May 3, 1747; Natick First Church Records, msc, New England Historical and Genealogical Society, January 6, 1744; Salem Third Church Records, ms, October 2, 1754; Stoneham First Church Records, ms, August 25, 1752; Suffield First Church Records, undated but c. 1741; Wenham First Church Records, msc, June 21, 1751; "Weston First Church Records," 534–535.

66. Haverhill First Church Records, ms, November 28, 1731.

67. Halifax First Church Records, ts, October 27, 1763.

68. Edwards, Sermon on Deut. 1:13–18, June 1748, L. 21r.

69. Given that Edwards's church practiced open communion, the membership obviously would have been more "mixt" in Northampton than in other churches. But Edwards's sermon reflects a belief that regardless of admissions requirements, churches contained apathetic and unqualified voters; the Northampton minister clearly favored the adoption of lay committees in churches throughout the colony.

70. North Andover First Church Records, ms; "Topsfield First Church Records"; and Halifax First Church Records, ts. Patterns were similar in many other churches whose records seem to be detailed and complete. The First Church of Boston exercised virtually no discipline during the 1750s, while the First Church of Hanover disciplined only one member during that decade. The First Church of Revere heard only two cases from 1751 to 1759. It censured eight members from 1762 to 1767, but seven of those cases involved fornication. The Wenham First Church Records contain only one disciplinary case from 1751 to 1765. For other examples see the records dating from 1750 to 1770 of the Boston Seventh Church; Byfield First Church; Bradford First Church; Cambridge First Church; Marblehead Second Church; Methuen First Church; Truro First Church; and Salem Third Church.

71. Methuen First Church Records, April 27, 1763; Scituate First Church Records, ms, Sturgis Library, Barnstable, Mass., May 24, 1764, March 6, 1759; Newburyport First Church Records, ms, entry dated June 1746.

72. Wenham First Church Records, msc, February 7, 1751, through January 15, 1753.

73. As is the case with rates of church discipline, the fragmentary nature of church records renders impossible precise calculations concerning the frequency of church councils. Some indication of frequency can be gleaned through an examination of the records of individual churches that appear to be regular and complete. Several churches that were often called upon by neighboring churches prior to the 1750s received far fewer requests in later decades. The Reading First Church, which was invited to 21 councils from 1743 to 1755, received no invitations from 1756 to 1770. The Wenham First Church attended no councils from 1756 to 1770. The First Church of Revere attended no councils from 1751 to 1769. The Boston First Church attended only one council from 1754 to 1762.

74. The case of Josiah Fairfield described earlier, for example, embroiled the First Church of Wenham for three years, though neither lay liberties nor clerical authority were central to the affair. The controversy surrounding the firing of Jonathan Edwards, on the other hand, did include both practical and theoretical discussion of decision-making authority, Congregational procedures, and the *Cambridge Platform*. Edwards, "Narrative of Communion Controversy," in Hall, ed., *Edwards' Ecclesiastical Writings*; Tracy, *Jonathan Edwards*, chapters 7 and 8.

75. William Upham, ed., "Beverly First Church Records," Essex Institute, *Historical Collections*, 41 (1905), 214–215; Revere First Church Records; Haverhill Fourth Church Records, ms, Haverhill Public Library. Many church record books that are complete and detailed through the 1740s become sketchy in the 1750s or the 1760s. For some particularly good examples, see Beverly Second Church Records; *Boston First Church Records*; Cohasset First Church Records, vol. 2, ms, Cohasset First Congregational Church; Groveland First Church Records; Hopkinton First Church Records; Methuen First Church Records; Middleboro First Church Records.

76. Edward Goddard, *A Brief Account*, 4.

77. Reading First Church Records, ts, 87, April 30, 1746, August 1746; see also 90, January, 1747. For examples of doctrinal complaints see Beverly Second Church Records, ms, July 22, 1757, which detail complaints over doctrine in the First Church of Leominster; *Brewster First Church Records*, 98, November 6, 1749; Georgetown First Church Records, ms, February 10, 1751, February 21, 1754, January 21, 1759; Halifax First Church Records, ts, 72, October 28, 1762; Haverhill First Church Records, ms, November 26, 1757; Hull First Church Records, ms, July 13, 1767; Methuen First Church Records, msc, October 2, 1754; Springfield First Church Records, ms, March 1, 1759; Tewksbury First Church Records, ms, August 23, 1754.

78. See Harry S. Stout, "The Great Awakening in New England Reconsidered: The New England Clergy," *Journal of Social History*, 7 (1974), 27–28; Gaustad, *The Great Awakening in New England*, 75.

79. These conclusions, of course, pertain strictly to Congregational churches. Many New Lights and Separates broke off to establish or join Baptist organizations in the aftermath of the Great Awakening. Though no study has carefully analyzed the decision-making process in these churches from the vantage point of their church records, historians have argued that Baptist practices were more democratic than those in Standing churches. See Goen, *Revivalism and Separatism*, and William G. McLoughlin, *New England Dissent, 1630–1833: The Baptists and the Separation of Church and State*, 2 vols. (Cambridge, Mass., 1971).

80. Increase Mather, *A Sermon wherein it is Shewed That the Ministers of the Gospel need . . . the Prayers of the Lord's People for Them* (Boston, 1718), 15.

Afterword

1. The quotation appears in Perry Miller, *Jonathan Edwards* (New York, 1949), 224. Among the best of the many analyses of Edwards's dismissal is found in Patricia J. Tracy, *Jonathan Edwards, Pastor: Religion and Society in Eighteenth-Century Northampton* (New York, 1979), chapters 7 and 8. See also Jonathan Edwards, "Narrative of Communion Controversy," in David D. Hall, ed., *The Works of Jonathan Edwards*, vol. 12, *Ecclesiastical Writings* (New Haven, 1994), 505–619.

2. See "The Economic Thought of Jonathan Edwards," *Church History*, 60 (March 1991), 37–54, and Gerald R. McDermott, *One Holy and Happy Society: The Public Theology of Jonathan Edwards* (University Park, Pa., 1992).

3. The First Churches of Harvard, Stoneham, and Grafton, for example, each expressed their commitment to the *Cambridge Platform* in the late 1740s and, through the 1760s, held regular church meetings, maintained mutual watch, exercised discipline, and conducted all affairs with lay consent. Government in the First Church of Abington was neither more nor less "democratic" after the Great Awakening; rather, practices changed little during Samuel Brown's thirty-five year ministry. Continuities also marked practices at the First Church of Berkeley under the forty-four years of Samuel Tobey's pastorate. Tobey's congregation formally endorsed the *Cambridge Platform* in 1743, elected two ruling elders in 1748, and maintained active church discipline through the 1760s.

4. Medford First Church Records, 11, ms, Medford Town Hall; "Weston First Church Records," 533; Sturbridge First Church Records, ms, 21.

5. Many ministers assumed the role of "moderator" (sometimes formally, sometimes informally) during the 1740s and beyond, whose purpose was simply to preside over and maintain order in church meetings. Apparently this development began in prudential concerns and eventually extended to meetings concerning all church affairs. In 1734, for example, the First Church of Boston appointed a moderator for a meeting of the church and town concerning fiscal matters. Lay people served as moderators in the absence of a ministers. By the 1770s, most Congregational churches employed lay or clerical moderators regardless of the nature of the decisions. The office is first mentioned outside of prudential affairs in Framingham in 1747, Wenham in 1749, Weston in 1750, Revere in 1755, Hull in the 1760s, Wakefield in 1765, and in the Boston Seventh Church in 1776. Some ministers formally identified themselves as moderators or "clerks," and others did not, though in practice they had assumed that role. See Pierce, *Boston First Church Records*, 167; Framingham First Church Records, ts, Framingham Public Library, 118; Wenham First Church Records, msc, 27; "Weston First Church Records," 532; Revere First Church Records, 88; Hull First Church Records, manuscript, New England Historical and Genealogical Society, 163; Wakefield First Church Records, 107; Boston Seventh Church Records, msc, New England Historical and Genealogical Society, 174.

6. Samuel Cooke, *A Sermon Preached at Cambridge in the Audience of His Honor Thomas Hutchinson* (Boston, 1770) in A.W. Plumstead, ed., *The Wall and the Garden: Selected Massachusetts Election Sermons 1660–1775* (Minneapolis, 1968), 328.

7. Joseph S. Clark, *A Historical Sketch of the Congregational Churches in Massachusetts, from 1620 to 1858* (Boston, 1858), 12–13; [Benjamin Prescott], *A Letter to a friend relating to the differences in the First Church in Salem, wherein the proceedings of the Ecclesiastical Councils concerned in that affair are vindicated, and the objections raised against them answered* (Boston, 1735), 4.

Index